Perl Best Practices

Damian Conway

Beijing · Cambridge · Farnham · Köln · Paris · Sebastopol · Taipei · Tokyo

Perl Best Practices
by Damian Conway

Copyright © 2005 O'Reilly Media, Inc. All rights reserved.
Printed in the United States of America.

Published by O'Reilly Media, Inc., 1005 Gravenstein Highway North, Sebastopol, CA 95472.

O'Reilly books may be purchased for educational, business, or sales promotional use. Online editions are also available for most titles (*safari.oreilly.com*). For more information, contact our corporate/institutional sales department: (800) 998-9938 or *corporate@oreilly.com*.

Editors:	Allison Randal
	Tatiana Apandi
Production Editor:	Genevieve d'Entremont
Cover Designer:	Ellie Volckhausen
Interior Designer:	David Futato

Printing History:

July 2005:	First Edition.

 This book uses RepKover™, a durable and flexible lay-flat binding.

ISBN: 0-596-00173-8
ISBN13: 978-0-596-00173-5
[M]

For Linda

Table of Contents

Preface

This book is designed to help you write better Perl code: in fact, the best Perl code you possibly can. It's a collection of 256 guidelines covering various aspects of the art of coding, including layout, name selection, choice of data and control structures, program decomposition, interface design and implementation, modularity, object orientation, error handling, testing, and debugging. These guidelines have been developed and refined over a programming career spanning 22 years. They're designed to work well together, and to produce code that is clear, robust, efficient, maintainable, and concise.

Mind you, that's not easy to achieve. Conciseness can be the natural enemy of clarity; efficiency the nemesis of maintainability. And armouring code to make it sufficiently robust can undermine clarity, efficiency, conciseness, *and* maintainability. Sometimes it's a case of: "Choose any one."

This book doesn't try to offer *the* one true universal and unequivocal set of best practices. There are as many ways of measuring code quality, and as many dimensions in which code can be judged, as there are programmers to make those assessments. Each programmer and each programming team will have their own opinions about the most important and desirable attributes of code.

What this book offers instead is *a* set of best practices: a set that is coherent, widely applicable, balanced in its aims, and that is based on real-world experience of how code is actually written, rather than on someone's ivory-tower theories on how code ought to be created. Most of all, it's a set of practices that actually work, and that many developers around the world are already using. Much like Perl itself, these guidelines are about helping you to get your job done, without getting in the way.

If you're an experienced developer, it's almost certain that you won't like all of the suggestions that follow. You will find some of them unnatural or counterintuitive; others may feel excessively rigid and un-Perlish. Maybe they'll just seem unnecessarily different from the ways you're used to writing software, and from the long-ingrained coding habits you find so comfortable.

Try to put those feelings aside as you read through the advice in this book. Review it as you would any other proposed code enhancement: analyze the arguments that are made for these new practices; ask yourself whether you've ever fallen into the traps they seek to avoid; consider whether the coding techniques suggested here might be worth trying.

Just thinking about these issues—becoming conscious of the way you currently write code—can be of enormous benefit, even if you don't adopt a single one of the recommendations that follow.

Contents of This Book

Chapter 1, *Best Practices*, explains why it might be worth reassessing your current coding practices. It discusses how coding styles are evolved, and sets out three broad criteria against which any existing or proposed coding practice can be assessed. The chapter also explains why good coding habits matter and suggests how they can be developed.

Chapter 2, *Code Layout*, tackles the many contentious issues of code layout. It suggests how to set out block delimiters; how to visually distinguish built-ins and keywords from subroutines and variables; where to place operators, terminators, delimiters, and other punctuation; how to improve readability by the consistent use of whitespace; the optimal width for code lines and block indents; how to set out lists of values; and where to break long expressions. It concludes by recommending a convenient tool that automates most of these layout tasks.

Chapter 3, *Naming Conventions*, presents a series of guidelines that can help you choose more descriptive names for variables, subroutines, and namespaces. It also demonstrates how the various components of a consistent naming scheme can work together to improve the overall maintainability of code, both by making it more readable and by reducing the need for deobfuscatory comments.

Chapter 4, *Values and Expressions*, provides a simple set of rules that can help you avoid common pitfalls when creating character strings, numbers, and lists. Topics include how to avoid unintended variable interpolation (and non-interpolation), reliable and readable approaches to nonprintable characters, defining constants, avoiding barewords, and taming heredocs, commas, long numbers, and lists.

Chapter 5, *Variables*, explores a robust approach to using variables. It explains the inherent drawbacks of package or punctuation variables, suggesting safer alternatives where possible, and safer practices where there are no alternatives. The second half of the chapter presents several efficient and maintainable techniques of handling data in arrays and hashes using the "container slicing" mechanism.

Chapter 6, *Control Structures*, examines Perl's rich variety of control structures, encouraging the use of those that are easier to maintain, less error-prone, or more efficient. The chapter provides a set of simple guidelines for deciding which of for, while, or map is most appropriate for a given task. The effective use of iterator variables is also discussed, including the common case of needing to iterate hash entries by key and value simultaneously.

Chapter 7, *Documentation*, suggests a series of techniques that can make documenting your code less tedious, and therefore more likely. It advocates a template-based approach to both user and technical documentation, and discusses when, where, and how to write useful and accurate comments.

Chapter 8, *Built-in Functions*, discusses better ways of using some of Perl's most popular built-in functions, including sort, reverse, scalar, eval, unpack, split, substr, values, select, sleep, map, and grep. It also summarizes the many other useful "non-built-in" builtins provided by two modules from the standard Perl distribution and one from CPAN.

Chapter 9, *Subroutines*, describes efficient and maintainable ways to write subroutines in Perl, including the use of positional, named, and optional arguments, argument validation and defaults, safe calling and return conventions, predictable return values in various contexts, and why subroutine prototypes and implicit returns should be avoided.

Chapter 10, *I/O*, explains how to open and close files reliably, when to use line-based input, how to correctly detect interactive applications, the importance of prompting, and how best to provide feedback to users during long non-interactive tasks.

Chapter 11, *References*, offers advice on demystifying Perl's many dereferencing syntaxes, discusses why symbolic references create more problems than they solve, and recommends ways to prevent cyclic reference chains from causing memory leaks.

Chapter 12, *Regular Expressions*, presents guidelines for using regular expressions. It recommends the use of extended formatting, suggests a simple but unusual fix for Perl's confusing "single-line" and "multiline" matching modes, warns of the perils of matching whitespace too precisely, shows how to avoid using the error-prone numeric variables, presents a robust approach to building complex regexes that are still maintainable, gives several hints on optimizing slow matches, and concludes by explaining when *not* to use regular expressions.

Chapter 13, *Error Handling*, advocates a coherent exception-based approach to error handling, and explains why exceptions are preferable to special return values or flags. It also recommends the use of exception objects, and explores in detail how they can be declared, created, thrown, caught, and handled.

Chapter 14, *Command-Line Processing*, addresses the design and implementation of command-line interfaces, both for individual programs and for application suites. It recommends several modules that can make your command-line interfaces more consistent and predictable, and at the same time can considerably reduce the effort required to implement those interfaces.

Chapter 15, *Objects*, and Chapter 16, *Class Hierarchies*, offer a robust and efficient approach to creating objects and class hierarchies in Perl. This approach provides fully encapsulated objects with no performance penalty, and supports single and multiple inheritance without the usual problems of attribute collision, incomplete initialization, partial destruction, or incorrect method autoloading. Chapter 16 also introduces a new module that allows these robust and efficient classes to be built semi-automatically.

Chapter 17, *Modules*, looks at non-object-oriented modules, exploring the best ways to create them, design their interfaces, declare and check their version numbers, and refactor existing code into them. This chapter also discusses the many existing modules that are freely available as part of the Perl standard library and on CPAN.

Chapter 18, *Testing and Debugging*, encourages the use of testing, advocating test-driven design and development using the core `Test::` modules. It also offers tips on effective debugging techniques, including a description of various modules and other free tools that can make debugging easier.

Chapter 19, *Miscellanea*, offers several additional guidelines on miscellaneous topics such as revision control, interfacing to code written in other languages, processing configuration files, text formatting, tied variables, benchmarking and profiling your code, caching techniques, and some general advice on refactoring.

Appendix A, *Essential Perl Best Practices*, summarizes the 30 most important guidelines in the book in three one-page lists. Appendix B, *Perl Best Practices*, lists all 256 guidelines, with cross-references to their chapters and locations. Appendix C, *Editor Configurations*, provides some useful configuration options for the Vim, Vile, Emacs, TextWrangler, and BBEdit text editors. Appendix D, *Recommended Modules and Utilities*, lists and cross-references the various modules recommended throughout the book, and provides a brief summary of their most useful subroutines. Appendix E offers a short bibliography.

Conventions Used in This Book

The following typographical conventions are used in the text of this book:

Italic

> Indicates emphasis, new terms, URLs, email addresses, filenames, paths, and Unix utilities.

`Constant-width regular`

> Indicates commands, variables, attributes, functions, classes, namespaces, methods, modules, values, the contents of files, the output from commands, and code examples that break recommended practices.

`Constant-width bold`

> Indicates commands and other text that should be typed literally by the user, and code examples that demonstrate recommended practices.

Constant-width italic

Indicates text that should be replaced with user-supplied values and comments within code examples.

Code Examples

This book is intended to help you get your job done. In general, you may use the code in this book in your programs and documentation. You do not need to contact O'Reilly for permission unless you're reproducing a significant portion of the code. For example, writing a program that uses several chunks of code from this book does not require permission. Selling or distributing a CD-ROM of examples from O'Reilly books does require permission. Answering a question by citing this book and quoting example code does not require permission. Incorporating a significant amount of example code from this book into your product's documentation does require permission.

O'Reilly appreciates, but does not require, attribution. An attribution usually includes the title, author, publisher, and ISBN. For example: "*Perl Best Practices,* by Damian Conway. Copyright 2005 O'Reilly Media, Inc., ISBN: 0-596-00173-8".

If you feel that your use of code examples may fall outside fair use or the given permission guidelines, feel free to send a specific request to *permissions@oreilly.com.*

Feedback

Please address comments and questions concerning this book to the publisher:

O'Reilly Media, Inc.
1005 Gravenstein Highway North
Sebastopol, CA 95472
(800) 998-9938 (in the United States or Canada)
(707) 829-0515 (international or local)
(707) 829-0104 (fax)

There is a web page for this book that lists errata, examples, and any additional information. You can access this page at:

http://www.oreilly.com/catalog/perlbp

To comment or ask technical questions about this book, send email to:

bookquestions@oreilly.com

For more information about books, conferences, Resource Centers, and the O'Reilly Network, see:

http://www.oreilly.com

Acknowledgments

Every book is the work of a multitude. In writing this one, I have benefitted from the help, advice, and support of many of the most talented people in the Perl community. I would like to express my deepest gratitude:

To Linda Mui, my first editor, for her seemingly limitless patience and continuing faith, which gave me the freedom to eventually find my true subject.

To Nat Torkington, my second editor, for refiring my enthusiasm for writing, and for his extraordinary encouragement, support, and mateship over the past decade.

To Allison Randal and Tatiana Apandi, my third editors, for their grace, composure, understanding, good advice, quiet efficiency, and very practical assistance.

To Sean M. Burke, for his careful technical analysis, invaluable grammatical advice, salient questions, and for an especially brilliant footnote that I sorely wish I could have used.

To Nancy Kotary, for gently improving my writing with her superb copy-editing.

To Genevieve d'Entremont, for heroic typesetting far beyond the call of duty.

To Lucie Haskins, whose superb index so elegantly complements the original manuscript.

To Larry Wall, for his friendship and wisdom over the past five years, and for teaching me so much in that time, not the least of all: humility.

To Abigail, for bringing a no-nonsense approach to Perl coding and for invaluable advice on many topics—in particular, regular expressions and inside-out objects.

To Nate Bailey, for his unfailing support over the past few years, for helping me craft sentences that make sense the first time, and for his expert second-hand knowledge of sociopathy.

To Hildo Biersma, for his professional perspective on the realities of developing in large team environments, and for considerably more good suggestions than I was able to use in a single book.

To chromatic, for his rapier wit, for unveiling the mysteries of testing, and for his invaluable assistance in getting the message out to the wider Perl community.

To Chris Devers, for consistently better wordings throughout the book, and for saving me from writing an entire extra chapter, when a paragraph turned out to be enough.

To Richard Dice, for marshalling compelling economic arguments to keep the review process on track, and for finding me the perfect business-like operands.

To Stephen Edmonds, for unearthing three very subtle coding errors that would otherwise have passed most annoyingly into print.

To Paul Fenwick, for the much-needed teacher's perspective he brought to the presentation of these ideas, and for duly withholding biscuits when I broke my own guidelines.

To Garrett Goebel, for his extraordinary attention to detail and his remarkable ability to extrapolate from those particulars to excellent general advice.

To Mick Goulish, for enthusiastic encouragement, sound skeptical advice when I was under pressure, and some of the best laughs I've ever had, right when I most needed them.

To Uri Guttman, for seeing things no-one else did, in ways that no-one else could.

To Trey Harris, for so ably representing the expert programmer and thereby inspiring me to find better ways, instead of just easy ways.

To Brand Hilton, for unsurpassed typo correction, his uncanny ability to spot bugs in code samples, and his valiant defence of "unless".

To Steven Lembark, for so many excellent suggestions, and for helping to keep me focused on the needs of real-world developers.

To Andy Lester, for inspiring me with his deep understanding of, and passion for, the best coding practices.

To Greg London, for his insights into the needs of real programmers, and for telling me honestly when the humour didn't work.

To Tim Maher, for his friendship and support over many years, and for occasionally being the essential voice of dissent.

To Bill Odom, for sharing so much of his wisdom and experience, and graciously allowing me to steal so many of his best ideas.

To Jacinta Richardson, for her many excellent suggestions, both grammatical and syntactical, and for her uncompromising opposition to lazy writing.

To Bill Ricker, for his invaluable documenting of guidelines, modules, and versions; his eagle eye for corporate-unfriendly suggestions; and his extraordinary knowledge of computing theory, practice, and history.

To Randal Schwartz, for finding the time to offer feedback on my book despite the heavy demands of concurrently revising two of his own.

To Peter Scott, for sharing his unparalleled experience, knowledge, and wisdom, and for his and Grace's kindness and support in times of sorrow.

To Mike Stok, for his unique perspective on Perl programming, and the many insightful suggestions that flowed from it.

To Tony Stubblebine, for not being afraid to criticize when criticism was warranted, and especially for his sound advice on documentation.

To Andrew Sundstrom, for the unique way he blends the warrior, the philosopher, and the poet in all aspects of his life, including his programming.

To Bennett Todd, whose encouragement and advice I have now relied upon across five years and two books.

To Merijn Broeren, Dave Cross, and Tom Christiansen for their generous offers to help with this book.

To Dave Rolsky, Brian Ingerson, and Eric J. Roode, for being so open to my impertinent suggestions for improving their already excellent modules.

To my fellow Perl Monks: Joe Hourcle, for his detailed and timely help with BBEdit and TextWrangler; John McNamara, Jim Mahoney, Scott Lanning, and Michael Joyce, to whom belongs all credit for the Emacs advice herein; and all the other acolytes, monks, friars, abbots, and saints who helped me put together the editor configuration appendix: *artist*, *barrachois*, *Fletch*, *InfiniteLoop*, *jplindstrom*, *leriksen*, *Limbic~Region*, *runrig*, *Smylers*, and *stefp*.

To my parents, Sandra and Jim Conway, and my parents-in-law Fred and Corallie Stock, for their unfailing belief in me.

And above all, to my beloved Linda, who is the wellspring of all my inspiration, and the reason for everything I do.

## CHAPTER 1

Best Practices

*We do not all have to write like Faulkner, or program
like Dijkstra. I will gladly tell people what my
programming style is, and I will even tell them where I
think their own style is unclear or makes me jump
through mental hoops.*

*But I do this as a fellow programmer, not as the Perl
god…stylistic limits should be self-imposed, or at most
policed by consensus among your buddies.*

—Larry Wall
Natural Language Principles in Perl

Code matters. Analysis, design, decomposition, algorithms, data structures, and control flow mean *nothing* until they are made real, given form and power in the statements of some programming language. It is code that allows abstractions and ideas to control the physical world, that enables mathematical procedures to govern real-world processes, that converts data into information and information into knowledge.

Code matters. So the way in which you code matters too. Every programmer has a unique approach to writing software; a unique coding style. Programmers' styles are based on their earliest experiences in programming—the linguistic idiosyncrasies of their first languages, the way in which code was presented in their initial textbooks, and the stylistic prejudices of their early instructors. That style will develop and change as the programmer's experience and skills increase. Indeed, most programmers' style is really just a collection of coding habits that have evolved in response to the opportunities and pressures they have experienced throughout their careers.

Just as in natural evolution, those opportunities and pressures may lead to a coding style that is fit, strong, and well-adapted to the programmer's needs. Or it may lead to a coding style that is nasty, brutish, and underthought. But what it most often leads to is something even worse: Intuitive Programmer Syndrome.

Many programmers code by instinct. They aren't conscious of the hundreds of choices they make every time they code: how they format their source, the names they use for variables, the kinds of loops they use (while vs for vs map), whether to put that extra semicolon at the end of the block, whether to grep with a regex or a block, where and when to put comments, whether to use an object-oriented or procedural approach, how to explain their programs in their documentation, whether to return undef or throw an exception on failure, how to decompose the different components of a system into subroutines, how to bundle those subroutines into modules, how to interact with the program's user.

Developers are usually focused entirely on the problems they're solving, the solutions they're creating, and the algorithms they're implementing. So when it comes to choosing a variable name, they use the first one that comes to mind*; when it comes to using a loop they use the one they always use†; and when it comes to that trailing semicolon, well, sometimes they do and sometimes they don't. Just as the spirit moves them.

In *The Importance of Being Earnest*, Oscar Wilde captures the nature of the Intuitive Programmer perfectly:

> *Lady Bracknell:*
>
>> Good afternoon, dear Algernon, I hope you are behaving very well.
>
> *Mr Moncreif:*
>
>> I'm feeling very well, Aunt Augusta.
>
> *Lady Bracknell:*
>
>> That isn't the same thing at all.
>
>> In fact in my experience the two things rarely go together.

And so it is with many programmers. They write their code in the way that seems natural, that happens intuitively, and that feels good.

Unfortunately, if you're earnest about your profession, comfort isn't enough. "Behaving very well" may seem stuffy and conventional and uncreative and completely at odds with the whole outlaw hacker ethos, but it has one important advantage: it works. Good social manners help societies run smoothly; good programming manners help programs—and programming teams—do the same.

Rules, conventions, standards, and practices help programmers communicate and coordinate with one another. They provide a uniform and predictable framework for thinking about problems, and a common language for expressing solutions. This is especially critical in Perl, where the language itself is deliberately designed to offer many ways to accomplish the same task, and consequently supports many incompatible dialects in which to express any solution.

The goal of this book is to help you to develop a conscious programming style: to train yourself—and your team—to do things consistently in a way you've decided is

---

* Often whatever is short, vaguely relevant, and easy to spell: $value, @data, $next, %tmp, $obj, $key, @nums, %opt, $arg, $foo, $in, $to, $fh, $x, $y, @q, and so on.

† The three-part C-style for loop: "It's so flexible! What more do you need?"

correct, rather than in whatever way feels good at the time. Or, if you prefer your metaphors more Eastern than Edwardian: to help you move beyond the illusion of the sensual programming life, and become stylistically enlightened.

Three Goals

A good coding style is one that reduces the costs of your software project. There are three main ways in which a coding style can do that: by producing applications that are more robust, by supporting implementations that are more efficient, and by creating source code that is easier to maintain.

Robustness

When deciding how you will write code, choose a style that is likely to reduce the number of bugs in your programs. There are several ways that your coding style can do that:

- A coding style can minimize the chance of introducing errors in the first place. For example, appending _ref to the name of every variable that stores a reference (see Chapter 3) makes it harder to accidentally write $array_ref[$n] instead of $array_ref->[$n], because anything except an arrow after _ref will soon come to look wrong.

- A coding style can make it easy to detect incorrect edge cases, where bugs often hide. For example, constructing a regular expression from a table (see Chapter 12) can prevent that regex from ever matching a value that the table doesn't cover, or from failing to match a value that it does.

- A coding style can help you avoid constructs that don't scale well. For example, avoiding a cascaded if-elsif-elsif-elsif-... in favour of table look-ups (see Chapter 6) can ensure that the cost of any selection statement stays nearly constant, rather than growing linearly with the number of alternatives.

- A coding style can improve how code handles failure. For example, mandating a standard interface for I/O prompting (see Chapter 10) can encourage developers to habitually verify terminal input, rather than simply assuming it will always be correct.

- A coding style can improve how code reports failure. For example, a rule that every failure must throw an exception, rather than returning an undef (see Chapter 13), will ensure that errors cannot be quietly ignored or accidentally propagated into unrelated code.

- A coding style can improve the structure of code. For example, a prohibition against reusing code via cutting-and-pasting (see Chapter 17) can force developers to abstract program components into subroutines and then aggregate those subroutines into modules.

Efficiency

Of course, it doesn't matter how bug-free or error-tolerant your code is if it takes a week to predict tomorrow's weather, an hour to execute someone's stock trade, or even just one full second to deploy the airbags. Correctness *is* vital, but so is efficiency.

Efficient code doesn't have to be fragile, complex, or hard to maintain. Coding for efficiency is often simply a matter of working with Perl's strengths and avoiding its weaknesses. For example, reading an entire file of text (possibly gigabytes of it) into a variable just to change each occurrence of 'C#' to 'D-flat' is vastly slower than reading and changing the data line-by-line (see Chapter 10). On the other hand, when you *do* need to read an entire file into your program, then doing so line-by-line becomes woefully inefficient.

Efficiency can be a particularly thorny goal, though. Changes in Perl's implementation from version to version, and platform-specific differences within the same version, can change the relative efficiency of particular constructs. So whenever you're choosing between two possible solutions on the basis of efficiency, it's critical to benchmark each candidate on the actual platform on which you'll be deploying code, using real data (see Chapter 19).

Maintainability

You will typically spend at least four times longer maintaining code than you spent writing it[*]. So it makes sense to optimize your programming style for readability, not writability. Better yet, try to optimize for comprehensibility: easy-to-read and easy-to-understand aren't necessarily the same thing.

When you're developing a particular code suite over a long period of time, you eventually find yourself "in the zone". In that state, you seem to have the design and the control flow and the data structures and the naming conventions and the modular decomposition and every other aspect of the program constantly at your mental fingertips. You understand the code in a profound way. It's easy to "see" problems directly and locate bugs quickly, sometimes without even quite knowing how you knew. You truly *grok* the source.

Six months later, the code might just as well have been written by someone else[†]. You've moved on from it, forgotten the clever intricacies of the design, lost the implicit understanding of the control and data flows. And you have *no* idea why that

---

[*] The observation that maintenance costs tend to outweigh initial development costs about 4-to-1 is often referred to as Boehm's Law. The predominance of maintenance over development has been repeatedly observed in real-world studies over the past three decades, though the actual cost ratio varies from about 2-to-1 to well over 10-to-1.

[†] That's Eagleson's Law. Other experts bitterly assert that the critical interval is closer to three weeks.

critical variable was named `$nxt_eTofF_trig`, what it stores, what that value is used for, or how it might be implicated in this newly discovered bug.

By far the easiest way to fix that bug is to get yourself back into the zone: to recover the detailed mental model you had when you first wrote it. That means that to build software that's easy to maintain, you need to build software that's easy to re-*grok*. And to do that, you need to preserve as much of your mental model of the code as you can, in some medium more permanent and reliable than mere neurons. You need to encode your understanding in your documentation and, if possible, in the source itself.

Having a consistent and coherent approach to coding can help. Consistent coding habits allow you to carry part of your mental model through every project, and to stay at least partially in the same mindset every time you write code. Having an entire team with consistent coding habits extends those benefits much further, making it easier for someone else to reconstruct your intentions and your understanding, because your code looks and works the same as theirs.

This Book

To help you develop that consistent and coherent approach, the following 18 chapters explore a coordinated set of coding practices that have been specifically designed to enhance the robustness, efficiency, and maintainability of Perl code.

Each piece of advice is framed as a single imperative sentence—a "Thou shalt…" or a "Thou shalt not…", presented like this:

Always code as if the guy who ends up maintaining your code will be a violent psychopath who knows where you live.

Each such admonition is followed by a detailed explanation of the rule, explaining how and when it applies. Every recommendation also includes a summary of the reasoning behind the prescription or proscription, usually in terms of how it can improve the reliability, performance, or comprehensibility of your code.

Almost every guideline also includes at least one example of code that conforms to the rule (set in **`constant-width bold`**) as well as counterexamples that break it (set in `constant-width regular`). These code fragments aim to demonstrate the advantages of following the suggested practice, and the problems that can occur if you don't. All of these examples are also available for you to download and reuse from *http:// www.oreilly.com/catalog/perlbp*.

The guidelines are organized by topic, not by significance. For example, some readers will wonder why use strict and use warnings aren't mentioned on page 1. But if you've already seen the light on those two, they don't *need* to be on page 1. And if you haven't seen the light yet, Chapter 18 is soon enough. By then you'll have discovered several hundred ways in which code can go horribly wrong, and will be better able to appreciate these two ways in which Perl can help your code go right.

Other readers may object to "trivial" code layout recommendations appearing so early in the book. But if you've ever had to write code as part of a group, you'll know that layout is where most of the arguments start. Code layout is the medium in which all other coding practices are practised, so the sooner everyone can admit that code layout *is* trivial, set aside their "religious" convictions, and agree on a coherent coding style, the sooner your team can start getting useful work done.

As you consider these pieces of advice, think about each of them in the context of the type of coding you typically do. Question your current practice in the particular area being discussed, and compare it against the recommended approach. Evaluate the robustness, efficiency, and maintainability of your current coding habits and consider whether a change is justified.

But remember that each piece of advice is a *guideline*: a fellow programmer gladly telling you what his programming style is, and where he thinks other styles are unclear or make him jump through mental hoops. Whether or not you agree with all of them doesn't matter. What matters is that you become aware of the coding issues these guidelines address, think through the arguments made in their favour, assess the benefits and costs of changing your current practices, and then consciously decide whether to adopt the solutions offered here.

Then consider whether they will work for everyone else on your project as well. Coding is (usually) a collaborative effort; developing and adopting a team coding style is too. Mainly because a team coding standard will *stay* adopted only if every member of your team is willing to sign off on it, support it, use it, and encourage other team members to follow it as well.

Use this book as a starting point for your discussions. Negotiate a style that suits you all. Perhaps everyone will eventually agree that—although their personal style is self-evidently superior to anything else imaginable—they are nevertheless graciously willing to abide by the style suggested here as a reasonable compromise. Or perhaps someone will point out that particular recommendations just aren't appropriate for your circumstances, and suggest something that would work better.

Be careful, though. It's amazing how many arguments about coding practice are actually just rationalizations: carefully constructed excuses that ultimately boil down to either "It's not my present habit!" or "It's just too much effort to change!" Not changing your current practices *can* be a valid choice, but not for either of those reasons.

Keep in mind that the goal of any coding style is to reduce your development costs by increasing the maintainability, robustness, and efficiency of your code. Be wary of any argument—either for or against change—that doesn't directly address at least one of those issues.

Rehabiting

People cling to their current coding habits even when those habits are manifestly making their code buggy, slow, and incomprehensible to others. They cling to those habits because it's easier to live with their deficiencies than it is to fix them. *Not* thinking about how you code requires no effort. That's the whole point of a habit. It's a skill that has been compiled down from a cerebral process and then burnt into muscle memory; a microcoded reflex that your fingers can perform without your conscious control.

For example, if you're an aficionado of the BSD style of bracketing (see Chapter 2), then it's likely that your fingers can type Closingparen-Return-Openingcurly-Return-Tab without your ever needing to think about it—which makes it especially hard if your development team decides to adopt K&R bracketing instead, because now you have to type Closingparen-Return-Openingcurly-Return-*dammit!*-Backspace-Backspace-Backspace-Space-Openingcurly-Return-Tab for a couple of months until your fingers learn the new sequence.

Likewise, if you're used to writing Perl like this:

```
@tcmd= grep /^.*;$/ => @cmd;
```

then abiding by the guidelines in this book and writing this instead:

```
@terminated_commands
    = grep { m/ \A [^\n]* ; \n? \z /xms } @raw_commands;
```

will be deeply onerous. At least, it will be at first, until you break your existing habits and develop new ones.

But that's the great thing about programming habits: they're incredibly easy to change. All you have to do is *consciously* practise things the new way for long enough, and eventually your coding habits will automatically re-formulate themselves around that new behaviour.

So, if you decide to adopt the recommendations in the following chapters, try to adopt them zealously. See how often you can catch yourself (or others in your team) breaking the new rules. Stop letting your fingers do the programming. Recorrect each old habit the instant you notice yourself backsliding. Be strict with your hands. Rather than letting them type what feels good, force them to type what works well.

Soon enough you'll find yourself typing Closingparen-Space-Openingcurly-Return-Tab, and g-r-e-p-Space-Openingcurly-Space, and Closingslash-x-m-s, all without even thinking about it. At which point, having reprogrammed your intuitions correctly, you will once again be able to program "correctly"…by intuition.

## CHAPTER 2

Code Layout

Most people's [...] programs should be indented
six feet downward and covered with dirt.
—Blair P. Houghton

Formatting. Indentation. Style. Code layout. Whatever you choose to call it, it's one of the most contentious aspects of programming discipline. More and bloodier wars have been fought over code layout than over just about any other aspect of coding.

So what is the best practice here? Should you use classic Kernighan & Ritchie (K&R) style? Or go with BSD code formatting? Or adopt the layout scheme specified by the GNU project? Or conform to the Slashcode coding guidelines?

Of course not! Everyone knows that *[insert your personal coding style here]* is the One True Layout Style, the only sane choice, as ordained by *[insert your favorite Programming Deity here]* since Time Immemorial! Any other choice is manifestly absurd, willfully heretical, and self-evidently a Work of Darkness!!!

And that's precisely the problem. When deciding on a layout style, it's hard to decide where rational choices end and rationalized habits begin.

Adopting a coherently designed approach to code layout, and then applying that approach consistently across all your coding, is fundamental to best practice programming. Good layout can improve the readability of a program, help detect errors within it, and make the structure of your code much easier to comprehend. Layout matters.

But most coding styles—including the four mentioned earlier—confer those benefits almost equally well. So while it's true that having a consistent code layout scheme matters very much indeed, the *particular* code layout scheme you ultimately decide upon...

does not matter at all!

All that matters is that you adopt a single, coherent style; one that works for your entire programming team. And, having agreed upon that style, that you then apply it consistently across all your development.

The layout guidelines suggested in this chapter have been carefully and consciously selected from many alternatives, in a deliberate attempt to construct a coding style that is self-consistent and concise, that improves the readability of the resulting code, that makes it easy to detect coding mistakes, and that works well for a wide range of programmers in a wide range of development environments.

Undoubtedly, there will be some layout guideline here that you disagree with. Probably violently. When you find it, come back and reread the five words at the top of this page. Then decide whether your reasons for your disagreement outweigh the reasons given for the guideline. If they do, then not following that particular guideline won't matter at all.

Bracketing

Brace and parenthesize in K&R style.

When setting out a code block, use the K&R* style of bracketing. That is, place the opening brace at the end of the construct that controls the block. Then start the contents of the block on the next line, and indent those contents by one indentation level. Finally, place the closing brace on a separate line, at the same indentation level as the controlling construct.

Likewise, when setting out a parenthesized list over multiple lines, put the opening parenthesis at the end of the controlling expression; arrange the list elements on the subsequent lines, indented by one level; and place the closing parenthesis on its own line, outdenting it back to the level of the controlling expression. For example:

```
my @names = (
    'Damian',    # Primary key
    'Matthew',   # Disambiguator
    'Conway',    # General class or category
);

for my $name (@names) {
    for my $word ( anagrams_of(lc $name) ) {
        print "$word\n";
    }
}
```

---

* "K&R" are Brian Kernighan and Dennis Ritchie, authors of the book *The C Programming Language* (Prentice Hall, 1988).

Don't place the opening brace or parenthesis on a separate line, as is common under the BSD and GNU styles of bracketing:

```
# Don't use BSD style...
my @names =
(
    'Damian',    # Primary key
    'Matthew',   # Disambiguator
    'Conway',    # General class or category
);

for my $name (@names)
{
    for my $word (anagrams_of(lc $name))
    {
        print "$word\n";
    }
}


# And don't use GNU style either...

for my $name (@names)
  {
    for my $word (anagrams_of(lc $name))
      {
        print "$word\n";
      }
  }
```

The K&R style has one obvious advantage over the other two styles: it requires one fewer line per block, which means one more line of actual code will be visible at any time on your screen. If you're looking at a series of blocks, that might add up to three or four extra code lines per screen.

The main counter-argument in favour of the BSD and GNU styles is usually that having the opening bracket* on its own line makes it easier to visually match up the start and end of a block or list. But this argument ignores the fact that it's equally easy to match them up under K&R style. You just scroll upwards until you "bump your head" on the overhanging control construct, then scroll right to the end of the line.

Or, more likely, you'd just hit whatever key your editor uses to bounce between matched brackets. In *vi* that's %. *Emacs* doesn't have a native "bounce" command, but it's easy to create one by adding the following to your *.emacs* file†:

---

* Throughout this book, the word "bracket" will be used as a generic term to refer to any of the four types of paired delimiters: "braces" ({...}), "parentheses" ((...)), "square brackets" ([...]), and "angle brackets" (<...>).

† The editor configurations suggested throughout this book are collected in Appendix C, *Editor Configurations*. They are also available to download from *http://www.oreilly.com/catalog/perlbp*.

```
;; Use % to match various kinds of brackets...
(global-set-key "%" 'match-paren)
  (defun match-paren (arg)
    "Go to the matching paren if on a paren; otherwise insert %."
    (interactive "p")
    (cond ((string-match "[[{(<]"  next-char) (forward-sexp 1))
          ((string-match "[\]})>]" prev-char) (backward-sexp 1))
          (t (self-insert-command (or arg 1)))))
```

More importantly, finding the matching brace or parenthesis is rarely a goal in itself. Most often you're interested in the closing bracket only because you need to determine where the current construct (for loop, if statement, or subroutine) ends. Or you want to determine which construct a particular closing bracket terminates. Both those tasks are marginally *easier* under K&R style. To find the end of a construct, just look straight down from the construct's keyword; to find what construct a particular bracket terminates, scan straight up until you hit the construct's keyword.

In other words, the BSD and GNU styles make it easy to match the *syntax* of brackets, whereas K&R makes it easy to match the *semantics* of brackets. That being said, there is nothing wrong with the BSD or GNU styles of bracketing. If you, and your fellow developers, find that vertically aligned brackets improve your comprehension of code, then use them instead. What matters most is that all the members of your programming team agree on a single style and use it consistently.

Keywords

Separate your control keywords from the following opening bracket.

Control structures regulate the dynamic behaviour of a program, so the keywords of control structures are amongst the most critical components of a program. That's why it's important that those keywords stand out clearly in the source code.

In Perl, most control structure keywords are immediately followed by an opening parenthesis, which can make it easy to confuse them with subroutine calls. It's important to distinguish the two. To do this, use a single space between a keyword and the following brace or parenthesis:

```
for my $result (@results) {
    print_sep();
    print $result;
}

while ($min < $max) {
    my $try = ($max - $min) / 2;
    if ($value[$try] < $target) {
        $max = $try;
    }
```

```
        else {
            $min = $try;
        }
    }
```

Without the intervening space, it's harder to pick out the keyword, and easier to mistake it for the start of a subroutine call:

```
for(@results) {
    print_sep();
    print;
}

while($min < $max) {
    my $try = ($max - $min) / 2;
    if($value[$try] < $target) {
        $max = $try;
    }
    else{
        $min = $try;
    }
}
```

Subroutines and Variables

**Don't separate subroutine or variable names
from the following opening bracket.**

In order for the previous rule to work properly, it's important that subroutines and variables *not* have a space between their names and any following brackets. Otherwise, it's too easy to mistake a subroutine call for a control structure, or misread the initial part of an array element as an independent scalar variable.

So cuddle subroutine calls and variable names against their trailing parentheses or braces:

```
my @candidates = get_candidates($marker);

CANDIDATE:
for my $i (0..$#candidates) {
    next CANDIDATE if open_region($i);

    $candidates[$i]
        = $incumbent{ $candidates[$i]{region} };
}
```

Spacing them out only makes them harder to recognize:

```
my @candidates = get_candidates ($marker);

CANDIDATE:
```

```
for my $i (0..$#candidates) {
    next CANDIDATE if open_region ($i);

    $candidates [$i]
        = $incumbent {$candidates [$i] {region}};
}
```

Builtins

Don't use unnecessary parentheses
for builtins and "honorary" builtins.

Perl's many built-in functions are effectively keywords of the language, so they can legitimately be called without parentheses, except where it's necessary to enforce precedence.

Calling builtins without parentheses reduces clutter in your code, and thereby enhances readability. The lack of parentheses also helps to visually distinguish between subroutine calls and calls to builtins:

```
while (my $record = <$results_file>) {
    chomp $record;
    my ($name, $votes) = split "\t", $record;
    print 'Votes for ',
        substr($name, 0, 10),          # Parens needed for precedence
        ": $votes (verified)\n";
}
```

Certain imported subroutines, usually from modules in the core distribution, also qualify as "honorary" builtins, and may be called without parentheses. Typically these will be subroutines that provide functionality that ought to be in the language itself but isn't. Examples include carp and croak (from the standard Carp module—see Chapter 13), first and max (from the standard List::Util module—see Chapter 8), and prompt (from the IO::Prompt CPAN module—see Chapter 10).

Note, however, that in any cases where you find that you need to use parentheses in builtins, they should follow the rules for subroutines, not those for control keywords. That is, treat them as subroutines, with no space between the builtin name and the opening parenthesis:

```
while (my $record = <$results_file>) {
    chomp( $record );
    my ($name, $votes) = split("\t", $record);
    print(
        'Votes for ',
        substr($name, 0, 10),
        ": $votes (verified)\n"
    );
}
```

Don't treat them as control keywords (by adding a trailing space):

```
while (my $record = <$results_file>) {
    chomp ($record);
    my ($name, $votes) = split ("\t", $record);
    print (
        'Votes for ',
        substr ($name, 0, 10),
        ": $votes (verified)\n"
    );
}
```

Keys and Indices

Separate complex keys or indices from their surrounding brackets.

When accessing elements of nested data structures (hashes of hashes of arrays of whatever), it's easy to produce a long, complex, and visually dense expression, such as:

```
$candidates[$i] = $incumbent{$candidates[$i]{get_region( )}};
```

That's especially true when one or more of the indices are themselves indexed variables. Squashing everything together without any spacing doesn't help the readability of such expressions. In particular, it can be difficult to detect whether a given pair of brackets is part of the inner or outer index.

Unless an index is a simple constant or scalar variable, it's much clearer to put spaces between the indexing expression and its surrounding brackets:

```
$candidates[$i] = $incumbent{ $candidates[$i]{ get_region() } };
```

Note that the determining factors here are both the complexity and the overall length of the index. Occasionally, "spacing-out" an index makes sense even if that index *is* just a single constant or scalar. For example, if that simple index is unusually long, it's better written as:

```
print $incumbent{ $largest_gerrymandered_constituency };
```

rather than:

```
print $incumbent{$largest_gerrymandered_constituency};
```

Operators

Use whitespace to help binary operators stand out from their operands.

Long expressions can be hard enough to comprehend without adding to their complexity by jamming their various components together:

```
    my $displacement=$initial_velocity*$time+0.5*$acceleration*$time**2;

    my $price=$coupon_paid*$exp_rate+(($face_val+$coupon_val)*$exp_rate**2);
```

Give your binary operators room to breathe, even if it requires an extra line to do so:

```
    my $displacement
        = $initial_velocity * $time  +  0.5 * $acceleration * $time**2;

    my $price
        = $coupon_paid * $exp_rate  +  ($face_val + $coupon_paid) * $exp_rate**2;
```

Choose the amount of whitespace according to the precedence of the operators, to help the reader's eyes pick out the natural groupings within the expression. For example, you might put additional spaces on either side of the lower-precedence + to visually reinforce the higher precedence of the two multiplicative subexpressions surrounding it. On the other hand, it's quite appropriate to sandwich the ** operator tightly between its operands, given its very high precedence and its longer, more easily identified symbol.

A single space is always sufficient whenever you're also using parentheses to emphasize (or to vary) precedence:

```
    my $velocity
        = $initial_velocity + ($acceleration * ($time + $delta_time));

    my $future_price
        = $current_price * exp($rate - $dividend_rate_on_index) * ($delivery - $now);
```

Symbolic unary operators should always be kept with their operands:

```
    my $spring_force = !$hyperextended ? -$spring_constant * $extension : 0;

    my $payoff = max(0, -$asset_price_at_maturity + $strike_price);
```

Named unary operators should be treated like builtins, and spaced from their operands appropriately:

```
    my $tan_theta = sin $theta / cos $theta;

    my $forward_differential_1_year = $delivery_price * exp -$interest_rate;
```

Semicolons

Place a semicolon after every statement.

In Perl, semicolons are statement separators, not statement terminators, so a semicolon isn't required after the very last statement in a block. Put one in anyway, even if there's only one statement in the block:

```
    while (my $line = <>) {
        chomp $line;
```

```
    if ( $line =~ s{\A (\s*) -- (.*)}{$1#$2}xms ) {
        push @comments, $2;
    }

    print $line;
}
```

The extra effort to do this is negligible, and that final semicolon confers two very important advantages. It signals to the reader that the preceding statement is finished, and (perhaps more importantly) it signals to the *compiler* that the statement is finished. Telling the compiler is more important than telling the reader, because the reader can often work out what you really meant, whereas the compiler reads only what you actually wrote.

Leaving out the final semicolon usually works fine when the code is first written (i.e., when you're still paying proper attention to the entire piece of code):

```
while (my $line = <>) {
    chomp $line;

    if ( $line =~ s{\A (\s*) -- (.*)}{$1#$2}xms ) {
        push @comments, $2
    }

    print $line
}
```

But, without the semicolons, there's nothing to prevent later additions to the code from causing subtle problems:

```
while (my $line = <>) {
    chomp $line;

    if ( $line =~ s{\A (\s*) -- (.*)}{$1#$2}xms ) {
        push @comments, $2
        /shift/mix
    }

    print $line
    $src_len += length;
}
```

The problem is that those two additions don't actually add new statements; they just absorb the existing ones. So the previous code actually means:

```
while (my $line = <>) {
    chomp $line;

    if ( $line =~ s{\A (\s*) -- (.*)}{$1#$2}xms ) {
        push @comments, $2 / shift() / mix()
    }

    print $line ($src_len += length);
}
```

This is a very common mistake, and an understandable one. When extending existing code, you will naturally focus on the new statements you're adding, on the assumption that the existing ones will continue to work correctly. But, without its terminating semicolon, an existing statement may be assimilated into the new one instead.

Note that this rule does not apply to the block of a map or grep if that block consists of only a single statement. In that case, it's better to omit the terminator:

```
my @sqrt_results
    = map { sqrt $_ } @results;
```

because putting a semicolon in the block makes it much more difficult to detect where the full statement ends:

```
my @sqrt_results
    = map { sqrt $_; } @results;
```

Note that this exception to the stated rule is not excessively error-prone, as having more than one statement in a map or grep is relatively unusual, and often a sign that a map or grep was not the right choice in the first place (see "Complex Mappings" in Chapter 6).

Commas

Place a comma after every value in a multiline list.

Just as semicolons act as separators in a block of statements, commas act as separators in a list of values. That means that exactly the same arguments apply in favour of treating them as terminators instead.

Adding an extra trailing comma (which is perfectly legal in any Perl list) also makes it much easier to reorder the elements of the list. For example, it's much easier to convert:

```
my @dwarves = (
    'Happy',
    'Sleepy',
    'Dopey',
    'Sneezy',
    'Grumpy',
    'Bashful',
    'Doc',
);
```

to:

```
my @dwarves = (
    'Bashful',
    'Doc',
```

```
        'Dopey',
        'Grumpy',
        'Happy',
        'Sleepy',
        'Sneezy',
    );
```

You can manually cut and paste lines or even feed the list contents through *sort*.

Without that trailing comma after 'Doc', reordering the list would introduce a bug:

```
    my @dwarves = (
        'Bashful',
        'Doc'
        'Dopey',
        'Grumpy',
        'Happy',
        'Sleepy',
        'Sneezy',
    );
```

Of course, that's a trivial mistake to find and fix, but why not adopt a coding style that eliminates the very possibility of such problems?

Line Lengths

Use 78-column lines.

In these modern days of high-resolution 30-inch screens, anti-aliased fonts, and laser eyesight correction, it's entirely possible to program in a terminal window that's 300 columns wide.

Please don't.

Given the limitations of printed documents, legacy VGA display devices, presentation software, and unreconstructed managerial optics, it isn't reasonable to format code to a width greater than 80 columns. And even an 80-column line width is not always safe, given the text-wrapping characteristics of some terminals, editors, and mail systems.

Setting your right margin at 78 columns maximizes the usable width of each code line whilst ensuring that those lines appear consistently on the vast majority of display devices.

In *vi*, you can set your right margin appropriately by adding:

```
    set textwidth=78
```

to your configuration file. For *Emacs*, use:

```
    (setq fill-column 78)
    (setq auto-fill-mode t)
```

Another advantage of this particular line width is that it ensures that any code fragment sent via email can be quoted at least once without wrapping:

```
From: boss@headquarters
To: you@saltmines
Subject: Please explain

I came across this chunk of code in your latest module.
Is this your idea of a joke???

> $;=$/;seek+DATA,undef$/,!$s;$_=<DATA>;$s&&print||(*{q;::\;
> ;}=sub{$d=$d-1?$d:$0;s;';\t#$d#;,$_})&&$g&&do{$y=($x||=20)*($y||8);sub
> i{sleep&f}sub'p{print$;x$=,join$;,$b=~/.{$x}/g,$;}sub'f{pop||1}sub'n{substr($b
> ,&f%$y,3)=~tr,0,0,}sub'g{@_[@_]=@_;--($f=&f);$m=substr($b,&f,1);($w,$w,$m,0)
> [n($f-$x)+n($x+$f)-(${m}eq+0=>)+n$f]||$w}$w="\40";$b=join'',@ARGV?<>:$_,$w
> x$y;$b=~s).)$&=~/\w/?0:$w)gse;substr($b,$y)=q++;$g='$i=0;$i?$b:$c=$b;
> substr+$c,$i,1,g$i;$g=~s?\d+?($&+1)%$y?e;$i-$y+1?eval$g:do{$b=$c;p;i}';
> sub'e{eval$g;&e};e}||eval||die+No.$;

Please see me at once!!

Y.B.
```

Indentation

Use four-column indentation levels.

Indentation depth is far more controversial than line width. Ask four programmers the right number of columns per indentation level and you'll get four different answers: two-, three-, four-, or eight-column indents. You'll usually also get a heated argument.

The ancient coding masters, who first cut code on teletypes or hardware terminals with fixed tabstops, will assert that eight columns per level of indentation is the only acceptable ratio, and support that argument by pointing out that most printers and software terminals still default to eight-column tabs. Eight columns per indentation level ensures that your code looks the same everywhere:

```
while (my $line = <>) {
        chomp $line;
        if ( $line =~ s{\A (\s*) -- ([^\n]*) }{$1#$2}xms ) {
                push @comments, $2;
        }
        print $line;
}
```

Yes (agree many younger hackers), eight-column indents ensure that your code looks *equally ugly and unreadable* everywhere! Instead, they insist on no more than two or three columns per indentation level. Smaller indents maximize the number of levels of nesting available across a fixed-width display: about a dozen levels under a two- or three-column indent, versus only four or five levels with eight-column indents. Shallower indentation also reduces the horizontal distance the eye has to track, thereby keeping indented code in the same vertical sight-line and making the context of any line of code easier to ascertain:

```
while (my $line = <>) {
    chomp $line;
    if ( $line =~ s{\A (\s*) -- ([^\n]*) }{$1#$2}xms ) {
        push @comments, $2;
    }
    print $line;
}
```

The problem with this approach (cry the ancient masters) is that it can make indentations impossible to detect for anyone whose eyes are older than 30, or whose vision is worse than 20/20. And that's the crux of the problem. Deep indentation enhances structural readability at the expense of contextual readability; shallow indentation, vice versa. Neither is ideal.

The best compromise[*] is to use four columns per indentation level. This is deep enough that the ancient masters can still actually see the indentation, but shallow enough that the young hackers can still nest code to eight or nine levels[†] without wrapping:

```
while (my $line = <>) {
    chomp $line;
    if ( $line =~ s{\A (\s*) -- (.*)}{$1#$2}xms ) {
        push @comments, $2;
    }
    print $line;
}
```

Tabs

Indent with spaces, not tabs.

Tabs are a bad choice for indenting code, even if you set your editor's tabspacing to four columns. Tabs do not appear the same when printed on different output devices, or pasted into a word-processor document, or even just viewed in someone

---

[*] According to the research reported in "Program Indentation and Comprehensibility" (*Communications of the ACM*, Vol. 26, No. 11, pp. 861–867).

[†] But don't do that! If you need more than four or five levels of indentation, you almost certainly need to factor some of that nested code out into a subroutine or module. See Chapters 9 and 17.

else's differently tabspaced editor. So don't use tabs alone or (worse still) intermix tabs with spaces:

```
sub addarray_internal {
»    my ($var_name, $need_quotemeta) = @_;

»    $raw .= $var_name;

»    my $quotemeta = $need_quotemeta ? q{ map {quotemeta $_} }
»    »   »   »   » :                     $EMPTY_STR
»    ··············;

····my $perl5pat
····»    = qq{(??{join q{|}, $quotemeta \@{$var_name}})};

»    push @perl5pats, $perl5pat;

»    return;
}
```

The only reliable, repeatable, transportable way to ensure that indentation remains consistent across viewing environments is to indent your code using only spaces. And, in keeping with the previous rule on indentation depth, that means using four space characters per indentation level:

```
sub addarray_internal {
····my ($var_name, $need_quotemeta) = @_;

····$raw .= $var_name;

····my $quotemeta = $need_quotemeta ? q{ map {quotemeta $_} }
··················:··················$EMPTY_STR
··················;

····my $perl5pat
········= qq{(??{join q{|}, $quotemeta \@{$var_name}})};

····push @perl5pats, $perl5pat;

····return;
}
```

Note that this rule *doesn't* mean you can't use the Tab key to indent your code; only that the result of pressing that key can't actually be a tab. That's usually very easy to ensure under modern editors, most of which can easily be configured to convert tabs to spaces. For example, if you use *vim*, you can include the following directives in your *.vimrc* file:

```
set tabstop=4        "An indentation level every four columns"
set expandtab        "Convert all tabs typed into spaces"
set shiftwidth=4     "Indent/outdent by four columns"
set shiftround       "Always indent/outdent to the nearest tabstop"
```

Or in your *.emacs* initialization file (using "cperl" mode):

```
(defalias 'perl-mode 'cperl-mode)

;; 4 space indents in cperl mode
'(cperl-close-paren-offset -4)
'(cperl-continued-statement-offset 4)
'(cperl-indent-level 4)
'(cperl-indent-parens-as-block t)
'(cperl-tab-always-indent t)
```

Ideally, your code should not contain a single instance of the tab character. In your layout, they should have been transformed to spaces; in your literal strings, they should all be specified using \t (see Chapter 4).

Blocks

Never place two statements on the same line.

If two or more statements share one line, each of them becomes harder to comprehend:

```
RECORD:
while (my $record = <$inventory_file>) {
    chomp $record; next RECORD if $record eq $EMPTY_STR;
    my @fields = split $FIELD_SEPARATOR, $record; update_sales(\@fields);$count++;
}
```

You're already saving vertical space by using K&R bracketing; use that space to improve the code's readability, by giving each statement its own line:

```
RECORD:
while (my $record = <$inventory_file>) {
    chomp $record;
    next RECORD if $record eq $EMPTY_STR;
    my @fields = split $FIELD_SEPARATOR, $record;
    update_sales(\@fields);
    $count++;
}
```

Note that this guideline applies even to map and grep blocks that contain more than one statement. You should write:

```
my @clean_words
    = map {
        my $word = $_;
        $word =~ s/$EXPLETIVE/[DELETED]/gxms;
        $word;
    } @raw_words;
```

not:

```
my @clean_words
    = map { my $word = $_; $word =~ s/$EXPLETIVE/[DELETED]/gxms; $word } @raw_words;
```

Chunking

Code in paragraphs.

A paragraph is a collection of statements that accomplish a single task: in literature, it's a series of sentences conveying a single idea; in programming, it's a series of instructions implementing a single step of an algorithm.

Break each piece of code into sequences that achieve a single task, placing a single empty line between each sequence. To further improve the maintainability of the code, place a one-line comment at the start of each such paragraph, describing what the sequence of statements does. Like so:

```
# Process an array that has been recognized...
sub addarray_internal {
    my ($var_name, $needs_quotemeta) = @_;

    # Cache the original...
    $raw .= $var_name;

    # Build meta-quoting code, if requested...
    my $quotemeta = $needs_quotemeta ?  q{map {quotemeta $_} } : $EMPTY_STR;

    # Expand elements of variable, conjoin with ORs...
    my $perl5pat = qq{(??{join q{|}, $quotemeta \@{$var_name}})};

    # Insert debugging code if requested...
    my $type = $quotemeta ? 'literal' : 'pattern';
    debug_now("Adding $var_name (as $type)");
    add_debug_mesg("Trying $var_name (as $type)");

    return $perl5pat;
}
```

Paragraphs are useful because humans can focus on only a few pieces of information at once[*]. Paragraphs are one way of aggregating small amounts of related information, so that the resulting "chunk" can fit into a single slot of the reader's limited short-term memory. Paragraphs enable the physical structure of a piece of writing to reflect and emphasize its logical structure. Adding comments at the start of each paragraph further enhances the chunking by explicitly summarizing the purpose[†] of each chunk.

---

[*] An idea made famous in 1956 by George A. Miller in "The Magical Number Seven, Plus or Minus Two" (*The Psychological Review*, 1956, Vol. 63, pp. 81–97).

[†] The *purpose*, not the *actions*. Paragraph comments need to explain why the code is needed, not merely paraphrase what it's doing.

Note, however, that the comments of paragraphs are only of secondary importance here. It is the vertical gaps separating each paragraph that are critical. Without them, the readability of the code declines dramatically, even if the comments are retained:

```
sub addarray_internal {
    my ($var_name, $needs_quotemeta) = @_;
    # Cache the original...
    $raw .= $var_name;
    # Build meta-quoting code, if required...
    my $quotemeta = $needs_quotemeta ?  q{map {quotemeta $_} } : $EMPTY_STR;
    # Expand elements of variable, conjoin with ORs...
    my $perl5pat = qq{(??{join q{|}, $quotemeta \@{$var_name}})};
    # Insert debugging code if requested...
    my $type = $quotemeta ? 'literal' : 'pattern';
    debug_now("Adding $var_name (as $type)");
    add_debug_mesg("Trying $var_name (as $type)");
    return $perl5pat;
}
```

Elses

Don't cuddle an else.

A "cuddled" else looks like this:

```
} else {
```

An uncuddled else looks like this:

```
}
else {
```

Cuddling saves an additional line per alternative, but ultimately it works against the readability of code in other ways, especially when that code is formatted using K&R bracketing. A cuddled else keyword is no longer in vertical alignment with its controlling if, nor with its own closing bracket. This misalignment makes it harder to visually match up the various components of an if-else construct.

More importantly, the whole point of an else is to distinguish an alternate course of action. But cuddling the else makes that distinction less distinct. For a start, it removes the near-empty line provided by the closing brace of the preceding if, which reduces the visual gap between the if and else blocks. Squashing the two blocks together in that way undermines the paragraphing inside the two blocks (see the previous guideline, "Chunking"), especially if the contents of the blocks are themselves properly paragraphed with empty lines between chunks.

Cuddling also moves the else from the leftmost position on its line, which means that the keyword is harder to locate when you are scanning down the code. On the other hand, an uncuddled else improves both the vertical separation of your code and the identifiability of the keyword:

```
if ($sigil eq '$') {
    if ($subsigil eq '?') {
        $sym_table{ substr($var_name,2) } = delete $sym_table{$var_name};

        $internal_count++;
        $has_internal{$var_name}++;
    }
    else {
        ${$var_ref} = q{$sym_table{$var_name}};

        $external_count++;
        $has_external{$var_name}++;
    }
}
elsif ($sigil eq '@' && $subsigil eq '?') {
    @{ $sym_table{$var_name} }
        = grep {defined $_} @{$sym_table{$var_name}};
}
elsif ($sigil eq '%' && $subsigil eq '?') {
    delete $sym_table{$var_name}{$EMPTY_STR};
}
else {
    ${$var_ref} = q{$sym_table{$var_name}};
}
```

In contrast, a cuddled else or elsif reduces readability by obscuring both the chunking of the blocks and the visibility of the keywords:

```
if ($sigil eq '$') {
    if ($subsigil eq '?') {
        $sym_table{ substr($var_name,2) } = delete $sym_table{$var_name};

        $internal_count++;
        $has_internal{$var_name}++;
    } else {
        ${$var_ref} = q{$sym_table{$var_name}};

        $external_count++;
        $has_external{$var_name}++;
    }
} elsif ($sigil eq '@' && $subsigil eq '?') {
    @{$sym_table{$var_name}}
        = grep {defined $_} @{$sym_table{$var_name}};
} elsif ($sigil eq '%' && $subsigil eq '?') {
    delete $sym_table{$var_name}{$EMPTY_STR};
} else {
    ${$var_ref} = q{$sym_table{$var_name}};
}
```

Vertical Alignment

Align corresponding items vertically.

Tables are another familiar means of chunking related information, and of using physical layout to indicate logical relationships. When setting out code, it's often useful to align data in a table-like series of columns. Consistent indentation can suggest equivalences in structure, usage, or purpose.

For example, initializers for non-scalar variables are often much more readable when laid out neatly using extra whitespace. The following array and hash initializations are very readable in tabular layout:

```
my @months = qw(
    January   February   March
    April     May        June
    July      August     September
    October   November   December
);

my %expansion_of = (
    q{it's}    => q{it is},
    q{we're}   => q{we are},
    q{didn't}  => q{did not},
    q{must've} => q{must have},
    q{I'll}    => q{I will},
);
```

Compressing them into lists saves lines, but also significantly reduces their readability:

```
my @months = qw(
    January February March April May June July August September
    October November December
);

my %expansion_of = (
    q{it's} => q{it is}, q{we're} => q{we are}, q{didn't} => q{did not},
    q{must've} => q{must have}, q{I'll} => q{I will},
);
```

Take a similar tabular approach with sequences of assignments to related variables, by aligning the assignment operators:

```
$name   = standardize_name($name);
$age    = time - $birth_date;
$status = 'active';
```

rather than:

```
$name = standardize_name($name);
$age = time - $birth_date;
$status = 'active';
```

Alignment is even more important when assigning to a hash entry or an array element. In such cases, the keys (or indices) should be aligned in a column, with the surrounding braces (or square brackets) also aligned. That is:

```
$ident{ name   } = standardize_name($name);
$ident{ age    } = time - $birth_date;
$ident{ status } = 'active';
```

Notice how this tabular layout emphasizes the keys of the entries being accessed, and thereby highlights the purpose of each assignment. Without that layout, your attention is drawn instead to the "column" of $ident prefixes, and the keys are consequently much harder to discern:

```
$ident{name} = standardize_name($name);
$ident{age} = time - $birth_date;
$ident{status} = 'active';
```

Aligning the assignment operators but not the hash keys is better than not aligning either, but still not as readable as aligning both:

```
$ident{ name }    = standardize_name($name);
$ident{ age }     = time - $birth_date;
$ident{ status } = 'active';
```

Breaking Long Lines

Break long expressions before an operator.

When an expression at the end of a statement gets too long, it's common practice to break that expression after an operator and then continue the expression on the following line, indenting it one level. Like so:

```
push @steps, $steps[-1] +
    $radial_velocity * $elapsed_time +
    $orbital_velocity * ($phase + $phase_shift) -
    $DRAG_COEFF * $altitude;
```

The rationale is that the operator that remains at the end of the line acts like a continuation marker, indicating that the expression continues on the following line.

Using the operator as a continuation marker seems like an excellent idea, but there's a serious problem with it: people rarely look at the right edge of code. Most of the semantic hints in a program—such as keywords—appear on the left side of that code. More importantly, the structural cues for understanding code—for example, indenting—are predominantly on the left as well (see the upcoming "Keep Left" sidebar). This means that indenting the continued lines of the expression actually gives a false impression of the underlying structure, a misperception that the eye must travel all the way to the right margin to correct.

Keep Left

The left edge of code is the most prominent location because, like English, Perl is fundamentally a left-to-right language, and in such languages the left-most portion of a statement is most salient.

At the start of a statement, readers are "fresh"; they don't have to remember anything that has gone before. In contrast, by the end of a statement, their short-term memory buffers will be full, they will be preoccupied trying to interpret the whole line, or they may have lost focus entirely.

Linguists call this effect the "end-weight problem" and recommend that important information not be saved till last:

> *Because, after a long night of hacking, in a horrible dream, there came to me the damnèd souls responsible for ANSI C++, I ran screaming.*

Placing that information up front makes it easier to pay attention to it, even if the remainder of the sentence blurs a little:

> *I ran screaming because the damnèd souls responsible for ANSI C++ came to me in a horrible dream after a long night of hacking.*

It's entirely possible to design a programming language where the important stuff comes last—Forth and PostScript are two examples—but, thankfully, Perl isn't that kind of language.

A cleaner solution is to break long lines *before* an operator. That approach ensures that each line of the continued expression will start with an operator, which is unusual in Perl code. That way, as the reader's eye scans down the left margin of the code, it's immediately obvious that an indented line is merely the continuation of the previous line, because it starts with an operator.

The indenting of the second and subsequent lines of the expression is also critical. Continued lines should not simply be indented to the next indentation level. Instead, they should be indented to the starting column of the expression to which they belong. That is, instead of:

```
push @steps, $steps[-1]
    + $radial_velocity * $elapsed_time
    + $orbital_velocity * ($phase + $phase_shift)
    - $DRAG_COEFF * $altitude
    ;
```

you should write:

```
push @steps, $steps[-1]
             + $radial_velocity * $elapsed_time
             + $orbital_velocity * ($phase + $phase_shift)
             - $DRAG_COEFF * $altitude
             ;
```

This style of layout has the added advantage that it keeps the two arguments of the push visually separated in the horizontal, and thereby makes them easier to distinguish.

When a broken expression is continued over multiple lines, it is good practice to place the terminating semicolon on a separate line, indented to the same column as the start of the continued expression. As the reader's eye scans down through the leading operators on each line, encountering a semicolon instead makes it very clear that the continued expression is now complete.

Non-Terminal Expressions

Factor out long expressions in the middle of statements.

The previous guideline applies only if the long expression to be broken is the last value in a statement. If the expression appears in the middle of a statement, it is better to factor that expression out into a separate variable assignment. For example:

```
my $next_step = $steps[-1]
                + $radial_velocity * $elapsed_time
                + $orbital_velocity * ($phase + $phase_shift)
                - $DRAG_COEFF * $altitude
                ;
add_step( \@steps, $next_step, $elapsed_time);
```

rather than:

```
add_step( \@steps, $steps[-1]
                + $radial_velocity * $elapsed_time
                + $orbital_velocity * ($phase + $phase_shift)
                - $DRAG_COEFF * $altitude
                , $elapsed_time);
```

Breaking by Precedence

Always break a long expression at the operator of the lowest possible precedence.

As the examples in the previous two guidelines show, when breaking an expression across several lines, each line should be broken before a low-precedence operator. Breaking at operators of higher precedence encourages the unwary reader to misunderstand the computation that the expression performs. For example, the following layout might surreptitiously suggest that the additions and subtractions happen before the multiplications:

```
push @steps, $steps[-1] + $radial_velocity
              * $elapsed_time + $orbital_velocity
              * ($phase + $phase_shift) - $DRAG_COEFF
              * $altitude
              ;
```

If you're forced to break on an operator of less-than-minimal precedence, indent the broken line one additional level relative to the start of the expression, like so:

```
push @steps, $steps[-1]
              + $radial_velocity * $elapsed_time
              + $orbital_velocity
                  * ($phase + $phase_shift)
              - $DRAG_COEFF * $altitude
              ;
```

This strategy has the effect of keeping the subexpressions of the higher precedence operation visually "together".

Assignments

Break long assignments before the assignment operator.

Often, the long statement that needs to be broken will be an assignment. The preceding rule does work in such cases, but leads to code that's unaesthetic and hard to read:

```
$predicted_val = $average
              + $predicted_change * $fudge_factor
              ;
```

A better approach when breaking assignment statements is to break before the assignment operator itself, leaving only the variable being assigned to on the first line. Then indent one level, and place the assignment operator at the start of the next line—once again indicating a continued statement:

```
$predicted_val
    = $average + $predicted_change * $fudge_factor;
```

Note that this approach often allows the entire righthand side of an assignment to be laid out on a single line, as in the preceding example. However, if the righthand expression is still too long, break it again at a low-precedence operator, as suggested in the previous guideline:

```
$predicted_val
    = ($minimum + $maximum) / 2
        + $predicted_change * max($fudge_factor, $local_epsilon);
```

A commonly used alternative layout for broken assignments is to break after the assignment operator, like so:

```
$predicted_val =
    $average + $predicted_change * $fudge_factor;
```

This approach suffers from the same difficulty described earlier: it's impossible to detect the line continuation without scanning all the way to the right of the code, and the "unmarked" indentation of the second line can mislead the casual reader. This problem of readability is most noticeable when the variable being assigned to is itself quite long:

```
$predicted_val{$current_data_set}[$next_iteration] =
    $average + $predicted_change * $fudge_factor;
```

which, of course, is precisely when such an assignment would most likely need to be broken. Breaking before the assignment operator makes long assignments much easier to identify, by keeping the assignment operator visually close to the start of the variable being assigned to:

```
$predicted_val{$current_data_set}[$next_iteration]
    = $average + $predicted_change * $fudge_factor;
```

Ternaries

Format cascaded ternary operators in columns.

One operator that is particularly prone to creating long expressions is the ternary operator. Because the ? and : of a ternary have very low precedence, a straightforward interpretation of the expression-breaking rule doesn't work well in this particular case, since it produces something like:

```
my $salute = $name eq $EMPTY_STR ? 'Customer'
           : $name =~ m/\A((?:Sir|Dame) \s+ \S+)/xms ? $1
           : $name =~ m/(.*), \s+ Ph[.]?D \z/xms ? "Dr $1" : $name;
```

which is almost unreadable.

The best way to lay out a series of ternary selections is in two columns, like so:

```
                # When their name is...              Address them as...
my $salute = $name eq $EMPTY_STR                  ? 'Customer'
           : $name =~ m/\A((?:Sir|Dame) \s+ \S+) /xms ? $1
           : $name =~ m/(.*), \s+ Ph[.]?D \z    /xms ? "Dr $1"
           :                                            $name
           ;
```

In other words, break a series of ternary operators before every colon, aligning the colons with the operator preceding the first conditional. Doing so will cause the conditional tests to form a column. Then align the question marks of the ternaries so that the various possible results of the ternary also form a column. Finally, indent the last result (which has no preceding question mark) so that it too lines up in the results column.

This special layout converts the typical impenetrably obscure ternary sequence into a simple look-up table: for a given condition in column one, use the corresponding result from column two.

You can use the tabular layout even if you have only a single ternary:

```
my $name = defined $customer{name} ? $customer{name}
         :                           'Sir or Madam'
         ;
```

Starting out this way makes it easier for maintainers to subsequently add new alternatives to the table. This idea is explored further in the "Tabular Ternaries" guideline in Chapter 6.

Lists

Parenthesize long lists.

The comma operator is really an operator only in scalar contexts. In lists, the comma is an item separator. Consequently, commas in multiline lists are best treated as item terminators. Moreover, multiline lists are particularly easy to confuse with a series of statements, as there is very little visual difference between a , and a ; .

Given the potential for confusion, it's important to clearly mark a multiline list as being a list. So, if you need to break a list across multiple lines, place the entire list in parentheses. The presence of an opening parenthesis highlights the fact that the subsequent expressions form a list, and the closing parenthesis makes it immediately apparent that the list is complete.

When laying out a statement containing a multiline list, place the opening parenthesis on the same line as the preceding portion of the statement. Then break the list after every comma, placing the same number of list elements on each separate line and indenting those lines one level deeper than the surrounding statement. Finally, outdent the closing parenthesis back to the same level as the statement. Like so:

```
my @months = qw(
    January   February   March
    April     May        June
    July      August     September
    October   November   December
);
```

```
for my $item (@requested_items) {
    push @items, (
        "A brand new $item",
        "A fully refurbished $item",
        "A ratty old $item",
    );
}

print (
    'Processing ',
    scalar(@items),
    ' items at ',
    time,
    "\n",
);
```

Note that the final item in the list should still have a comma, even though it isn't required syntactically.

When writing multiline lists, always use parentheses (with K&R-style bracketing), keep to the same number of items on each line, and remember that in list contexts a comma isn't an operator, so the "break-before-an-operator rule" doesn't apply. In other words, not like this:

```
my @months = qw( January   February   March   April   May   June   July   August
                 September  October   November  December
               );

for my $item (@requested_items) {
    push @items, "A brand new $item"
               , "A fully refurbished $item"
               , "A ratty old $item"
               ;
}

print 'Processing '
    , scalar(@items)
    , ' items at '
    , time
    , "\n"
    ;
```

The "Thin Commas" guideline in Chapter 4 presents several other good reasons for parenthesizing lists.

Automated Layout

Enforce your chosen layout style mechanically.

In the long term, it's best to train yourself and your team to code in a consistent, rational, and readable style such as the one suggested earlier. However, the time and commitment necessary to accomplish that isn't always available. In such cases, a reasonable compromise is to prescribe a standard code-formatting tool that must be applied to all code before it's committed, reviewed, or otherwise displayed in public.

There is now an excellent code formatter available for Perl: *perltidy*. It's freely available from SourceForge at *http://perltidy.sourceforge.net* and provides an extensive range of user-configurable options for indenting, block delimiter positioning, column-like alignment, and comment positioning.

Using *perltidy*, you can convert code like this:

```perl
if($sigil eq '$'){
    if($subsigil eq '?'){
        $sym_table{substr($var_name,2)}=delete $sym_table{locate_orig_var($var)};
        $internal_count++;$has_internal{$var_name}++
    } else {
        ${$var_ref} =
            q{$sym_table{$var_name}}; $external_count++; $has_external{$var_name}++;
}} elsif ($sigil eq '@'&&$subsigil eq '?') {
    @{$sym_table{$var_name}} = grep
        {defined $_} @{$sym_table{$var_name}};
} elsif ($sigil eq '%' && $subsigil eq '?') {
delete $sym_table{$var_name}{$EMPTY_STR}; } else
{
${$var_ref}
=
q{$sym_table{$var_name}}
}
```

into something readable:

```perl
if ( $sigil eq '$' ) {
    if ( $subsigil eq '?' ) {
        $sym_table{ substr( $var_name, 2 ) }
            = delete $sym_table{ locate_orig_var($var) };
        $internal_count++;
        $has_internal{$var_name}++;
    }
    else {
        ${$var_ref} = q{$sym_table{$var_name}};
        $external_count++;
        $has_external{$var_name}++;
    }
}
elsif ( $sigil eq '@' && $subsigil eq '?' ) {
    @{ $sym_table{$var_name} }
        = grep {defined $_} @{ $sym_table{$var_name} };
}
elsif ( $sigil eq '%' && $subsigil eq '?' ) {
    delete $sym_table{$var_name}{$EMPTY_STR};
}
else {
    ${$var_ref} = q{$sym_table{$var_name}};
}
```

Notice how closely the tidied version follows the various formatting guidelines in this chapter. To achieve that result, you need to configure your *.perltidyrc* file like this:

```
-l=78    # Max line width is 78 cols
-i=4     # Indent level is 4 cols
-ci=4    # Continuation indent is 4 cols
-st      # Output to STDOUT
-se      # Errors to STDERR
-vt=2    # Maximal vertical tightness
-cti=0   # No extra indentation for closing brackets
-pt=1    # Medium parenthesis tightness
-bt=1    # Medium brace tightness
-sbt=1   # Medium square bracket tightness
-bbt=1   # Medium block brace tightness
-nsfs    # No space before semicolons
-nolq    # Don't outdent long quoted strings
-wbb="% + - * / x != == >= <= =~ !~ < > | & **= += *= &= <<= &&= -=
        /= |= >>= ||= .= %= ^= x="
         # Break before all operators
```

Mandating that everyone use a common tool to format their code can also be a simple way of sidestepping the endless objections, acrimony, and dogma that always surround any discussion on code layout. If *perltidy* does all the work for them, then it will cost developers almost no effort to adapt to the new guidelines. They can simply set up an editor macro that will "straighten" their code whenever they need to.

CHAPTER 3
Naming Conventions

Names are but noise and smoke,
Obscuring heavenly light

—Johann Wolfgang von Goethe
    Faust: Part I

Consistent and coherent code layout is vital, because it determines what the reader of your code sees. But naming conventions are even more important, because they determine how the reader *thinks* about your program.

Well-chosen identifier names convey to the reader the meaning of the data in variables, the behaviour and results of subroutines, and the features and purpose of classes and other data types. They can help to make the data structures and algorithms used in a program explicit and unambiguous. They can also function as a reliable form of documentation, and as a powerful debugging aid.

Best practice in naming consists of finding a consistent way of assigning identifiers to variables, subroutines, and types. There are two principal components of this method: syntactic consistency and semantic consistency.

Syntactic consistency means that all identifiers should conform to a predictable and recognizable grammatical structure. That is, you should not name one variable $max_ velocity and then name another $displacementMax, or $mxdsp, or $Xmaximal. In other words, if one variable name has an *adjective_noun* structure, all variable names should be *adjective_noun*. Similarly, if one variable uses underscores to separate components of the name, then others shouldn't omit similar separators elsewhere, or use interCapStyle instead. Your approach to abbreviation—both what to abbreviate and how to abbreviate it—has to be consistent as well.

Semantic consistency means that the names you choose should clearly and accurately reflect the purpose, usage, and significance of whatever you're naming. In other words, a name like @data is a poor choice (compared to, say, @sales_records) because it fails to tell the reader anything important about the contents of the array or their significance in your program. Likewise, naming an indexing variable $i or $n doesn't serve to make the meaning of $sales_records[$i] any clearer, especially when compared to something like $sales_records[$largest_sale_today] or $sales_records[$cancelled_transaction_number].

This chapter explores all these issues, offering a consistent and easy-to-use approach to generating names for the various types of nameable referents in Perl.

Identifiers

Use grammatical templates when forming identifiers.

The single most important practice when creating names is to devise a set of grammar rules to which all names must conform. A grammar rule specifies one or more templates (e.g., *Noun :: Adjective :: Adjective*) that describe how to form the entity on the left of the arrow (e.g., *namespace*). Placeholders in templates, such as *Noun* and *Adjective*, are replaced by the corresponding parts of speech: nouns like "Disk" and adjectives like "Audio". For a Perlish introduction to the concepts of grammars, see the *tutorial.html* file that accompanies the Parse::RecDescent CPAN module.

Develop a set of "name templates" for your packages' subroutines and variables, learn them by heart, and use them consistently. This practice will ensure that you always generate names that have a standard internal structure.

A suitable grammar rule for naming packages and classes is:

```
namespace  →  Noun :: Adjective :: Adjective
            | Noun :: Adjective
            | Noun
```

This rule might produce package names such as:

```perl
package Disk;
package Disk::Audio;
package Disk::DVD;
package Disk::DVD::Rewritable;
```

In this scheme, specialized versions of an existing namespace are named by adding adjectives to the name of the more general namespace. Hence you would expect that Disk::DVD::Rewritable represents a class derived from Disk::DVD, which in turn inherits from the general Disk class. Placing the adjectives last (in defiance of the usual English convention[*]) ensures that the most prominent feature of any class or package name is the hierarchy in which the class belongs.

---

[*] The approach advocated here is much more like the Linnaean system of biological taxonomy: a "genus" name followed by one or more increasingly specific modifiers. Such schemes make it easy to detect that the common *Camelus dromedarius* and the less-common *Camelus bactrianus* are two species of the same genus, that the endangered *Camelus bactrianus ferus* is a particular subspecies of *Camelus bactrianus*, and that all three creatures are wholly unrelated to the elusive *Nessiteras rhombopteryx*.

It's important to remember, however, that Perl won't automatically enforce the hierarchical relationships indicated by this naming scheme. You still have to specify those relationships explicitly:

```perl
package Disk;

package Disk::DVD;
use base qw( Disk );

package Disk::DVD::Rewritable;
use base qw( Disk::DVD );
```

The naming scheme is purely to help human readers of the code identify and remember the relationships you specify.

Variables should be named according to the data they will store, and as specifically as possible. Variables that are used in more than one block should always have a two-part (or longer) name. Reserve single-word names for variables of very limited scope and, even then, consider whether a longer name would be clearer. The recommended grammar rule is very simple. A variable is named with a noun, preceded by zero or more adjectives:

variable → *[adjective _]* noun*

The choice of nouns and adjectives is critical. The nouns in particular should indicate what the variable does in terms of the problem domain, not in terms of the implementation. For example:

```perl
my $next_client;            # not: $next_elem
my $prev_appointment;       # not: $prev_elem
my $estimated_net_worth;    # not: $value

my $next_node;              # not: $node
my $root_node;              # not: $root

my $final_total;            # not: $sum
my $cumulative_total;       # not: $partial_sum
```

The use of adjectives to make an identifier more specific is strongly encouraged. The more specific a name, the easier it is to detect mistakes such as:

```perl
my $total = 0;
my $count = 0;

while (my $next = get_next_score_for($curr_player)) {
    $total++;
    $count += $next;
}
```

That algorithmic error would be much easier to pick out if the variables had more explicit names:

```perl
my $total_score = 0;
my $games_count = 0;
```

```
while (my $next_score = get_next_score_for($curr_player)) {
    $total_score++;
    $games_count += $next_score;
}
```

Incrementing a "total score" is dubious; adding a "score" to a "count" is almost certainly wrong.

Furthermore, the use of qualifiers on variable names can help reinforce the reader's understanding. For example, if a cumulative total is to be printed on each iteration, it would be better to name the variable like so:

```
my $running_total = 0;
my $games_count   = 0;

while (my $next_score = get_next_score_for($curr_player)) {
    $running_total += $next_score;
    $games_count++;
    print "After $games_count: $running_total\n";
}
```

This style leaves the maintainer of the code in no doubt that you really did intend to track cumulative intermediate scores, rather than just the final total. That would be especially obvious if you had accidentally mistyped:

```
my $running_total = 0;
my $games_count   = 0;

while (my $next_score = get_next_score_for($curr_player)) {
    $running_total += $next_score;
    $games_count++;
}
print "After $games_count: $running_total \n";
```

Note that the rules for creating variables ($*adjective_noun*) are the opposite of those for naming classes and packages (*Noun::Adjective*). This is deliberate, and designed to help readers distinguish between the two types of names. The more conventional grammatical structure (adjective before the noun) is used for the more frequently used type of name (i.e., for variables), which improves the overall readability of the code. At the same time, namespace names stand out better because of their unusual reversed syntax.

There is one extra grammatical variation that applies only to hashes and arrays that are used as look-up tables:

lookup_variable → *[adjective _]* noun preposition*

Adding a preposition to the end of the name makes hash and array accesses much more readable:

```
my %title_of;
my %ISBN_for;
my @sales_from;
```

```
# and later...

while (my $month = prompt -menu => $MONTH_NAMES) {
    for my $book ( @catalog ) {
        print "$ISBN_for{$book}  $title_of{$book}: $sales_from[$month]\n";
    }
}
```

For subroutines and methods, a suitable grammatical rule for forming names is:

```
routine  →  imperative_verb  [ _ adjective]?  _  noun  _  preposition
         |  imperative_verb  [ _ adjective]?  _  noun  _  participle
         |  imperative_verb  [ _ adjective]?  _  noun
```

This rule results in subroutine names such as:

```
sub get_record;                        # imperative_verb noun
sub get_record_for;                    # imperative_verb noun preposition

sub eat_cookie;                        # imperative_verb noun
sub eat_previous_cookie;               # imperative_verb adjective noun

sub build_profile;                     # imperative_verb noun
sub build_execution_profile;           # imperative_verb adjective noun
sub build_execution_profile_using;     # imperative_verb adjective noun participle
```

These naming rules—particularly the two that put participles or prepositions at the ends of names—create identifiers that read far more naturally, often eliminating the need for any additional comments:

```
@config_options = get_record_for($next_client);

for my $option (@config_options) {
    build_execution_profile_using($next_client, $option);
}
```

Booleans

Name booleans after their associated test.

A special case can be made for subroutines that return boolean values, and for variables that store them. These should be named for the properties or predicates they test, in such a way that the resulting conditional expressions read naturally. Often that rule will mean they begin with is_ or has_, but not always. For example:

```
sub is_valid;
sub metadata_available_for;
sub has_end_tag;

my $loading_finished;
my $has_found_bad_record;
```

```
    # and later...

    if (is_valid($next_record) && !$loading_finished) {
        METADATA:
        while (metadata_available_for($next_record)) {
            push @metadata, get_metadata_for($next_record);
            last METADATA if has_end_tag($next_record);
        }
    }
    else {
        $has_found_bad_record = 1;
    }
```

Again, explicit and longer names are strongly preferred. Compare the readability of the previous code with the following:

```
    sub ok;
    sub metadata;
    sub end_tag;

    my $done;
    my $bad;

    # and later...

    if (ok($next_record) && !$done) {               # Ok in what sense? What is done?
        METADATA:
        while (metadata($next_record)) {            # Metadata exists? Defined? True?
            push @metadata, get_metadata_for($next_record);
            last METADATA if end_tag($next_record); # Does this set an end tag?
        }
    }
    else {
        $bad = 1;                                    # What's bad? In what way?
    }
```

Reference Variables

Mark variables that store references with a `_ref` suffix.

In Perl, you can't give a variable a specific type to ensure that it's able to store only particular kinds of values (integer, string, reference, and so on). That's usually not a problem, because Perl's automatic type conversions paper over most of the cracks very neatly[*].

Except when it comes to references.

---

[*] If it *is* a problem for you, take a look at the Attribute::Types module on CPAN.

It's an all-too-common mistake to put a reference into a scalar, and then subsequently forget to use the all-important dereferencing arrow:

```perl
sub pad_str {
    my ($text, $opts) = @_;

    my $gap   = $opts{cols} - length $text;        # Oops! Should be: opts->{cols}
    my $left  = $opts{centred} ? int($gap/2) : 0;  # Should be: opts->{centred}
    my $right = $gap - $left;

    return $SPACE x $left . $text . $SPACE x $right;
}
```

Of course, use strict qw(vars) (see Chapter 18) is supposed to pick up precisely this transgression. And it usually will. Unless, of course, there also happens to be a valid %opts hash in the same scope.

You can minimize the chances of making this mistake in the first place by always appending the suffix _ref to any variable that is supposed to store a reference. Of course, naming reference variables this way doesn't *prevent* this particular mistake, or even catch it for you when you do. But it does make the error much more visually obvious:

```perl
sub pad_str {
    my ($text, $opts_ref) = @_;

    my $gap   = $opts_ref{cols} - length $text;
    my $left  = $opts_ref{centred} ? int($gap/2) : 0;
    my $right = $gap - $left;

    return $SPACE x $left . $text . $SPACE x $right;
}
```

If you adopt this coding practice[*], your eyes will soon come to expect an arrow after any occurrence of _ref, and the absence of such a dereferencer will become glaringly obvious.

You could also write a very short Perl script to detect and correct such mistakes:

```perl
#! /usr/bin/perl -w

while (my $src_line = <>) {
    $src_line =~ s{ _ref \s* (?= [\{[(] ) }   # If _ref precedes opening bracket...
                  {_ref->}gxms;               # ...insert an arrow

    print $src_line;
}
```

---

[*] The only piece of "Hungarian notation" recommended in this book.

Arrays and Hashes

Name arrays in the plural and hashes in the singular.

A hash is a mapping from distinct keys to individual values, and is most commonly used as a random-access look-up table. On the other hand, arrays are usually ordered sequences of multiple values, and are most commonly processed collectively or iteratively.

Because hash entries are typically accessed individually, it makes sense for the hash itself to be named in the singular. That convention causes the individual accesses to read more naturally in the code. Moreover, because hashes often store a property that's related to their key, it's often even more readable to name a hash with a singular noun followed by a preposition. For example:

```
my %option;
my %title_of;
my %count_for;
my %is_available;

# and later...

if ($option{'count_all'} && $title_of{$next_book} =~ m/$target/xms) {
    $count_for{$next_book}++;
    $is_available{$next_book} = 1;
}
```

On the other hand, array values are more often processed collectively, in loops or in map or grep operations. So it makes sense to name them in the plural, after the group of items they store:

```
my @events;
my @handlers;
my @unknowns;

# and later...

for my $event (@events) {
    push @unknowns, grep { ! $_->handle($event) } @handlers;
}

print map { $_->err_msg } @unknowns;
```

If, however, an array is to be used as a random-access look-up table, name it in the singular, using the same conventions as for a hash:

```
# Initialize table of factorials
my @factorial = (1);
for my $n (1..$MAX_FACT) {
    $factorial[$n] = $n * $factorial[$n-1];
}
```

```
# Check availability and look up in table
sub factorial {
    my ($n) = @_;

    croak "Can't compute factorial($n)"
        if $n < 0 || $n > $MAX_FACT;

    return $factorial[$n];
}
```

Underscores

Use underscores to separate words in multiword identifiers.

In English, when a name consists of two or more words, those words are typically separated by spaces or hyphens—for example, "input stream", "key pressed", "end-of-file", "double-click".

Since neither spaces nor hyphens are valid characters in Perl identifiers, use the next closest available alternative: the underscore. Underscores correspond better to the default natural-language word separator (a space) because they impose a visual gap between the words in an identifier. For example:

```
FORM:
for my $tax_form (@tax_form_sequence) {
    my $notional_tax_paid
        = $tax_form->{reported_income} * $tax_form->{effective_tax_rate};

    next FORM if $notional_tax_paid  < $MIN_ASSESSABLE;

    $total_paid
        += $notional_tax_paid - $tax_form->{allowed_deductions};
}
```

TheAlternativeInterCapsApproachIsHarderToReadAndInParticularDoesn'tGeneralizeWellToALLCAPSCONSTANTS:

```
FORM:
for my $taxForm (@taxFormSequence) {
    my $notionalTaxPaid
        = $taxForm->{reportedIncome} * $taxForm->{effectiveTaxRate};

    next FORM if $notionalTaxPaid  < $MINASSESSABLE;

    $totalPaid
        += $notionalTaxPaid - $taxForm->{allowedDeductions};
}
```

Capitalization

Distinguish different program components by case.

In a Perl program, an identifier might refer to a variable, a subroutine, a class or package name, an I/O stream, a format, or a typeglob. More importantly, sometimes the same identifier can refer to two or more of those in the same scope:

```
# Print command line files, prefixing each line with the filename...
if (@ARGV) {
    while (my $line = <ARGV>) {
        print "$ARGV: $line";
    }
}
```

To help make it clear what kind of referent an identifier is naming:

- Use lowercase only for the names of subroutines, methods, variables, and labeled arguments ($controller, new( ), src=>$fh).
- Use mixed-case for package and class names (IO::Controller).
- Use uppercase for constants ($SRC, $NODE)*.

For example:

```
my $controller
    = IO::Controller->new(src=>$fh,  mode=>$SRC|$NODE);
```

These case distinctions can then serve as useful clues to the purpose and role of each identifier, with visual differences reinforcing semantic differences. In contrast, it's much harder to distinguish between the variables, constants, methods, and classes in any of the following:

```
my $controller
    = io::controller->new(src=>$fh,  mode=>$src|$node);

my $Controller
    = Io::Controller->New(Src=>$Fh,  Mode=>$Src|$Node);

my $CONTROLLER
    = IO::CONTROLLER->NEW(SRC=>$FH,  MODE=>$SRC|$NODE);
```

Of course, the approach suggested here is by no means the only possible set of conventions. But they *are* the same conventions (adapted for Perl's unique syntax) that are already applied in many languages and software libraries. In addition, they are already widely used throughout the Perl community, and therefore familiar to many programmers.

---

* Yes, constants with sigils. See "Constants" in Chapter 4.

Note that the only exception to this guideline should be in identifiers that include a proper name, a standard abbreviation, or a unit of measurement. These should keep their familiar capitalizations, regardless of the construct they're used in. For example, write:

```
my $expended_MJoules
    = $LaTeX_FUDGE_FACTOR * HTTP_transfer_rate() * $W3C::XHTML->entropy_factor( );
```

not:

```
my $expended_mjoules
    = $LATEX_FUDGE_FACTOR * http_transfer_rate() * $W3c::Xhtml->entropy_factor( );
```

Abbreviations

Abbr idents by prefx.

If you choose to abbreviate an identifier, abbreviate it by retaining the start of each word. This generally produces much more readable names than other approaches. Fr xmpl, bbrvtng wrds by rmvng vwls cn prdc mch lss rdbl nms*.

This example is easily comprehended:

```
use List::Util qw( max );

DESC:
for my $desc (@orig_strs) {
    my $len = length $desc;
    next DESC if $len > $UPPER_LIM;
    $max_len = max($max_len, $len);
}
```

This usage is not nearly as simple to decipher:

```
use List::Util qw( max );

DSCN:
for my $dscn (@rgnl_strgs) {
    my $lngh = length $dscn;
    next DSCN if $lngh > $UPPR_LMT;
    $mx_lngh = max($mx_lngh, $lngh);
}
```

Note that, when you're abbreviating identifiers by prefixing, it's acceptable—and often desirable—to keep the last consonant as well ($orig_strs, prefx( ), and so on), especially if that consonant is a plural suffix.

---

* Dmttdly, ts nt *mpssbl* t dcphr dsmvwld dntfrs r thr bbrvtn schms, bt t *ds* tk mch mr ffrt wtht cnfrrng ny clr bnfts (prt frm mby llwng y t ptch cd v SMS, nd pssbly csng yr pnty-hrd bss's hd t xpld!). Lk hw mch tm yv lrdy wstd jst nrvllng ths ftnt!

This rule need not be applied to identifiers that are well-known standard abbreviations. In such cases, it's better to use the "native" abbreviation strategy:

```
$ctrl_char = '\N{ESCAPE}';

$connection_Mbps  = get_bitrate( ) / 1e6;

$is_tty = -t $msg_src;
```

"Ctrl" is preferable because it appears on most keyboards, whereas $con_char could be misread as "continuation character". "Mbps" is the standard unit, and the alternative ($connection_Mbits_per_sec) is far too unwieldy. As for "tty", "src", and "msg" (or "mesg"), they're all in common use, and the alternatives—"term", "sou", or "mess"—are either ambiguous, obscure, or just plain silly.

Ambiguous Abbreviations

Abbreviate only when the meaning remains unambiguous.

Well-chosen abbreviations can improve the readability of code by reducing the length of identifiers, which can then be recognized as a single visual chunk. Abbreviation is, in effect, a form of visual hashing.

Unfortunately, as with most other hashing schemes, abbreviation suffers from the problem of collisions. When a single abbreviation could be the shortened form of two or more common words, the few characters saved by abbreviating will be paid for over and over again in time lost deciphering the resulting code

```
$term_val       # terminal value or termination valid?
    = $temp     # temperature or temporary?
      * $dev;   # device or deviation?
```

On the other hand, abbreviating down to even a single character can occasionally be appropriate:

```
# Run the standard dynamic and kinematic calculations...
$a = $f / $m;
$v = $u + $a*$t;
$s = $u*$t + 0.5*$a*$t**2;
```

The standard single letter iterator variables—$i, $j, $k, $n, $x, $y, $z—are also often acceptable in nested loops, especially when the indices are coordinates of some kind:

```
sub swap_domain_and_range_of {
    my ($table_ref) = @_;

    my @pivotted_table;
    for my $x (0..$#{$table_ref}) {
        for my $y (0..$#{$table_ref->[$x]}) {
            $pivotted_table[$y][$x] = $table_ref->[$x][$y];
```

```
        }
    }

    return \@pivotted_table;
}
```

Ambiguous Names

Avoid using inherently ambiguous words in names.

It's not only abbreviations that can introduce ambiguities in your identifiers. Complete words often have two or more homonyms, in which case any name containing them will be inherently ambiguous.

One of the worst offenders in this respect is the word "last". A variable named $last_record might refer to the record that was most recently processed (in which case it should be called $prev_record), or it might refer to the ultimate record in a list (in which case it should be called $final_record).

The word "set" is another major stumbling block. A subroutine named get_set() might retrieve a collection of values (in which case, call it retrieve_collection()), or it might test whether the "get" option has been enabled (in which case, call it get_is_enabled()), or it might mediate both fetch and store operations of some value (in which case, call it fetch_or_store()).

Other commonly used words to avoid include:

- "left" (the direction *vs* what remains)
- "right" (the other direction *vs* being correct *vs.* an entitlement)
- "no" (the negative *vs* the abbreviation for number)
- "abstract" (theoretical *vs* a précis *vs* to summarize)
- "contract" (make smaller *vs* a legal agreement)
- "record" (an extreme outcome *vs* a data aggregation *vs* to log)
- "second" (the ordinal position *vs* the unit of time)
- "close" (near *vs* to shut)
- "bases" (more than one base *vs* more than one basis)

Any homograph can potentially cause difficulties if it has a distinct, non-programming-related sense that is relevant to your particular problem domain.

Keep in mind that it may not be immediately obvious to you that a given identifier is ambiguous. Indeed, the alternate interpretation might come to light only when someone else is (mis)reading your code, or when you are puzzling over theirs. If a particular identifier ever leads to this form of confusion, then it should be renamed

---

immediately. However, in your initial coding it probably suffices just to avoid "last" and "set".

Utility Subroutines

Prefix "for internal use only" subroutines with an underscore.

A *utility subroutine* exists only to simplify the implementation of a module or class. It is never supposed to be exported from its module, nor ever to be used in client code.

Always use an underscore as the first "letter" of any utility subroutine's name. A leading underscore is ugly and unusual and reserved (by ancient C/Unix convention) for non-public components of a system. The presence of a leading underscore in a subroutine call makes it immediately obvious when part of the implementation has been mistaken for part of the interface.

For example, if you had a function fib( ) for computing Fibonacci numbers[*] (like the one shown in Example 3-1), then it would be an error to call:

```
print "Fibonacci($n) = ", _find_fib($n), "\n";
```

because _find_fib( ) doesn't return a useful value. You almost certainly wanted:

```
print "Fibonacci($n) = ", fib($n), "\n";
```

By naming _find_fib( )with an initial underscore, the call to it stands out far more clearly, and the misuse is brought immediately to the attention of anyone familiar with the convention.

Example 3-1. Iterative on-demand Fibonacci computations

```
# Cache of previous results, minimally initialized...
my @fib_for = (1,1);

# Extend cache when needed...
sub _find_fib {
    my ($n) = @_;

    # Walk up cache from last known value, applying Fn = Fn-1 + Fn-2...
    for my $i (@fib_for..$n) {
        $fib_for[$i] = $fib_for[$i-1] + $fib_for[$i-2];
    }
}
```

---

[*] Much like the weather, everybody talks about Fibonacci numbers, but nobody ever seems to do anything with them. That's a pity, because the Fibonacci sequence does have important real-world uses: reallocating increasing amounts of memory for data structures whose ultimate size is unknown; estimating reasonable timeouts under uncertain connectivity; scaling retry intervals to resolve lock contentions; or anywhere else that you need to keep retrying some operation, but want it to be bigger, longer, or slower each time.

Example 3-1. Iterative on-demand Fibonacci computations (continued)

```
    return;
}

# Return Fibonacci number N
sub fib {
    my ($n) = @_;

    # Verify argument in computable range...
    croak "Can't compute fib($n)" if $n < 0;

    # Extend cache if necessary...
    if ( !defined $fib_for[$n] ) {
        _find_fib($n);
    }

    # Look up value in cache...
    return $fib_for[$n];
}
```

## CHAPTER 4

Values and Expressions

Data is semi-animate…sort of like programmers.
—Arthur Norman

Constructing and using values ought to be trivial. After all, there are very few components of a Perl program simpler than a character string or a number or a + operator.

Unfortunately, the syntax of Perl's literal values is so rich that there are plenty of ways to mess them up. Variables can interpolate unexpectedly, or fail to interpolate at all. Character escape codes and literal numbers can mysteriously appear in the wrong base. Delimiters can be just about anything you like.

And Perl's operators are even worse. Several of them are polymorphic: silently changing their behaviour depending on the type of argument they're applied to. Others are monomorphic: silently changing their arguments to fit their behaviour. Others are just plain inefficient in some usages.

This chapter suggests some appropriate coding habits that can help you avoid the pitfalls associated with creating values and manipulating them in expressions.

String Delimiters

Use interpolating string delimiters only for strings that actually interpolate.

Unexpectedly interpolating a variable in a character string is a common source of errors in Perl programs. So is unexpected *non*-interpolation. Fortunately, Perl provides two distinct types of strings that make it easy to specify exactly what you want.

If you're creating a literal character string and you definitely intend to interpolate one or more variables into it, use a double-quoted string:

```
my $spam_name = "$title $first_name $surname";
my $pay_rate  = "$minimal for maximal work";
```

If you're creating a literal character string and not intending to interpolate any variables into it, use a single-quoted string:

```
my $spam_name = 'Dr Lawrence Mwalle';
my $pay_rate  = '$minimal for maximal work';
```

If your uninterpolated string includes a literal single quote, use the q{...} form instead:

```
my $spam_name = q{Dr Lawrence ('Larry') Mwalle};
my $pay_rate  = q{'$minimal' for maximal work};
```

Don't use backslashes as quote delimiters; they only make it harder to distinguish the content from the container:

```
my $spam_name = 'Dr Lawrence (\'Larry\') Mwalle';
my $pay_rate  = '\'$minimal\' for maximal work';
```

If your uninterpolated string includes both a literal single quote and an unbalanced brace, use square brackets as delimiters instead:

```
my $spam_name = q[Dr Lawrence }Larry{ Mwalle];
my $pay_rate  = q['$minimal' for warrior's work {{:-)];
```

Reserving interpolating quoters for strings that actually do interpolate something[*] can help you avoid unintentional interpolations, because the presence of a $ or @ in a single-quoted string then becomes a sign that something might be amiss. Likewise, once you become used to seeing double quotes only on interpolated strings, the absence of any variable in a double-quoted string becomes a warning sign. So these rules also help highlight missing intentional interpolations.

The four distinct rules are fine for isolated literals, but when you're creating a set of related string values, mixing and matching the rules can severely reduce the readability of your code:

```
my $title        = 'Perl Best Practices';
my $publisher    = q{O'Reilly};
my $end_of_block = '}';
my $closing_delim = q['}];
my $citation     = "$title ($publisher)";
```

For sequences of "parallel" strings, choose the most general delimiters required and use them consistently throughout the set:

```
my $title        = q[Perl Best Practices];
my $publisher    = q[O'Reilly];
my $end_of_block = q[}];
my $closing_delim = q['}];
my $citation     = qq[$title ($publisher)];
```

---

[*] Note that "interpolation" includes the expansion of character escapes like "\n" and "\t".

Note that there's a two-column gap between the assignment operator and each q[...] character string. This aligns the string delimiters with those of the lone qq[...] string, which helps its keyword stand out and draws attention to its different semantics.

Empty Strings

Don't use "" or ' ' for an empty string.

An important exception to the preceding rules is the empty string. You can't use "", as an empty string doesn't interpolate anything. It doesn't contain a literal quote or brace either, so the previous rules call for it to be written like so:

```
$error_msg = '';
```

But that's not a good choice. In many display fonts, it's far too easy to mistake ' ' (single-quote, single-quote) for " (a lone double-quote), which means that you need to apply the second rule for non-interpolated strings, and write each empty string like so, preferably with a comment highlighting it:

```
$error_msg = q{};    # Empty string
```

Also see the "Constants" guideline later in this chapter.

Single-Character Strings

Don't write one-character strings in visually ambiguous ways.

Character strings that consist of a single character can present a variety of problems, all of which make code harder to maintain.

A single space in quotes is easily confused with an empty string:

```
$separator = ' ';
```

Like an empty string, it should be specified more verbosely:

```
$separator = q{ };    # Single space
```

Literal tabs are even worse (and not just in single-character strings):

```
$separator  = ' ';         # Empty string, single space, or single tab???
$column_gap = '        '; # Spaces? Tabs? Some combination thereof?
```

Always use the interpolated \t form instead:

```
$separator  = "\t";
$column_gap = "\t\t\t";
```

Literal single-quote and double-quote characters shouldn't be specified in quotation marks either, for obvious aesthetic reasons: '"', "\"", '\'', "'". Use q{"} and q{'} instead.

You should also avoid using quotation marks when specifying a single comma character. The most common use of a comma string is as the first argument to a join:

```perl
my $printable_list = '(' . join(',', @list) . ')';
```

The ',', sequence is unnecessarily hard to decipher, especially when:

```perl
my $printable_list = '(' . join(q{,}, @list) . ')';
```

is just as easy to write, and stands out more clearly as being a literal. See the "Constants" guideline later in this chapter for an even cleaner solution.

Escaped Characters

Use named character escapes instead of numeric escapes.

Some ASCII characters that might appear in a string—such as DEL or ACK or CAN—don't have a "native" Perl representation. When one or more of those characters is required, the standard solution is to use a numeric escape: a backslash followed by the character's ASCII value inside double-quotes. For example, using octal escapes:

```perl
$escape_seq = "\127\006\030Z";        # DEL-ACK-CAN-Z
```

or hexadecimal escapes:

```perl
$escape_seq = "\x7F\x06\x22Z";        # DEL-ACK-CAN-Z
```

But not everyone who subsequently reads your code will be familiar with the ASCII values for these characters, which means they will have to rely on the associated comments. That's a real shame too, because both of the previous examples are wrong! The correct sequence was:

```perl
$escape_seq = "\177\006\030Z";        # Octal DEL-ACK-CAN-Z
```

or:

```perl
$escape_seq = "\x7F\x06\x18Z";        # Hexadecimal DEL-ACK-CAN-Z
```

Errors like that are particularly hard to track down. Even if you do know the ASCII table by heart, it's still easy to mistakenly type "\127" for DEL because the ASCII code for DEL *is* 127. At least, in base 10 it is. Unfortunately, backslashed escapes in strings are specified in base 8. And once your brain has accepted the 127-is-DEL relationship, it becomes exceptionally hard to see the mistake. After all, it *looks* right.

That's why it's better to use *named escapes* for those characters that have no explicit Perl representation. Named escapes are available in Perl 5.6 and later, and are enabled via the use charnames pragma. Once they're operational, instead of using a numeric escape you can put the name of the required character inside a \N{...} sequence within any double-quoted string. For example:

```
use charnames qw( :full );

$escape_seq = "\N{DELETE}\N{ACKNOWLEDGE}\N{CANCEL}Z";
```

Note that there's no need for a comment here; when you use the actual names of the characters within the string, the escapes become self-documenting.

Constants

Use named constants, but don't use constant.

Raw numbers that suddenly appear in the middle of a program are often mysterious, frequently confusing, and always a potential source of errors. Certain types of unprintable character strings—for example, initialization strings for modems—are similarly awkward.

A line like this:

```
print $count * 42;
```

is unsatisfactory, as the reader may have no idea from the context why the variable is being multiplied by that particular number. Is it 42: the number of dots on a pair of dice? Or 42: the decimal ASCII value of asterisk? Or 42: the number of chromosomes in common wheat? Or 42: the angular spread of a rainbow? Or 42: the number of lines per page in the Gutenberg Bible? Or 42: the number of gallons per barrel of oil?

Replace these kinds of raw literals with a read-only lexical variable whose name explains the meaning of the number:

```
use Readonly;
Readonly my $MOLYBDENUM_ATOMIC_NUMBER => 42;

# and later...

print $count * $MOLYBDENUM_ATOMIC_NUMBER;
```

The Readonly CPAN module exports a single subroutine (Readonly( )) that expects two arguments: a scalar, array, or hash variable, and a value. The value is assigned to the variable, and then the variable's "read-only" flag is set, to prevent any further assignments. Note the use of all-uppercase in the variable name (in accordance with the guideline in Chapter 3) and the use of the fat comma (because the constant name and its value form a natural pair—see "Fat Commas" later in this chapter).

If you accidentally try to assign a new value to a constant:

```
$MOLYBDENUM_ATOMIC_NUMBER = $CARBON_ATOMIC_NUMBER * $NITROGEN_ATOMIC_NUMBER;
```

the interpreter immediately throws an exception:

```
Modification of a read-only value attempted at nuclear_lab.pl line 13
```

Even when the constant is instantly recognizable, and highly unlikely ever to change, it's still better to give it a name. Naming the constant improves the level of abstraction, and therefore the readability, of the resulting code:

```
use Readonly;
Readonly my $PI => 3.1415926;

# and later...

$area = $PI * $radius**2;
```

The same approach is also particularly helpful when dealing with empty strings:

```
use Readonly;
Readonly my $EMPTY_STR => q{};

# and later...

my $error_msg = $EMPTY_STR;
```

This named constant is far less likely to be overlooked or misinterpreted than a raw '' might be. It's also less mystifying to inexperienced Perl programmers than a q{}. Likewise, the other visually ambiguous literals can be made much clearer with:

```
Readonly my $SPACE        => q{ };
Readonly my $SINGLE_QUOTE => q{'};
Readonly my $DOUBLE_QUOTE => q{"};
Readonly my $COMMA        => q{,};
```

The obvious question at this point is: *why* use Readonly *instead of* use constant? After all, the constant pragma comes standard with Perl, and the constants it creates don't have those annoying sigils.

Well, it turns out those annoying sigils are actually highly useful, because they allow Readonly-generated constants to be interpolated into other strings. For example:

```
use Readonly;
Readonly my $DEAR      => 'Greetings to you,';
Readonly my $SINCERELY => 'May Heaven guard you from all misfortune,';

$msg = <<"END_MSG";
$DEAR $target_name

$scam_pitch

$SINCERELY

$fake_name
END_MSG
```

Bareword constants can't be interpolated, so you have to write:

```
use constant {
    DEAR     => 'Greetings to you,',
    SINCERELY => 'May Heaven guard you from all misfortune,',
};

# and later...

$msg = DEAR . $target_name
     . "$scam_pitch\n\n"
     . SINCERELY
     . "\n\n$fake_name";
```

which is both harder to read and easier to get wrong (for example, there's a space missing between the DEAR and the $target_name).

The sigils also ensure that constants behave as expected in autostringifying contexts:

```
use Readonly;
Readonly my $LINES_PER_PAGE => 42;        # Gutenberg-compatible

# and later...

$margin{$LINES_PER_PAGE}                   # sets $margin{'42'}
    = $MAX_LINES - $LINES_PER_PAGE;
```

In contrast, constants created by use constant are treated as barewords anywhere a string is expected:

```
use constant (
    LINES_PER_PAGE => 42
);

# and later...

$margin{LINES_PER_PAGE}                    # sets $margin{'LINES_PER_PAGE'}
    = MAX_LINES - LINES_PER_PAGE;
```

But perhaps most importantly, use Readonly allows you to create lexically scoped constants at runtime:

```
EVENT:
while (1) {
    use Readonly;
    Readonly my $EVENT => get_next_event();

    last EVENT if not defined $EVENT;

    if ($VERBOSE) {
        print $EVENT->desc(), "\n";
    }

    # process event here...
}
```

whereas use `constant` creates package-scoped constant subroutines at compile time:

```
EVENT:
while (1) {
    use constant EVENT => get_next_event();

    last EVENT if not defined EVENT;

    if (VERBOSE) {
        print EVENT->desc(), "\n";
    }

    # process event here...
}
```

That difference is critical here, because the use `constant` version will call `get_next_event()` only once—at compile time. If no event is available at that time, the subroutine will presumably return `undef`, and the loop will terminate before completing even a single iteration. The behaviour will be even worse if an event *is* available at compile time, in which case that event will be bound forever to the `EVENT` constant, and the loop will never terminate. The `Readonly` version doesn't suffer the same problem, because it executes at runtime, reinitializing the `$EVENT` constant each time the loop iterates.

Note that to get the full benefits of `Readonly`, you need to be using Perl 5.8 and have installed the associated `Readonly::XS` module, which requires precompilation. Be sure to read the module's documentation for a careful description of the pros and cons of using `Readonly` under earlier versions of Perl or without the precompiled helper module.

If you decide not to use the `Readonly` module in production code (for performance or political reasons), then using `constant` is still better than using literal values.

Leading Zeros

Don't pad decimal numbers with leading zeros.

Several of the guidelines in this book recommend laying out data in table format, and aligning that data vertically. For example:

```
use Readonly;

Readonly my %ATOMIC_NUMBER => (
    NITROGEN    =>     7,
    NIOBIUM     =>    41,
    NEODYNIUM   =>    60,
    NOBELIUM    =>   102,
);
```

But sometimes the desire to make columns line up cleanly can be counterproductive. For example, you might be tempted to pad the atomic number values with zeros to make them uniform:

```
use Readonly;

Readonly my %ATOMIC_NUMBER => (
    NITROGEN   =>  007,
    NIOBIUM    =>  041,
    NEODYNIUM  =>  060,
    NOBELIUM   =>  102,
);
```

Unfortunately, that also makes them wrong. Even though leading zeros aren't significant in mathematics, they *are* significant in Perl. Any integer that begins with a zero is interpreted as an octal number, not a decimal. So the example zero-padded version is actually equivalent to:

```
use Readonly;

Readonly my %ATOMIC_NUMBER => (
    NITROGEN   =>    7,
    NIOBIUM    =>   33,
    NEODYNIUM  =>   48,
    NOBELIUM   =>  102,
);
```

To avoid this covert transmutation of the numbers, never start a literal integer with zero. Even if you *do* intend to specify octal numbers, don't use a leading zero, as that may still mislead inattentive future readers of your code.

If you need to specify octal values, use the built-in oct function, like so:

```
use Readonly;

Readonly my %PERMISSIONS_FOR => (
    USER_ONLY      => oct(600),
    NORMAL_ACCESS  => oct(644),
    ALL_ACCESS     => oct(666),
);
```

Long Numbers

Use underscores to improve the readability of long numbers.

Large numbers can be difficult to sanity check:

```
$US_GDP              = 10990000000000;
$US_govt_revenue     =  1782000000000;
$US_govt_expenditure =  2156000000000;
```

Those figures are supposed to be in the trillions, but it's very hard to tell if they have the right number of zeros. So Perl provides a convenient mechanism for making large numbers easier to read: you can use underscores to "separate your thousands":

```
# In the US they use thousands, millions, billions, trillions, etc...
$US_GDP              = 10_990_000_000_000;
$US_govt_revenue     =  1_782_000_000_000;
$US_govt_expenditure =  2_156_000_000_000;
```

Prior to Perl 5.8, these separators could only be placed in front of every third digit of an integer (i.e., to separate the thousands, millions, billions, etc.). From 5.8 onwards, underscores can be placed between *any* two digits. For example:

```
# In India they use lakhs, crores, arabs, kharabs, etc...
$India_GDP              = 30_33_00_00_00_000;
$India_govt_revenue     =    86_69_00_00_000;
$India_govt_expenditure =  1_14_60_00_00_000;
```

Separators can also now be used in floating-point numbers and non-decimals, to make them easier to comprehend as well:

```
use bignum;
$PI = 3.141592_653589_793238_462643_383279_502884_197169_399375;

$subnet_mask= 0xFF_FF_FF_80;
```

Multiline Strings

Lay out multiline strings over multiple lines.

If a string has embedded newline characters, but the entire string won't fit on a single source line, then break the string after each newline and concatenate the pieces:

```
$usage = "Usage: $0 <file> [-full]\n"
         . "(Use -full option for full dump)\n"
         ;
```

In other words, the internal appearance of the string should mirror its external (printed) appearance as closely as possible.

Don't, however, be tempted to make the newline implicit, by wrapping a single string across multiple lines, like so:

```
$usage = "Usage: $0 <file> [-full]
(Use -full option for full dump)
";
```

Even though actual line breaks inside such a string *do* become newline characters within the string, the readability of such code suffers severely. It's harder to verify the line structure of the resulting string, because the first line is indented whilst the remaining lines have to be fully left-justified. That justification can also compromise your code's indentation structure.

Here Documents

Use a heredoc when a multiline string exceeds two lines.

The "break-after-newlines-and-concatenate" approach is fine for a small number of lines, but it starts to become inefficient—and ugly—for larger chunks of text.

For multiline strings that exceed two lines, use a heredoc:

```
$usage = <<"END_USAGE";
Usage: $0 <file> [-full] [-o] [-beans]
Options:
    -full  : produce a full dump
    -o     : dump in octal
    -beans : source is Java
END_USAGE
```

instead of:

```
$usage = "Usage: $0 <file> [-full] [-o] [-beans]\n"
       . "Options:\n"
       . "    -full  : produce a full dump\n"
       . "    -o     : dump in octal\n"
       . "    -beans : source is Java\n"
       ;
```

Heredoc Indentation

Use a "theredoc" when a heredoc would compromise your indentation.

Of course, even if your lines *are* all simple strings, the problem with using a heredoc in the middle of code is that its contents must be left-justified, regardless of the indentation level of the code it's in:

```
if ($usage_error) {
    warn <<'END_USAGE';
Usage: qdump <file> [-full] [-o] [-beans]
Options:
    -full  : produce a full dump
    -o     : dump in octal
    -beans : source is Java
END_USAGE
}
```

A better practice is to factor out any such heredoc into a predefined constant or a subroutine (a "theredoc"):

```
use Readonly;
Readonly my $USAGE => <<'END_USAGE';
Usage: qdump file [-full] [-o] [-beans]
Options:
    -full  : produce a full dump
    -o     : dump in octal
    -beans : source is Java
END_USAGE

# and later...

if ($usage_error) {
    warn $USAGE;
}
```

If the heredoc needs to interpolate variables whose values are not known at compile time, use a subroutine instead, and parameterize the variables:

```
sub build_usage {
    my ($prog_name, $filename) = @_;

    return <<"END_USAGE";
Usage: $prog_name $filename [-full] [-o] [-beans]
Options:
    -full  : produce a full dump
    -o     : dump in octal
    -beans : source is Java
END_USAGE
}

# and later...

if ($usage_error) {
    warn build_usage($PROGRAM_NAME, $requested_file);
}
```

The heredoc does compromise the indentation of the subroutine, but that's now a small and isolated section of the code, so it doesn't significantly impair the overall readability of your program.

Heredoc Terminators

Make every heredoc terminator a single uppercase identifier with a standard prefix.

You can use just about anything you like as a heredoc terminator. For example:

```
    print <<'end list';              # Prints 3 lines then [DONE]
    get name
    set size
    put next
    end list

    print "[DONE]\n";
```

or:

```
    print <<'';                      # Prints 4 lines (up to the empty line) then [DONE]
    get name
    set size
    put next
    end list

    print "[DONE]\n";
```

or even:

```
    print <<'print "[DONE]\n";';     # Prints 5 lines but no [DONE]!
    get name
    set size
    put next
    end list

    print "[DONE]\n";
```

Please don't. Heredocs are tough enough to understand as it is. Using bizarre terminators only makes them more difficult. It's a far better practice to stick with terminators that are capitalized (so they stand out better in mixed-case code) and free of whitespace (so only a single visual token has to be recognized).

For example, compared to the previous examples, it's much easier to tell what the contents of the following heredoc are:

```
    print <<'END_LIST';
    get name
    set size
    put next
    END_LIST
```

But even with a single identifier as terminator, both the contents and the termination marker of a heredoc still have to be left-justified. So it can still be difficult to detect the end of a heredoc. By naming every heredoc marker with a standard, easily recognized prefix, you can make them much easier to pick out.

'END_...' is the recommended choice for this prefix. That is, instead of:

```
    Readonly my $USAGE => <<"USAGE";
    Usage: $0 <file> [-full] [-o] [-beans]
    Options:
        -full  : produce a full dump
        -o     : dump in octal
        -beans : source is Java
    USAGE
```

delimit your heredocs like so:

```
Readonly my $USAGE => <<"END_USAGE";
Usage: $0 <file> [-full] [-o] [-beans]
Options:
    -full  : produce a full dump
    -o     : dump in octal
    -beans : source is Java
END_USAGE
```

It helps to think of the << heredoc introducer as being pronounced "Everything up to…", so that the previous code reads as: *the read-only* $USAGE *variable is initialized with everything up to* END_USAGE.

Heredoc Quoters

When introducing a heredoc, quote the terminator.

Notice that all the heredoc examples in the previous guidelines used either single or double quotes after the <<. Single-quoting the marker forces the heredoc to not interpolate variables. That is, it acts just like a single-quoted string:

```
Readonly my $GRIPE => <<'END_GRIPE';
$minimal for maximal work
END_GRIPE

print $GRIPE;      # Prints: $minimal for maximal work
```

Double-quoting the marker ensures that the heredoc string *is* interpolated, just like a double-quoted string:

```
Readonly my $GRIPE => <<"END_GRIPE";
$minimal for maximal work
END_GRIPE

print $GRIPE;      # Prints: 4.99 an hour for maximal work
```

Most people aren't sure what the default interpolation behaviour is if you don't use any quotes on the marker:

```
Readonly my $GRIPE => <<END_GRIPE;
$minimal for maximal work
END_GRIPE

print $GRIPE;      # ???
```

Do you know? Are you sure? And even if you *are* sure you know, are you sure that your colleagues all know?

And that's the whole point. Heredocs aren't used as frequently as other types of strings, so their default interpolation behaviour isn't as familiar to most Perl programmers.

Adding the explicit quotes around the heredoc marker takes almost no extra effort, but it relieves every reader of the considerable extra effort of having to remember the default behaviour*. Or, more commonly, of having to look up the default behaviour every time.

It's always best practice to say precisely what you mean, and to record as much of your intention as possible in the actual source code—even if saying what you mean makes the code a little more verbose.

Barewords

Don't use barewords.

In Perl, any identifier that the compiler doesn't recognize as a subroutine (or as a package name or filehandle or label or built-in function) is treated as an unquoted character string. For example:

```
$greeting = Hello . World;
print $greeting, "\n";                    # Prints: HelloWorld
```

Barewords are fraught with peril. They're inherently ambiguous, because their meaning can be changed by the introduction or removal of seemingly unrelated code. In the previous example, a Hello( ) subroutine might somehow come to be defined before the assignment, perhaps when a new version of some module started to export that subroutine by default. If that were to happen, the former Hello bareword would silently become a zero-argument Hello( ) subroutine call.

Even without such pre-emptive predeclarations, barewords are unreliable. If someone refactored the previous example into a single print statement:

```
print Hello, World, "\n";
```

then you'd suddenly get a compile-time error:

```
No comma allowed after filehandle at demo.pl line 1
```

That's because Perl always treats the first bareword after a print as a named filehandle†, rather than as a bareword string value to be printed.

Barewords can also crop up accidentally, like this:

```
my @sqrt = map {sqrt $_} 0..100;
for my $N (2,3,5,8,13,21,34,55) {
    print $sqrt[N], "\n";
}
```

---

* Which happens to be: interpolate like a double-quoted string.

† Technically speaking, it treats the bareword as a symbolic reference to the current package's symbol table entry, from which the print then extracts the corresponding filehandle object.

And your brain will "helpfully" gloss over the critical difference between $sqrt[$N] and $sqrt[N]. The latter is really $sqrt['N'], which in turn becomes $sqrt[0] in the numeric context of the array index; unless, of course, there's a sub N() already defined, in which case anything might happen.

All in all, barewords are far too error-prone to be relied upon. So don't use them at all. The easiest way to accomplish that is to put a use strict qw(subs), or just a use strict, at the start of any source file (see Chapter 18). The strict pragma will then detect any barewords at compile time:

```
use strict 'subs';

my @sqrt = map {sqrt $_} 0..100;
for my $N (2,3,5,8,13,21,34,55) {
    print $sqrt[N], "\n";
}
```

and throw an exception:

```
Bareword "N" not allowed while "strict subs" in use at sqrts.pl line 5
```

Fat Commas

Reserve => for pairs.

Whenever you are creating a list of key/value or name/value pairs, use the "fat comma" (=>) to connect the keys to their corresponding values. For example, use it when constructing a hash:

```
%default_service_record  = (
    name   => '<unknown>',
    rank   => 'Recruit',
    serial => undef,
    unit   => ['Training platoon'],
    duty   => ['Basic training'],
);
```

or when passing named arguments to a subroutine (see Chapter 9):

```
$text = format_text({ src=>$raw_text,  margins=>[1,62], justify=>'left' });
```

or when creating a constant:

```
Readonly my $ESCAPE_SEQ => "\N{DELETE}\N{ACKNOWLEDGE}\N{CANCEL}Z";
```

The fat comma visually reinforces the connection between the name and the following value. It also removes the need to quote the key string, as long as you use only valid Perl identifiers* as keys. Compare the readability of the previous examples with the following comma-only versions:

```
%default_service_record  = (
    'name',    '<unknown>',
    'rank',    'Recruit',
    'serial', undef,
    'unit',    ['Training platoon'],
    'duty',    ['Basic training'],
);

$text = format_text('src', $raw_text, 'margins', [1,62], 'justify', 'left');

Readonly my $ESCAPE_SEQ, "\N{DELETE}\N{ACKNOWLEDGE}\N{CANCEL}Z";
```

An alternative criterion that is sometimes used when considering a => is whether you can pronounce the symbol as some kind of *process verb*, such as "becomes" or "produces" or "implies" or "goes into" or "is sent to". For example:

```
# The substring of $name becomes whatever's in $new_name
substr $name, $from, $len => $new_name;

# Send this signal to this process
send_signal($signal => $process);

# Open a handle to a particular file
open my $binary => '<:raw', $filename
    or croak "Can't open '$filename': $OS_ERROR";
```

Underlying this approach is the idea of using the prominence of the fat comma to mark the boundary of two distinct subsets within an argument list. At the same time, the arrow-like appearance of the operator is supposed to convey a sense of moving or changing or mapping values. The problem here is that it's far too easy to misinterpret the direction and destination of the "movement" being represented. For example:

```
# The substring of $name GOES INTO $new_name (No it doesn't!)
substr $name, $from, $len => $new_name;

# Open a handle GOING OUT TO a particular file (No it won't!)
open my $binary => $filename;
```

Moreover, the original pronunciation-based criterion for using a fat comma can easily be forgotten. Thereafter, the => is likely to be used indiscriminately, often counterintuitively, and occasionally as a kind of "wish-fulfillment operator":

```
# This may or may not send the signal to the process
# (depending on the order in which send_msg() expects its arguments)
send_msg($signal => $process);
```

---

* A valid Perl identifier is an alphabetic character or underscore, optionally followed by one or more alphanumeric characters or underscores.

```
# This doesn't find the index of the target in the text (it's vice versa)
$found_at = index $target => $text;

# An excellent money-making plan ... for the casino
push @casino_money => @my_wallet;
```

Considering the potential for confusion, it's better to reserve the fat comma exclusively for hash entries, named arguments, and other name/value pairs.

Thin Commas

Don't use commas to sequence statements.

Perl programmers from a C/C++ background are used to writing C-style for loops in Perl:

```
# Binary chop search...
SEARCH:
for ($min=0,$max=$#samples, $found_target=0; $min<=$max; ) {
    $pos = int(($max+$min)/2);
    my $test_val = $samples[$pos];

    if ($target == $test_val) {
        $found_target = 1;
        last SEARCH;
    }
    elsif ($target < $test_val) {
        $max = $pos-1;
    }
    else {
        $min = $pos+1;
    }
}
```

Each comma within the for initialization acts as a kind of "junior semicolon", separating substatements within the first compartment of the for.

After seeing commas used that way, people sometimes think that it's also possible to use "junior semicolons" within a list:

```
print 'Sir ',
    (check_name($name), $name),
    ', KBE';
```

The intent seems to be to check the person's name just before it's printed, with check_name( ) throwing an exception if the name is wrong (see Chapter 13). The underlying assumption is that using a comma would mean that only the final value in the parentheses was passed on to print.

Unfortunately, that's not what happens. The comma actually has two distinct roles in Perl. In a scalar context, it is (as those former C programmers expect) a sequencing operator: "do this, then do that". But in a list context, such as the argument list of a print, the comma is a list *separator*, not technically an operator at all.

The subexpression (check_name($name), $name) is merely a sublist. And a list context automatically flattens any sublists into the main list. That means that the previous example is the same as:

```
print 'Sir ',
      check_name($name),
      $name,
      ', KBE';
```

which will probably not produce the desired effect:

```
Sir 1Tim Berners-Lee, KBE
```

The best way to avoid such problems is to adopt a style that limits commas to a single role: that of separating the items of lists. Then there can be no confusion between scalar comma operators and list comma separators.

If two or more statements need to be treated as a single statement, don't use scalar commas as "junior semicolons". Instead, use a do block and real semicolons:

```
# Binary chop search...
SEARCH:
for (do{$min=0; $max=$#samples;  $found_target=0;}; $min<=$max; ) {
    # etc, as before
}

print 'Sir ',
      do{ check_name($name); $name; },
      ', KBE';
```

Or, better still, find a way to factor the sequence of statements out of the expression entirely:

```
($min, $max, $found_target) = (0, $#samples, 0);

SEARCH:
while ($min<=$max) {
    # [Binary chop implementation as shown earlier]
}

check_name($name);
print "Sir $name, KBE";
```

Low-Precedence Operators

Don't mix high- and low-precedence booleans.

Perl's low-precedence logical not reads much better than its corresponding high-precedence ! operator. So it's tempting to write:

```
next CLIENT if not $finished;    # Much nicer than: if !$finished
```

However, the extremely low precedence of not can lead to problems if that condition is later extended:

```
next CLIENT if not $finished || $result < $MIN_ACCEPTABLE;
```

It's likely that at least some readers of your code will mistake the behaviour of that statement and assume that it's equivalent to:

```
next CLIENT if (not $finished) || $result < $MIN_ACCEPTABLE;
```

It's not. It actually means:

```
next CLIENT if not( $finished || $result < $MIN_ACCEPTABLE );
```

Even if the choice of || was deliberate, and implements the desired test correctly, there is nothing in the code to indicate that the mixing of precedence was intentional. So, while the novice reader is left to wonder about the meaning of the expression, the more experienced reader is left to wonder about its correctness.

Replacing the || with an or would solve the precedence problem (if indeed there were one), since or is even lower precedence than not:

```
next CLIENT if not $finished or $result < $MIN_ACCEPTABLE;
```

And then adding a pair of parentheses would explicitly indicate whether the intention was:

```
next CLIENT if not($finished or $result < $MIN_ACCEPTABLE);
```

or:

```
next CLIENT if not($finished) or $result < $MIN_ACCEPTABLE;
```

On the other hand, the high-precedence boolean operators don't seem to invoke the same levels of fear, uncertainty, or doubt, probably because they're used much more frequently. It's safer and more comprehensible to use only high-precedence booleans in conditional expressions:

```
next CLIENT if !$finished || $result < $MIN_ACCEPTABLE;
```

and then use parentheses when you need to vary precedence:

```
next CLIENT if !( $finished || $result < $MIN_ACCEPTABLE);
```

To maximize the comprehensibility of conditional tests, avoid and and not completely, and reserve low-precedence or for specifying "fallback positions" on fallible builtins:

```
open my $source, '<', $source_file
    or croak "Couldn't access source code: $OS_ERROR";
```

(but see also "Builtin Failures" in Chapter 13).

Lists

Parenthesize every raw list.

The precedence of the comma operator is so low that, even when it's in a list context, it may not act the way that a casual reader expects. For example, the following assignment:

```
@todo = 'Patent concept of 1 and 0', 'Sue Microsoft and IBM', 'Profit!';
```

is identical to:

```
@todo = 'Patent concept of 1 and 0';
'Sue Microsoft and IBM';
'Profit!';
```

That's because the precedence of the comma is less than that of assignment, so the previous example is really a set of "junior semicolons":

```
(@todo = 'Patent concept of 1 and 0'), 'Sue Microsoft and IBM', 'Profit!';
```

For that reason it's a good practice to ensure that comma-separated lists of values are always safely enclosed in parentheses, to boost the precedence of the comma-separators appropriately:

```
@todo = ('Patent concept of 1 and 0', 'Sue Microsoft and IBM', 'Profit!');
```

But be careful to avoid the all-too-common error of using square brackets instead of parentheses:

```
@todo = ['Patent concept of 1 and 0', 'Sue Microsoft and IBM', 'Profit!'];
```

This example produces a @todo array with only a single element, which is a reference to an anonymous array containing the three strings.

List Membership

**Use table-lookup to test for membership in lists of strings;
use** any( ) **for membership of lists of anything else.**

Like grep, the any( ) function from List::MoreUtils (see "Utilities" in Chapter 8) takes a block of code followed by a list of values. Like grep, it applies the code block to each value in turn, passing them as $_. But, unlike grep, any( ) returns a true value as soon as any of the values causes its test block to succeed. If none of the values ever makes the block true, any( ) returns false.

This behaviour makes any( ) an efficient general solution for testing list membership, because you can put any kind of equivalence test in the block. For example:

```
# Is the index number already taken?
if ( any { $requested_slot == $_ } @allocated_slots ) {
    print "Slot $requested_slot is already taken. Please select another: ";
    redo GET_SLOT;
}
```

or:

```
# Is the bad guy at the party under an assumed name?
if ( any { $fugitive->also_known_as($_) } @guests ) {
    stay_calm( );
    dial(911);
    do_not_approach($fugitive);
}
```

But don't use any( ) if your list membership test uses eq:

```
Readonly my @EXIT_WORDS => qw(
    q quit bye exit stop done last finish aurevoir
);

# and later...

if ( any { $cmd eq $_ } @EXIT_WORDS ) {
    abort_run( );
}
```

In such cases it's much better to use a look-up table instead:

```
Readonly my %IS_EXIT_WORD
    = map { ($_ => 1) } qw(
            q quit bye exit stop done last finish aurevoir
        );

# and later...

if ( $IS_EXIT_WORD{$cmd} ) {
    abort_run( );
}
```

The hash access is faster than a linear search through an array, even if that search can short-circuit. The code implementing the test is far more readable as well.

## CHAPTER 5

Variables

Variables won't. Constants aren't.
—Osborn's Law

Compared to most mainstream languages, Perl has an embarrassingly rich variety of built-in variables. The largest group of these are the global *punctuation variables*—$_, $/, $|, @_, @+, %!, %^H—which control a wide range of fundamental program behaviours, and which are largely responsible for Perl's unwarranted reputation as "executable line-noise". Other standard variables have more obvious names—@ARGV, %SIG, ${^TAINT}—but are still global in their scope, and in their effects as well.

Perl also provides self-declaring package variables. These will silently spring into existence the first time they're referred to, helpfully converting typos into valid, but incorrect, code.

This chapter presents a series of coding practices that can minimize the problems associated with Perl's sometimes over-helpful built-in variables. It also offers some techniques for making the most efficient use of variables you create yourself.

Lexical Variables

Avoid using non-lexical variables.

Stick to using only lexical variables (my), unless you genuinely need the functionality that only a package or punctuation variable can provide.

Using non-lexical variables increases the "coupling" of your code. If two otherwise unrelated sections of code both use a package variable, those two pieces of code can interact with each other in very subtle ways, just by the way they each interact with that shared variable. In other words, without full knowledge of every other piece of code that is called from a particular statement, it is impossible to know whether the value of a given non-lexical variable will somehow be changed by executing that statement.

Some of Perl's built-in non-lexical variables, such as $_, @ARGV, $AUTOLOAD, or $a and $b, are impossible to avoid. But most of the rest are not required in general programming, and there are usually better alternatives. Table 5-1 lists the commonly used Perl built-in variables and what you should use instead. Note that prior to Perl 5.8, you may need to specify use IO::Handle explicitly before using the suggestions that involve method calls on filehandles.

Table 5-1. Alternatives to built-in variables

Variable	Purpose	Alternative
$1, $2, $3, etc.	Store substrings captured from the previous regex match	Assign captures directly using list context regex matching, or unpack them into lexical variables immediately after the match (see Chapter 12). Note that these variables *are* still acceptable in the replacement string of a substitution, because there is no alternative. For example: `s{($DD)/($MMM)/($YYYY)}{$3-$2-$1}xms`
$&	Stores the complete substring most recently matched by a regex	Place an extra set of capturing parentheses around the entire regex, or use Regexp::MatchContext (see the "Match Variables" guideline later in this chapter).
$`	Stores the substring that preceded the most recent successful regex match	Place a ((?s).*?) at the beginning of the regex to capture everything up to the start of the pattern you are actually interested in, or use Regexp::MatchContext.
$'	Stores the substring that followed the most recent successful regex match	Place a ((?s).*) at the end of the regex to capture everything after the pattern you are actually interested in, or use Regexp::MatchContext.
$*	Controls newline matching in regexes	Use the /m regex modifier.
$.	Stores the current line number of the current input stream	Use $fh->input_line_number( ).
$|	Controls autoflushing of the current output stream	Use $fh->autoflush( ).
$"	Array element separator when interpolating into strings	Use an explicit join.
$%, $=, $-, $~, $^, $:, $^L, $^A	Control various features of Perl's format mechanism	Use Perl6::Form::form instead (see Chapter 19).
$[	Determines the starting index of arrays and strings	Never change the starting index from zero.
@F	Stores the result of autosplitting the current line	Don't use the -a command-line flag when invoking *perl*.
$^W	Controls warnings	Under Perl 5.6.1 and later, specify use warnings instead.

Package Variables

Don't use package variables in your own development.

Even if you're occasionally forced to use Perl's built-in non-lexical variables, there's no reason to use ordinary package variables in your own development.

For example, don't use package variables to store state inside a module:

```
package Customer;

use Perl6::Export::Attrs;     # See Chapter 17

# State variables...
our %customer;
our %opt;

sub list_customers : Export {
    for my $id (sort keys %customer) {
        if ($opt{terse}) {
            print "$customer{$id}{name}\n";
        }
        else {
            print $customer{$id}->dump();
        }
    }
    return;
}


# and later in...
package main;
use Customer qw( list_customers );

$Customer::opt{terse} = 1;

list_customers();
```

Lexical variables are a much better choice. And if they need to be accessed outside the package, provide a separate subroutine to do that:

```
package Customer;

use Perl6::Export::Attrs;

# State variables...
my %customer;
my %opt;
```

```
sub set_terse {
    $opt{terse} = 1;
    return;
}

sub list_customers : Export {
    for my $id (sort keys %customer) {
        if ($opt{terse}) {
            print "$customer{$id}{name}\n";
        }
        else {
            print $customer{$id}->dump( );
        }
    }
    return;
}

# and elsewhere...

package main;
use Customer qw( list_customers );

Customer::set_terse( );

list_customers( );
```

If you never use package variables, there's no possibility that people using your module could accidentally corrupt its internal state. Developers who are using your code simply cannot access the lexical state variables outside your module, so there is no possibility of incorrectly assigning to them.

Using a subroutine call like Customer::set_terse( ) to store or retrieve module state means that you (the module writer) retain control over how state variables are modified. For example, later in the development cycle it might be necessary to integrate a more general reporting package into the source code:

```
package Customer;

use Perl6::Export::Attrs;

# State variables...
my %customer;
my %opt;

use Reporter;

sub set_terse {
    return Reporter::set_terseness_for({ name => 1 });
}
```

```
sub list_customers : Export {
    for my $id (sort keys %customer) {
        Reporter::report({ name => $customer{$id} });
    }
    return;
}
```

Note that, although there is no longer a $opt{terse} variable inside the package, any code that calls Customer::set_terse( ) will continue to work without change. If $opt{terse} had been a package variable, you would now have to either track down every assignment to it and change that code to call Reporter::set_terseness_for( ), or replace $opt{terse} with a tied variable (see Chapter 19).

Generally speaking, it's bad practice to use variables anywhere in a module's interface. Chapter 17 discusses this point further.

Localization

If you're forced to modify a package variable, localize it.

Occasionally you will have no choice but to use a package variable, usually because some other developer has made it part of the module's public interface. But if you change the value of that variable, you're making a permanent decision for every other piece of code in your program that uses the module:

```
use YAML;
$YAML::Indent = 4;        # Indent hereafter 4 everywhere that YAML is used
```

By using a local declaration when making that change, you restrict its effects to the dynamic scope of the declaration:

```
use YAML;
local $YAML::Indent = 4; # Indent is 4 until control exits current scope
```

That is, by prefacing the assignment with the word local, you can temporarily replace the package variable $YAML::Indent until control reaches the end of the current scope. So any calls to the various subroutines in the YAML package from within the current scope will see an indent value of 4. And after the scope is exited, the previous indent value (whatever it was) will be restored.

This is much more neighbourly behaviour. Rather than imposing your personal preferences on the rest of the program, you're imposing them only on your small corner of the code.

Initialization

Initialize any variable you localize.

Many people seem to think that a localized variable keeps its pre-localization value. It doesn't. Whenever a variable is localized, its value is reset to undef[*].

So this probably won't work as expected:

```
use YAML;
# Localize the current value...    (No it doesn't!)
local $YAML::Indent;

# Then change it, if necessary...
if (defined $config{indent}) {
    $YAML::Indent = $config{indent};
}
```

Unless the if statement executes, the localized copy of $YAML::Indent will retain its post-localization value of undef.

To correctly localize a package variable but still retain its pre-localization value, you need to write this instead:

```
use YAML;
# Localize the current value...
local $YAML::Indent = $YAML::Indent;

# Then change it, if necessary...
if (defined $config{indent}) {
    $YAML::Indent = $config{indent};
}
```

This version might look odd, redundant, and very possibly wrong, but it's actually both correct and necessary[†]. As with any other assignment, the righthand side of the localized assignment is evaluated first, yielding the original value of $YAML::Indent. Then the variable is localized, which installs a new container inside $YAML::Indent. Finally, the assignment—of the old value to the new container—is performed.

Of course, you may not have wanted to preserve the former indentation value, in which case you probably needed something like:

```
Readonly my $DEFAULT_INDENT => 4;

# and later...
```

---

[*] Or, more accurately, the storage associated with the variable's name is temporarily replaced by a new, uninitialized storage.

[†] Okay, so it still *looks* odd. Two out of three ain't bad.

```
use YAML;
local $YAML::Indent = $DEFAULT_INDENT;
```

Even if you specifically did want that variable to be undefined, it's better to say so explicitly:

```
use YAML;
local $YAML::Indent = undef;
```

That way any readers of the code can immediately see that the lack of definition is intentional, rather than wondering whether it's an oversight.

Punctuation Variables

use English **for the less familiar punctuation variables.**

Avoiding punctuation variables completely is, unfortunately, not a realistic option. For a few of the less commonly used variables, there is no good alternative. Or you may be maintaining code that is already structured around the extensive use of these variables, and reworking that code is impractical.

For example:

```
local $| = 1;        # Autoflush output
local $" = qq{\0};   # Hash subscript separator
local $; =  q{, };   # List separator
local $, =  q{, };   # Output field separator
local $\ = qq{\n};   # Output record separator

eval {
    open my $pipe, '<', '/cdrom/install |'
        or croak "open failed: $!";

    @external_results = <$pipe>;

    close $pipe
        or croak "close failed: $?, $!";
};

carp "Internal error: $@" if $@;
```

In such cases, the best practice is to use the "long" forms of the variables instead, as provided by use English. The *English.pm* module gives readable identifiers to most of the punctuation variables. With it, you could greatly improve the readability and robustness of the previous example:

```
use English qw( -no_match_vars );   # See the "Match Variables" guideline later

local $OUTPUT_AUTOFLUSH      = 1;
local $SUBSCRIPT_SEPARATOR   = qq{\0};
local $LIST_SEPARATOR        = q{, };
```

```
local $OUTPUT_FIELD_SEPARATOR   = q{, };
local $OUTPUT_RECORD_SEPARATOR  = qq{\n};

eval {
    open my $pipe, '/cdrom/install |'
        or croak "open failed: $OS_ERROR";

    @extrenal_results = <$pipe>;

    close $pipe
        or croak "close failed: $CHILD_ERROR, $OS_ERROR";
};

carp "Internal error: $EVAL_ERROR"
    if $EVAL_ERROR;
```

The readability improvement is easy to see, but the greater robustness is perhaps less obvious. Take another look at the localization of the five variables:

```
local $OUTPUT_AUTOFLUSH        = 1;
local $SUBSCRIPT_SEPARATOR     = qq{\0};
local $LIST_SEPARATOR          = q{, };
local $OUTPUT_FIELD_SEPARATOR  = q{, };
local $OUTPUT_RECORD_SEPARATOR = qq{\n};
```

and compare it with the non-English version:

```
local $| = 1;        # Autoflush output
local $" = qq{\0};   # Hash subscript sep
local $; = q{, };    # List separator
local $, = q{, };    # Output field sep
local $\ = qq{\n};   # Output record sep
```

Did you spot the mistake in the "punctuated" version? The comment on the second assignment claims that it is setting the hash subscript separator variable. But in fact the code is setting $", which is the list separator variable. Meanwhile, the third line's comment claims to be setting the list separator, whereas it's actually setting the hash-subscript separator variable: $;.

Somehow during development or maintenance those two variables were switched. Unfortunately, the values being assigned to them *weren't* swapped, nor were the comments. But, because these particular punctuation variables are relatively uncommon, it's easy to just trust the comments*, which can blind you to the actual problem.

In comparison, the use English version doesn't even *have* comments. It doesn't need them. The long variable names document the purpose of each variable directly. And it's unlikely you'll mistakenly assign a value meant for the hash-subscript separator to the list separator instead. No matter how bad your spelling, the odds of accidentally typing $SUBSCRIPT_SEPARATOR when you meant to type $LIST_SEPARATOR are very slight.

---

* Don't. Ever.

There is one exception to this rule that all inescapable punctuation variables ought to be replaced with their use English synonyms. That exception is the $ARG variable:

```
@danger_readings = grep { $ARG > $SAFETY_LIMIT } @reactor_readings;
```

Using $ARG is likely to make your code *less* clear to the average reader, compared with its original punctuation form:

```
@danger_readings = grep { $_ > $SAFETY_LIMIT } @reactor_readings;
```

The general principle here is simple: If you had to look up a punctuation variable in the *perlvar* documentation when you were writing or maintaining the code, then most people will have to look it up when they read the code. And they'll probably have to look that variable up every single time they read the code.

So the *first* time you have to look up a punctuation variable in *perlvar*, replace it with the alternative construct suggested in Table 5-1, or else with its use English equivalent.

Localizing Punctuation Variables

If you're forced to modify a punctuation variable, localize it.

The problems described earlier under "Localization" can also crop up whenever you're forced to change the value in a punctuation variable (often in I/O operations). All punctuation variables are global in scope. They provide explicit control over what would be completely implicit behaviours in most other languages: output buffering, input line numbering, input and output line endings, array indexing, et cetera.

It's usually a grave error to change a punctuation variable without first localizing it. Unlocalized assignments can potentially change the behaviour of code in entirely unrelated parts of your system, even in modules you did not write yourself but are merely using.

Using local is the cleanest and most robust way to temporarily change the value of a global variable. It should always be applied in the smallest possible scope, so as to minimize the effects of any "ambient behaviour" the variable might control:

```
Readonly my $SPACE => q{ };

if (@ARGV) {
    local $INPUT_RECORD_SEPARATOR  = undef;   # Slurp mode
    local $OUTPUT_RECORD_SEPARATOR = $SPACE;  # Autoappend a space to every print
    local $OUTPUT_AUTOFLUSH        = 1;       # Flush buffer after every print

    # Slurp, mutilate, and spindle...
    $text = <>;
    $text =~ s/\n/[EOL]/gxms;
    print $text;
}
```

A common mistake is to use unlocalized global variables, saving and restoring their original values at either end of the block, like so:

```
Readonly my $SPACE => q{ };

if (@ARGV) {
    my $prev_irs = $INPUT_RECORD_SEPARATOR;
    my $prev_ors = $OUTPUT_RECORD_SEPARATOR;
    my $prev_af  = $OUTPUT_AUTOFLUSH;

    $INPUT_RECORD_SEPARATOR  = undef;
    $OUTPUT_RECORD_SEPARATOR = $SPACE;
    $OUTPUT_AUTOFLUSH        = 1;

    $text = <>;
    $text =~ s/\n/[EOL]/gxms;
    print $text;

    $INPUT_RECORD_SEPARATOR  = $prev_irs;
    $OUTPUT_RECORD_SEPARATOR = $prev_ors;
    $OUTPUT_AUTOFLUSH        = $prev_af;

}
```

This way is slower and far less readable. It's prone to cut-and-paste errors, mistyping, mismatched assignments, forgetting to restore one of the variables, or one of the other classic blunders. Use local instead.

Match Variables

Don't use the regex match variables.

Whenever you use English, it's important to load the module with a special argument:

```
use English qw( -no_match_vars );
```

This argument prevents the module from creating the three "match variables": $PREMATCH (or $`), $MATCH (or $&), and $POSTMATCH (or $'). Whenever these variables appear anywhere in a program, they force every regular expression in that program to save three extra pieces of information: the substring the match initially skipped (the "prematch"), the substring it actually matched (the "match"), and the substring that followed the match (the "postmatch").

Every regex has to do this every time any pattern match succeeds, because these punctuation variables are global in scope, and hence available everywhere. So the regex that sets them might not be in the same lexical scope, the same package, or even the same file as the code that next uses them. The compiler can't know which regex will have been the most recently successful at any point, so it has to play it safe and set the match variables every time any regex anywhere matches, in case that particular match is the one that precedes the use of one of the match variables.

This particular problem neatly illustrates why all non-lexical variables cause difficulties. The presence of $`, $&, or $' immediately couples a particular piece of code to (potentially) every single regex in your program. Leaving aside the extra workload that connection imposes on every pattern match, this also means that debugging pattern matches can be potentially much more difficult. If one of the match variables doesn't contain what you expected, it's possible that's because it was actually set by some pattern match other than the one you thought was setting it. And that pattern match could be *anywhere* in your source code.

Don't ever use the match variables:

```
use English;

my ($name, $birth_year)
    = $manuscript =~ m/(\S+) \s+ was \s+ born \s+ in \s+ (\d{4})/xms;

if ($name) {
    print $PREMATCH,
          qq{<born date="$birth_year" name="$name">},
          $MATCH,
          q{</born>},
          $POSTMATCH;
}
```

It's better to use extra capturing parentheses to retain the required context information:

```
my ($prematch, $match, $name, $birth_year, $postmatch)
    = $manuscript =~ m{ (\A.*?)       # capture prematch from start
                        (             # then capture entire match...
                            (\S+) \s+ was \s+ born \s+ in \s+ (\d{4})
                        )
                        (.*\z)        # then capture postmatch to end
                      }xms;
if ($name) {
    print $prematch,
          qq{<born date="$birth_year" name="$name">},
          $match,
          q{</born>},
          $postmatch;
}
```

This solution avoids imposing a performance penalty on every regex match when you're only using the match variables from one. However, it does penalize this particular regex in another way: by making it much uglier, and burying the significant part of the regex under a mound of extra parentheses. It can also be tricky to remember that the entire match is now the second capture, and so the $match variable has to be declared ahead of $name and $birth_year. Indeed, having the entire match captured ahead of parts of the match may seem counterintuitive to subsequent readers of the code.

A cleaner solution is to use the `Regexp::MatchContext` CPAN module. This module extends the Perl regex syntax with a new metasyntactic construct: `(?p)`. The module also exports three subroutines named `PREMATCH()`, `MATCH()`, and `POSTMATCH()`. These subroutines return those respective parts of the match context of the most recent regex with a `(?p)` marker anywhere inside it.

You could simplify the previous example by rewriting it like this:

```
use Regexp::MatchContext;

my ($name, $birth_year)
    = $manuscript =~ m/(?p) (\S+) \s+ was \s+ born \s+ in \s+ (\d{4})/xms;

if ($name) {
    print PREMATCH(),
          qq{<born date="$birth_year" name="$name">},
          MATCH(),
          q{</born>},
          POSTMATCH();
}
```

Note how close this example is to the original version of the code. Apart from using three subroutines instead of three global variables, the only change from the original version is that you have to put a `(?p)` marker in the regex. That's a tiny bit more work, but it confers several significant advantages. For a start, it explicitly marks which regex is capturing the match variables, so it's easier to work out which code to debug when a match variable goes wrong.

Better still, unlike `English`, the `Regexp::MatchContext` module does the extra match-variable-preservation work only for those particular regexes that have a `(?p)` marker, so there's no longer an overhead imposed on all the other regexes in your program. And even in those regexes that *do* set the match variables, `Regexp::MatchContext` does most of the extra work lazily. That is, the information is extracted only when you actually use one of the match variables, not when the regex is originally matched.

Yet another advantage to using `Regexp::MatchContext` is that the subroutines it exports return a genuine `substr`-like substring, rather than a read-only copy. You can assign a value to `MATCH()` and that assignment will change the corresponding sections of the original string. For example, you could rework the following slightly obscure substitution:

```
$html =~ s{.*? (<body> .* </body>) .*}     # Locate components of page
          {   $STD_HEADER                   # Ensure standard header is used
            . verify_body($1)               # Check contents
            . '</html>'                      # Remove any trailing extras
          }exms;
```

replacing it with a more readable match-and-reassign version:

```
use Regexp::MatchContext;

if ($html =~ m{(?p) <body> .* </body>}xms) {    # Locate body of page (with context)
    PREMATCH( )  = $STD_HEADER;                  # Ensure standard header is used
    MATCH( )     = verify_body( MATCH( ) );      # Check contents
    POSTMATCH( ) = '</html>';                    # Remove any trailing extras
}
```

Dollar-Underscore

Beware of any modification via $_.

One particularly easy way to introduce subtle bugs is to forget that $_ is often an alias for some other variable. Any assignment to $_ or any other form of transformation on it, such as a substitution or transliteration, is probably changing some other variable. So any change applied to $_ needs to be scrutinized particularly carefully.

This problem can be especially insidious when $_ isn't actually being named explicitly. For example, suppose you needed a subroutine that would return a copy of any string passed to it, with the leading and trailing whitespace trimmed from the copy. And suppose you also want that subroutine to default to trimming $_ if no explicit argument is provided (just as the built-in chomp does). You might write such a subroutine like this:

```
sub trimmed_copy_of {
    # Trim explicit arguments...
    if (@_ > 0) {
        my ($string) = @_;
        $string =~ s{\A \s* (.*?) \s* \z}{$1}xms;
        return $string;
    }
    # Otherwise, trim the default argument (i.e. $_)...
    else {
        s{\A \s* (.*?) \s* \z}{$1}xms;
        return $_;
    }
}
```

and then use it like so:

```
print trimmed_copy_of($error_mesg);

for (@diagnostics) {
    print trimmed_copy_of;
}
```

Unfortunately, that implementation of trimmed_copy_of( ) is fatally flawed. After using the function in the previous code, the contents of $error_mesg are unchanged (as they should be), but each of the elements of @diagnostics has been unexpectedly shaved. That's because `trimmed_copy_of()` correctly deals with explicit arguments by copying them into a separate variable and then changing that copy:

```
if (@_ > 0) {
    my ($string) = @_;
    $string =~ s{\A \s* (.*?) \s* \z}{$1}xms;
    return $string;
}
```

But the subroutine applies its substitution directly to the (implicit) `$_`, without first copying its contents:

```
else {
    s{\A \s* (.*?) \s* \z}{$1}xms;
    return $_;
}
```

Within the `for` loop, the `$_` variable is sequentially aliased to each element of the array:

```
for (@diagnostics) {
    print trimmed_copy_of;
}
```

which means that the substitution applied to `$_` inside `trimmed_copy_of()` will alter the original array elements.

Something has clearly gone wrong in the design or the implementation. Either `trimmed_copy_of()` should never change the string it's trimming, or it should always change it. If it should never trim the original, the subroutine needs to be written:

```
sub trimmed_copy_of {
    my $string = (@_ > 0) ? shift : $_;
    $string =~ s{\A \s* (.*?) \s* \z}{$1}xms;
    return $string;
}
```

On the other hand, if the intention was that the subroutine consistently modify its (explicit or implicit) argument, then it should have been written like so:

```
sub trim_str {
    croak 'Useless use of trim_str() in non-void context'
        if defined wantarray;

    for my $orig_arg ( @_ ? @_ : $_ ) {            # all args or just $_
        $orig_arg =~ s{\A \s* (.*?) \s* \z}{$1}xms;  # change the actual args
    }

    return;
}
```

in which case it would be used differently, too:

```
for my $warning ($error_mesg, @diagnostics) {
    trim_str $warning;
    print $warning;
}
```

There are several features of this second version of the subroutine that are worth noting. First, because the behaviour of the subroutine changed, its name also needs to change. trimmed_copy_of( ) returns a trimmed copy, so it's named with a past participle that describes how the argument was modified. trim_str( ) does something to its actual argument, so it's named with an imperative verb indicating the action to be carried out.

Next, there's the rather unusual test and exception in this second version:

```
croak 'Useless use of trim_str( ) in non-void context'
        if defined wantarray;
```

You're probably more familiar with exceptions that warn about the useless use of constructs in void contexts, but here the subroutine dies if the context specifically *isn't* void. That's because the trim_str( ) subroutine exists solely to modify its arguments. It doesn't return a useful value, so anyone using it in a scalar context:

```
$tidy_text = trim_str $raw_text;
```

or a list context:

```
print trim_str $message;
```

is making a mistake. Killing them for it immediately is probably a kindness.

Finally, the heart of the trimming operation is:

```
for my $orig_arg ( @_ ? @_ : $_ ) {            # all args or just $_
    $orig_arg =~ s{\A \s* (.*?) \s* \z}{$1}xms;
}
```

In other words, if there is at least one element in the subroutine's argument list (@_), then iterate through those arguments, changing each of them. Otherwise, iterate through only $_, changing it. The use of (@_ ? @_ : $_) to generate the for loop's list is sufficiently unusual and line-noisy that it warrants clarification with an end-of-line comment.

Note too that that loop could have been written as:

```
for ( @_ ? @_ : $_ ) {                         # all args or just $_
    s{\A \s* (.*?) \s* \z}{$1}xms;
}
```

but it would then almost certainly have been harder to comprehend and maintain. In that version, the implicit $_ alias within the for loop would be aliased either sequentially to the elements of @_ (which are themselves aliases to the subroutine's actual arguments) or to whatever the $_ *outside* the loop was aliased to. At which point your brain explodes.

Similar problems caused by unintended modifications via $_ can also crop up within the block of a map or grep. See "List Processing Side Effects" in Chapter 6 for specific advice on avoiding that particular kind of pedesagittry.

Array Indices

Use negative indices when counting from the end of an array.

The last, second last, third last, *n*th last elements of an array can be accessed by counting backwards from the length of the array, like so:

```
# Replace broken frames...
$frames[@frames-1] = $active{top};        # Final frame
$frames[@frames-2] = $active{prev};       # Penultimate frame
$frames[@frames-3] = $active{backup};     # Antepenultimate frame
```

Alternatively, you can work backwards from the final index ($#array_name), like so:

```
# Replace broken frames...
$frames[$#frames   ] = $active{top};      # Final frame
$frames[$#frames-1] = $active{prev};      # Penultimate frame
$frames[$#frames-2] = $active{backup};    # Antepenultimate frame
```

However, Perl provides a much cleaner notation for accessing the terminal elements of an array. Whenever an array access is specified with a negative number, that number is taken as an ordinal position in the array, counting backwards from the last element.

The preceding assignments are much better written as:

```
# Replace broken frames...
$frames[-1] = $active{top};        # 1st-last frame (i.e., final frame)
$frames[-2] = $active{prev};       # 2nd-last frame
$frames[-3] = $active{backup};     # 3rd-last frame
```

Using negative indices is good practice, because the leading minus sign makes the index stand out as unusual, forcing the reader to think about what that index means and marking any "from the end" indices with an obvious prefix.

Equally importantly, the negative indices are unobscured by any repetition of the variable name within the square brackets. In the previous two versions, notice how similar the three indices are (in that all three start with either [@frames-... or [$#frames...). Each index differs by only around 20%: two characters out of nine or ten. In contrast, in the negative-index version, every index differs by 50%, making those differences much easier to detect visually.

Using negative indices consistently also increases the robustness of your code. Suppose @frames contains only two elements. If you wrote:

```
$frames[@frames-1] = $active{top};        # Final frame
$frames[@frames-2] = $active{prev};       # Penultimate frame
$frames[@frames-3] = $active{backup};     # Antepenultimate frame
```

you'd be assigning values to $frames[1] (the last element), $frames[0] (the first element), and $frames[-1] (the last element again!) On the other hand, using -1, -2, and

-3 as indices causes the interpreter to throw an exception when you try to assign to a nonexistent element:

```
Modification of non-creatable array value attempted, subscript -3 at frames.pl line 33.
```

Slicing

Take advantage of hash and array slicing.

The previous examples would be even less cluttered (and hence more readable) using an array slice and a hash slice:

```
@frames[-1,-2,-3]
    = @active{'top', 'prev', 'backup'};
```

An array slice is a syntactic shortcut that allows you to specify a list of array elements, without repeating the array name for each one. A slice looks similar to a regular array access, except that the array keeps its leading @ and you're then allowed to specify more than one index in the square brackets. An array slice like:

```
@frames[-1,-2,-3]
```

is exactly the same as:

```
($frames[-1], $frames[-2], $frames[-3])
```

just much less work to type in, or read. There's a similar syntax for accessing several elements of a hash: you change the leading $ of a regular hash access to @, then add as many keys as you like. The slice:

```
@active{'top', 'prev', 'backup'}
```

is exactly the same as:

```
($active{'top'}, $active{'prev'}, $active{'backup'})
```

The sliced version of the frames assignment will be marginally faster than three separate scalar assignments, though the difference in performance is probably not significant unless you're doing hundreds of millions of repetitions. The real benefit is in comprehensibility and extensibility.

Be careful, though. This version:

```
@frames[-1..-3]
    = @active{'top', 'prev', 'backup'};
```

is not identical in behaviour. In fact it's a no-op, since the -1..-3 range generates an empty list, just like any other range whose final value is less than its initial value. So the "negative range" actually selects an empty slice, which makes the previous code equivalent to:

```
() = @active{'top', 'prev', 'backup'};
```

To successfully use a range of negative numbers in an array slice, you would need to reverse the order, and remember to reverse the order of keys in the hash slice, too:

```
@frames[-3..-1]
    = @active{'backup', 'prev', 'top'};
```

That's subtle enough that it's almost certainly not worth the effort. In slices, ranges that include negative indices are generally more trouble than they're worth.

Slice Layout

Use a tabular layout for slices.

A slice-to-slice assignment like:

```
@frames[-1,-2,-3]
    = @active{'top', 'prev', 'backup'};
```

can also be written as:

```
    @frames[ -1,     -2,      -3    ]
= @active{'top', 'prev', 'backup'};
```

This second version makes it immediately apparent which hash entry is being assigned to which array element. Unfortunately, this approach is useful only when the number of keys/indices in the slices is small. As soon as either list exceeds a single line, the readability of the resulting code is made much worse by vertical alignments:

```
    @frames[ -1,     -2,      -3,        -4,           -5,       -6,
               -7,             -8      ]
= @active{'top', 'prev', 'backup', 'emergency', 'spare', 'rainy day',
          'alternate', 'default'};
```

Slice Factoring

Factor large key or index lists out of their slices.

As the final example in the previous guideline demonstrates, slices can quickly become unwieldy as the number of indices/keys increases.

A more readable and more scalable approach in such cases is to factor out the index/key equivalences in a separate tabular data structure:

```
Readonly my %CORRESPONDING => (
  # Key of          Index of
  # %active...      @frames...
    'top'        =>  -1,
    'prev'       =>  -2,
    'backup'     =>  -3,
    'emergency'  =>  -4,
    'spare'      =>  -5,
    'rainy day'  =>  -6,
    'alternate'  =>  -7,
    'default'    =>  -8,
);
```

```
@frames[ values %CORRESPONDING ] = @active{ keys %CORRESPONDING };
```

Each key in %CORRESPONDING is one of the keys of %active, and each value in %CORRESPONDING is the corresponding index of @frames. So the righthand side of the assignment (@active{ keys %CORRESPONDING }) is a hash slice of %active that includes all the entries whose keys are listed in %CORRESPONDING. Similarly, @frames[values %CORRESPONDING] is an array slice of @frames that includes all the corresponding indices listed in %CORRESPONDING. That means that the assignment copies entries from %active to the corresponding elements of @frames, with the correspondence being specified by the key/value pairs in %CORRESPONDING.

Storing that key/value correspondence in a hash works because the values and keys functions always traverse the entries of a hash in the same order, so the Nth value returned by values will always be the value of the Nth key returned by keys. Because the two builtins preserve the order of the entries of %CORRESPONDING, the assignment between the two slices copies $active{'top'} into $frames[-1], $active{'prev'} into $frames[-2], $active{'backup'} into $frames[-3], etc.

This approach improves the maintainability of the code, as the %CORRESPONDING hash very clearly and prominently lists the mapping from %active keys to @frames indices. The actual assignment statement is also made considerably simpler. In addition, factoring out the correspondence between keys and indices makes the code very much easier to maintain. Adding an extra assignment now only requires listing an extra key/index pair; changing a key or index only requires updating an existing pair.

And, of course, this technique is not restricted to negative indices, nor do the indices need to be specified in any particular order. If there are a large number of fields being transferred, it can be useful to arrange the keys alphabetically, to make them easier for humans to look up. For example:

```
Readonly my %CORRESPONDING => (
    age        =>  1,
    comments   =>  6,
    fraction   =>  8,
    hair       =>  9,
```

```
        height      => 2,
        name        => 0,
        occupation  => 5,
        office      => 11,
        shoe_size   => 4,
        started     => 7,
        title       => 10,
        weight      => 3,
    );

    @staff_member_details[ values %CORRESPONDING ]
        = @personnel_record{ keys %CORRESPONDING };
```

Simple arrays can also be useful when refactoring the keys or indices of a single slice:

```
    # This is the order in which stat() returns its information:
    Readonly my @STAT_FIELDS
        => qw( dev ino mode nlink uid gid rdev size atime mtime ctime blksize blocks );

    sub status_for {
        my ($file) = @_;

        # The hash to be returned...
        my %stat_hash = ( file => $file );

        # Load each stat datum into an appropriately named entry of the hash...
        @stat_hash{@STAT_FIELDS} = stat $file;

        return \%stat_hash;
    }

    # and later...

    warn 'File was last modified at ', status_for($file)->{mtime};
```

This kind of table-driven programming is highly scalable and particularly easy to maintain. Numerous variations on this technique will be advocated in subsequent chapters.

## CHAPTER 6

Control Structures

Nothing is more difficult,
and therefore more precious,
than to be able to decide.
—Napoleon I

Control structures are all about choosing: choosing whether to do something, choosing between two or more alternatives, choosing how often to repeat something. As in real life, much programming grief springs either from making the wrong choice or from using the wrong approach when making a choice.

This chapter looks at a range of programming practices that can help to make your code's decision making less error-prone, more efficient, and easier to verify.

The basic principles are simple: make the decision stand out; make the consequences of any decision stand out; base the decision on as few criteria as possible; don't phrase the decision negatively; avoid flag variables and count variables; and make it very easy to detect variations in the flow of control.

If Blocks

Use block `if`, not postfix `if`.

One of the most effective ways to make decisions and their consequences stand out is to avoid using the postfix form of `if`. For example, it's easier to detect the decision and consequences in:

```
if (defined $measurement) {
    $sum += $measurement;
}
```

than in:

```
$sum += $measurement if defined $measurement;
```

Moreover, postfix tests don't scale well as the consequences increase. For example:

```
$sum += $measurement
and $count++
and next SAMPLE
    if defined $measurement;
```

and:

```
do {
    $sum += $measurement;
    $count++;
    next SAMPLE;
} if defined $measurement;
```

are both *much* harder to comprehend than:

```
if (defined $measurement) {
    $sum += $measurement;
    $count++;
    next SAMPLE;
}
```

So always use the block form of if.

Postfix Selectors

Reserve postfix if for flow-of-control statements.

The only exception to the previous guideline comes about because of another of the principles enumerated at the start of this chapter: "make it very easy to detect variations in the flow of control".

Such variations come about when a next, last, redo, return, goto, die, croak, or throw[*] occurs in the middle of other code. These commands break up the orderly downward flow of execution, so it is critical that they are easy to detect. And, although they are usually associated with some conditional test, the fact that they may potentially interrupt the control flow is more important than the conditions under which they are doing so.

---

[*] See Chapter 13 for an explanation of the throw( ) method.

Hence it's better to place the next, last, redo, return, goto, die, croak, and throw keywords in the most prominent position on their code line. In other words, they should appear as far to the left as possible (as discussed in the "Keep Left" sidebar in Chapter 2).

If an if is being used solely to determine whether to invoke a flow-control statement, use the postfix form. Don't hide the action over on the right:

```perl
sub find_anomolous_sample_in {
    my ($samples_ref) = @_;

    MEASUREMENT:
    for my $measurement (@{$samples_ref}) {
        if ($measurement < 0) { last MEASUREMENT; }

        my $floor = int($measurement);
        if ($floor == $measurement) { next MEASUREMENT; }

        my $allowed_inaccuracy = scale($EPSILON, $floor);
        if ($measurement-$floor > $allowed_inaccuracy) {
            return $measurement;
        }
    }
    return;
}
```

Be "up front" about it:

```perl
sub find_anomolous_sample_in {
    my ($samples_ref) = @_;

    MEASUREMENT:
    for my $measurement (@{$samples_ref}) {
        last MEASUREMENT if $measurement < 0;

        my $floor = int($measurement);
        next MEASUREMENT if $floor == $measurement;

        my $allowed_inaccuracy = scale($EPSILON, $floor);
        return $measurement
            if $measurement-$floor > $allowed_inaccuracy;
    }
    return;
}
```

Other Postfix Modifiers

Don't use postfix unless, for, while, **or** until.

The special dispensation to use postfix if in flow-control statements doesn't extend to any other types of statements. Nor does it extend to any of the other postfix statement modifiers.

The postfix looping modifiers create particular maintenance problems because they place the control flow (i.e., the loop specifier) to the right of the statement it controls. For example, a loop like:

```
print for grep {defined $_} @generated_lines;
```

makes it harder to notice the looped flow of control, especially if you also have statements like:

```
print $fh grep {defined $_} @generated_lines;
```

A proper for loop makes the iteration much more obvious:

```
for my $line (grep {defined $_} @generated_lines) {
    print $line;
}
```

Note too that it's not possible to give a readable name to the iterator variable of a postfix loop, nor to easily nest conditional tests inside such a loop. Instead of being able to write the code in a straightforward, explicit, easy-to-follow, and extensible way:

```
for my $line (@generated_lines) {
    if (defined $line) {
        print lc $line;
    }
}
```

you're forced to rely on boolean operations, and tempted by default behaviours:

```
defined and print lc for @generated_lines;
```

Worse still, using a postfix loop will sometime make it necessary to use explicit $_, which makes the resulting code much harder to understand:

```
$_ = lc for @generated_lines;
```

The same code is much clearer in block form:

```
for my $line (@generated_lines) {
    $line = lc $line;
}
```

This disparity in readability grows greater as the number of statements to be iterated increases:

```
defined
and print lc
and (s{\A cmd}{}xms or 1)
and push @non_cmds, $_
    for @generated_lines;
```

at which point most people would surely switch over to:

```
for my $line (@generated_lines) {
    if (defined $line) {
        print lc $line;
        $line =~ s{\A cmd}{}xms;
        push @non_cmds, $line;
    }
}
```

So why not start out that way? Starting with the postfix form means that you will almost inevitably have to rewrite some existing code using the block form. And rewriting existing code is a great way to introduce new bugs.

Negative Control Statements

Don't use `unless` or `until` at all.

Perl is unusual amongst programming languages in that it provides not only positive conditional tests (`if` and `while`), but also their negative counterparts (`unless` and `until`). Some people find that these keywords can make certain control structures read more naturally to them:

```
RANGE_CHECK:
until ($measurement > $ACCEPTANCE_THRESHOLD) {
    $measurement = get_next_measurement();
    redo RANGE_CHECK unless defined $measurement;
    # etc.
}
```

However, for many other developers, the relative unfamiliarity of these negated tests actually makes the resulting code harder to read than the equivalent "positive" version:

```
RANGE_CHECK:
while ($measurement <= $ACCEPTANCE_THRESHOLD) {
    $measurement = get_next_measurement();
    redo RANGE_CHECK if !defined $measurement;
    # etc.
}
```

More importantly, the negative tests don't scale well. They almost always become much harder to comprehend as soon as their condition has two or more components, especially if any of those components is itself expressed negatively. For example, most people have significantly more difficulty understanding the double negatives in:

```
VALIDITY_CHECK:
until ($measurement > $ACCEPTANCE_THRESHOLD && ! $is_exception{$measurement}) {
    $measurement = get_next_measurement();
    redo VALIDITY_CHECK unless defined $measurement && $measurement ne '[null]';
    # etc.
}
```

So unless and until are inherently harder to maintain. In particular, whenever a negative control statement is extended to include a negative operator, it will have to be re-cast as a positive control, which requires you to change both the keyword and the conditional:

```
VALIDITY_CHECK:
while ($measurement < $ACCEPTANCE_THRESHOLD && $is_exception{$measurement}) {
    $measurement = get_next_measurement();
    redo VALIDITY_CHECK if !defined $measurement || $measurement eq '[null]';
    # etc.
}
```

Not only is that extra effort, it's error-prone effort. Reworking conditionals in that way is an excellent opportunity to introduce new and subtle bugs into your program…just as the previous example did. The original until condition was:

```
until ($measurement > $ACCEPTANCE_THRESHOLD && ! $is_exception{$measurement}) {
```

The corresponding "positive" version *should* have been:

```
while ($measurement <= $ACCEPTANCE_THRESHOLD || $is_exception{$measurement}) {
```

This kind of mistake is unfortunately common, but very easy to avoid. If you never use an unless or until, then you'll never have to rewrite it as an if or while. Moreover, if your control statements are always "positive", your code will generally be more comprehensible to all readers*, regardless of the complexity of its logical expressions. Even in the simple cases, something like:

```
croak "$value is missing" if !$found;
```

is not appreciably harder to comprehend than:

```
croak "$value is missing" unless $found;
```

unless or until are minor conveniences that can easily become major liabilities. They're never necessary, and frequently counterproductive. Don't use them.

---

* Including yourself in six months' time…

Don't Fail Not to Use Chained Negatives

The "Negative Control Statements" guideline has proved to be one of the most controversial in this book. Though few people will miss until, many very good Perl programmers feel that unless is a valid choice, which improves readability in a limited number of circumstances.

If you, or your team, are persuaded by such arguments and decide to allow the use of unless as part of your coding practices, then make sure that you only ever use it in ways that genuinely improve the readability of your code. The best way to ensure that is to require that the conditional expression of any negative control statement must always itself be expressed using "positive" logic.

That is, *never* write an unless (or an until) in which the condition includes a "negative" operator, an inequality, or any kind of ordering test. Don't use any of the following operators with an unless or an until:

```
!   not                  # Negation of value
!~  !=  ne               # Inequality of value
<   >   <=  >=  <=>      # Numerical ordering
lt  gt  le  ge  cmp      # String ordering
```

Abiding by that rule would permit the following limited uses:

```
next NAME unless $name eq 'Harry';
redo NAME unless $name =~ m/Mud{1,2}/xms;

unless ($count == $MAX_COUNT) {
    carp 'Search terminated prematurely';
}
```

but would still prohibit confusing double-negatives and reversed inequalities like:

```
last NAME  unless $name ne 'Harry';
exit $FAIL unless $name !~ m/Mud{1,2}/xms;

unless ($count != $MAX_COUNT) {
    carp "Still searching...\n";
}
return $count
    unless $count < 10 || $tries >= $MAX_TRIES;

until ($input ne $EMPTY_STR) {
    $input = prompt '> ';
}
```

Remember too that, if you do choose to allow unless or until, extra attention will be required whenever a conditional expression is extended. In particular, if the extension adds a "negative" of any kind, then you will need to convert the negative control statement to the appropriate positive form, and rewrite of the original condition accordingly.

The added degree of complexity and awareness that this transformation always requires and the risk of introducing errors that it inevitably involves are two good reasons to reread the "Negative Control Statements" guideline, and to reconsider banning unless and until altogether.

C-Style Loops

The three-part for statements that Perl inherits from C are needed only for unusual loop control behaviour, such as iterating by twos, or in an irregular sequence. But even in such cases, these C-style loops provide that unusual behaviour in an obscure and harder-to-maintain way.

That's because the iterative behaviour of a three-part for statement is *emergent*, rather than explicit. In other words, the only way to know what a loop like:

```
for (my $n=4; $n<=$MAX; $n+=2) {
    print $result[$n];
}
```

is going to do is to sit down and work out the abstract logic of the three components:

"Let's see: n starts at 4, and continues up to MAX, incrementing by two each time. So the sequence is 4, 6, 8, etc. So the loop iterates through all the even n's from 4 up to and including MAX (if MAX itself is even)."

But you could write the same loop without the C-style for, like this:

```
RESULT:
for my $n (4..$MAX) {
    next RESULT if odd($n);
    print $result[$n];
}
```

The advantage with this version is that subsequent readers of the code no longer have to work out the logic of the loop. The code itself says explicitly:

"n from 4 to MAX, skipping values that are odd."

The code is clearer, which means it's more maintainable and less susceptible to subtle bugs or nasty edge-cases.

The usual counter-argument is that this second example has to iterate twice as many times for the same effect, and has to call a subroutine (odd( )) each of those times. Should $MAX become large, that additional cost might become prohibitive.

In practice, many loops don't iterate enough times for those overheads to matter. And often the actual work done by the loop will swamp the costs of iteration anyway. But, if benchmarking indicates that the clearer-but-slower code *is* having a noticeable effect on performance, then a better solution is usually to "inline" the call to odd( ), replacing it with a direct check on each $n value:

```
RESULT:
for my $n (4..$MAX) {
    next RESULT if $n % 2;      # $n%2!=0 when $n is odd
```

```
        print $result[$n];
    }
```

In a simple example like this one, it can be hard to see the benefits of the more readable non-C-style for loops. But those benefits become clearer as the complexity of the loop control increases. Take a few moments to work out what the following three-part for loop does:

```
SALE:
for (my ($sales, $seats)=(0,$CAPACITY);
        $sales < $TARGET && $seats > $RESERVE;
        $sales += sell_ticket(), $seats--
) {
    prompt -yn, "[$seats seats remaining] Sell another? "
        or last SALE;
}
```

The fact that working out what that loop does really does take a few moments is a good indicator that the code is not sufficiently readable—especially when compared with the following non-C-style version:

```
my $sales = 0;
my $seats = $CAPACITY;

SALE:
while ($sales < $TARGET && $seats > $RESERVE) {
    prompt -yn, "[$seats seats remaining] Sell another? "
        or last SALE;

    $sales += sell_ticket();
    $seats--;
}
```

The three-part for loop is rarely used as a pure for loop (i.e., to iterate a fixed number of times). More often, it's used as a complex while loop, which means that using an actual while loop in such cases is a much better practice.

Unnecessary Subscripting

Avoid subscripting arrays or hashes within loops.

Unless you actually need to know the indices of the array elements you're processing, iterate the values of an array directly:

```
for my $client (@clients) {
    $client->tally_hours();
    $client->bill_hours();
    $client->reset_hours();
}
```

Iterating the indices and then doing repeated array accesses is significantly slower, and less readable:

```
for my $n (0..$#clients) {
    $clients[$n]->tally_hours();
    $clients[$n]->bill_hours();
    $clients[$n]->reset_hours();
}
```

Repeated indexing is repeated computation; duplicated effort that incurs an extra cost but provides no added benefit. Iterating indices is also prone to off-by-one errors. For example:

```
for my $n (1..@clients) {
    $clients[$n]->tally_hours();
    $clients[$n]->bill_hours();
    $clients[$n]->reset_hours();
}
```

Likewise, if you're processing the entries of a hash and you need only the values of those entries, don't iterate the keys and then look up the values repeatedly:

```
for my $original_word (keys %translation_for) {
    if ( $translation_for{$original_word} =~ m/ $PROFANITY /xms) {
        $translation_for{$original_word} = '[DELETED]';
    }
}
```

Repeated hash look-ups are even more costly than repeated array indexing. Just iterate the hash values directly:

```
for my $translated_word (values %translation_for) {
    if ( $translated_word =~ m/ $PROFANITY /xms) {
        $translated_word = '[DELETED]';
    }
}
```

Note that this last example works correctly because, in Perl 5.6 and later, the values function returns a list of aliases to the actual values of the hash, rather than just a list of copies (see "Hash Values" in Chapter 8). So if you change the iterator variable (for example, assigning '[DELETED]' to $translated_word), you're actually changing the corresponding original value inside the hash.

The only situation where iterating values doesn't work correctly is when you need to delete the entries from the hash:

```
for my $translated_word (values %translation_for) {
    if ( $translated_word =~ m/ $PROFANITY /xms) {
        delete $translated_word;                    # Compile-time error
    }
}
```

Here, aliasing isn't enough, because the delete builtin needs to know the key as well, so it will only accept actual hash look-ups as arguments. The correct solution is to use a hash slice instead (see Chapter 5):

```
my @unacceptable_words
    = grep {$translation_for{$_} =~ m/ $PROFANITY /xms}
        keys %translation_for;

delete @translation_for{@unacceptable_words};
```

The grep collects all those keys whose values must be removed, and stores that list in @unacceptable_words. The list of keys is then used to create a slice of the original hash (i.e., a list of hash look-ups), which *can* be passed to delete.

By Any Other Name...

An *alias* may sometimes seem like magic, but it's based in a very simple idea.

In a Perl program, a normal variable consists of two distinct components: a storage location in memory, and a name (such as $foo) by which the program refers to that storage location. In other words, every variable is a box, with a "Hi-my-name-is..." sticker on it.

Aliasing is the process of putting a second (or third, or *n*th) "Hi-my-name-is-also..." sticker on a single box. Perl subroutines do this all the time. For example, if you call get_passwd($user), then inside the call to get_passwd( ) the name $_[0] is temporarily attached to the container whose original name is $user. That container now has two names: one that's used inside the subroutine and one that's used outside.

Anything you do to an alias (e.g., get its value, increment it, print it, assign a new value to it) is really being done to the original variable—because there's really only *one* variable, no matter how many separate names you give it.

Necessary Subscripting

Never subscript more than once in a loop.

Sometimes you have no choice: you really do need to know the index of each value you're iterating over, as well as the value itself. But, even when it *is* necessary to iterate indices or keys, be sure to extract the value only once:

```
for my $agent_num (0..$#operatives) {        # Iterate indices
    my $agent = $operatives[$agent_num];     # Extract value once

    print "Checking agent $agent_num\n";     # Use index
    if ($on_disavowed_list{$agent}) {         # Use value
        print "\t...$agent disavowed!\n";    # Use value again
    }
}
```

Never extract it repeatedly in the same iteration:

```
for my $agent_num (0..$#operatives) {          # Iterate indices
    print "Checking agent $agent_num\n";        # Use index
    if ($on_disavowed_list{$operatives[$agent_num]}) {   # Extract value
        print "\t...$operatives[$agent_num] disavowed!\n";  # Extract value again
    }
}
```

Apart from the fact that repeated array look-ups are repeatedly expensive, they also clutter the code, and increase the maintenance effort if either the array name or the name of the iterator variable subsequently has to be changed.

Occasionally a mere copy of the value won't do, because you need to iterate both indices and values, *and* still be able to modify the values. It's easy to do that too—just use the Data::Alias CPAN module*:

```
use Data::Alias;

for my $agent_num (0..$#operatives) {          # Iterate indices
    alias my $agent = $operatives[$agent_num];  # Rename value

    print "Checking agent $agent_num\n";        # Use index
    if ($on_disavowed_list{$agent}) {           # Use value
        $agent = '[DISAVOWED]';                 # Change value
    }
}
```

The technique here is the same as before: iterate indices, then look up the value once. But in this case, instead of copying the value, the loop block creates a lexically scoped alias to it.

The alias function takes a variable as its only argument, and converts that variable into an *alias variable*. Assigning directly to the alias variable as you declare it:

```
alias my $agent                    # Alias variable
    = $operatives[$agent_num];     # Assigned expression
```

causes the alias variable to become another name for the assigned expression (usually another variable).

Once the aliasing is accomplished, anything that is done to the alias variable (including subsequent assignments) is actually being done to the variable to which it was aliased. Thus assigning to $agent actually assigns to $operatives[$agent_num]. The only difference is that there's no array element look-up involved, so accessing the alias is actually faster.

Exactly the same approach can be taken when it's necessary to iterate the keys and values of a hash:

---

* Or the Lexical::Alias module if you're running under a version of Perl earlier than 5.8.1.

```
    for my $name (keys %client_named) {            # Iterate keys
        alias my $client_info = $client_named{$name};  # Rename value

        print "Checking client $name\n";           # Use key
        if ($client_info->inactivity( ) > $ONE_YEAR) {  # Use value
            $client_info                           # Change value...
                = Client::Moribund->new({ from => $client_info });  # ...using value
        }
    }
```

Note that you can't use Perl's built-in each function for this kind of thing:

```
    while (my ($name, $client_info) = each %client_named) {  # Iterate key/value
        print "Checking client $name\n";           # Use key
        if ($client_info->inactivity( ) > $ONE_YEAR) {  # Use value
            $client_info                           # Change copy (!)
                = Client::Moribund->new({ from => $client_info });  # ...using value
        }
    }
```

If you use each, the $client_info variable receives only a *copy* of each hash value, not an alias to it. So changing $client_info has no effect on the original values inside %client_named.

Extracting or renaming values is also a good practice if those values are nested inside a deeper data structure, or are the result of a subroutine call. For example, if the previous code needed to choose different responses for clients with different periods of inactivity, it would be cleaner and more efficient to extract that information only once:

```
    for my $name (keys %client_named) {            # Iterate keys
        alias my $client_info = $client_named{$name};  # Rename value
        my $inactive = $client_info->inactivity( );  # Extract value once

        print "Checking client $name\n";           # Use key

        $client_info
            # Reuse value many times...   To decide new status of client...
            = $inactive > $ONE_YEAR    ? Client::Moribund->new({ from => $client_info })
            : $inactive > $SIX_MONTHS ?   Client::Silver->new({ from => $client_info })
            : $inactive > $SIX_WEEKS  ?     Client::Gold->new({ from => $client_info })
            :                           Client::Platinum->new({ from => $client_info })
            ;
    }
```

Iterator Variables

Use named lexicals as explicit `for` **loop iterators.**

From a readability standpoint, $_ is a terrible name for a variable, especially for an iterator variable. It conveys nothing about the nature or purpose of the values it stores, except that they're currently being iterated in the innermost enclosing loop. For example:

```
for (@candidates) {
    if (m/\[ NO \] \z/xms) {
        $_ = reconsider($_);

        $have_reconsidered{lc()}++;
    }
    else {
        print "New candidate: $_\n";

        $_ .= accept_or_reject($_);

        $have_reconsidered{lc()} = 0;
    }
}
```

This piece of code starts off well enough: "For each of these candidates, if *it** matches a certain pattern...". But things go downhill very quickly from there.

On the third line, the call to lc has its argument omitted, so the function defaults to using $_. And the maintainability of the code immediately suffers. Whoever wrote the code obviously knew that lc defaults to $_ in this way; in fact, that's probably part of the reason they used $_ as the loop iterator in the first place. But will future maintainers of the code know about that default behaviour? If not, they'll have to look up lc to check, which makes their job just a little harder. Unnecessarily harder.

The usual reply at this point is that those maintainers *should* know Perl well enough to know that lc defaults to lowercasing $_. But that's the crumbling edge of a very slippery slope. Which of the following built-in functions also default to $_?

abs	close	printf	sleep
chdir	die	require	-t
chroot	localtime	select	-T

Even if you knew[†], and were confident that you knew, are you equally confident that your teammates know?

Taking advantage of the default behaviour of any builtin forces the reader to "fill in the gaps", and therefore makes the resulting code harder to read. And much harder to debug. Saying explicitly what you mean takes only a little extra coding effort— effort that is repaid many times over when the code is being maintained.

Meanwhile, the example gets worse:

```
else {
    print "New candidate: $_\n";
```

---

* In Perl, the best way to pronounce $_ is usually "it".

† Of the 12 builtins listed, only abs, chroot, require, and -T default to operating on $_.

```
        $_ .= accept_or_reject($_);

        $have_reconsidered{lc()} = 0;
    }
```

Because $_ isn't a meaningful name in the context, it's hard to tell at a glance exactly what information is being printed by the first line of the else block. Likewise, it's impossible to tell what's being accepted or rejected by the following line, or what the result is being appended to.

All the problems of maintainability described so far can be eliminated simply by giving the iterator variable a human-readable name:

```
for my $name (@candidates) {
    if ($name =~ m/\[ NO \] \z/xms) {
        $name = reconsider($name);

        $have_reconsidered{lc($name)}++;
    }
    else {
        print "New candidate: $name\n";

        $name .= accept_or_reject($name);

        $have_reconsidered{lc($name)} = 0;
    }
}
```

In this version it's clear that the name of each candidate in the array is matched against a pattern. If the match succeeds, then the candidate's name has been (case-insensitively) reconsidered one more time. Otherwise, something is appended to their name, and it's noted that the name has not yet been reconsidered.

Now the reader doesn't need to remember default behaviours, because the code can't use them (as the iterator variable is no longer $_). Nor is there any need to mentally keep track of what the iterator variable actually contains, because it now has an explicit name that describes its contents.

Note that the recommendation to avoid $_ applies even if $_ is entirely implicit in the loop, and regardless of the type of loop:

```
while (<$bookmarks>) {
    if (m/phoenix|firebird/xms) {
        s/\s* \z/ (see firefox)\n/xms;
    }
    print;
}
```

For maintainability, that's still better written as:

```
while (my $record = <$bookmarks>) {
    if ($record =~ m/phoenix|firebird/xms) {
        $record =~ s/\s* \z/ (see firefox)\n/xms;
    }
```

```
    print $record;
}
```

Non-Lexical Loop Iterators

Always declare a `for` loop iterator variable with `my`.

When using an explicit iterator variable in a `for` loop, make sure it's explicitly declared as a *lexical* variable, using the `my` keyword. That is, never write a `for` loop like this:

```
my $client;

SEARCH:
for $client (@clients) {
    last SEARCH if $client->holding();
}

if ($client) {
    $client->resume_conversation();
}
```

If you leave off the `my`, Perl *doesn't* reuse the lexical variable declared above the loop. Instead, it silently declares a new lexical variable (which is also named `$client`) as the iterator variable. That new lexical is always scoped to the loop block, and it hides any variable of the same name from any outer scope.

This behaviour is contrary to all reasonable expectation. Everywhere else in Perl, when you declare a lexical variable, it's visible throughout the remainder of its scope, unless another explicit `my` declaration hides it. So it's natural to expect that the `$client` variable used in the `for` loop is the same lexical `$client` variable that was declared before the loop.

But it isn't. The previous example is actually equivalent to:

```
my $client;

SEARCH:
for my $some_other_variable_also_named_client (@clients) {
    last SEARCH if $some_other_variable_also_named_client->holding();
}

if ($client) {
    $client->resume_conversation();
}
```

Writing it that way makes the logical error in the code much more obvious. The loop isn't setting the outermost lexical `$client` to the first client who's on hold. It's setting an inner lexical variable (which is also named `$client` in the original version). Then it's throwing that variable away at the end of the loop. The outer lexical `$client` retains its original undefined value, and the `if` block is never executed.

Unfortunately, the first version shown doesn't make that error obvious at all. It looks like it ought to work. It *would* work if the loop construct was anything other than a for. And that's the problem. Finding this particular bug is made very much more difficult by the counter-intuitive semantics of loop iterators.

Fortunately, if you always use an explicitly declared lexical iterator instead, the problem never arises, because it's obvious that there are two distinct $client variables:

```
my $client;

SEARCH:
for my $client (@clients) {
    last SEARCH if $client->holding();
}

if ($client) {
    $client->resume_conversation();
}
```

Of course, the code is still broken. But now the declaration of a second lexical $client makes the problem obvious. Best practice isn't only about coding in a way that doesn't introduce errors. Sometimes it's also about coding in a way that doesn't *conceal* errors.

It's simply impossible to use the final value of a loop iterator variable after its for loop has terminated; iterator variables always cease to exist after the loop exits. So the correct solution here is to stop trying to reuse the iterator outside its loop and use a separate variable entirely:

```
my $holding_client;

SEARCH:
for my $client (@clients) {
    if ($client->holding()) {
        $holding_client = $client;
        last SEARCH;
    }
}

if ($holding_client) {
    $holding_client->resume_conversation();
}
```

Or better still, factor the search out into a subroutine:

```
sub get_next_holding_client {
    # Search for and return any client on hold...
    for my $client (@_) {
        return $client if $client->holding();
    }

    # Fail if no clients on hold...
    return;
}
```

```
# and later...

my $client_on_hold = get_next_holding_client(@clients);

if ($client_on_hold) {
    $client_on_hold->resume_conversation( );
}
```

Or, best of all, just use a core utility*:

```
use List::Util qw( first );

my $client_on_hold = first {$_->holding} @clients;

if ($client_on_hold) {
    $client_on_hold->resume_conversation( );
}
```

The first function is exactly like a short-circuiting version of grep. You give grep a block and a list of values, and it returns all those values for which the block evaluates true. You also give first a block and a list of values, but then it returns only the first value for which the block is true (and doesn't bother to check the rest of the values).

List Generation

Use map instead of for when generating new lists from old.

A for loop is so convenient that it's natural to reach for it in any situation where a fixed number of list elements is to be processed. For example:

```
my @sqrt_results;
for my $result (@results) {
    push @sqrt_results, sqrt($result);
}
```

But code like that can be very inefficient, because it has to perform a separate push for every transformed element. Those pushes usually require a series of internal memory reallocations, as the @sqrt_results array repeatedly fills up. It *is* possible to preallocate space in @sqrt_results, but the syntax to do that is a little obscure, which doesn't help readability:

```
my @sqrt_results;

# Preallocate as many elements as @results already has...
$#sqrt_results = $#results;

for my $next_sqrt_result (0..$#results) {
```

---

* Core in 5.8 and later. Available on the CPAN for earlier versions of Perl.

```
        $sqrt_results[$next_sqrt_result] = sqrt $results[$next_sqrt_result];
    }
```

You also have to use an explicit counter if you preallocate. You can't use push, because you just gave the array some number of preallocated elements, so push would put each new value *after* them.

The alternative is to use Perl's built-in map function. This function is specifically aimed at those situations when you want to process a list of values, to create some kind of related list. For example, to produce a list of square roots from a list of numbers:

```
    my @sqrt_results = map { sqrt $_ } @results;
```

Some of the benefits of this approach are very obvious. For a start, there's less code, so (provided you know what map does) the code is significantly easier to understand. Less code also means there are likely to be fewer bugs, as there are fewer places for things to go wrong.

There are a couple of other advantages that aren't quite as obvious. For example, when you use map, most of your looping and list generation is being done in heavily optimized compiled C code, not in interpreted Perl. So it's usually being done considerably faster.

In addition, the map knows in advance exactly how many elements it will eventually process, so it can preallocate sufficient space in the list it's returning. Or rather it can *usually* preallocate sufficient space. If the map's block returns more than one value for each element of the original list, then extra allocations will still be necessary. But, even then, not as many as the equivalent series of push statements would require.

Finally, on a more abstract level, a map is almost always used to transform a sequence of data, so seeing a map immediately suggests to the reader that a data transformation is intended. And the syntax of the function makes it easy to visually locate both the transformation itself (what's in the braces) and the data it's being applied to (what's after the braces).

List Selections

Use grep **and** first **instead of** for
when searching for values in a list.

The same principles apply when you want to refine a list by removing unwanted elements. Instead of a for loop:

```
    # Identify candidates who are unfit for the cut-and-thrust of politics...
    my @disqualified_candidates;
    for my $name (@candidates) {
        if (cannot_tell_a_lie($name)) {
            push @disqualified_candidates, $name;
        }
    }
```

just use a grep:

```
# Identify candidates who are unfit for the cut-and-thrust of politics...
my @disqualified_candidates
    = grep {cannot_tell_a_lie($_)} @candidates;
```

Likewise, don't use a for when you're searching a list for a particular element:

```
# Victimize someone at random...
my $scapegoat = $disqualified_candidates[rand @disqualified_candidates];

# Unless there's a juicier story...
SEARCH:
for my $name (@disqualified_candidates) {
    if (chopped_down_cherry_tree($name)) {
        $scapegoat = $name;
        last SEARCH;
    }
}

# Publish and be-damn...
print {$headline} "Disgraced $scapegoat Disqualified From Election!!!\n";
```

Using the first function often results in code that is both more comprehensible and more efficient:

```
use List::Util qw( first );

# Find a juicy story...
my $scapegoat
    = first { chopped_down_cherry_tree($_) }  @disqualified_candidates;

# Otherwise victimize someone at random...
if (!defined $scapegoat) {
    $scapegoat = $disqualified_candidates[rand @disqualified_candidates];
}

# Publish and be-damn...
print {$headline} "Disgraced $scapegoat Disqualified From Election!!!\n";
```

List Transformation

Use for instead of map when transforming a list in place.

There is, however, a particular case where map and grep are *not* better than an explicit for loop: when you're transforming an array *in situ*. In other words, when you have an array of elements or a list of lvalues and you want to replace each of them with a transformed version of the original.

For example, suppose you have a series of temperature measurements in Fahrenheit, and you need them in Kelvin instead. You could accomplish that transformation by applying a map to the data and then assigning it back to the original container:

```
@temperature_measurements = map { F_to_K($_) } @temperature_measurements;
```

But the map statement has to allocate extra memory to store the transformed values and then assign that temporary list back to the original array. That process could become expensive if the list is large or the transformation is repeated many times.

In contrast, the equivalent for block can simply reuse the existing memory in the array:

```
for my $measurement (@temperature_measurements) {
    $measurement = F_to_K($measurement);
}
```

Note that this second version also makes it slightly more obvious that elements of the array are being replaced. To detect that fact in the map version, you have to compare the array names at both ends of a long assignment statement. In the for-loop version, the more compact statement:

```
$measurement = F_to_K($measurement);
```

makes it easier to see that each measurement is being replaced with some transformed version of its original value.

Complex Mappings

Use a subroutine call to factor out complex list transformations.

When a map, grep, or first is applied to a list, the block performing the transformation or conditional test can sometimes become quite complex[*]. For example:

```
use List::Util qw( max );

Readonly my $JITTER_FACTOR => 0.01;    # Jitter by a maximum of 1%

my @jittered_points
    = map { my $x = $_->{x};
            my $y = $_->{y};

            my $max_jitter = max($x, $y) / $JITTER_FACTOR;
```

---

[*] map blocks rarely start out complex, but the complexity of any critical piece of code will tend to grow over time. This fall from grace seems to be caused not so much by the Second Law of Thermodynamics as by the First Law of Murphy.

```
             { x => $x + gaussian_rand({mean=>0, dev=>0.25, scale=>$max_jitter}),
               y => $y + gaussian_rand({mean=>0, dev=>0.25, scale=>$max_jitter}),
             }
        } @points;
```

This large block is very hard to read, especially since the final anonymous hash constructor looks more like a nested block. So the temptation is to use a `for` instead:

```
my @jittered_points;
for my $point (@points) {
    my $x = $point->{x};
    my $y = $point->{y};

    my $max_jitter = max($x, $y) / $JITTER_FACTOR;

    my $jittered_point = {
        x => $x + gaussian_rand({ mean=>0, dev=>0.25, scale=>$max_jitter }),
        y => $y + gaussian_rand({ mean=>0, dev=>0.25, scale=>$max_jitter }),
    };

    push @jittered_points, $jittered_point;
}
```

That certainly does help the overall readability, but it's still far from optimal. A better solution is to factor out the complex calculation into a separate subroutine, then call that subroutine within a now much simpler and more readable `map` expression:

```
my @jittered_points = map { jitter($_) } @points;

# and elsewhere...

# Add a random Gaussian perturbation to a point...
sub jitter {
    my ($point) = @_;
    my $x = $point->{x};
    my $y = $point->{y};

    my $max_jitter = max($x, $y) / $JITTER_FACTOR;

    return {
        x => $x + gaussian_rand({ mean=>0, dev=>0.25, scale=>$max_jitter }),
        y => $y + gaussian_rand({ mean=>0, dev=>0.25, scale=>$max_jitter }),
    };
}
```

List Processing Side Effects

Never modify $_ in a list function.

One particular feature of the way the `map`, `grep`, and `first` functions work can easily become a source of subtle errors. These functions all use the $_ variable to pass each list element into their associated block. But, for better efficiency, these functions alias $_ to each list value they're iterating, rather than copying each value into $_.

You probably don't often think of map, grep, and first as creating aliases. You probably just think of those functions as taking a list and returning a second, independent list. And, most importantly, you almost certainly don't expect them to *change* the original list.

However, if the block you give to a map, grep, or first modifies $_ in any way, then it's actually modifying an alias to some element of the function's list. That means it's actually modifying the original element itself, which is almost certainly an error.

This kind of mistake commonly occurs in code like this:

```
# Select .pm files for which no corresponding .pl file exists...
@pm_files_without_pl_files
    = grep { s/.pm\z/.pl/xms && !-e } @pm_files;
```

The intention here is almost certainly virtuous. The thought process was probably something like:

> The implicit $_ successively holds a copy of each of the filenames in @pm_files. I'll replace the .pm suffix of that copy with .pl, then see if the resulting file exists. If it doesn't, then the original (.pm) filename will be passed through the grep to be collected in @pm_files_without_pl_files.

The mistake is simple, but deadly: $_ doesn't successively hold a *copy* of anything. It successively holds *aliases*. So the actual effect of the grep is far more sinister. $_ is an *alias*—that is, just another name—for each of the filenames in @pm_files. So the substitution in the grep block replaces the .pm suffix of each *original* filename with .pl; then the -e checks whether the resulting file exists. If the file doesn't exist, then the filename (now ending in .pl) will be passed through to @pm_files_without_pl_files. And, regardless of whether that name is passed through or not, the block will have modified the original element in @pm_files.

Oops!

Not only did that grep statement unintentionally mess up the contents of @pm_files, it didn't even do the job it was supposed to do. Because it changes each $_ on the way through, what you actually get back are the names of the .pl files that were M.I.A., *not* the .pm files that were looking for them.

This kind of error can occur anywhere that the block of any list-processing function uses any of Perl's numerous $_-modifying features. For example:

```
# Find the first "chunk" that spans more than one line
$next_multi_line_chunk
    = first { chomp; m/\n/xms; } @file_chunks;
```

Here, the first block chomps the actual elements of @file_chunks, because the raw chomp chomps $_, which is successively aliased to each element of @file_chunks. But the first stops calling its block as soon as one of those post-chomped elements is found to still have a newline in it (m/\n/xms).

So, after this assignment statement executes, the `first` will have surreptitiously chomped each element in `@file_chunks`, up to and including the first element that contained a newline. But, because `first` will have stopped checking at that point, none of the elements after the first match will have been modified at all. So `@file_chunks` is left in a state that is simultaneously unexpected (it's not obvious that the array was being modified at all), inconsistent (only part of the array has been modified), and unpredictable (how much was modified depends on the contents of the array).

Of course, there is no limit to human iniquity, and occasionally that kind of subtle nastiness is actually *intentional*. For example:

```
use List::MoreUtils qw( uniq );

# Remove directory pathnames from filenames and collect separately...
@dir_paths = uniq map { s{ \A (.*/) }{}xms ? $1 : './' } @file_paths;
```

In this case, the sneaky substitution within the `map` block is deliberate. The implementer genuinely wants to chop off any leading `'some/path/here/'` from each element of `@file_paths`, and at the same time collect those off-cuts into the `@dir_paths` array. Ten-out-of-ten for Perl *savoir-faire*, but minus several million for maintainability.

The rule here is simple: no `map`, `grep`, or `first` block should *ever* have a side effect. In particular, no `map`, `grep`, or `first` block should ever modify `$_`.

If your block really does need to modify a copy of each list element, then create the copy explicitly within the block:

```
@pm_files_without_pl_files
    = grep {
        my $file = $_;
        $file =~ s/.pm\z/.pl/xms;
        !-e $file;
    } @pm_files;
```

In this version, the substitution is applied to an explicit copy of the filename (in `$file`), so the original strings in `@pm_files` will be unchanged, and the filenames that flow through to `@pm_files_without_pl_files` will retain their original `.pm` suffixes.

On the other hand, if you find you really do need side effects in your `map`, `grep`, or `first` block, then don't use `map` or `grep` or `first` at all. Rewrite the code as a `for` loop instead. That way, the side-effects in the loop can easily be detected and understood:

```
# Track directory paths to ensure uniqueness...
my %seen_dir;

FILE_PATH:
for my $file (@file_paths) {
    # Default to current directory...
    my $dir_path = './';
```

```
    # Capture and remove any actual directory path and use it as the path...
    if ($file =~ s{ \A (.*/) }{}xms) {
        $dir_path = $1;
    }

    # Reject repeated directory paths...
    next FILE_PATH if $seen_dir{$dir_path}++;

    # Record the extracted path...
    push @dir_paths, $dir_path;
}
```

Multipart Selections

Avoid cascading an `if`.

Avoid cascades of `if-elsif-elsif-else` statements wherever possible. They tend to produce code with poor readability that is also expensive to execute.

The readability of an `if` cascade suffers because the blocks associated with each alternative have to be placed between the alternatives themselves. That can easily cause the entire construct to expand beyond a single screen or page. Any kind of code that extends over a visual boundary is very much more difficult to understand, because the reader is then forced to mentally cache parts of the construct as they scroll through it.

Even if the code doesn't cause a mental page fault, the alternation of condition-action-condition-action-condition-action can make it difficult to compare the conditions and hence to verify that the logic you're implementing is correct. For example, it can be hard to verify that, collectively, your conditions cover all the important alternatives. It can also be difficult to ensure that they are mutually exclusive.

Likewise, if the actions are very similar (e.g., assigning different values to the same variable), it's relatively easy to induce errors (mistyping the variable name in one branch, for example) or to introduce subtleties (such as deliberately using a different variable name in one branch).

The performance of an `if` cascade can also be suboptimal. Unless you are able to put the most common cases first, a cascaded `if` is going to have to test, on average, one-half of its alternative conditions before it can execute any of its blocks. And often it's simply not possible to put the common cases first, either because you don't know which cases will be the common ones or because you specifically need to check the special cases first.

The following guidelines examine specific types of cascaded `if`, and suggest alternative code structures that are more robust, readable, and efficient.

Value Switches

Use table look-up in preference to cascaded equality tests.

Sometimes an if cascade selects its action by testing the same variable against a fixed number of predefined values. For example:

```
sub words_to_num {
    my ($words) = @_;

    # Treat each sequence of non-whitespace as a word...
    my @words = split /\s+/, $words;

    # Translate each word to the appropriate number...
    my $num = $EMPTY_STR;
    for my $word (@words) {
        if ($word =~ m/ zero | zéro /ixms) {
            $num .= '0';
        }
        elsif ($word =~ m/ one | un | une /ixms) {
            $num .= '1';
        }
        elsif ($word =~ m/ two | deux /ixms) {
            $num .= '2';
        }
        elsif ($word =~ m/ three | trois /ixms) {
            $num .= '3';
        }
        # etc. etc. until...
        elsif ($word =~ m/ nine | neuf /ixms) {
            $num .= '9';
        }
        else {
            # Ignore unrecognized words
        }
    }

    return $num;
}

# and later...

print words_to_num('one zero eight neuf');    # prints: 1089
```

A cleaner and more efficient solution is to use a hash as a look-up table, like so:

```
my %num_for = (
#   English       Français        Française
    'zero' => 0,  'zéro' => 0,
    'one'  => 1,   'un'  => 1,     'une' => 1,
    'two'  => 2,  'deux' => 2,
```

```
      'three' => 3,  'trois' => 3,
#          etc.          etc.
      'nine' => 9,   'neuf' => 9,
);

sub words_to_num {
    my ($words) = @_;

    # Treat each sequence of non-whitespace as a word...
    my @words = split /\s+/, $words;

    # Translate each word to the appropriate number...
    my $num = $EMPTY_STR;
    for my $word (@words) {
        my $digit = $num_for{lc $word};
        if (defined $digit) {
            $num .= $digit;
        }
    }

    return $num;
}

# and later...

print words_to_num('one zero eight neuf');     # prints: 1089
```

In this second version, words_to_num( ) looks up the lowercase form of each word in
the %num_for hash and, if that look-up provides a defined result, appends it to the
number being created.

The primary advantage here is that the code in the for loop never need change, no
matter how many extra words you subsequently add to the look-up table. For example, if we wished to cater for Hindi digits as well, then you'd need to change the if'd
version in 10 separate places:

```
for my $word (@words) {
        if ($word =~ m/ zero | zéro | shunya /ixms) {
            $num .= '0';
        }
        elsif ($word =~ m/ one | un | une | ek /ixms) {
            $num .= '1';
        }
        elsif ($word =~ m/ two | deux | do /ixms) {
            $num .= '2';
        }
        elsif ($word =~ m/ three | trois | teen /ixms) {
            $num .= '3';
        }
        # etc.
        elsif ($word =~ m/ nine | neuf | nau /ixms) {
            $num .= '9';
        }
```

```
        else {
            # Ignore unrecognized words
        }
    }
```

But, in the look-up table version, the only change would be to add an extra column to the table itself:

```
my %num_for = (
#     English          Français          Française          Hindi
    'zero' => 0,      'zéro' => 0,                        'shunya' => 0,
     'one' => 1,       'un' => 1,       'une' => 1,          'ek' => 1,
     'two' => 2,      'deux' => 2,                           'do' => 2,
   'three' => 3,     'trois' => 3,                         'teen' => 3,
#       etc.             etc.                                 etc.
    'nine' => 9,      'neuf' => 9,                          'nau' => 9,
);
```

Factoring the translations out into a table also improves the readability of the code, both because the code is more compact, and because tables are a familiar and comprehensible way to structure information.

The values to be looked up in a table don't have to be scalar constants. For example, here's a simple module that installs a debug( ) function, whose behaviour can be configured when the module is loaded:

```
package Debugging;

use Carp;
use Log::Stdlog  { level => 'debug' };

# Choice of actions when debugging...
my %debug_mode = (
  # MODE              DEBUGGING ACTION
    off    => sub {},
    logged => sub { return print {*STDLOG} debug =>  @_; },
    loud   => sub {                   carp 'DEBUG: ', @_; },
    fatal  => sub {                   croak 'DEBUG: ', @_; },
);

# Change debugging behaviour whenever module is used...
sub import {
    my $package = shift;
    my $mode    = @_ > 0 ? shift : 'loud';    # Default to carping

    # Locate appropriate behaviour, or die trying...
    my $debugger = $debug_mode{$mode};
    croak "Unknown debugging mode ('$mode')" if !defined $debugger;

    # Install new behaviour...
    use Sub::Installer;
    caller()->reinstall_sub(debug  => $debugger);

    return;
}
```

The module's `import()` subroutine (which is called whenever the module is loaded) takes a string that specifies how the newly created `debug()` subroutine should behave. For example:

```
use Debugging qw( logged );    # debug() logs messages
```

That string is unpacked into `$mode` within the `import` subroutine, and then used as a look-up key into the `%debug_mode` hash. The look-up returns an anonymous subroutine that is then installed (via the `Sub::Installer` module) as the caller's `debug()` subroutine.

Once again, the advantage is that the logic of the `import()` subroutine doesn't have to change when additional debugging alternatives become available. You can simply add the new behaviour (as an anonymous subroutine) to the `%debug_mode` table. For example, to provide a debugging mode that counts messages:

```
# Choice of actions when debugging...
my %debug_mode = (
   # MODE            DEBUGGING ACTION
     off      => sub {},
     logged   => sub { return print {*STDLOG} debug => @_;    },
     loud     => sub {                  carp 'DEBUG: ', @_; },
     fatal    => sub {                  croak 'DEBUG: ', @_; },
     counted  =>  do {
                       my $count = 1;     # Private variable for sub
                       sub { carp "DEBUG: [$count] ", @_; $count++; }
                    },
);
```

Tabular Ternaries

When producing a value, use tabular ternaries.

Hash-based table look-ups aren't always feasible. Sometimes decisions have to be made based on a series of tests, rather than on a particular value. However, if each alternative course of action results in a simple value, then it's still possible to avoid explicit cascaded `if`s and preserve a tabular layout in your code. The trick is to use the ternary operator (`?:`) instead.

For example, to produce a suitable string for a salutation in a form letter, you might write something like:

```
my $salute;
if ($name eq $EMPTY_STR) {
    $salute = 'Dear Customer';
}
elsif ($name =~ m/\A ((?:Sir|Dame) \s+ \S+)/xms) {
    $salute = "Dear $1";
}
```

```
    elsif ($name =~ m/([^\n]*), \s+ Ph[.]?D \z/xms) {
        $salute = "Dear Dr $1";
    }
    else {
        $salute = "Dear $name";
    }
```

The repeated assignments to $salute suggest that a cleaner solution, using only a single assignment, may be possible. Indeed, you could build a simple tabular structure to determine the correct salutation, by cascading ternaries instead of ifs, like so:

```
                    # Name format...                              # Salutation...
    my $salute = $name eq $EMPTY_STR                           ? 'Dear Customer'
              : $name =~ m/ \A((?:Sir|Dame) \s+ \S+) /xms ? "Dear $1"
              : $name =~ m/ (.*), \s+ Ph[.]?D \z      /xms ? "Dear Dr $1"
              :                                                "Dear $name"
              ;
```

The efficiency of this series of tests will be exactly the same as the preceding cascaded-if version, so there's no advantage in that respect. The advantages of this approach are in terms of readability and comprehensibility. For a start, it's very obvious that this extended construct is, despite the many alternatives it considers, really just a single assignment statement. And it's very easy to confirm that the correct variable is being assigned to[*].

A second advantage of the ternary version is that (if you squint a little) it looks like a table: one column of tests on $name and a second column listing the corresponding salutations. It even has column borders of a kind: the vertical rows of colons and question marks.

The ternary version is also considerably more compact, and requires two-thirds fewer lines than the equivalent cascaded if. That makes it far easier to keep the code on one screen as additional alternatives are added.

The final advantage of using ternaries instead of an if cascade is that the syntax of the ternary operator is much stricter. In a regular cascaded if statement, it's easy to accidentally leave off the final unconditional else. For example:

```
    my $salute;
    if ($name eq $EMPTY_STR) {
        $salute = 'Dear Customer';
    }
    elsif ($name =~ m/\A ((?:Sir|Dame) \s+ \S+)/xms) {
        $salute = "Dear $1";
    }
    elsif ($name =~ m/(.*), \s+ Ph[.]?D\z/xms) {
        $salute = "Dear Dr $1";
    }
```

---

[*] Did you notice the cascaded-if version has a bug in its third alternative? That branch doesn't assign to $salute; it assigns to $sa1ute.

In which case, $salute might sometimes unexpectedly remain undefined.

However, there is no way to make the same mistake using a ternary cascade:

```
                 # Name format...                          Salutation...
my $salute = $name eq $EMPTY_STR                     ? 'Dear Customer'
           : $name =~ m/\A((?:Sir|Dame) \s+ \S+)/xms ? "Dear $1"
           : $name =~ m/(.*), \s+ Ph[.]?D \z     /xms ? "Dear Dr $1"
           ;
```

If you do, Perl will immediately (and lethally) inform you that leaving out the final alternative is a syntax error.

do-while Loops

Don't use do...while **loops.**

Like any other postfix looping construct, a do...while loop is intrinsically hard to read, because it places the controlling condition at the end of the loop, rather than at the beginning.

More importantly, in Perl a do...while loop isn't a "first-class" loop at all. Specifically, you can't use the next, last, or redo commands within a do...while. Or, worse still, you *can* use those control directives; they just won't do what you expect.

For example, the following code looks like it should work:

```
sub get_big_int {
    my $int;

    TRY:
    do {
        # Request an integer...
        print 'Enter a large integer: ';
        $int = <>;

        # That's not an integer!...
        next TRY if $int !~ /\A [-+]? \d+ \n? \z/xms;

        # Otherwise tidy it up a little...
        chomp $int;
    } while $int < 10;    # Until the input is more than a single digit

    return $int;
}

# and later...

for (1..$MAX_NUMBER_OF_ATTEMPTS) {
    print sqrt get_big_int(), "\n";
}
```

That looks okay, but it isn't. Specifically, if a non-integer is ever entered and the next
TRY command is invoked, that next starts looking for an appropriately labeled loop to
re-iterate. But the do...while isn't actually a loop; it's a postfix-modified do block. So
the next ignores the TRY: label attached to the do. Control passes out of the do block,
and then out of the subroutine call (a subroutine isn't a loop either), until it returns
to the for loop. But the for loop isn't labeled TRY:, so control passes outwards again,
this time right out of the program.

In other words, if the user ever enters a value that isn't a pure integer, the entire
application will immediately terminate—not a very robust or graceful way to
respond to errors. That kind of bug is particularly hard to find too, because it's one
of those rare cases of a Perl construct not doing what you mean. It looks right, but it
works wrong.

The best practice is to avoid do...while entirely. The simple way to do that is to use
a regular while loop instead, but to "counter-initialize" the $int variable, to guaran-
tee that the loop executes at least once:

```
sub get_big_int {
    my $int = 0;    # Small value so the while loop has to iterate at least once

    TRY:
    while ($int < 10) {
        print 'Enter a large integer: ';
        $int = <>;

        next TRY if $int !~ /\A [-+]? \d+ \n? \z/xms;

        chomp $int;
    }

    return $int;
}
```

Sometimes, however, the condition to be met is too complex to permit counter-
initialization, or perhaps no counter-initial value is possible. This most commonly
occurs when the test is performed by a separate subroutine. In such cases, either
use a flag:

```
sub get_big_int {
    my $tried = 0;
    my $int;

    while (!$tried || !is_big($int)) {
        print 'Enter a valid integer: ';
        $int = <>;

        chomp $int;

        $tried = 1;
    }
```

```
        return $int;
    }
```

or, better still, use a return to explicitly escape from an infinite loop:

```
    sub get_big_int {
        while (1) {
            print 'Enter a valid integer: ';
            my $int = <>;

            chomp $int;

            return $int if is_big($int);
        }

        return;
    }
```

Linear Coding

Reject as many iterations as possible, as early as possible.

Chapter 2 recommends the practice of "coding in paragraphs" as a way to chunk code and improve its comprehensibility. Taking this idea one step further, it is also good practice to "process in paragraphs". That is, don't wait until you have all your data assembled before you start checking it. It's more efficient, and often more comprehensible, to verify as you go.

Checking data as soon as it's available means that you can short-circuit sooner if the data is unacceptable. More importantly, the resulting "paragraphs" of code are then specific to each piece of data, rather than to one phase of the processing. That means your code chunks are better focused on the distinct elements of the problem domain, rather than on the more complex interactions between those elements.

For example, instead of:

```
    for my $client (@clients) {
        # Compute current and future client value...
        my $value     = $client->{volume} * $client->{rate};
        my $projected = $client->{activity} * $value;

        # Verify client is active, worth watching, and worth keeping...
        if ($client->{activity}
            && $value >= $WATCH_LEVEL
            && $projected >= $KEEP_LEVEL
        ) {
            # If so, add in the client's expected contribution...
            $total += $projected * $client->{volatility};
        }
    }
```

you can generate-and-test each datum sequentially, like so:

```
CLIENT:
for my $client (@clients) {
    # Verify active client...
    next CLIENT if !$client->{activity};

    # Compute current client value and verify client is worth watching...
    my $value = $client->{volume} * $client->{rate};
    next CLIENT if $value < $WATCH_LEVEL;

    # Compute likely client future value and verify client is worth keeping...
    my $projected = $client->{activity}* $value;
    next CLIENT if $projected < $KEEP_LEVEL;

    # Add in client's expected contribution...
    $total += $projected * $client->{volatility};
}
```

Note that this second version deals with each part of the decision separately, instead of lumping them together in one bloated, multiline conditional test. This sequential approach makes it easier to see the different criteria that are being tested, as you can focus on one criterion—and its associated data—at a time. Linear coding also typically reduces the number of nested blocks that are required, which can further improve readability.

Better still, the second version is potentially much more efficient. The first version computes $value and $projected for every single client, whether or not the loop eventually uses that data. The second version does no work at all on inactive clients, because its first next statement terminates each iteration as soon as torpor is detected. Similarly, the loop block does only half as much work on the clients who are active but not worth watching.

Distributed Control

Don't contort loop structures just to consolidate control.

The bloated conditional tests mentioned in the previous guideline can also appear in the conditions of loop structures, where they usually indicate the (mis)application of structured programming techniques.

Proponents of structured programming usually insist that every loop should have only a single exit point: the conditional expression that's controlling the loop. The very laudable intent of that rule is to make it easier to determine the correctness of the loop by consolidating all information about its termination behaviour in a single place.

Unfortunately, blind adherence to this principle frequently produces code that looks like this:

```
Readonly my $INTEGER => qr/\A [+-]? \d+ \n? \z/xms;

my $int   = 0;
my $tries = 0;
my $eof   = 0;

while (!$eof
       && $tries < $MAX_TRIES
       && ( $int !~ $INTEGER || $int < $MIN_BIG_INT )
) {
    print 'Enter a big integer: ';
    $int = <>;
    if (defined $int) {
        chomp $int;

        if ($int eq $EMPTY_STR) {
            $int = 0;
            $tries--;
        }
    }
    else {
        $eof = 1;
    }
    $tries++;
}
```

The loop conditional typically contains a mixture of positive and negative tests on several flag variables. The block itself then contains multiple nested if tests, mainly to set the termination flags or to pre-empt further execution if an exit condition is encountered within the block.

When a loop has been contorted in this manner, it's often extremely difficult to understand. Take a moment to work through the previous example code and determine exactly what it does.

Now compare that convoluted code with the following version (which provides exactly the same behaviour):

```
Readonly my $INTEGER => qr/\A [+-]? \d+ \n? \z/xms;

my $int;

INPUT:
for my $attempt (1..$MAX_TRIES) {
    print 'Enter a big integer: ';
    $int = <>;

    last INPUT if not defined $int;
    redo INPUT if $int eq "\n";
    next INPUT if $int !~ $INTEGER;

    chomp $int;
    last INPUT if $int >= $MIN_BIG_INT;
}
```

This version requires no flag variables. It has fewer lines of code. It has no nested conditionals or multipart tests. You can easily work out what it does on end-of-file or when the input is an empty line or when given a non-integer simply by working through the linear sequence of tests within the block.

Herding loop flags into a single location only gives the illusion of consolidating control. A complex exit condition still relies on other tests within the loop to set the appropriate flags, so the actual control is still implicitly distributed.

Perl provides clean ways to distribute control *explicitly* throughout a loop. Use them.

Redoing

Use `for` and `redo` **instead of an irregularly counted** `while`.

In the final version of the input code shown in the previous guideline, a `while` loop plus a count variable (`$tries`) was replaced by a `for` loop. This is a good practice in any situation where a `while` loop is controlled by a variable that is linearly incremented on each iteration. Using a `for` makes explicit your intention to loop a fixed number of times. It also eliminates both the count variable and the need to explicitly test that variable against some maximal value. That, in turn, removes the possibility of forgetting to increment the variable and the risk of off-by-one errors in the explicit test.

However, this kind of loop refactoring is satisfactory only when the count variable is uniformly incremented on every iteration. There are plenty of situations where that is not quite the case; where the count is usually incremented each time, but not always. Such exceptions obviously create a serious problem in a fixed-repetition `for` loop.

For example, the previous example didn't count an empty input line as a legitimate "try". That was easy to accommodate in the "`while ($tries < $MAX_TRIES)`" version; you simply don't increment `$tries` in that case. But, in a `for` loop, the expected number of iterations is fixed before the loop even starts, and you have no control over the incrementing of the loop variable. So it would seem that a `for` loop is contraindicated whenever the iteration-counting is irregular.

Fortunately, the `redo` statement allows a loop to have its cake (i.e., be a `for` loop instead of a `while`) and eat it too (by still discounting certain iterations). That's because a `redo` sends the execution back to the start of the *current* iteration of the loop block: "Do not pass `for`. Do not collect another iterated value."

Using a `redo` allows you to take advantage of the fixed-iteration semantics of a `for` loop (with their cleaner and more maintainable syntax), but still allows controlled deviations from a fixed number of iterations when necessary. It also makes the program's control flow more obvious and comprehensible. There is no longer any need to decode the implicit behaviour caused by (non-)changes to the value of a count variable. Instead, every exception to the fixed number of repetitions promised by the for loop is explicitly marked with a redo keyword.

For these reasons it's a good practice to replace any "counted" while loop with a for loop, and then to use a redo in any situation where the count should not be incremented for that particular iteration.

Unfortunately, this practice does not generalize to situations where the count must be decremented in any way or increased by more than one. In such cases, a while-plus-$count is the correct solution.

Loop Labels

Label every loop that is exited explicitly, and use the label with every next, last, **or** redo.

The next, last, and redo statements make it much easier to specify sophisticated flow of control in a readable manner. And that readability is further enhanced if the reader doesn't have to puzzle out which particular loop a given next, last, or redo is controlling.

The easiest way to accomplish that is to label every loop in which a next, last, or redo is used. Then use the same label on each next, last, and redo in that loop. The reader can then match up the name on the keyword against the labels on the surrounding loops to determine which loop's flow of control is being altered.

So you should write:

```
INPUT:
for my $try (1..$MAX_TRIES) {
    print 'Enter an integer: ';
    $int = <>;

    last INPUT if not defined $int;
    redo INPUT if $int eq "\n";

    chomp $int;
    last INPUT if $int =~ $INTEGER;
}
```

instead of:

```
for my $try (1..$MAX_TRIES) {
    print 'Enter an integer: ';
    $int = <>;

    last if not defined $int;
    redo if $int eq "\n";

    chomp $int;
```

```
        last if $int =~ $INTEGER;
    }
```

Another, less obvious benefit of following this guideline is that the presence of the label at the start of any loop alerts the reader to the fact that the loop has embedded flow control.

Place the label on the line preceding the loop keyword, at the same level of indentation, and with an empty line (or a paragraph comment) above it. That way, the label helps the loop stand out, but leaves the actual loop keyword on the left margin, where it's easy to see.

When you're labeling a loop, choose a label that helps to document the purpose of the loop, and of the flow control statements. In particular, don't name loops LOOP:

```
LOOP:
for my $try (1..$MAX_TRIES) {
    print 'Enter an integer: ';
    $int = <>;

    last LOOP if not defined $int;
    redo LOOP if $int eq "\n";

    chomp $int;
    last LOOP if $int =~ $INTEGER;
}
```

That's as bad as naming a variable $var or calling a subroutine func( ).

Labelling loops is especially important for maintainability. A typical mistake is to initially write code that correctly exits from a loop like so:

```
while (my $client_ref = get_client()) {
    # Retrieve phone number...
    my $phone = $client_ref->{phone};

    # Skip client if "do not call" was requested...
    next if $phone =~ m/do \s+ not \s+ call/ixms;

    # Profit!
    send_sms_to($phone, $advert);
}
```

Later, a change of internal data structure may make it necessary to add an inner loop, at which point the flow of control can easily go awry:

```
while (my $client_ref = get_client()) {
    my $preferred_phone;

    # Retrieve phone number (clients can now have more than one)...
    for my $phone ( @{ $client_ref->{phones} } ) {
        # Skip client if "do not call" was requested...
        next if $phone =~ m/do \s+ not \s+ call/ixms;

        # Select phone number...
        $preferred_phone = $phone;
```

```
        last;
    }

    # Profit!
    send_sms_to($preferred_phone, $advert);
}
```

The problem here is that the intention was to give up trying to contact clients if any of their numbers is marked "Do Not Call". But moving the next if... inside a nested for loop means that the next no longer moves the loop on to the next client, just on to the next phone number of the current client. Apart from causing you to annoy clients who have specifically asked you not to, this error also introduces the possibility that $preferred_phone will be undefined when it's finally passed to send_sms_to().

In contrast, if your policy is to always label every loop that has a flow control statement inside it:

```
CLIENT:
while (my $client_ref = get_client()) {
    # Retrieve phone number...
    my $phone = $client_ref->{phone};

    # Skip client if "do not call" was requested...
    next CLIENT if $phone =~ m/do \s+ not \s+ call/ixms;

    # Profit!
    send_sms_to($phone, $advert);
}
```

then either the updated code will be automatically correct:

```
CLIENT:
while (my $client_ref = get_client()) {
    my $preferred_phone;

    # Retrieve phone number (clients can now have more than one)...
    PHONE_NUMBER:
    for my $phone ( @{ $client_ref->{phones} } ) {
        # Skip client if "do not call" was requested...
        next CLIENT if $phone =~ m/do \s+ not \s+ call/ixms;

        # Select phone number...
        $preferred_phone = $phone;
        last PHONE_NUMBER;
    }

    # Profit!
    send_sms_to($preferred_phone, $advert);
}
```

or the error will be obvious, as the comment and the target of the next will then be manifestly inconsistent:

```
    # Skip client if "do not call" was requested...
    next PHONE_NUMBER if $phone =~ m/do \s+ not \s+ call/ixms;
```

CHAPTER 7
Documentation

*Documentation is like sex: when it's good, it's very, very
good; and when it's bad, it's still better than nothing.*
—Dick Brandon

Documentation: for most development programmers it's a millstone, but for maintenance programmers it's a life-line. More importantly, very few programmers are exclusively in one role or the other. Most developers write code that they then have to maintain themselves. Or else they have to maintain other people's code in order to develop their own.

The problem is that any code of your own that you haven't looked at for six or more months might as well have been written by someone else[*]. The young, smart, optimistic you—who's creating the code—will undoubtedly find it tedious to document your understanding of what that code does and how it does it. But the older, wiser, sadder you—who later has to fix, extend, and adapt that code—will treasure the long-forgotten insights that your documentation preserves.

In that sense, documentation is a love letter that you write to your future self.

Types of Documentation

Distinguish user documentation from technical documentation.

End users will rarely read your code, or your comments. If they read anything at all, they'll run your module or application through *perldoc*[†] and read whatever emerges.

---

[*] Eagleson's Law again.

[†] *perldoc* is a command-line utility that comes standard with Perl. It locates, extracts, and presents documentation from the Perl manpages, the standard library, and any other modules installed on your system. A good place to start is:

```
> perldoc perldoc
```

On the other hand, maintainers and other developers may also read your POD[*], but they'll spend far more of their time looking directly at your code.

So it makes sense to put user documentation in the "public" sections of your code's POD (i.e., in the =head1, =head2, and =over/=item/=back sections), and relegate the technical documentation to "non-public" places (i.e., to the =for and =begin/=end POD sections and to comments).

More importantly, *distinguish* between the content of user and technical documentation. In particular, don't put implementation details in user documentation. It wastes your time and it annoys the user. Tell the user what the code does, not how the code does it, unless those details are somehow relevant to the users' use of that code.

For example, when documenting a set of list operations for users, tell them that pick( ) takes a list and selects one element at random, that shuffle( ) takes a list and returns a randomly reordered version of that list, and that zip( ) takes two or more array references and produces a single list that interleaves the array values. You may choose to mention that pick( ) and shuffle( ) do their jobs in a genuinely random and unbiased manner, but there's no need to explain how that miracle is achieved.

On the other hand, your module may also provide a set of specialist sorting routines: sort_radix( ), sort_shell( ), sort_pigeonhole( ). When documenting these, you will obviously need to at least mention the different algorithms they employ, and the conditions under which each might be a superior choice.

Boilerplates

Create standard POD templates for modules and applications.

One of the main reasons documentation can often seem so unpleasant is the "blank page effect". Many programmers simply don't know how to start, or what to say.

One of the best ways to make writing documentation less forbidding (and hence more likely to actually occur) is to circumvent that initial empty screen by providing a template that developers can cut and paste into their code.

For a module, that documentation template might look something like Example 7-1. For an application, the variation shown in Example 7-2 is more appropriate. Of course, the specific details that your templates provide may vary from those shown here, according to your other coding practices. The most likely variation will be in the licence and copyright, but you may also have specific in-house conventions

---

[*] POD is the "Plain Old Documentation" format, a simple mark-up language for embedded documentation that is recognized by the Perl compiler. If you're unfamiliar with it, take a look at the *perlpod* manpage.

regarding version numbering (see Chapter 17), or the grammar of diagnostic messages (see Chapter 13), or the attribution of authorship.

Example 7-1. User documentation template for modules

```
=head1 NAME

<Module::Name> - <One-line description of module's purpose>


=head1 VERSION

The initial template usually just has:

This documentation refers to <Module::Name> version 0.0.1.


=head1 SYNOPSIS

    use <Module::Name>;
    # Brief but working code example(s) here showing the most common usage(s)

    # This section will be as far as many users bother reading,
    # so make it as educational and exemplary as possible.


=head1 DESCRIPTION

A full description of the module and its features.
May include numerous subsections (i.e., =head2, =head3, etc.).


=head1 SUBROUTINES/METHODS

A separate section listing the public components of the module's interface.
These normally consist of either subroutines that may be exported, or methods
that may be called on objects belonging to the classes that the module provides.
Name the section accordingly.

In an object-oriented module, this section should begin with a sentence of the
form "An object of this class represents...", to give the reader a high-level
context to help them understand the methods that are subsequently described.


=head1 DIAGNOSTICS

A list of every error and warning message that the module can generate
(even the ones that will "never happen"), with a full explanation of each
problem, one or more likely causes, and any suggested remedies.
(See also "Documenting Errors" in Chapter 13.)
```

Example 7-1. User documentation template for modules (continued)

```
=head1 CONFIGURATION AND ENVIRONMENT
```

*A full explanation of any configuration system(s) used by the module,
including the names and locations of any configuration files, and the
meaning of any environment variables or properties that can be set. These
descriptions must also include details of any configuration language used.
(See also "Configuration Files" in Chapter 19.)*


```
=head1 DEPENDENCIES
```

*A list of all the other modules that this module relies upon, including any
restrictions on versions, and an indication of whether these required modules are
part of the standard Perl distribution, part of the module's distribution,
or must be installed separately.*


```
=head1 INCOMPATIBILITIES
```

*A list of any modules that this module cannot be used in conjunction with.
This may be due to name conflicts in the interface, or competition for
system or program resources, or due to internal limitations of Perl
(for example, many modules that use source code filters are mutually
incompatible).*


```
=head1 BUGS AND LIMITATIONS
```

*A list of known problems with the module, together with some indication of
whether they are likely to be fixed in an upcoming release.*

*Also a list of restrictions on the features the module does provide:
data types that cannot be handled, performance issues and the circumstances
in which they may arise, practical limitations on the size of data sets,
special cases that are not (yet) handled, etc.*

The initial template usually just has:

```
There are no known bugs in this module.
Please report problems to <Maintainer name(s)>  (<contact address>)
Patches are welcome.

=head1 AUTHOR
```

<Author name(s)> (<contact address>)

Example 7-1. User documentation template for modules (continued)

```
=head1 LICENCE AND COPYRIGHT

Copyright (c) <year> <copyright holder> (<contact address>). All rights reserved.

followed by whatever licence you wish to release it under.
For Perl code that is often just:

This module is free software; you can redistribute it and/or
modify it under the same terms as Perl itself. See L<perlartistic>.

This program is distributed in the hope that it will be useful,
but WITHOUT ANY WARRANTY; without even the implied warranty of
MERCHANTABILITY or FITNESS FOR A PARTICULAR PURPOSE.
```

Example 7-2. User documentation template for applications

```
=head1 NAME

<application name> - <One-line description of application's purpose>


=head1 VERSION

The initial template usually just has:

This documentation refers to <application name> version 0.0.1.


=head1 USAGE

    # Brief working invocation example(s) here showing the most common usage(s)

    # This section will be as far as many users ever read,
    # so make it as educational and exemplary as possible.


=head1 REQUIRED ARGUMENTS

A complete list of every argument that must appear on the command line.
when the application  is invoked, explaining what each of them does, any
restrictions on where each one may appear (i.e., flags that must appear
before or after filenames), and how the various arguments and options
may interact (e.g., mutual exclusions, required combinations, etc.)

If all of the application's arguments are optional, this section
may be omitted entirely.
```

Example 7-2. User documentation template for applications (continued)

```
=head1 OPTIONS

A complete list of every available option with which the application
can be invoked, explaining what each does, and listing any restrictions,
or interactions.

If the application has no options, this section may be omitted entirely.


=head1 DESCRIPTION

A full description of the application and its features.
May include numerous subsections (i.e., =head2, =head3, etc.).


=head1 DIAGNOSTICS

A list of every error and warning message that the application can generate
(even the ones that will "never happen"), with a full explanation of each
problem, one or more likely causes, and any suggested remedies. If the
application generates exit status codes (e.g., under Unix), then list the exit
status associated with each error.


=head1 CONFIGURATION AND ENVIRONMENT

A full explanation of any configuration system(s) used by the application,
including the names and locations of any configuration files, and the
meaning of any environment variables or properties that can be set. These
descriptions must also include details of any configuration language used.
(See also "Configuration Files" in Chapter 19.)


=head1 DEPENDENCIES
=head1 INCOMPATIBILITIES
=head1 BUGS AND LIMITATIONS
=head1 AUTHOR
=head1 LICENCE AND COPYRIGHT

These sections are the same as in Example 7-1.
```

You could make it easy to load these files from templates by configuring your text editor appropriately. In your *vim* configuration file:

```
iab papp  ^]:r ~/.code_templates/perl_application.pl^M
```

Or in your *Emacs* configuration:

```
;; Load an application template in a new unattached buffer...
(defun application-template-pl ( )
  "Inserts the standard Perl application template"  ; For help and info.
  (interactive "*")                                 ; Make this user accessible.
  (switch-to-buffer "application-template-pl")
```

```
    (insert-file "~/.code_templates/perl_application.pl"))
;; Set to a specific key combination...
(global-set-key "\C-ca" 'application-template-pl)
```

Extended Boilerplates

Extend and customize your standard POD templates.

The two templates recommended in the previous section represent only the *minimum* amount of information that should be provided to the user. There are many more possibilities that your team might choose to add to its standard template, such as:

=head1 EXAMPLES

Many people learn better by example than by explanation, and most learn better by a combination of the two. Providing a */demo* directory stocked with well-commented examples is an excellent idea, but your users might not have access to the original distribution, and the demos are unlikely to have been installed for them. Adding a few illustrative examples in the documentation itself can greatly increase the "learnability" of your code.

=head1 FREQUENTLY ASKED QUESTIONS

Incorporating a list of correct answers to common questions may seem like extra work (especially when it comes to maintaining that list), but in many cases it actually *saves* time. Frequently asked questions are frequently emailed questions, and you already have too much email to deal with. If you find yourself repeatedly answering the same question by email, in a newsgroup, on a web site, or in person, answer that question in your documentation as well. Not only is this likely to reduce the number of queries on that topic you subsequently receive, it also means that anyone who *does* ask you directly can simply be directed to read the fine manual.

=head1 COMMON USAGE MISTAKES

This section is really "Frequently Unasked Questions". With just about any kind of software, people inevitably misunderstand the same concepts and misuse the same components. By drawing attention to these common errors, explaining the misconceptions involved, and pointing out the correct alternatives, you can once again pre-empt a large amount of unproductive correspondence. Perl itself provides documentation of this kind, in the form of the *perltrap* manpage.

=head1 SEE ALSO

Often there will be other modules and applications that are possible alternatives to using your software. Or other documentation that would be of use to the users of your software. Or a journal article or book that explains the ideas on which the software is based. Listing those in a "See Also" section allows people to understand your software better and to find the best solution for their problem themselves, without asking you directly*.

=head1 (DISCLAIMER OF) WARRANTY

This subsection is essential in any software that is likely to be used outside your own organization. It should be in a section separate from the "Copyright and Licence", and it should be drafted by a competent legal professional (so you have someone else to sue if someone sues you). If you're not part of a corporation and don't have your own attack lawyers, a useful starting point might be clauses 11 and 12 of the GNU Public License (*http://www.gnu.org/copyleft/gpl.html*)†.

=head1 ACKNOWLEDGEMENTS

Acknowledging any help you received in developing and improving your software is plain good manners. But expressing your appreciation isn't only courteous; it's also enlightened self-interest. Inevitably people will send you bug reports for your software. But what you'd much prefer them to send you are bug reports accompanied by working bug fixes. Publicly thanking those who have already done that in the past is a great way to remind people that patches are always welcome.

Location

Put user documentation in source files.

Having decided what to provide as user documentation, the next question is *where* to provide it. The answer is: put the documentation in the same file as the module or application itself (i.e., in the relevant *.pm* or *.pl* file).

The other common alternative is to put the documentation in its own separate *.pod* file. This is possible because *perldoc* is smart enough to look for POD files as well as source files when searching for documentation. The problem is that this approach works only if the appropriate *.pod* document has been installed along with the module or application, and has been installed somewhere in *perldoc*'s search path, which is unlikely.

In contrast, if the user documentation is placed directly in the appropriate *.pm* or *.pl* file, it will automatically be available anywhere the module or application itself is.

---

* By now you have no doubt detected the ulterior motive for providing more extensive user manuals and written advice. User documentation is all about not having to actually talk to users.

† However, the author is not a competent legal professional and this suggestion is offered for information purposes only and in no way constitutes legal advice. This recommendation is distributed in the hope that it will be useful, but WITHOUT ANY WARRANTY; without even the implied warranty of MERCHANTABILITY or FITNESS FOR A PARTICULAR PURPOSE.

Contiguity

Keep all user documentation in a single place within your source file.

Even though Perl allows you to interleave POD sections between chunks of source code, don't.

User documentation that is fragmented into numerous small pieces distributed throughout the code is *much* harder to maintain in a consistent state, because you have to sift through the intervening code fragments to find it or compare it.

It is sometimes argued that having documentation near the code that it documents can help maintain consistency between the two. In practice, the opposite often seems to be the case: the necessity to go elsewhere in a file in order to update documentation after a code change actually seems to make it *more* likely that developers will do so. When the documentation is right on hand it's somehow easier to overlook or ignore. Of course, that's not going to be the case for everyone. Many people do find documenting a subroutine easier when the documentation is immediately to hand.

A more important reason not to intersperse code and documentation is that doing so usually produces either contorted code or confused documentation. Keeping documentation near the code it explains will frequently force you to lay the code out in an unnatural order, so as to ensure sensible exposition in the documentation. Or else it will force you to present your documentation in an unnatural order, so as to ensure a sensible layout of the code. Neither of these outcomes is desirable, and both can be avoided by keeping the documentation in its own separate, coherent section of the source file.

Position

Place POD as close as possible to the end of the file.

Having decided to keep the documentation together, the obvious question is whether to place it at the start or the end of the file.

There seems to be no particular reason to place it at the beginning. Anyone who is looking at the source is presumably most interested in the code itself, and will appreciate seeing it immediately when they open the file, rather than having to wade though several hundred lines of user documentation first. Moreover, the compiler is able to do a slightly more efficient job it if doesn't have to skip POD sections before it finds any code to compile.

So place your POD at the end of the file, preferably after the __END__ marker so that the compiler doesn't have to look at it at all. Or, if you're using a __DATA__ section in your implementation, wrap the documentation in =pod/=cut directives and place it just before the __DATA__ marker.

Technical Documentation

Subdivide your technical documentation appropriately.

When it comes to technical documentation, use separate *.pod* or plain-text files for your external documentation, design documents, data dictionaries, algorithm overviews, change log, and so on. Make sure that the "See Also" section of your user documentation refers to these extra files.

Use comments (and "invisible" POD directives) for internal documentation, explanations of implementation, maintenance notes, et cetera. The following guidelines give details on each of these points.

Comments

Use block templates for major comments.

Create comment templates that are suitable for your team. For example, to internally document a subroutine or method, you might use something like:

```
#############################################
# Usage      : ????
# Purpose    : ????
# Returns    : ????
# Parameters : ????
# Throws     : no exceptions
# Comments   : none
# See Also   : n/a
```

which might be filled in like so:

```
#############################################
# Usage      : Config::Auto->get_defaults()
# Purpose    : Defaults for 'new'
# Returns    : A hash of defaults
# Parameters : none
# Throws     : no exceptions
# Comments   : No corresponding attribute,
#            : gathers data from each
#            : attr_def attribute
# See Also   : $self->set_default()
```

Structured comments like that are usually better than free-form comments:

```
# This method returns a hash containing the defaults currently being
# used to initialize configuration objects. It takes no arguments.
# There isn't a corresponding class attribute; instead it collects
# the necessary information from the various attr_def attributes. There's
# also a set_default( ) method.
```

Templates produce commenting that is more consistent and easier to read. They're also much more coder-friendly because they allow developers to simply "fill in a form". Comment templates also make it more feasible to ensure that all essential information is provided, and to identify missing information easily, by searching for any field that still has a ???? in its "slot".

Your team might prefer to use some other template for structured comments—maybe even just this:

```
### CLASS METHOD/INSTANCE METHOD/INTERFACE SUB/INTERNAL UTILITY ###
# Purpose:  ????
# Returns:  ????
```

In this version, the type of subroutine can be specified by retaining one of the four titles, and only the essential information is recorded:

```
### CLASS METHOD ###
# Purpose:  Defaults for 'new'
# Returns:  A hash of defaults
```

Note that it's particularly useful to indicate how the subroutine is expected to be used—either with a Usage: field, or with a title like CLASS METHOD. In Perl, the sub keyword is used to declare normal subroutines, class methods, instance methods, internal-use-only utilities, as well as the implementation of overloaded operators. Knowing which role (or roles) a particular subroutine is supposed to play makes it much easier to understand the subroutine, to use it correctly, and to maintain it.

A templated block comment like those recommended earlier should be used to document each component of a module or application. "Components" in this context means subroutines, methods, packages, and the main code of an application.

Algorithmic Documentation

Use full-line comments to explain the algorithm.

Chapter 2 recommends coding in paragraphs. Part of that advice is to prefix each paragraph with a single-line comment.

That comment should explain at a high level what the associated paragraph contributes to the overall process implemented by the code. Ideally, if all the paragraph comments were to be extracted, they should summarize the algorithm by which the code performs its task.

Keep each such comment strictly to a single line. Any more than that interrupts the code excessively, making it harder to follow. If the paragraph is doing something too complicated to be explained in a single line, that is a sign that the code either needs to be split into several paragraphs, or else refactored out into a subroutine (which can then be given a more expansive block comment).

For example:

```perl
sub addarray_internal {
    my ($var_name, $needs_quotemeta) = @_;

    # Record original...
    $raw .= $var_name;

    # Build meta-quoting code, if required...
    my $quotemeta = $needs_quotemeta ? 'map {quotemeta $_}'
                                      : $EMPTY_STR
                                      ;

    # Expand elements of variable, conjoin with ORs...
    my $perl5pat
        = qq{(??{join q{|}, $quotemeta \@{$var_name}})};

    # Insert debugging code if requested...
    my $type = length $quotemeta ? 'literal' : 'pattern';
    debug_now("Adding $var_name (as $type)");
    add_debug_mesg("Trying $var_name (as $type)");

    # Add back-translation...
    push @perl5pats, $perl5pat;

    return;
}
```

Note, however, that the very first paragraph—which will always be unpacking the subroutine's parameters (see Chapter 9)—does not require a comment. Nor does the final return statement.

Elucidating Documentation

Use end-of-line comments to point out subtleties and oddities.

The guidelines in this book aim to help you write code that's self-documenting, so most lines within a single paragraph shouldn't require extra "hints" in order to understand them.

But self-documentation is always in the eye of the original author, and code that seemed perfectly clear when it was written may be somewhat less intelligible when it's re-read six months later.

Comprehensibility can suffer particularly badly when the code incorporates jargon from the problem domain. Terms that were extremely familiar to the original designers and implementers might mean nothing to those who later have to maintain the source. For example, you could inherit code like this:

```
my $QFETM_func_ref;

if ($QFETM_func_ref  = get_GET()) {
    make_futtock($QFETM_func_ref);
}

$build_mode = oct $arg{mode};
```

in which case, the judicious application of trailing comments is appropriate:

```
my $QFETM_func_ref;  # stores Quantum Field Effect Transfer Mode function

# Build futtock representation if remote data is available...
if ($QFETM_func_ref  = get_GET()) {    # instead of get_POST()
    make_futtock($QFETM_func_ref);        # futtock: a rib of a ship's frame
}

$build_mode = oct $arg{mode};   # *From* octal, not *to* octal
```

End-of-line comments should be kept pithy. If you feel that an elucidating comment needs more than the remainder of the current line, then use a discursive comment instead (see "Discursive Documentation" later in this chapter).

Defensive Documentation

Comment anything that has puzzled or tricked you.

The final line in the previous example demonstrates the use of an in-line comment to overcome a maintainer's personal stumbling block:

```
$build_mode = oct $arg{mode};   # *From* octal, not *to* octal
```

Many programmers mistakenly assume that the oct builtin returns the octal version of its argument, when it actually converts its argument from an octal representation to decimal. That comment may have been added when the code was originally written (presumably in a *d'oh!* moment after several hours of fruitless debugging), or it may have been appended by a subsequent maintainer (to immortalize their own Homeric realization). Either way, by commenting it explicitly, that same false expectation will thereafter be averted every time someone new reads the code.

An in-line comment is appropriate whenever you encounter a subtle bug, or whenever you write some subtle code. "Subtle" has a very precise definition here: it means that you either had to look something up in a manual, or had to spend more than five seconds thinking about it before you understood its syntax or semantics.

For example, this:

```
@options = map +{ $_ => 1 }, @flags;
```

needs to be commented:

```
@options = map +{ $_ => 1 }, @flags;    # Anon hash ctor, not map block!
```

In general, if it puzzled or tricked you once, it will puzzle or trick you—or whoever comes after you—again. To avoid that, leave a *Hyre Be Dragones* comment in the code.

Indicative Documentation

Consider whether it's better to rewrite than to comment.

More often than not, the need to leave hints in the code indicates that the code itself is in need of reworking. For example, if the final example of the previous section had used a map block (as suggested in the "Mapping and Grepping" guideline in Chapter 8), then it would look like this instead:

```
@options = map { {$_ => 1} } @flags;
```

in which case the trailing comment would probably not be necessary. The outer braces after the map would obviously be block delimiters, because under the Chapter 8 guideline *every* map is followed by a block. The inner braces might still be slightly disconcerting, but as the map block is expected to return a value, it would be easy enough to deduce that those inner brackets must be producing a value, and hence must be a hash constructor.

Of course, if that still weren't obvious enough, a trailing comment would be appropriate. But now it could be much more to the point:

```
@options = map { {$_ => 1} } @flags;    # map block returns hash ref
```

Discursive Documentation

Use "invisible" POD sections for longer technical discussions.

The =for and =begin/=end POD directives provide an easy way to create large blocks of text that are ignored by the compiler and don't produce any visible output when the surrounding file is processed by a POD formatter. So these directives provide an easy way to embed extended pieces of internal documentation within your source.

The =for directive is identical to a =begin/=end pair, except that it allows only a single paragraph of content, terminated by an empty line. This might well be construed as a feature, in that it encourages conciseness*. But note that you still have to provide a trailing =cut, to switch the compiler back from skipping documentation to compiling Perl code.

Both these forms of block commenting take a "format name" after the keyword. Normally this name would be used to indicate which formatting tool the documentation is intended for (e.g., =for html ..., =for groff ..., =for LaTeX ...), but it is far more useful as a means to specify the kind of internal documentation you are writing. Then, provided the description you choose doesn't match the name of one of the standard POD formatters, the resulting POD block will be effectively invisible outside the source code. An easy way to ensure that invisibility is to capitalize the description and put a colon at the end of it.

For example, you can use this approach to record your rationale for unusual design or implementation decisions:

```
=for Rationale:
    We chose arrays over hashes here because profiling indicated over
    99% of accesses were iterated over the entire set, rather than being
    random. The dataset is expected to grow big enough that the better
    access performance and smaller memory footprint of a big array will
    outweigh the awkwardness of the occasional binary-chop search.

=cut
```

You can make notes on possible improvements that you don't currently have time to design or implement:

```
=for Improvement:
    Would be handier if this subroutine also accepted UMT values

=cut
```

Or explain any obscure pieces of domain-specific information that necessitated unusual implementation approaches:

```
=for Domain:
    No observation is ever recorded without an error bound. Hence the
    use of interval arithmetic in the next three subroutines.

=cut
```

Or mark sections that might benefit from optimization or that ought to be rewritten, making note of the conditions under which that might be possible:

---

* The only thing harder than finally convincing coders to write comments is then convincing them to write short comments.

```
=for Optimization:
    This parser would almost certainly benefit from the use of
    progressive matching with m/\G.../gcxms, rather than relying
    on successive prefix substitutions.
    Reconsider when everyone is using at least Perl 5.6.1.

=cut
```

Or highlight workarounds necessitated by limitations in Perl itself (or *perl* itself):

```
=for Workaround:
    Have to use a localized package variable here, rather than a
    lexical. A closure would be better of course, but lexicals don't seem
    to propagate properly into regexes under 5.8.3 (or earlier). This
    problem has been reported via perlbug.

=cut
```

Avoid the =begin/=end form unless the annotation is large and requires multiple paragraphs or embedded code examples:

```
=begin Optimization:

    This parser would almost certainly benefit from the use of
    progressive matching with m/\G.../gcxms, as in:

        while (pos $text < length $text) {
            if (m/\G ($TYPENAME)/gcxms) {
                push @tokens, Token::Type->new({ name => $1 });
            }
            elsif (m/\G ($VARNAME)/gcxms) {
                push @tokens, Token::Var->new({ alias => $1 });
            }
            # etc.
            else {
                croak q{Don't understand '},
                    substr($text, pos $text, 20),
                    "'\n";
            }
        }

    Reconsider when everyone is using at least Perl 5.6.1.

=end Optimization

=cut
```

Note that, unlike the consolidated "visible" POD written for user documentation, the "invisible" POD containing these technical discussions should be kept as close as possible to the code it refers to. Furthermore, since this documentation is "for internal use only" and never intended for any POD formatter, don't use POD mark-up within these sections.

Proofreading

Check the spelling, syntax, and sanity of your documentation.

The point of all documentation is communication: either with the users of your code, or with those who maintain it. To be effective, documentation must communicate effectively. It must be without distractions (like spelling mistakes), it must be comprehensible (i.e., syntactically correct), it must be unambiguous, and it must make sense.

So, although it's important to write your documentation, it's far more important to *read* it after it's written, to make sure it will do the job you created it to do.

The best way to proofread a document is to look at a "rendered" version of it. That is, don't simply reread the POD source you just wrote. Instead, convert that POD to plain text (using *perldoc*) or to HTML (via *pod2html*) or even to LaTeX (with *pod2latex*), and then read through it using the appropriate display tool.

Better still, have someone who's unfamiliar with the code read through your documentation. A new reader will be far better able to recognize when some part of your explanation is confusing, ambiguous, or otherwise unenlightening.

## CHAPTER 8

Built-in Functions

Bloody instructions which, being taught,
return to plague their inventor
—William Shakespeare
Macbeth, Act 1, Scene 7

The single most important recommendation about Perl's built-in functions is also the simplest: use them.

If Perl already provides a way to solve your problem, and that way is integrated into the language itself, then it doesn't make sense to reinvent it. It's likely that Perl's built-in solution is faster and far better debugged than anything you'll have time to write yourself.

However, some of Perl's built-in functions are sufficiently complex, and their behaviour sufficiently subtle, that there are still right and wrong ways to use them. This chapter explores some of these ways.

Sorting

Don't recompute sort keys inside a `sort`.

Doing expensive computations inside the block of a sort is inefficient. By default, the Perl interpreter now uses merge-sorting to implement sort[*], which means that every sort will call the sort block O(N log N) times. For example, suppose you needed to set up a collection of script files for binary-chop searching. In that case, you might

---

[*] Prior to 5.8, the quicksort algorithm was used. Quicksort's average performance is slightly better than mergesort for small lists, but its worst-case performance can be significantly worse. With the move to merge-sort, Perl's default sorting behaviour is now also "stable". That is, it preserves the ordering of list elements that are equivalent.

need to sort a set of scripts by their SHA-512 digests. Doing that the obvious way is needlessly slow, because each script is likely to be re-SHA'd several times:

```
Use Digest::SHA qw( sha512 );

# Sort by SHA-512 digest of scripts
@sorted_scripts
    = sort { sha512($a) cmp sha512($b) } @scripts;
```

Digests

SHA-512 is one of a family of *cryptographic hash functions*. It's something like Perl's built-in crypt function, but much more robust.

A hash function takes an input text of any size (or, sometimes, any size up to some ridiculously huge limit) and returns a sequence of bits—a *digest*—that identifies the original text. Such functions are also referred to as *one-way hash algorithms*, because a given input text always produces the same digest, but a digest cannot be reverse-engineered to recover the original text.

Cryptographic hash functions are also designed so that a prohibitive amount of computation would be required to discover two different input texts that produce the same digest.

Together, these properties ensure that two people can reliably compare the contents of two text files, without revealing those contents to each other or to any third party, simply by comparing the digests of the two files.

See the documentation of the standard Digest module for an overview of the numerous cryptographic hash functions available in Perl.

A better solution is to cache the SHA values you've computed and avoid recalculating them. There are various standard techniques for doing that. The most straightforward is known as the Orcish Manœuvre[*]:

```
# Sort by SHA-512 digest of scripts
# (optimized with an on-the-fly key cache)
@sorted_scripts
    = do {
        my %sha512_of;
        sort { ($sha512_of{$a} ||= sha512($a))
                    cmp
               ($sha512_of{$b} ||= sha512($b))
             }
             @scripts;
    };
```

---

[*] Joseph Hall, who invented the technique, dubbed it "Orcish" because it "ORs a cache". Aren't you sorry you asked?

The sort block uses a hash (%sha512_of) to record each digest it computes. So, when comparing two scripts, it checks to see whether it already knows their SHA-512 values ($sha512_of{$a} cmp $sha512_of{$b}). If either look-up fails to find a cached value for the digest of its key, it returns undef instead, in which case the ||= will be evaluated. The sha512( ) call to its right then computes the appropriate value, which is assigned to the corresponding entry of the look-up table, for future reference.

Note the use of a do block to limit the scope of the %sha512_of cache to the particular call to sort. If two or more sorts were likely to be applied to some of the same scripts, it would be more efficient to preserve the cache between sorts by moving the declaration of %sha512_of to some suitable outer scope, in which case the do block would no longer be required:

```
# Declare cache...
my %sha512_of;

# and later...

# Sort by SHA-512 digest of scripts
# (optimized with an on-the-fly key cache)
@sorted_scripts
    = sort { ($sha512_of{$a} ||= sha512($a))
                    cmp
               ($sha512_of{$b} ||= sha512($b))
           }
           @scripts;
```

Alternatively, rather than building the cache on the fly, you could precompute all the digests and store them in a look-up table via a sliced assignment:

```
# Sort by SHA-512 digest of scripts
# (optimized with a precomputed key cache)
my %sha512_of;
@sha512_of{@scripts} = map { sha512($_) } @scripts;

@sorted_scripts = sort { $sha512_of{$a} cmp $sha512_of{$b} } @scripts;
```

The resulting code is much cleaner and just as efficient, unless there is a chance that the sort block might throw an exception and prematurely abort the sorting, in which case you'll have done some of that precomputation needlessly.

Another approach would be to prebuild a list of digest/script pairs, sort on the digests, and then keep only the original scripts:

```
# Sort by SHA512 digest of scripts
# (optimized with the Schwartzian Transform)
@sorted_scripts
    = map  { $_->[0] }              # 3. Extract only scripts
       sort { $a->[1] cmp $b->[1] }  # 2. Sort on digests
        map  { [$_, sha512($_)] }    # 1. Precompute digests, store with scripts
          @scripts;
```

This pipelined solution is known as the Schwartzian Transform. Note the special layout, with the three steps lined up under each other. This format is used because it emphasizes the characteristic map-sort-map structure of the transform, making it much easier to identify when the technique is being used.

Probably the cleanest and most maintainable solution (albeit slightly slower than direct caching or precomputation) is to *memoize* the sha512( ) subroutine itself:

```
use Digest::SHA qw( sha512 );

# Make the SHA-512 digest function self-caching...
use Memoize;
memoize('sha512');

# Sort by auto-cached SHA-512 digest of scripts...
@sorted_scripts = sort { sha512($a) cmp sha512($b) } @scripts;
```

Memoizing a subroutine causes it to remember every value it ever returns and to immediately return that same value (without recomputing it) the next time the subroutine is called with the same arguments.

The Memoize module is standard in Perl 5.8 and later, and available from the CPAN for earlier versions of Perl. It's a very clean way to introduce caching into your code without littering that code with the ugly mechanics of an explicit cache. See Chapter 19 for a more detailed discussion of caching and memoization.

All of the previous solutions have distinct performance characteristics and trade-offs, which are likely to vary depending on the size of the list to be sorted, the complexity of the function you're using to compare keys, and even the platform you're running on. In some cases, it might even be faster to just leave the (re-)computations in the sort block. So, if you decide to optimize your sort using one of these techniques, it's vitally important to benchmark the performance of whichever approach you decide to use. See Chapter 19 for more discussion of benchmarking. The "Automating Sorts" guideline later in this chapter suggests another easy way to build optimized sorts.

Reversing Lists

Use reverse **to reverse a list.**

By default, the sort builtin sorts strings by ascending ASCII sequence. To make it sort by descending sequence instead, you might write:

```
@sorted_results = sort { $b cmp $a } @unsorted_results;
```

But the operation would be much more comprehensible if you wrote:

```
@sorted_results = reverse sort @unsorted_results;
```

That is, if you sorted using the default ordering and then reversed the sorted results afterwards.

Interestingly, in many versions of Perl, it's just as fast (or occasionally even faster) to use an explicitly reversed sort. In recent releases, the reverse sort sequence is recognized and optimized. In older releases, sorting with any explicit block was *not* optimized, so calling sort without a block is significantly faster, even when the extra cost of the reverse is taken into account.

Another situation in which reversing a list can significantly improve maintainability, without seriously compromising performance, is when you need to iterate "downwards" in a for loop. Instead of writing:

```
for (my $remaining=$MAX; $remaining>=$MIN; $remaining--) {
    print "T minus $remaining, and counting...\n";
    sleep $INTERVAL;
}
```

write:

```
for my $remaining (reverse $MIN..$MAX) {
    print "T minus $remaining, and counting...\n";
    sleep $INTERVAL;
}
```

This approach makes it clear that you intended to count in reverse, as well as making the precise range of $remaining much easier to determine. And, once again, the difference in iteration speed is usually not even noticeable.

The loop itself is also more robust. In the first version, the C-like for relies on correct coordination among its three components to achieve the appropriate iteration behaviour. But in the second version, the Perl-like for is given an exact range to iterate, so it's less prone to incorrect choices of comparison operator, inappropriate updating of the iterator variable, or other bad interactions.

Reversing Scalars

Use scalar reverse **to reverse a scalar.**

The reverse function can also be called in scalar context to reverse the characters in a single string:

```
my $visible_email_address = reverse $actual_email_address;
```

However, it's better to be explicit that a string reversal is intended there, by writing:

```
my $visible_email_address = scalar reverse $actual_email_address;
```

Both of these examples happen to work correctly, but leaving off the scalar specifier can cause problems in code like this:

```
add_email_addr(reverse $email_address);
```

which will *not* reverse the string inside $email_address. That particular call to reverse is in the argument list of a subroutine. That means it's in list context, so it reverses the order of the (one-element) list that it's passed. Reversing a one-element list gives you back the same list, in the same order, with the same single element unaltered by the reordering.

In such cases, you're working against the native context, so you have to be explicit:

```
add_email_addr(scalar reverse $email_address);
```

Rather than having to puzzle out contexts every time you want to reverse a string, it's much easier—and more reliable—to develop the habit of always explicitly specifying a scalar reverse when that's what you want.

Fixed-Width Data

Use unpack to extract fixed-width fields.

Fixed-width text data:

```
X123-S000001324700000199
SFG-AT000000010200009099
Y811-Q000010030000000033
```

is still widely used in many data processing applications. The obvious way to extract this kind of data is with Perl's built-in substr function. But the resulting code is unwieldy and surprisingly slow:

```
# Specify field locations...
Readonly my %FIELD_POS => (ident=>0,  sales=>6,   price=>16);
Readonly my %FIELD_LEN => (ident=>6,  sales=>10,  price=>8);

# Grab each line/record...
while (my $record = <$sales_data>) {

    # Extract each field...
    my $ident = substr($record, $FIELD_POS{ident}, $FIELD_LEN{ident});
    my $sales = substr($record, $FIELD_POS{sales}, $FIELD_LEN{sales});
    my $price = substr($record, $FIELD_POS{price}, $FIELD_LEN{price});

    # Append each record, translating ID codes and
    # normalizing sales (which are stored in 1000s)...
    push @sales, {
        ident => translate_ID($ident),
        sales => $sales * 1000,
```

```
        price => $price,
    };
}
```

Using regexes to capture the various fields produces slightly cleaner code, but the matches are still not optimally fast:

```
# Specify order and lengths of fields...
Readonly my $RECORD_LAYOUT
    => qr/\A (.{6}) (.{10}) (.{8}) /xms;

# Grab each line/record...
while (my $record = <$sales_data>) {

    # Extract all fields...
    my ($ident, $sales, $price)
        = $record =~ m/ $RECORD_LAYOUT /xms;

    # Append each record, translating ID codes and
    # normalizing sales (which are stored in 1000s)...
    push @sales, {
        ident => translate_ID($ident),
        sales => $sales * 1000,
        price => $price,
    };
}
```

The built-in unpack function is optimized for this kind of task. In particular, a series of 'A' specifiers can be used to extract a sequence of multicharacter substrings:

```
# Specify order and lengths of fields...
Readonly my $RECORD_LAYOUT => 'A6 A10 A8';   # 6 ASCII, then 10 ASCII, then 8 ASCII

# Grab each line/record...
while (my $record = <$sales_data>) {

    # Extract all fields...
    my ($ident, $sales, $price)
        = unpack $RECORD_LAYOUT, $record;

    # Append each record, translating ID codes and
    # normalizing sales (which are stored in 1000s)...
    push @sales, {
        ident => translate_ID($ident),
        sales => $sales * 1000,
        price => $price,
    };
}
```

Some fixed-width formats insert one or more empty columns between the fields of each record, to make the resulting data more readable to humans. For example:

```
X123-S  0000013247  00000199
SFG-AT  0000000102  00009099
Y811-Q  0000100300  00000033
```

When extracting fields from such data, you should use the '@' specifier to tell unpack where each field starts. For example:

```
# Specify order and lengths of fields...
Readonly my $RECORD_LAYOUT
    => '@0 A6 @8 A10 @20 A8';    # At column zero extract 6 ASCII chars
                                 # then at column 8 extract 10,
                                 # then at column 20 extract 8.


# Grab each line/record...
while (my $record = <$sales_data>) {

    # Extract all fields...
    my ($ident, $sales, $price)
        = unpack $RECORD_LAYOUT, $record;

    # Append each record, translating ID codes and
    # normalizing sales (which are stored in 1000s)...
    push @sales, {
        ident => translate_ID($ident),
        sales => $sales * 1000,
        price => $price,
    };
}
```

This approach scales extremely well, and can also cope with non-spaced data or variant layouts (i.e., with reordered fields). In particular, the unpack function doesn't require that '@' specifiers be specified in increasing column order. This means that an unpack can roam back and forth through a string (much like seek-ing a filehandle) and thereby extract fields in any convenient order. For example:

```
# Specify order and lengths of fields...
Readonly my %RECORD_LAYOUT  => (
                #  Ident   Sales    Price
    Unspaced => '   A6      A10       A8',    # Legacy layout
      Spaced => ' @0 A6  @8 A10  @20 A8',     # Standard layout
     ID_last => '@21 A6  @0 A10  @12 A8',     # New, more convenient layout
);

# Select record layout...
my $layout_name = get_layout($filename);

# Grab each line/record...
while (my $record = <$sales_data>) {

    # Extract all fields...
    my ($ident, $sales, $price)
        = unpack $RECORD_LAYOUT{$layout_name}, $record;

    # Append each record, translating ID codes and
    # normalizing sales (which are stored in 1000s)...
    push @sales, {
        ident => translate_ID($ident),
```

```
        sales => $sales * 1000,
        price => $price,
    };
}
```

The loop body is very similar to those in the earlier examples, except for the record layout now being looked up in a hash. The three variations in formatting and sequence have been cleanly factored out into a table.

Note that the entry for $RECORD_LAYOUT{ID_last}:

```
ID_last => '@21 C6  @0 C10  @12 C8',
```

makes use of non-monotonic '@' specifiers. By jumping to column 21 first, then back to column 0, and on again to column 12, this ID_last format ensures that the call to unpack within the loop:

```
my ($ident, $sales, $price)
    = unpack $RECORD_LAYOUT{$layout_name}, $record;
```

will extract the record ID before the sales amount and the price, even though the ID field comes *after* those other two fields in the file.

Separated Data

Use `split` **to extract simple variable-width fields.**

For data that is laid out in fields of varying width, with defined separators (such as tabs or commas) between the fields, the most efficient way to extract those fields is using a split. For example, if a single comma is the field separator:

```
# Specify field separator...
Readonly my $RECORD_SEPARATOR => q{,};
Readonly my $FIELD_COUNT       => 3;

# Grab each line/record...
while (my $record = <$sales_data>) {
    chomp $record;

    # Extract all fields...
    my ($ident, $sales, $price)
        = split $RECORD_SEPARATOR, $record, $FIELD_COUNT+1;

    # Append each record, translating ID codes and
    # normalizing sales (which are stored in 1000s)...
    push @sales, {
        ident => translate_ID($ident),
        sales => $sales * 1000,
        price => $price,
    };
}
```

Note the use of the third argument to split. Typically, split is called with only two arguments: the separator itself ($RECORD_SEPARATOR), and then the string from which the fields are to be split out ($record). If a third argument is provided, however, it specifies the maximum number of distinct fields that the split should return.

It's good practice to always provide this extra information if it's known, because otherwise split splits its input as many times as possible, builds a (potentially very long) list of the results, and returns it. The assignment would then throw away all but the first three elements of the returned list, so it's a (potentially very expensive) waste of time to create them in the first place.

In some circumstances, the optimizer can work out how many return values you were expecting, and will automatically supply the third argument itself. However, being explicit is still the better practice, because your code will stay efficient when someone later modifies your statement to something that isn't automatically optimized.

It can also be useful to capture the "residue" that's left after you've split out the fields you expected. For example, to warn about suspect records:

```
my ($ident, $sales, $price, $unexpected_data)
        = split $RECORD_SEPARATOR, $record, $FIELD_COUNT+1;

carp "Unexpected trailing garbage at end of record id '$ident':\n",
    "\t$unexpected_data\n"
        if $unexpected_data;
```

Using the third argument is highly recommended, but caution is also required. A common error here is to use the actual number of fields you want as the third argument:

```
my ($ident, $sales, $price)
        = split $RECORD_SEPARATOR, $record, $FIELD_COUNT;
```

instead of that number plus one. If you're trying to extract the first three fields of each record, the field count has to be four, because you need to break the record into four parts: the first three fields (which will be captured in the variables) *plus* the remainder of the string (which will be ignored). Using $FIELD_COUNT instead of $FIELD_COUNT+1 tells split to return three pieces, so it would break $record twice and return the resulting three substrings: *ID*, *sales*, and *price-plus-whatever-else-followed-it-in-the-original-string*.

Variable-Width Data

Use Text::CSV_XS **to extract complex variable-width fields.**

Perl's built-in functions aren't always the right answer. Using split to extract variable-width fields is efficient and easy, provided those fields *really are* always delimited by a simple separator. More often though, even if your records start out as purely comma-delimited:

```
Readonly my $RECORD_SEPARATOR => q{,};
Readonly my $FIELD_COUNT      => 3;

my ($ident, $sales, $price) = split $RECORD_SEPARATOR, $record, $FIELD_COUNT+1;
```

it soon becomes necessary to extend the format rules to cope with human vagaries (such as ignoring whitespace around commas):

```
Readonly my $RECORD_SEPARATOR => qr/\s* , \s*/xms;
Readonly my $FIELD_COUNT      => 3;

my ($ident, $sales, $price) = split $RECORD_SEPARATOR, $record, $FIELD_COUNT+1;
```

Or else someone will need to include a comma in a field and will decide to escape it with a backslash, in which case you'll need:

```
Readonly my $RECORD_SEPARATOR => qr/ \s* (?<!\\) , \s* /xms;  # Unbackslashed comma
```

And from there it's "Oh, we ought to be able to backslash a backslash too" and then "Hey, let's allow double-quoted fields so we don't have to backslash any of the commas in them". At which point your attempts to write a suitable separator regex for split have become a whirling vortex of pain, as you struggle to reinvent the "Comma-Separated Values" encoding. Badly.

The split function is ideal for simple cases, but scales very poorly when some variant of CSV is being parsed. As soon as your record format goes beyond a simple separator that can be recognized with a (non-lookbehind) regex, consider whether you can respecify your data format and rewrite your code to use the Text::CSV_XS module instead:

```
use Text::CSV_XS;

# Specify format...
my $csv_format
    = Text::CSV_XS->new({
          sep_char    => q{,},    # Fields are comma-separated
          escape_char => q{\\},   # Backslashed chars are always data
          quote_char  => q{"},    # Fields can be double-quoted
      });

# Grab each line/record...
RECORD:
while (my $record = <$sales_data>) {
    # Verify record is correctly formatted (or skip it)...
    if (!$csv_format->parse($record)) {
        warn 'Record ', $sales_data->input_line_number(), " not valid: '$record'";
        next RECORD;
    }

    # Extract all fields...
    my ($ident, $sales, $price) = $csv_format->fields();
```

```perl
        # Append each record, translating ID codes and
        # normalizing sales (which are stored in 1000s)...
        push @sales, {
            ident => translate_ID($ident),
            sales => $sales * 1000,
            price => $price,
        };
    }
```

This solution first constructs a specialized CSV parser (Text::CSV_XS->new( )), specifying what characters to use as the field separator, the escape character, and the field
quoting delimiters. Then, the while loop checks whether each line conforms to the
CSV syntax ($csv_format->parse($record)) and, if so, retrieves the fields that the call
to parse( ) successfully extracted.

In fact, the previous code structure ("read, parse, extract, repeat") is so common that
it has been encapsulated into an even cleaner solution: the Text::CSV::Simple module. Using that module, the previous example becomes:

```perl
    use Text::CSV::Simple;

    # Specify format...
    my $csv_format
        = Text::CSV::Simple->new({
            sep_char    => q{,},    # Fields are comma-separated
            escape_char => q{\\},   # Backslashed chars are always data
            quote_char  => q{"},    # Fields can be double-quoted
        });

    # Specify field names in order (any other fields will be ignored)...
    $csv_format->field_map( qw( ident sales price ) );

    # Grab each line/record...
    for my $record_ref ($csv_format->read_file($sales_data)) {
        push @sales, {
            ident => translate_ID($record_ref->{ident}),
            sales => $record_ref->{sales} * 1000,
            price => $record_ref->{price},
        };
    }
```

This version first creates a Text::CSV::Simple object, passing it the same configuration arguments as before (because it's actually just a wrapper around a Text::CSV_XS
object). The call to field_map( ) then tells the object the name of each field, in the
order they occur within the data. A single call to read_file( ) then reads in the entire
file and converts it to a list of hashes, one for each record that was read in. Finally,
the for loop processes each hash that was returned, extracting the appropriately
named fields ($record_ref->{ident}, $record_ref->{sales}, $record_ref->{price})

Note however that, as the name implies, the Text::CSV_XS module is written in C,
compiled to a library, and made available to Perl using the "XS" bridging mecha-

nism[*]. If you need to run your code on a system where using compiled modules of this kind is not feasible, the Text::CSV module provides a (slower, much less configurable) alternative that is implemented in pure Perl.

String Evaluations

Avoid string eval.

There are numerous reasons why the string form of eval:

```
use English qw( -no_match_vars );

eval $source_code;
croak $EVAL_ERROR if $EVAL_ERROR; # ALWAYS check for an error after any eval
```

is better avoided. For a start, it has to re-invoke the parser and the compiler every time you call it, so it can be expensive and can cause expected processing delays, especially if the eval is inside a loop.

More importantly, a string eval doesn't provide compile-time warnings on the code that it creates. It does produce run-time warnings, of course, but encountering those warnings then depends on the thoroughness of your testing regime (see Chapter 18).

This is a serious problem, because writing code that generates other code that is then eval'd is typically *much* harder (and therefore more error-prone) than writing normal code. And code-generating code is likewise very much harder to maintain.

Perhaps the most common rationale for using a string eval is to create new subroutines that are built around some expression the user supplies. For example, you might need to generate a range of sorting routines using different, user-provided keys. Example 8-1 demonstrates how to do that with a string eval.

Example 8-1. Creating subroutines via run-time compilation

```
sub make_sorter {
    my ($subname, $key_code) = @_;
    my $package = caller();

    # Create and compile the source of a new subroutine in the caller's namespace
    eval qq{
        # Go to the caller's namespace...
        package $package;

        # Define a subroutine of the specified name...
        sub $subname {
```

---

[*] See the *perlxs* manpage for the horrifying details.

Example 8-1. Creating subroutines via run-time compilation (continued)

```
                # That subroutine does a Schwartzian transform...
                return map  { \$_->[0] }                    # 3. Return original value
                       sort { \$a->[1] cmp \$b->[1] }       # 2. Compare keys
                       map  { my (\$key) = do {$key_code};  # 1. Extract keys as asked,
                              [\$_, \$key];                 #    and cache with values
                            }
                            \@_;                            # 0. Sort full arg list
        }
    };

    # Confirm that the eval worked...
    use English qw( -no_match_vars );
    croak $EVAL_ERROR if $EVAL_ERROR;

    return;
}

# and then...

make_sorter(sort_sha => q{ sha512($_)    } );   # sorts by SHA-512 of each value
make_sorter(sort_ids => q{ /ID:(\d+)/xms } );   # sorts by ID field from each value
make_sorter(sort_len => q{ length        } );   # sorts by length of each value

# and later...

@names_shortest_first = sort_len(@names);
@names_digested_first = sort_sha(@names);
@names_identity_first = sort_ids(@names);
```

That approach certainly works, provided you get all your backslashes in the right places. But it leaves make_sorter( ) at the run-time mercy of whoever calls it. If the caller passes a key-extraction string that is not itself valid code:

```
    make_sorter(sort_sha => q{ sha512($_  } );
```

then the error message will be generated only at runtime, and even then it will not be particularly informative:

```
    syntax error at (eval 11) line 11, at EOF
    Global symbol "$key" requires explicit package name at (eval 11) line 12.
            main::make_sorter('sort_sha',' sha512($_      ') called at demo.pl line 42
```

Worse still, if (like almost everyone else) you forget to include the post-eval error test in make_sorter( ):

```
        croak $EVAL_ERROR if $EVAL_ERROR;
```

then no error message will be seen at all. Or, rather, no error message will be produced until callers attempt to call their new sort_sha( ) subroutine, at which point they'll be curtly and unhelpfully informed:

```
    Undefined subroutine &sort_sha called at demo.pl line 86.
```

A cleaner solution is to use anonymous subroutines to specify each key extractor. Then you can use another anonymous subroutine to implement each new sorter, and install those sorters yourself using the Sub::Installer module, as shown in Example 8-2.

Example 8-2. Creating subroutines via anonymous closures

```
# Generate a new sorting routine whose name is the string in $sub_name
# and which sorts on keys extracted by the subroutine referred to by $key_sub_ref
sub make_sorter {
    my ($sub_name, $key_sub_ref) = @_;

    # Create a new anonymous subroutine that implements the sort...
    my $sort_sub_ref = sub {
        # Sort using the Schwartzian transform...
        return map  { $_->[0] }                    # 3. Return original value
                sort { $a->[1] cmp $b->[1] }        # 2. Compare keys
                map  { [$_, $key_sub_ref->()] }     # 1. Extract key, cache with value
                    @_;                             # 0. Perform sort on full arg list
    };

    # Install the new anonymous sub into the caller's namespace
    use Sub::Installer;
    caller->install_sub($sub_name, $sort_sub_ref);

    return;
}

# and then...
make_sorter(sort_sha => sub{ sha512($_) } );
make_sorter(sort_ids => sub{ /^ID:(\d+)/ } );
make_sorter(sort_len => sub{ length     } );

# and later...

@names_shortest_first = sort_len(@names);
@names_digested_first = sort_sha(@names);
@names_identity_first = sort_ids(@names);
```

In this second version, instead of passing make_sorter( ) the key-extracting code as a string, you pass it a small anonymous subroutine. The critical difference is that these anonymous subroutines are syntax checked at compile time, so you'll get a compile-time error if there's a mistake in any of them. For example:

```
    make_sorter(sort_sha => sub{ sha512($_ } );
```

would produce the very accurate fatal compile-time error:

```
    syntax error at demo.pl line 42, near "$_ }"
```

Assuming it's passed a valid key extractor, the make_sorter( ) subroutine then creates its own anonymous subroutine (which it temporarily stores in $sort_sub_ref). Once again, this anonymous subroutine is syntax checked at compile time, so any errors are likely to be discovered before the code is shipped, whether or not `make_sorter( )` is ever actually called during testing. And because the subroutine is real code, there's no need to "backslash" any of it, so it's easier to read and understand.

The `$sort_sub_ref` subroutine implements the requested sorting algorithm, but in this version it extracts its keys by calling the key-extraction subroutine that was passed to `make_sorter( )` (and which is now held in `$key_sub_ref`).

Finally, having created the new sort subroutine, `make_sorter( )` installs it in the caller's namespace, using the facilities provided by the `Sub::Installer` module. Once this module has been loaded, every package namespace automatically has its own `install_sub( )` method. Subroutines can then be installed in a particular namespace simply by calling that namespace's `install_sub( )` method and passing it the name by which the subroutine is to be known, followed by a reference to the subroutine itself.

In other words, each time this second version of `make_sorter( )` is called, it takes the key-extractor subroutine it was passed and wraps that key-extractor up in a new anonymous sorting subroutine, which it then installs back in the namespace where `make_sorter( )` was originally called. But every piece of code involved in that process is checked at compile time. No run-time evaluations are required.

Automating Sorts

Consider building your sorting routines with `Sort::Maker`.

Using a subroutine like `make_sorter( )` to create efficient sorts is a very good practice. It allows you to focus on specifying your sort criteria correctly, instead of on the mechanics of sorting. It also factors out the comparatively large amounts of coding infrastructure needed to optimize your sorts.

You don't even have to write `make_sorter( )` yourself. The `Sort::Maker` CPAN module provides a very sophisticated implementation of the subroutine. It has options for building sorting subroutines using Orcish or Schwartzian optimizations, as well as the more advanced Guttman-Rosler Transform.

Using the module, Example 8-2 could be simplified to:

```
use Sort::Maker;

# Create sort subroutines (ST flag enables Schwartzian transform)...
make_sorter(name => 'sort_sha', code => sub{ sha512($_)    }, ST => 1 );
make_sorter(name => 'sort_ids', code => sub{ /ID:(\d+)/xms }, ST => 1 );
make_sorter(name => 'sort_len', code => sub{ length        }, ST => 1 );

# and later...
```

```
@names_shortest_first = sort_len(@names);
@names_digested_first = sort_sha(@names);
@names_identity_first = sort_ids(@names);
```

Note that, unlike the version shown in Example 8-2, the make_sorter( ) subroutine provided by Sort::Maker supports a large set of options, and so uses labeled arguments (see Chapter 9).

The module even has a declarative syntax for creating commonly needed sorts. For example, to create a sort_max_first( ) subroutine that sorts its argument list in descending numeric order:

```
make_sorter( name => 'sort_max_first', qw( plain number descending ) ) ;
```

The Sort::Maker module is highly recommended.

Substrings

Use 4-arg substr **instead of lvalue** substr.

The substr builtin is unusual in that it can be used as an lvalue (i.e., a target of assignment). So you can write things like:

```
substr($addr, $country_pos, $COUNTRY_LEN)
    = $country_name{$country_code};
```

This statement first locates the substring of the string in $addr which starts at $country_pos and runs for $COUNTRY_LEN characters. Then that substring is replaced with the string in $country_name{$country_code}. Effectively, it's an assignment into part of the string value in a variable.

But to readers who are unused to this particular feature, an assignment to a function call can be confusing, or even scary, and therefore less comprehensible. So substr assignments become an issue of maintainability.

Of course, it's not hard to look up the *perlfunc* manual and learn about the special semantics of substr assignments, so their impact on maintainability is marginal. Then again, almost every maintainability issue is, by itself, marginal. It's only collectively that subtleties, clevernesses, and esoterica begin to sabotage comprehensibility. And it's only collectively that obviousness, straightforwardness, and conformity to standards can help to enhance it. Every small choice when coding contributes in one direction or the other.

However you choose to assess their cognitive load, there is another problem with assignments to substrings: they're relatively slow. The call to substr has to locate the required substring, create an interim representation of it, return that interim representation, perform the assignment to it, re-identify the required substring, and then replace it.

To avoid those extra steps, in Perl 5.6.1 and later substr also comes in a four-argument model. That is, if you provide a fourth argument to the function, that argument is used as the string with which to replace the substring identified by the first three arguments. So the previous example could be rewritten more efficiently as:

```
substr $addr, $country_pos, $COUNTRY_LEN , $country_name{$country_code};
```

Because that assignment now takes place within the original call, there's no need to create and return an interim representation, and no effort wasted re-identifying the substring during the assignment. That means a four-argument substr call is always faster than the equivalent assignment to a three-argument substr call.

Hash Values

Make appropriate use of lvalue values.

Another builtin that can sometimes be used in an lvalue manner is the values function for hashes, though only in Perl 5.005_04 and later. Specifically, in recent Perls the values function returns a list of the *original* values of the hash, not a list of copies (as it did in Perl 5.005_03 and earlier).

This list of lvalues cannot be used in direct assignments:

```
values(%seen_files) = ( );    # Compile-time error
```

but it *can* be used indirectly: in a for loop. That is, if you need to transform every value of a hash in some generic fashion, you don't have to index repeatedly within a loop:

```
for my $party (keys %candidate_for) {
    $candidate_for{$party} =~ s{($MATCH_ANY_NAME)}
                               {\U$1}gmxs;
}
```

You can just use the result of values as individual lvalues:

```
for my $candidate (values %candidate_for) {
    $candidate =~ s{($MATCH_ANY_NAME)}
                   {\U$1}gxms;
}
```

The performance of the values-based version is also better. The loop's iterator variable is directly aliased to each hash value, so there's no need for (expensive) hash loop-ups inside the loop.

Stick with the indexing approach, however, if your code also has to support pre-5.6 compilers.

Globbing

Use glob, not < . . . >.

The <...> syntax is heavily associated with I/O in most people's minds. So something like this:

```
my @files = <*.pl>;
```

is easy to mistake for a normal readline operation:

```
my @files = <$fh>;
```

Unfortunately, the first version isn't an input operation at all. Angle brackets are input operators only when they're empty (<>), or when they contain a bareword identifier (<DATA>), or when they contain a simple scalar variable (<$input_file>). If anything else appears inside the angles, they perform shell-based directory look-up instead.

In other words, the <*.pl> operation takes the contents of the angle brackets (i.e., *.pl), passes them to the csh system shell[*], collects the list of filenames that match this shell pattern, and returns those names.

It's not bad enough that this "file glob" is easy to confuse with a popular I/O operation. Far worse, if you apply other best practices when writing it—such as factoring the fixed shell pattern out into a named constant—it suddenly transforms into the very I/O operation it previously only looked like:

```
Readonly my $FILE_PATTERN => '*.pl';

# and later...

my @files = <$FILE_PATTERN>;    # KABOOM! (probably)
```

As mentioned earlier, a scalar variable in angles is one of the three valid forms that invoke a readline call in Perl, which means that the refactored operation *isn't* a file glob specification any more. Instead, the angles attempt to do a readline, discover that $FILE_PATTERN contains the string '*.pl', and head straight off to the symbol table looking for a filehandle of that name. Unless the coder has been truly evil, there won't be such a filehandle[†] and, instead of the expected file list appearing in @files, a 'readline() on unopened filehandle' exception will be thrown.

---

[*] Under more recent versions of Perl, the shell pattern is expanded by the interpreter itself. See the standard File::Glob module for details.

[†] They would have to have written something like:

```
no strict 'refs'; open *{'*.pl'}, '<', $filename;
```

in which case the calamity that is about to befall them is a clear case of Instant Justice.

A construct that breaks when you attempt to improve its readability is, by definition, unmaintainable. The file globbing operation has a proper name:

```
my @files = glob($FILE_PATTERN);
```

Use it, and keep the angle brackets strictly for input operations.

Sleeping

Avoid a raw `select` for non-integer sleeps.

Perl's built-in `sleep` function will only pause your program for an integer number of seconds, even if you give it a floating-point duration:

```
sleep 1.5;          # same as sleep(int(1.5)), so sleeps 1 second
```

Worse still, if you ask it to sleep only a fraction of a second, it's effectively a no-op:

```
sleep 0.5;          # same as sleep(int(0.5)), so sleeps 0 seconds
```

Some systems are not capable of sleeping for fractions of a second, but if yours is, the easiest way to achieve that is to use the `Time::HiRes` module (which comes standard in Perl 5.8 and later):

```
use Time::HiRes qw( sleep );
sleep 0.5;             # now sleeps half a second
```

For even more accuracy (within the limitations of your underlying platform), you can import the `Time::HiRes::usleep( )` function instead and specify the length of your nap as an integral number of microseconds:

```
use Time::HiRes qw( usleep );
usleep 500_001;        # now sleeps just over half a second
```

Prior to the availability of the `Time::HiRes` module, the usual way to sleep for fractions of seconds was to use a side effect of Perl's built-in select function. The `select` function is supposed to poll sets of I/O streams to determine which of them are ready for reading or writing, and which have exceptions pending[*].

But the most useful part of this builtin turned out to be its fourth argument, which is supposed to tell `select` how long to conduct its poll before timing out. It was quickly realized that because this timeout value could be specified in fractions of a second, if select was called with a timeout value but without any streams to poll, like so:

```
select undef, undef, undef, $duration;
```

---

[*] If that brief explanation didn't help, don't worry about it. What select is supposed to do isn't important here; what's important is how hackers have perverted it to further their own evil designs.

then it would just sit there until the timeout expired, thereby sleeping for that fractional duration.

So if `Time::HiRes` isn't available, you can always sleep half a second by calling:

```
select undef, undef, undef, 0.5;
```

But finding something like that crawling around loose in your code is just plain nasty. It uses a mysterious and poorly understood builtin in a sneaky and improbable way. If you need to fall back on select-based sleeping, at least encapsulate the unpleasantness cleanly:

```
sub sleep_for {
    my ($duration) = @_;
    select undef, undef, undef, $duration;
    return;
}

# and then...

sleep_for(0.5);
```

Wrapping the select call in a subroutine will have negligible impact on the accuracy of the sleep interval. On most systems, the subroutine call overhead will be much smaller than the smallest interval for which select can reliably pause.

Mapping and Grepping

Always use a block with a map and grep.

The map and grep builtins each have two valid syntaxes:

```
map BLOCK LIST          grep BLOCK LIST
map EXPR, LIST          grep EXPR, LIST
```

That is, the code that tells map how to transform a list, or tells grep how to filter it, can be specified either as a single expression or in a block.

But when the first argument to a map or grep is specified as an expression, it becomes harder to distinguish from the remaining arguments:

```
print grep valid($_), @candidates;

@args = map substr($_, 0, 1), @flags, @files, @options;
```

The block form makes the transform or filter stand out more clearly:

```
print grep { valid($_) } @candidates;

@args = map {substr $_, 0, 1} @flags, @files, @options;
```

Using a block also avoids mistakes like:

```
@args = map substr $_, 0, 1, @flags, @files, @options;
```

Here the programmer seems to have thought that substr would somehow work out that it should consume only the first three arguments ($_, 0, 1), to magically produce an "extract the first character" expression that the map can then apply to the remaining arguments. Unfortunately, what happens instead is that the compiler notices that substr was given six arguments and complains:

```
Too many arguments for substr at demo.pl line 42, near "@options;"
```

Using the block form instead:

```
@args = map {substr $_, 0, 1} @flags, @files, @options;
```

makes the intent clear—both to the compiler and to subsequent readers.

More importantly, the expression forms of map and grep don't scale well as their transforms or filters become more complicated. If additional statements need to be added to a map or grep expression (for example, to inject a lexical variable, as shown in "List Processing Side Effects" in Chapter 6), that expression almost always has to be converted to a block. Starting out with a block reduces the amount of rewriting that's then required, and hence decreases the chances of new bugs being introduced.

Utilities

Use the "non-builtin builtins".

This guideline covers a number of common wheels that ought not be re-invented. Perl itself encourages the re-use of existing wheels by providing so many built-in functions in the first place. But there are a few gaps in its coverage; a few common tasks that it doesn't provide a convenient builtin to handle.

That's where the Scalar::Util, List::Util, and List::MoreUtils modules can help. They provide commonly needed list and scalar processing functions, which are implemented in C for performance. Scalar::Util and List::Util* are part of the Perl standard library (since Perl 5.8), and all three are also available on CPAN.

The Scalar::Util module provides the following functions:

blessed $scalar
   If $scalar contains a reference to an object, blessed( ) returns a true value (specifically, the name of the class). Otherwise, it returns undef.

---

* There is also a standard Hash::Util module in 5.8 and later, but its use is not recommended. See Chapter 15.

`refaddr $scalar`

> If `$scalar` contains a reference, `refaddr()` returns an integer representing the memory address that reference points to. If `$scalar` doesn't contain a reference, the subroutine returns `undef`. This result is useful for generating unique identifiers for variables or objects (see Chapter 15).

`reftype $scalar`

> If `$scalar` contains a reference, `reftype()` returns the standard string that describes the type of the referent (e.g., `'SCALAR'`, `'HASH'`, `'ARRAY'`, `'CODE'`, `'Regexp'`). In particular, if the reference is to a blessed object, `reftype()` still returns the standard string representing the underlying (pre-blessed) type of the object. If `$scalar` doesn't contain a reference, `reftype()` returns `undef`.

`readonly $scalar`

> Returns a true value if `$scalar` has been marked as read-only (e.g., via the Readonly module).

`tainted $scalar`

> Returns a true value if `$scalar` contains data from an untrusted source. See the *perlsec* manpage.

`openhandle $scalar`

> Returns the contents of `$scalar` if those contents can be used as a filehandle and the resulting filehandle is already open. Otherwise, returns `undef`. Handy for verifying arguments to I/O subroutines that are supposed to be passed a usable filehandle.

`weaken $scalar`

> This subroutine expects `$scalar` to contain a reference to something. It takes that reference and "hides" it from the reference-counting garbage collector. See "Cyclic References" in Chapter 11 for an example of why this might be a useful thing to do.

`is_weak $scalar`

> Returns a true value if `$scalar` contains a reference that has already been weakened.

`looks_like_number $scalar`

> Returns a true value if the entire contents of `$scalar` is something that Perl can treat as a number (e.g., an actual number, or a string that can be wholly converted to a number, or a reference). If `$scalar` contains a string that could only *partially* be converted to a number—such as `'802.11b'`—then `looks_like_number()` will return false. This function is often a better choice for verifying numeric input than simply relying on Perl's implicit numeric conversions. On the other hand, `looks_like_number()` also accepts the strings `'Inf'` and `'Infinity'` as numbers. Whether this is a bug or a feature will depend on your personal mathematical philosophy.

`Scalar::Util` also provides a several other exportable subroutines that are not described here. Those additional subroutines are not recommended, because their intended uses—such as identifying vstrings and setting subroutine prototypes—directly contravene specific guidelines in this book.

The `List::Util` module allows you to export any of the following functions:

`first {<condition>} @list`
> Returns the first element of `@list` that satisfies the condition specified in the block. `first( )` is similar to grep, but stops processing the list as soon as it finds the first successful match. See Chapters 6 and 9 for examples.

`max @list`
> Returns the largest element of `@list`, as determined by numeric comparison (>).

`maxstr @list`
> Returns the largest element of `@list`, as determined by string comparison (gt).

`min @list`
> Returns the smallest element of `@list`, as determined by numeric comparison (<).

`minstr @list`
> Returns the smallest element of `@list`, as determined by string comparison (lt).

`shuffle @list`
> Returns the elements of `@list` in an unbiased (pseudo-)randomized order[*].

`sum @list`
> Returns the sum of the individual elements of `@list` (that is: `$list[0] + $list[1] + $list[2] +...+ $list[$#list]`).

`reduce {<binary_op>} @list`
> Applies the specified binary operation to each adjacent pair of elements in `@list`. The binary operation must be specified in terms of operands `$a` and `$b` (like a sort block uses). For example, to multiply all the elements of a list together:

> ```
> my $overall_probablity = reduce { $a * $b } @partial_probabilities;
> ```

> Or to flatten a list of array references into a single array reference:

> ```
> my $universal_set_ref = reduce { [ uniq @{$a}, @{$b} ] } @individual_sets;
> ```

> In this last example, `reduce( )` takes every pair of adjacent array references inside `@individual_sets` (calling them `$a` and `$b` inside its block), dereferences them (`@{$a}` and `@{$b}`), concatenates the resulting lists (`@{$a}`, `@{$b}`), keeps only the unique elements (`uniq @{$a}, @{$b}`), and then puts the result into a new anonymous array (`[ @{$a}, @{$b} ]`).

The `List::MoreUtils` CPAN module provides efficient implementations for many additional list processing functions. Some of the most useful include:

---

[*] "Fairness" in a shuffle is actually quite tricky to get right. Which makes this particular wheel one that's especially worth not re-inventing. See "Randomizing an Array" in Chapter 4 of *Perl Cookbook* (O'Reilly, 2003) for a full discussion.

all {*<condition>*} @list

> Returns true if all of the items in @list satisfy the condition specified in the block. There are also any( ), notall( ), and none( ) variants, which test whether the corresponding numbers of list elements satisfy the condition. For example:

```
croak q{Can't handle an undefined value}
    if any {!defined} @args;
carp "All values are large. This may take a while...\n"
    if all {$_ > $FAST_LIMIT} @args;
```

first_index {*<condition>*} @list

> Returns the index of the first element in @list for which the condition in the block is true. There is also a last_index( ) version.

apply {*<transform>*} @list

> This function applies the operation(s) in the block to *copies* of each list element (passed in $_), and then returns the list of those modified copies. For example, instead of:

```
my @nice_words
    = map {
            my $copy = $_;
            $copy =~ s/$EXPLETIVE/[DELETED]/gxms;
            $copy;
        } @words;
```

> you can simply write:

```
my @nice_words = apply { s/$EXPLETIVE/[DELETED]/gxms } @words;
```

pairwise {*<binary_op>*} @array1, @array2

> Walks through the elements of @array1 and @array2 in parallel, applying the binary operation specified in the block to one element of @array1 (accessed via $a) and the corresponding element of @array2 (accessed via $b). Returns a list of the results of each such binary operation. For example:

```
my @revenue_from_items = pairwise { $a * $b } @sales_of_items, @price_of_items;
```

zip @array1, @array2, ...

> Returns a list that interleaves the elements of each array: $array1[0], $array2[0], $array1[1], $array2[1], $array1[2], $array2[2], etc. The name derives from the interleaving of teeth in a zipper. This subroutine is particularly handy for populating an anonymous hash from two arrays:

```
my $hash_ref = { zip @keys, @values };
```

uniq @list

> Returns a list consisting of all the elements in @list, but with any repeated elements removed. Preserves the original order of the elements it does return. If called in a scalar context, returns the number of unique elements in @list. Note that the list doesn't have to be sorted, nor do the repeated elements have to be adjacent.

The functions in Scalar::Util, List::Util, and List::MoreUtils are efficiently implemented and widely used, so they're fast and thoroughly debugged. They are also well named, so using them can improve the readability of your code. For example, instead of writing:

```
my $max_sample = $samples[0];
for my $sample (@samples[1..$#samples]) {
    if ($sample > $max_sample) {
        $max_sample = $sample;
    }
}
```

it's cleaner, clearer, more robust, more scalable, more maintainable, and faster to write:

```
my $max_sample = max @samples;
```

Even when you're only deciding between two values:

```
my $upper_limit = $last_seen gt $last_predicted ? $last_seen : $last_predicted;
```

it's still better to write:

```
my $upper_limit = maxstr($last_seen, $last_predicted);
```

Although calling the subroutine is approximately 25% slower than using a "raw" ternary operator, it's still blisteringly fast. And the maxstr( ) version definitely wins on cleanliness, clarity, reliability, scalability, and extensibility.

## CHAPTER 9

Subroutines

If you have a procedure with ten parameters,
you probably missed some.
—Alan Perlis

Subroutines are one of the two primary problem-decomposition tools available in Perl, modules being the other. They provide a convenient and familiar way to break a large task down into pieces that are small enough to understand, concise enough to implement, focused enough to test, and simple enough to debug.

In effect, subroutines allow programmers to extend the Perl language, creating useful new behaviours with sensible names. Having written a subroutine, you can immediately forget about its internals, and focus solely on the abstracted process or function it implements.

So the extensive use of subroutines helps to make a program more modular, which in turn makes it more robust and maintainable. Subroutines also make it possible to structure the actions of programs hierarchically, at increasingly high levels of abstraction, which improves the readability of the resulting code.

That's the theory, at least. In practice, there are plenty of ways that using subroutines can make code less robust, buggier, less concise, slower, and harder to understand. The guidelines in this chapter focus on avoiding those outcomes.

Call Syntax

Call subroutines with parentheses but without a leading &.

It's possible to call a subroutine without parentheses, if it has already been declared in the current namespace:

```
sub coerce;
```

```
# and later...

    my $expected_count = coerce $input, $INTEGER, $ROUND_ZERO;
```

But that approach can quickly become much harder to understand:

```
    fix my $gaze, upon each %suspect;
```

More importantly, leaving off the parentheses on subroutines makes them harder to
distinguish from builtins, and therefore increases the mental search space when the
reader is confronted with either type of construct. Your code will be easier to read
and understand if the subroutines always use parentheses and the built-in functions
always don't:

```
    my $expected_count = coerce($input, $INTEGER, $ROUND_ZERO);

    fix(my $gaze, upon(each %suspect));
```

Some programmers still prefer to call a subroutine using the ancient Perl 4 syntax,
with an ampersand before the subroutine name:

```
    &coerce($input, $INTEGER, $ROUND_ZERO);

    &fix(my $gaze, &upon(each %suspect));
```

Perl 5 does support that syntax, but nowadays it's unnecessarily cluttered. Barewords are forbidden under use strict, so there are far fewer situations in which a
subroutine call has to be disambiguated.

On the other hand, the ampersand itself is visually ambiguous; it can also signify a
bitwise AND operator, depending on context. And context can be extremely subtle:

```
    $curr_pos  = tell &get_mask();    # means: tell(get_mask())
    $curr_time = time &get_mask();    # means: time() & get_mask()
```

Prefixing with & can also lead to other subtle (but radical) differences in behaviour:

```
    sub fix {
        my (@args) = @_ ? @_ : $_;     # Default to fixing $_ if no args provided

        # Fix each argument by grammatically transforming it and then printing it...
        for my $arg (@args) {
            $arg =~ s/\A the \b/some/xms;
            $arg =~ s/e \z/es/xms;
            print $arg;
        }

        return;
    }

    # and later...

    &fix('the race');    # Works as expected, prints: 'some races'
```

```
for ('the gaze', 'the adhesive') {
    &fix;                   # Doesn't work as expected: looks like it should fix($_),
                            # but actually means fix(@_), using this scope's @_!
                            # See the 'perlsub' manpage for details
}
```

All in all, it's clearer, less ambiguous, and less error-prone to reserve the &subname syntax for taking references to named subroutines:

```
set_error_handler( \&log_error );
```

Just use parentheses to indicate a subroutine call:

```
coerce($input, $INTEGER, $ROUND_ZERO);

fix( my $gaze, upon(each %suspect) );

$curr_pos  = tell get_mask();
$curr_time = time & get_mask();
```

And *always* use the parentheses when calling a subroutine, even when the subroutine takes no arguments (like get_mask()). That way it's immediately obvious that you intend a subroutine call:

```
curr_obj()->update($status);    # Call curr_obj() to get an object,
                                # then call the update()method on that object
```

and not a typename:

```
curr_obj->update($status);      # Maybe the same (if currobj() already declared),
                                # otherwise call update() on class 'curr_obj'
```

Homonyms

Don't give subroutines the same names as built-in functions.

If you declare a subroutine with the same name as a built-in function, subsequent invocations of that name will still call the builtin…except when occasionally they don't. For example:

```
sub lock {
    my ($file) = @_;
    return flock $file, LOCK_SH;
}

sub link {
    my ($text, $url) = @_;
    return qq{<a href="$url">$text</a>};
}

lock($file);                    # Calls 'lock' subroutine; built-in 'lock' hidden
print link($text, $text_url);   # Calls built-in 'link'; 'link' subroutine hidden
```

Perl considers some of its builtins (like link) to be "more built-in" than others (like lock), and chooses accordingly whether to call your subroutine of the same name. If the builtin is "strongly built-in", an ambiguous call will invoke it, in preference to any subroutine of the same name. On the other hand, if the builtin is "weakly built-in", an ambiguous call will invoke the subroutine of the same name instead.

Even if these subroutines did always work as expected, it's simply too hard to maintain code where the program-specific subroutines and the language's keywords overlap:

```
sub crypt { return "You're in the tomb of @_\n"   }
sub map   { return "You have found a map of @_\n" }
sub chop  { return "You have chopped @_\n"        }
sub close { return "The @_ is now closed\n"       }
sub hex   { return "A hex has been cast on @_\n"  }

print crypt( qw( Vlad Tsepes ) );              # Subroutine or builtin?

for my $reward (qw( treasure danger) ) {
    print map($reward, 'in', $location);       # Subroutine or builtin?
}

print hex('the Demon');                        # Subroutine or builtin?
print chop('the Demon');                       # Subroutine or builtin?
```

There is an inexhaustible supply of subroutine names available; names that are more descriptive and unambiguous. Use them:

```
sub in_crypt  { return "You're in the tomb of @_\n"   }
sub find_map  { return "You have found a map of @_\n" }
sub chop_at   { return "You have chopped @_\n"        }
sub close_the { return "The @_ is now closed\n"       }
sub hex_upon  { return "A hex has been cast on @_\n"  }

print in_crypt( qw( Vlad Tsepes ) );

for my $reward (qw( treasure danger )) {
    print find_map($reward, 'in', $location);
}

print hex_upon('the Demon');
print chop_at('the Demon');
```

Argument Lists

Always unpack @_ first.

Subroutines always receive their arguments in the @_ array. But accessing them via $_[0], $_[1], etc. directly is almost always a Very Bad Idea. For a start, it makes the code far less self-documenting:

```
Readonly my $SPACE => q{ };

# Pad a string with whitespace...
sub padded {
    # Compute the left and right indents required...
    my $gap   = $_[1] - length $_[0];
    my $left  = $_[2] ? int($gap/2) : 0;
    my $right = $gap - $left;

    # Insert that many spaces fore and aft...
    return $SPACE x $left
         . $_[0]
         . $SPACE x $right;
}
```

Using "numbered parameters" like this makes it difficult to determine what each argument is used for, whether they're being used in the correct order, and whether the computation they're used in is algorithmically sane. Compare the previous version to this one:

```
sub padded {
    my ($text, $cols_count, $want_centering) = @_;

    # Compute the left and right indents required...
    my $gap   = $cols_count - length $text;
    my $left  = $want_centering ? int($gap/2) : 0;
    my $right = $gap - $left;

    # Insert that many spaces fore and aft...
    return $SPACE x $left
         . $text
         . $SPACE x $right;
}
```

Here the first line unpacks the argument array to give each parameter a sensible name. In the process, that assignment also documents the expected order and intended purpose of each parameter. The sensible parameter names also make it easier to verify that the computation of $left and $right is correct.

A mistake when using numbered parameters:

```
    my $gap   = $_[1] - length $_[2];
    my $left  = $_[0] ? int($gap/2) : 0;
    my $right = $gap - $left;
```

is much harder to identify than when named variables are in the wrong places:

```
    my $gap   = $cols_count - length $want_centering;
    my $left  = $text ? int($gap/2) : 0;
    my $right = $gap - $left;
```

Moreover, it's easy to forget that each element of @_ is an alias for the original argument; that changing $_[0] changes the variable containing that argument:

```
# Trim some text and put a "box" around it...
sub boxed {
    $_[0] =~ s{\A \s+ | \s+ \z}{}gxms;
    return "[$_[0]]";
}
```

Unpacking the argument list creates a copy, so it's far less likely that the original arguments will be inadvertently modified:

```
# Trim some text and put a "box" around it...
sub boxed {
    my ($text) = @_;

    $text =~ s{\A \s+ | \s+ \z}{}gxms;
    return "[$text]";
}
```

It's acceptable to unpack the argument list using a single list assignment as the first line of the subroutine:

```
sub padded {
    my ($text, $cols_count, $want_centering) = @_;

    # [Use parameters here, as before]
}
```

Alternatively, you can use a series of separate shift calls as the subroutine's first "paragraph":

```
sub padded {
    my $text           = shift;
    my $cols_count     = shift;
    my $want_centering = shift;

    # [Use parameters here, as before]
}
```

The list-assignment version is more concise, and it keeps the parameters together in a horizontal list, which enhances readability, provided that the number of parameters is small.

The shift-based version is preferable, though, whenever one or more arguments has to be sanity-checked or needs to be documented with a trailing comment:

```
sub padded {
    my $text           = _check_non_empty(shift);
    my $cols_count     = _limit_to_positive(shift);
    my $want_centering = shift;

    # [Use parameters here, as before]
}
```

Note the use of utility subroutines (see "Utility Subroutines" in Chapter 3) to perform the necessary argument verification and adjustment. Each such subroutine acts like a filter: it expects a single argument, checks it, and returns the argument value if the test succeeds. If the test fails, the verification subroutine may either return a default value instead, or call croak( ) to throw an exception (see Chapter 13). Because of that second possibility, verification subroutines should be defined in the same package as the subroutines whose arguments they are checking.

This approach to argument verification produces very readable code, and scales well as the tests become more onerous. But it may be too expensive to use within small, frequently called subroutines, in which case the arguments should be unpacked in a list assignment and then tested directly:

```perl
sub padded {
    my ($text, $cols_count, $want_centering) = @_;
    croak  q{Can't pad undefined text}        if !defined $text;
    croak qq{Can't pad to $cols_count columns} if $cols_count <= 0;

    # [Use parameters here, as before]
}
```

The only circumstances in which leaving a subroutine's arguments in @_ is appropriate is when the subroutine:

- Is short and simple
- Clearly doesn't modify its arguments in any way
- Only refers to its arguments collectively (i.e., doesn't index @_)
- Refers to @_ only a small number of times (preferably once)
- Needs to be efficient

This is usually the case only in "wrapper" subroutines:

```perl
# Implement the Perl 6 print+newline function...
sub say {
    return print @_, "\n";
}

# and later...

say( 'Hello world!' );
say( 'Greetings to you, people of Earth!' );
```

In this example, copying the contents of @_ to a lexical variable and then immediately passing those contents to print would be wasteful.

Named Arguments

Better still, use named arguments for any subroutine that is ever *likely* to have more than three parameters.

Named arguments replace the need to remember an ordering (which humans are comparatively poor at) with the need to remember names (which humans are relatively good at). Names are especially advantageous when a subroutine has many optional arguments—such as flags or configuration switches—only a few of which may be needed for any particular invocation.

Named arguments should always be passed to a subroutine inside a single hash, like so:

```
sub padded {
    my ($arg_ref) = @_;

    my $gap   = $arg_ref->{cols} - length $arg_ref->{text};
    my $left  = $arg_ref->{centered} ? int($gap/2) : 0;
    my $right = $gap - $left;

    return $arg_ref->{filler} x $left
         . $arg_ref->{text}
         . $arg_ref->{filler} x $right;
}

# and then...
for my $line (@lines) {
    $line = padded({ text=>$line, cols=>20, centered=>1, filler=>$SPACE });
}
```

As tempting as it may be, don't pass them as a list of raw name/value pairs:

```
sub padded {
    my %arg = @_;

    my $gap   = $arg{cols} - length $arg{text};
    my $left  = $arg{centered} ? int($gap/2) : 0;
    my $right = $gap - $left;

    return $arg{filler} x $left
         . $arg{text}
         . $arg{filler} x $right;
}
```

```
# and then...
for my $line (@lines) {
    $line = padded( text=>$line, cols=>20, centered=>1, filler=>$SPACE );
}
```

Requiring the named arguments to be specified inside a hash ensures that any mismatch, such as:

```
$line = padded({text=>$line, cols=>20..21, centered=>1, filler=>$SPACE});
```

will be reported (usually at compile time) in the caller's context:

```
Odd number of elements in anonymous hash at demo.pl line 42
```

Passing those arguments as raw pairs:

```
$line = padded(text=>$line, cols=>20..21, centered=>1, filler=>$SPACE);
```

would cause the exception to be thrown at run time, and from the line inside the subroutine where the odd number of arguments were unpacked and assigned to a hash:

```
Odd number of elements in hash assignment at Text/Manip.pm line 1876
```

It is okay to mix positional and named arguments, if there are always one or two main arguments to the subroutine (e.g., the string that padded( ) is supposed to pad) and the remaining arguments are merely configuration options of some kind. In any case, when there are both positional arguments and named options, the unnamed positionals should come first, followed by a single reference to a hash containing the named options. For example:

```
sub padded {
    my ($text, $arg_ref) = @_;

    my $gap   = $arg_ref->{cols} - length $text;
    my $left  = $arg_ref->{centered} ? int($gap/2) : 0;
    my $right = $gap - $left;

    return $arg_ref->{filler} x $left . $text . $arg_ref->{filler} x $right;
}

# and then...
for my $line (@lines) {
    $line = padded( $line, {cols=>20, centered=>1, filler=>$SPACE} );
}
```

Note that using this approach also has a slight advantage in maintainability: it sets the options more clearly apart from the main positional argument.

By the way, you or your team might feel that three is not the most appropriate threshold for deciding to use named arguments, but try to avoid significantly larger values of "three". Most of the advantages of named arguments will be lost if you still have to plough through five or six positional arguments first.

Missing Arguments

Use definedness or existence to test for missing arguments.

It's a common mistake to use a boolean test to probe for missing arguments:

```
Readonly my $FILLED_USAGE => 'Usage: filled($text, $cols, $filler)';

sub filled {
    my ($text, $cols, $filler) = @_;

    croak $FILLED_USAGE
        if !$text || !$cols || !$filler;

    # [etc.]
}
```

The problem is that this approach can fail in subtle ways. If, for example, the filler character is '0' or the text to be padded is an empty string, then an exception will incorrectly be thrown.

A much more robust approach is to test for definedness:

```
use List::MoreUtils qw( any );

sub filled {
    my ($text, $cols, $filler) = @_;

    croak $FILLED_USAGE
        if any {!defined $_} $text, $cols, $filler;

    # [etc.]
}
```

Or, if a particular number of arguments is required, and undef is an acceptable value for one of them, test for mere existence:

```
sub filled {
    croak $FILLED_USAGE if @_ != 3;    # All three args must be supplied

    my ($text, $cols, $filler) = @_;
    # etc.
}
```

Existence tests are particularly efficient because they can be applied before the argument list is even unpacked. Testing for the existence of arguments also promotes more robust coding, in that it prevents callers from carelessly omitting a required argument, and from accidentally providing any extras.

Note that existence tests can also be used when some arguments are optional, because the recommended practice for this case—passing options in a hash—ensures

---

that the actual number of arguments passed is fixed (or fixed-minus-one, if the options hash happens to be omitted entirely):

```
sub filled {
    croak $FILLED_USAGE if @_ < 1 || @_ > 2;

    my ($text, $opt_ref) = @_;    # Cols and fill char now passed as options

    # etc.
}
```

Default Argument Values

Resolve any default argument values as soon as @_ is unpacked.

The fundamental rule of argument processing is: nothing happens in the subroutine until all the arguments are stable. Don't, for example, add in defaults on the fly:

```
Readonly my $DEF_PAGE_WIDTH => 78;
Readonly my $SPACE          => q{ };

sub padded {
    my ($text, $arg_ref) = @_;

    # Compute left and right spacings...
    my $gap   = ($arg_ref->{cols}||$DEF_PAGE_WIDTH) - length($text||=$EMPTY_STR);
    my $left  = $arg_ref->{centered} ? int($gap/2) : 0;
    my $right = $gap - $left;

    # Prepend and append space...
    my $filler = $arg_ref->{filler} || $SPACE;
    return $filler x $left . $text . $filler x $right;
}
```

Apart from making the gap computation much harder to read and to verify, using the || and ||= operators to select default values is equivalent to testing for truth, and therefore much more prone to error on the edge cases (such as a '0' fill character).

If default values are needed, set them up first. Separating out any initialization will make your code more readable, and simplifying the computational statements is likely to make them less buggy too:

```
sub padded {
    my ($text, $arg_ref) = @_;

    # Set defaults...
    #           If option given...      Use option          Else default
    my $cols   = exists $arg_ref->{cols}   ? $arg_ref->{cols}   : $DEF_PAGE_WIDTH;
    my $filler = exists $arg_ref->{filler} ? $arg_ref->{filler} : $SPACE;
```

```
# Compute left and right spacings...
my $gap   = $cols - length $text;
my $left  = $arg_ref->{centered} ? int($gap/2) : 0;
my $right = $gap - $left;

# Prepend and append space...
return $filler x $left . $text . $filler x $right;
}
```

If there are many defaults to set up, the cleanest way to do that is by factoring the defaults out into a table (i.e., a hash) and then pre-initializing the argument hash with that table, like so:

```
Readonly my %PAD_DEFAULTS => (
    cols     => 78,
    centered => 0,
    filler   => $SPACE,
    # etc.
);

sub padded {
    my ($text, $arg_ref) = @_;

    # Unpack optional arguments and set defaults...
    my %arg = ref $arg_ref eq 'HASH' ? (%PAD_DEFAULTS, %{$arg_ref})
            :                          %PAD_DEFAULTS;

    # Compute left and right spacings...
    my $gap   = $arg{cols} - length $text;
    my $left  = $arg{centered} ? int($gap/2) : 0;
    my $right = $gap - $left;

    # Prepend and append space...
    return $arg{filler} x $left . $text . $arg{filler} x $right;
}
```

When the %arg hash is initialized, the defaults are placed ahead of the arguments supplied by the caller ((%PAD_DEFAULTS, %{$arg_ref})). So the entries in the default table are assigned to %arg first. Those default values are then overwritten by any entries from $arg_ref.

Scalar Return Values

Always `return scalar` **in scalar returns.**

One of the more subtle features of Perl subroutines is the way that their call context propagates to their return statements. In most places in Perl, the context (list, scalar, or void) can be deduced at compile time. One place where it *can't* be determined in advance is to the right of a return. The argument of a return is evaluated in whatever context the subroutine itself was called.

That's a very handy feature, which makes it easy to factor out or rename specific uses of built-in functions. For example, if you found yourself repeatedly filtering undefined and negative values out of lists:

```
@valid_samples = grep {defined($_) && $_ >= 0} @raw_samples;
```

it would be better to encapsulate that complex filter and rename it more meaningfully:

```
sub valid_samples_in {
    return grep {defined($_) && $_ >= 0} @_;
}

# and then...

@valid_samples = valid_samples_in(@raw_samples);
```

Because the return expression is always evaluated in the same context as the surrounding call, it's also still okay to use this subroutine in scalar context:

```
if (valid_samples_in(@raw_samples) < $MIN_SAMPLE_COUNT) {
    report_sensor_malfunction();
}
```

When the subroutine is called in scalar context, its `return` statement imposes scalar context on the grep, which then returns the total number of valid samples—just as a raw grep would do in the same position.

Unfortunately, it's easy to forget about the contextual lycanthropy of a `return`, especially when you write a subroutine that is "only ever going to be used one way"[*]. For example:

```
sub how_many_defined {
    return grep {defined $_} @_;
}

# and "always" thereafter:

my $found = how_many_defined(@raw_samples);
```

But eventually someone will write:

```
my ($found) = how_many_defined(@raw_samples);
```

and introduce a very subtle bug. The parentheses around $found put it in a list context, which puts the call to how_many_defined( ) in a list context, which puts the grep inside how_many_defined( ) in a list context, which causes the `return` to return the list of defined samples, the first of which is then assigned to $found[†].

---

[*] Yep, that's the sound of alarm bells you're hearing.

[†] And if that sample happens to be an integer, then $found will be assigned a numeric value, exactly as expected. It will be the *wrong* numeric value, but hey, at least that will make the bug much more interesting to track down.

If there were even the slightest chance that this scalar-returning subroutine might ever be called in a list context, it should have been written as follows:

```
sub how_many_defined {
    return scalar grep {defined $_} @_;
}
```

There is no shame in using an explicit scalar anywhere you know you want a scalar but you're not confident of your context. And because you can never be confident of your context in a return statement, an explicit scalar is always acceptable there.

At very least, you should always add one anywhere that a previously mistaken expectation regarding context has already bitten you. That way, the same misconception won't bite whoever is eventually responsible for the care and feeding of your code (that is, most likely you again, six months later).

Contextual Return Values

Make list-returning subroutines return
the "obvious" value in scalar context.

There is only one kind of list in Perl, so returning in a list context is easy—you just return all the values you produced:

```
sub defined_samples_in {
    return grep {defined $_} @_;
}
```

But what should that subroutine return in a scalar context? It might legitimately return an integer count (like grep itself does), in which case the subroutine stays exactly the same:

```
sub defined_samples_in {
    return grep {defined $_} @_;
}
```

Or it might instead return some serialized string representation of the list (like localtime does in scalar context):

```
sub defined_samples_in {
    my @defined_samples = grep {defined $_} @_;

    # Return all defined args in list context...
    if (wantarray) {
        return @defined_samples;
    }
    # Otherwise a serialized version in scalar context...
    return join($COMMA, @defined_samples);
}
```

Or it might return the "next" value in a series (like readline does):

```
use List::Util qw( first );

sub defined_samples_in {
    # Return all defined args in list context...
    if (wantarray) {
        return grep {defined $_} @_;
    }

    # Or, in scalar context, extract the first defined arg...
    return first {defined $_} @_;
}
```

It might try to preserve as much information as possible and return the full list of values using an array reference (which no Perl 5 builtin does):

```
sub defined_samples_in {
    my @defined_samples = grep {defined $_} @_;

    # Return all defined args in list context...
    if (wantarray) {
        return @defined_samples;
    }
    # Return all defined args (indirectly) in scalar context...
    return \@defined_samples;
}
```

It might even give up in disgust (like sort does):

```
sub defined_samples_in {
    croak q{Useless use of 'defined_samples_in' in a non-list context}
        if !wantarray;

    return grep {defined $_} @_;
}
```

Perl's list-returning builtins don't have a consistent behaviour in scalar context. They try to "do the right thing" on a case-by-case basis. Mostly they get it right; the scalar context results of grep, and localtime, and readline are what most people expect them to be.

Unfortunately, they don't *always* get it right. The scalar return values of select, readpipe, splice, unpack, and the various get... functions can be surprising to infrequent users of these functions. They have to be either memorized or repeatedly looked up in the fine manual. For many people, this makes using those builtins harder than it should be.

Don't perpetuate those difficulties in your own development. If you're writing a library of subroutines, make them predictable. Make every list-returning subroutine return the "obvious" value in scalar context.

What's the "obvious" value? It's the value that the developers who use the subroutine actually expect it to return. For example, if they all use defined_samples_in( ) like so:

```
if ( defined_samples_in(@samples) > 0 ) {
    process(@samples);
}
```

then they obviously expect it to return a count of defined samples. So the "obvious" scalar context return value is that count.

On the other hand, if everyone uses it like this:

```
my $floor_samples_ref     = defined_samples_in(@floor_samples);
my $restocked_samples_ref = defined_samples_in(@restocked_samples);

# and later...

swap_arrays($floor_samples_ref, $restocked_samples_ref);
```

then the expectation is clearly that the subroutine returns a reference to the array of results. So *that's* the "obvious" scalar return value.

In other words, the "obvious" return value in a scalar context is whatever the people who use your code *think* it's going to be (before they read the fine manual). That definition of obviousness presents a dilemma, though. The way you work out whether your proposed scalar-context behaviour is obvious is by implementing it and seeing how many people it trips up. But once the subroutine is deployed and client code is relying on it, it's too late to change its return value if that value turns out not to be what most people expect.

The solution (which is discussed in greater detail in Chapter 17) is to "play test" the subroutine before it's deployed. That is, ask the people who will actually be using your subroutine what they expect it will do in scalar context. Or, better yet, have them write sample code that uses the subroutine, and see how they use it. If you get a consensus (or even just a simple majority opinion), implement that. If you don't get agreement on a single "obvious" behaviour, see the "Multi-Contextual Return Values" guideline later in this chapter.

Unfortunately, getting this kind of preliminary feedback isn't always feasible. In such cases, you should simply select a reasonable default, based on the three fundamental categories of list-returning subroutines: homogeneous, heterogeneous, and iterative.

A *homogeneous list-returning subroutine* is one that returns a list of data values that are all of a single type: a list of samples, a list of names, or a list of images. Perl's built-in map, grep, and sort are examples of this type of subroutine. Because no one value in a homogeneous list is more significant than any other, the only interesting property of the list in a scalar context is usually the number of values it contains. Hence, in scalar contexts, homogeneous subroutines are usually expected to return a count, as map and grep both do.

A *heterogeneous list-returning subroutine* is one that returns a list containing distinct pieces of information: name, rank, and serial number; account number, account name, and balance; year, month, day. For example, the stat, caller, and getpwent builtins are all heterogeneous. The lists returned by subroutines of this type often do have a single piece of information that is more significant than any other, and they're typically expected to return that value in scalar contexts. For example, caller returns the caller's package name, whilst getpwent returns the relevant username.

Alternatively, all of the information returned by a heterogeneous subroutine might be equally important. So this type of subroutine is sometimes expected to return some kind of serialized representation of that information in scalar context, as localtime and gmtime do.

An *iterative list-returning subroutine* is one that returns an iterated series of values, typically the result of successive input operations. The builtins readline and readdir work this way. Iterative subroutines are always used for stepping through sequences of data, so in a scalar context, they should always return the result of a single iteration.

Remember, though, that these suggested default behaviours are recommendations, not natural laws. You may find that your "play testing" suggests that some other return value is more appropriate—more expected—in your particular subroutine. In that case, you should implement and deploy that behaviour instead, and then explicitly document the reasons for your choice.

Multi-Contextual Return Values

**When there is no "obvious" scalar context return value,
consider** Contextual::Return **instead.**

Sometimes no single scalar return value is appropriate for a list-returning subroutine. Your play-testers simply can't agree: different developers consistently expect different behaviours in different scalar contexts.

For example, suppose you're implementing a get_server_status() subroutine that normally returns its information as a heterogeneous list:

```
# In list context, return all the available information...
my ($name, $uptime, $load, $users) = get_server_status($server_ID);
```

You may find that, in scalar contexts, some programmers expected it to return its numeric load value:

```
# Total load is sum of individual server loads...
$total_load += get_server_status($server_ID);
```

Others assumed it would return a boolean value indicating whether the server is up:

```
# Skip inactive servers...
next SERVER if ! get_server_status($server_ID);
```

Still others anticipated a string summarizing the current status:

```
# Compile report on all servers...
$servers_summary .= get_server_status($server_ID) . "\n";
```

While a fourth group hoped for a hash-reference, to give them convenient named access to the particular server information they wanted:

```
# Total users is sum of users on each server...
$total_users += get_server_status($server_ID)->{users};
```

In such cases, implementing any one of these four expectations is going to leave three-quarters of your developers unhappy.

At some point, every subroutine *will* be called in scalar context, and will have to return something. If that something isn't obvious to the majority of people, then inexperienced developers—who might not even realize their call is in scalar context—will suffer. And experienced developers will suffer too: ham-strung by the limitations of scalar context return and forced to work with your arbitrary choice of return value.

Perl's subroutines are context-sensitive for a reason: so that they can Do The Right Thing when used in different ways. But often in scalar contexts there is no one Right Thing. So developers give up and just pick the One Thing That Seems Rightest...to them. All too often, a decision like that leads to confusion, frustration, and buggy code.

Surprisingly, the underlying problem here isn't that Perl is context-sensitive. The problem is that Perl isn't context-sensitive *enough*.

Perl has one kind of list context and one kind of void context, so simple list-context and void-context returns are the perfect tools for those. On the other hand, Perl has at least a dozen distinct scalar subcontexts: boolean, integer, floating-point, string, and the numerous reference types. So, unless one of those return types is the clear and obvious candidate, simple scalar context return is totally inadequate: a sledge-hammer when you really need tweezers.

Fortunately, there's a simple way to allow subroutines like get_server_status() to cater for two or more different scalar-context expectations simultaneously. The Contextual::Return CPAN module provides a mechanism by which you can specify that a subroutine returns different scalar values in boolean, numeric, string, hash-ref, array-ref, and code-ref contexts. For example, to allow get_server_status() to simultaneously support all five return behaviours shown at the start of this guide-line, you could simply write:

```
use Contextual::Return;

sub get_server_status {
    my ($server_ID) = @_;
```

```
# Acquire server data somehow...
my %server_data
    = _ascertain_server_status($server_ID);

# Return different components of that data, depending on call context...
return (
    LIST    { @server_data{ qw( name uptime load users ) } };              }
    BOOL    { $server_data{uptime} > 0;                                    }
    NUM     { $server_data{load};                                          }
    STR     { "$server_data{name}: $server_data{uptime}, $server_data{load}"; }
    HASHREF { \%server_data;                                               }
);
}
```

Now, in a list context, get_server_status( ) uses a hash slice to extract the information in the expected order. In a boolean context, it returns true if the uptime is nonzero. In a numeric context, it returns the server load. In a string context, a string summarizing the server's status is returned. And when the return value is expected to be a hash reference, get_server_status( ) simply returns a reference to the entire %server_data hash.

Note that each of those alternative return values is lazily evaluated. That means, on any given call to get_server_status( ), only one of the five contextual return blocks is actually executed.

Even in cases where you don't need to distinguish between so many alternatives, the Contextual::Return module can still improve the maintainability of your code, compared to using the built-in wantarray. The module allows you to say explicitly what you want to happen in different return context, and to label each of those outcomes with an obvious keyword. For example, suppose you had a subroutine such as:

```
sub defined_samples_in {
    if (wantarray) {
        return grep {defined $_} @_;
    }

    return first {defined $_} @_;
}
```

Without changing its behaviour at all, you could make the code considerably more self-documenting, and emphasize the inherent symmetry of the list and scalar cases, by rewriting it with a single contextual return:

```
use Contextual::Return;

sub defined_samples_in {
    return (
        LIST   {  grep {defined $_} @_ }
        SCALAR { first {defined $_} @_ }
    );
}
```

Besides producing more explicit and less cluttered code, this approach is more maintainable, too. When you need to extend the return behaviour of the subroutine, to more precisely match the expectations of those who use it, you can just add extra labeled return contexts, anywhere in the return list:

```
use Contextual::Return;

sub defined_samples_in {
    return (
        LIST     {             grep {defined $_} @_  }  # All defined vals
        SCALAR   {            first {defined $_} @_  }  # One defined val
        NUM      { scalar  grep {defined $_} @_  }  # How many vals defined?
        ARRAYREF {        [ grep {defined $_} @_ ] }  # Return vals in an array
    );
}
```

Regardless of the order in which the alternatives appear, Contextual::Return will automatically select the most appropriate behaviour in each call context.

Prototypes

Don't use subroutine prototypes.

Subroutine prototypes allow you to make use of more sophisticated argument-passing mechanisms than Perl's "usual list-of-aliases" behaviour. For example:

```
sub swap_arrays (\@\@) {
    my ($array1_ref, $array2_ref) = @_;

    my @temp_array = @{$array1_ref};
    @{$array1_ref} = @{$array2_ref};
    @{$array2_ref} = @temp_array;

    return;
}

# and later...

swap_arrays(@sheep, @goats);      # Implicitly pass references
```

The problem is that anyone who uses swap_arrays( ), and anyone who subsequently has to maintain that code, has to know about that subroutine's special magic. Otherwise, they will quite naturally assume that the two arrays will be flattened into a single list and slurped up by the subroutine's @_, because that's what happens in just about every other subroutine they ever use.

Using prototypes makes it impossible to deduce the argument-passing behaviour of a subroutine call simply by looking at the call. They also make it impossible to deduce the context in which particular arguments are evaluated. A subtle but common mistake is to "improve" the robustness of an existing library by putting prototype specifiers on all the subroutines. So a subroutine that used to be defined:

```
use List::Util qw( min max );

sub clip_to_range {
    my ($min, $max, @data) = @_;

    return map { max( $min, min($max, $_) ) } @data;
}
```

is updated to:

```
sub clip_to_range($$@) {  # takes two scalars and an array
    my ($min, $max, @data) = @_;

    return map { max($min, min($max, $_)) } @data;
}
```

The problem is that clip_to_range( ) was being used with an elegant table-lookup scheme:

```
my %range = (
    normalized => [-0.5,0.5],
    greyscale  => [0,255],
    percentage => [0,100],
    weighted   => [0,1],
);

# and later...

my $range_ref = $range{$curr_range};
@samples = clip_to_range( @{$range_ref}, @samples);
```

The $range{$curr_range} hash look-up returns a reference to a two-element array corresponding to the range that's currently selected. That array reference is then dereferenced by putting a @{...} around it. Previously, when clip_to_range( ) was an ordinary subroutine, that dereferenced array found itself in the list context, so it flattened into a list, producing the required minimum and maximum values for the subroutine's first two arguments.

But now that clip_to_range( ) has a prototype, things go very wrong. The prototype starts with a $, which looks like it's telling Perl that the first argument must be a scalar. But that's not what prototypes do at all.

What that $ prototype does is tell Perl that the first argument must be *evaluated in a scalar context*. And what is the first argument? It's the array produced by @{$range{$curr_range}}. And what do you get when an array is evaluated in a scalar context? The size of the array, which is 2, no matter which entry in %range was actually selected.

The second argument specification in the prototype is also a $. So the second argument to clip_to_range( ) must also be evaluated in a scalar context. And that second argument? It's @samples. Evaluating that array in scalar context once again produces its size. The second argument becomes the number of samples.

The final specification in the prototype is a @, which specifies that any remaining arguments are evaluated in list context. Of course, there aren't any more arguments now, but the @ specifier doesn't complain about that. An empty list is still a list, as far as it's concerned.

Adding a prototype didn't really improve the robustness of the code very much. Before it was imposed, clip_to_range( ) would have been passed the selected minimum, followed by the selected maximum, followed by all the data samples. Now, thanks to the wonders of prototyping, clip_to_range( ) always gets a minimum of 2, followed by a maximum equal to the number of samples, followed by no data. And Perl doesn't complain at all, since the prototype *was* successfully matched by the given arguments, even though it hosed them in the process.

Prototypes cause far more trouble than they avert. Even when they are properly understood and used correctly, they create code that doesn't behave the way it looks like it ought to, which makes it harder to maintain code that uses them. Furthermore, in OO implementations they engender a completely false sense of security, because they're utterly ignored in any method call.

Don't use prototypes. The only real advantage they can confer is allowing array and hash arguments to effectively be passed by reference:

```
swap_arrays(@sheep, @goats);
```

But even then, if you need pass-by-reference semantics, it's far better to make that explicit:

```
sub swap_arrays {
    my ($array1_ref, $array2_ref) = @_;

    my @temp_array = @{$array1_ref};
    @{$array1_ref} = @{$array2_ref};
    @{$array2_ref} = @temp_array;

    return;
}

# and later...

swap_arrays(\@sheep, \@goats);        # Explicitly pass references
```

Note that the body of swap_arrays( ) shown here is exactly the same as in the prototyped version at the start of this guideline. Only the call syntax varies. With prototypes it's magical, and therefore misleading; without prototypes it's a little uglier, but shows at a glance exactly what the code is doing.

Implicit Returns

If a subroutine "falls off the end" without ever encountering an explicit return, the value of the last expression evaluated in a subroutine is returned. That can lead to completely unexpected return values.

For example, consider this subroutine, which is supposed to return the second odd number in its argument list, or undef if there isn't a second odd number in the list:

```
sub find_second_odd {
    my $prev_odd_found = 0;

    # Check through args...
    for my $num (@_) {
        # Find an odd number...
        if (odd($num)) {
            # Return it if it's not the first (must be the second)...
            return $num if $prev_odd_found;

            # Otherwise, remember it's been seen...
            $prev_odd_found = 1;
        }
    }
    # Otherwise, fail
}
```

When that subroutine is used, strange things happen:

```
if (defined find_second_odd(2..6)) {
    # find_second_odd() returns 5
    # so the if block does execute as expected
}
if (defined find_second_odd(2..1)) {
    # find_second_odd() returns undef
    # so the if block is skipped as expected
}

if (defined find_second_odd(2..4)) {
    # find_second_odd() returns an empty string (!)
    # so the if block is unexpectedly executed
}

if (defined find_second_odd(2..3)) {
    # find_second_odd() returns an empty string again (!)
    # so the if block is unexpectedly executed again
}
```

The subroutine works correctly when there *is* a second odd number to be found, and when there are no numbers at all to be considered, but it behaves—there's no other word for it—*oddly* for the in-between cases*. That anomalous empty string is returned because that's what a failed boolean test evaluates to in Perl. And a failed boolean test is the last expression evaluated in the loop. No, not the conditional in:

```
if (odd($num)) {
```

or in:

```
return $num if $prev_found;
```

The last expression is the (failed) conditional test of the while loop. What while loop? The implicit while loop that the Perl compiler secretly translates every for loop into.

That's the problem. In order to predict the implicit return value of anything but the simplest subroutine, you not only have to understand the control flow within the subroutine and how that flow may change under different argument lists, but also what sneaky manipulations the compiler is performing on your code before it's executed.

But none of those complications will ever trouble you if you simply ensure that your subroutines can never "fall off the end". And all that requires is that every subroutine finishes with an explicit return statement—even if you have to add one "gratuitously":

```
sub find_second_odd {
    my $prev_odd_found = 0;

    # Check through args...
    for my $num (@_) {
        # Find an odd number...
        if (odd($num)) {
            # Return it if it's not the first (must be the second)...
            return $num if $prev_odd_found;

            # Otherwise, remember it's been seen...
            $prev_odd_found = 1;
        }
    }
    # Otherwise, fail explicitly
    return;
}
```

Now the subroutine always behaves as expected:

```
if (defined find_second_odd(2..6)) {
    # find_second_odd( ) returns 5
    # so if the block is executed, as expected
}
if (defined find_second_odd(2..1)) {
    # find_second_odd( ) returns undef
    # so if the block is skipped, as expected
}
```

---

* They'd be the "edge-cases", except that, in this instance, they're conceptually in the middle of the full range of possibilities.

```
    if (defined find_second_odd(2..4)) {
        # find_second_odd( ) returns undef
        # so if the block is skipped, as expected
    }

    if (defined find_second_odd(2..3)) {
        # find_second_odd( ) returns undef
        # so if the block is skipped, as expected
    }
```

That extra return is a very small price to pay for perfect predictability.

Note that this rule applies even if your subroutine "doesn't return anything". For example, if you're writing a subroutine to set a global flag, don't write:

```
    sub set_terseness {
        my ($terseness) = @_;

        $default_terseness = $terseness;
    }
```

If the subroutine isn't supposed to return a meaningful value, make it do so explicitly:

```
    sub set_terseness {
        my ($terseness) = @_;

        $default_terseness = $terseness;

        return;   # Explicitly return nothing meaningful
    }
```

Otherwise, developers who use the code could misinterpret the lack of an explicit return as indicating a deliberate implicit return instead. So they may come to rely on set_terseness( ) returning the new terseness value. That misinterpretation will become a problem if you later realize that the subroutine actually ought to return the previous terseness value, because that change in behaviour will now break any client code that was previously relying on the "undocumented feature" provided by the implicit return.

Returning Failure

Use a bare `return` to return failure.

Notice that each final return statement in the examples of the previous guideline used a return keyword with no argument, rather than a more-explicit return undef.

Normally, relying on default behaviour is not best practice. But in the case of a return statement, relying on the default return value actually prevents a particularly nasty bug.

The problem with returning an explicit `return undef` is that—contrary to most people's expectations—a returned undef isn't always false.

Consider a simple subroutine like this:

```
use Contextual::Return;

sub guesstimate {
    my ($criterion) = @_;

    my @estimates;
    my $failed = 0;

    # [Acquire data for specified criterion]

    return undef if $failed;

    # [Do guesswork based on the acquired data]

    # Return all guesses in list context or average guess in scalar context...
    return (
        LIST    { @estimates                   }
        SCALAR { sum(@estimates)/@estimates; }
    );
}
```

The successful return values are both fine, and completely appropriate for the two contexts in which the subroutine might be called. But the failure value is a serious problem. Since guesstimate( ) specifically tests for calls in list context, it's obvious that the subroutine is expected to be called in list contexts:

```
if (my @melt_rates = guesstimate('polar melting')) {
    my $model = Std::Climate::Model->new({ polar_melting => \@melt_rates });

    for my $interval (1,2,5,10,50,100,500) {
        print $model->predict({ year => $interval })
    }
}
```

But if the guesstimate( ) subroutine fails, it returns a single scalar value: undef. And in a list context (such as the assignment to @melt_rates), that single scalar undef value becomes a one-element list: (undef). So @melt_rates is assigned that one-element list and then evaluated in the overall *scalar* context of the if condition. And in scalar context an array always evaluates to the number of elements in it, in this case 1. Which is true.

Oops!*

What should have happened, of course, is that `guesstimate()` should have returned a failure value that was false in whatever context it was called, i.e., `undef` in scalar context and an empty list in list context:

```
if ($failed) {
    return (
        LIST   { () }
        SCALAR { undef }
    );
}
```

But that's precisely what a `return` itself does when it's not given an argument: it returns whatever the appropriate false value is for the current call context. So, by always using a bare `return` to return a "failure value", you can ensure that you will never bring about the destruction of the entire planetary ecosystem because of an expectedly true `undef`.

Meanwhile, Chapter 13 presents a deeper discussion on the most appropriate ways to propagate failure from a subroutine.

---

* And here "Oops!" means: the `if` block executes despite the failure of `guesstimate()` to acquire any meaningful data. So, when the climate model requests a numerical polar melting rate, that `undef` is silently converted to zero. This dwimmery causes the model to show that polar melting rates have absolutely no connection to world climate in general, and to rising ocean levels in particular. So mankind can happily keep burning fossil fuels at an ever-greater rate, secure in the knowledge that it has no effect. Until one day, the only person left is Kevin Costner. On a raft.

## CHAPTER 10

I/O

On two occasions I have been asked [by members
of Parliament], "Pray, Mr. Babbage, if you put into
the machine wrong figures, will the
right answers come out?"
I am not able rightly to apprehend the kind of
confusion of ideas that could provoke such a question.
—Charles Babbage

Input and output are critical in any design, because they mediate the interface of an application or library. To most users of your software, what your I/O components do is their entire experience of what the software *is*. So good I/O practices are essential to usability.

I/O operations are also particularly susceptible to inefficiencies, especially on large data sets. I/O is frequently the bottleneck in a system, and usually doesn't scale well. So good I/O practices are essential to performance too.

Yet another concern is that I/O deals with the software's external environment, which is typically less reliable than its own internals. Dealing successfully with the multiple failure modes of operating systems, filesystems, network connections, and human beings requires careful and conservative programming. So good I/O practices are essential to robustness as well.

Filehandles

Don't use bareword filehandles.

One of the most efficient ways for Perl programmers to bring misery and suffering upon themselves and their colleagues is to write this:

```
open FILE, '<', $filename
    or croak "Can't open '$filename': $OS_ERROR";
```

Using a bareword like that as a filehandle causes Perl to store the corresponding input stream descriptor in the symbol table of the current package. Specifically, the stream descriptor is stored in the symbol table entry whose name is the same as the bareword; in this case, it's *FILE. By using a bareword, the author of the previous code is effectively using a package variable to store the filehandle.

If that symbol has already been used as a filehandle anywhere else in the same package, executing this open statement will close that previous filehandle and replace it with the newly opened one. That's going to be a nasty surprise for any code that was already relying on reading input with <FILE>*.

The writer of this particular code also chose the imaginative name FILE for this particular filehandle. That's one of the commonest names used for package filehandles†, so the chances of colliding with someone else's open filehandle are greatly enhanced.

As if these pitfalls with bareword filehandles weren't bad enough, barewords are even more unreliable if there's a subroutine of the same name currently in scope. And worse still, under those circumstances they may fail *silently*. For example:

```
# Somewhere earlier in the same package (but perhaps in a different file)...
use POSIX;

# and later...

# Open filehandle to the external device...
open EXDEV, '<', $filename
    or croak "Can't open '$filename': $OS_ERROR";

# And process data stream...
while (my $next_reading = <EXDEV>) {
    process_reading($next_reading);
}
```

The POSIX module will have quietly exported a subroutine representing the POSIX error-code *EXDEV* into the package's namespace (just as if that constant had been declared in a use constant pragma). So the open statement is really:

```
open EXDEV(), '<', $filename
    or croak "Can't open '$filename': $OS_ERROR";
```

When that statement executes, it will first call the EXDEV( ) subroutine, which happens to return the value 18. The open statement then uses *that* value as a bareword filehandle name, opens an input stream to the requested file, and stores the resulting filehandle in the package's *18 symbol table entry‡.

---

* Not that we should have *too* much sympathy for that code, as it's behaving just as badly by using the FILE bareword itself.

† The other Four Horsemen of the I/O-pocalypse being IN, OUT, FH, and HANDLE.

‡ Yes, it's a valid symbol name: the regex capture variable $18 lives there.

Unfortunately, the EXDEV( ) subroutine *isn't* visible within the angle brackets of a subsequent input operation (i.e., <EXDEV>), because the input operator always treats an enclosed bareword as the direct name of the package filehandle that it's supposed to read from. As a result, the angle brackets attempt to read from *EXDEV, which results in a completely accurate, but highly confusing error message:

```
readline( ) on unopened filehandle EXDEV
```

The usual conundrum at that point is: *how can the filehandle possibly be unopened, when the* open *statement on the immediately preceding line didn't throw an exception???* And if the obvious culprit (the use POSIX) is off in another file somewhere, it can be very difficult to track down what's going wrong.

Curiously, the code *would* work as intended if it were rewritten like so:

```
# And process data stream...
while (my $next_reading = <18>) {
    process_reading($next_reading);
}
```

But that's hardly an ideal solution. The ideal solution is not to use bareword filehandles at all.

Indirect Filehandles

Use indirect filehandles.

Indirect filehandles provide a much cleaner and less error-prone alternative to bareword filehandles, and from Perl 5.6 onwards they're as easy to use as barewords. Whenever you call open with an undefined scalar variable as its first argument, open creates an anonymous filehandle (i.e., one that isn't stored in any symbol table), opens it, and puts a reference to it in the scalar variable you passed.

So you can open a file and store the resulting filehandle in a lexical variable, all in one statement, like so:

```
open my $FILE, '<', $filename
    or croak "Can't open '$filename': $OS_ERROR";
```

The my $FILE embedded in the open statement first declares a new lexical variable in the current scope. That variable is created in an undefined state, so the open fills it with a reference to the filehandle it's just created, as described earlier.

Under versions of Perl prior to 5.6, open isn't able to create the necessary filehandle automatically, so you have to do it yourself, using the gensym( ) subroutine from the standard Symbol module:

```
use Symbol qw( gensym );

# and later...

my $FILE = gensym();
open $FILE, '<', $filename
    or croak "Can't open '$filename': $OS_ERROR";
```

Either way, once the open filehandle is safely stored in the variable, you can read from it like so:

```
$next_line = <$FILE>;
```

And now it doesn't matter that the name of that filehandle is $FILE (at least, not from the point of view of code robustness). Sure, it's still a lousy, lazy, unimaginative, uninformative name, but now it's a lousy, lazy, unimaginative, uninformative, *lexical* name, so it won't sabotage anyone else's lousy, lazy, unimaginative, uninformative name*.

Even if there's already another $FILE variable in the same scope, the open won't clobber it; you'll merely get a warning:

```
"my" variable $FILE masks earlier declaration in same scope
```

and the new $FILE will hide the old one until the end of its scope.

Apart from avoiding the perils of global namespaces and the confusion of barewords that are sometimes subroutine calls, lexical filehandles have yet another advantage: they close themselves automatically when their lexical variable goes out of scope.

This feature ensures that a filehandle doesn't accidentally outlive the scope in which it's opened, it doesn't unnecessarily consume system resources, and it's also less likely to lose unflushed output if the program terminates unexpectedly. Of course, it's still preferable to close filehandles explicitly (see the "Cleanup" guideline later in this chapter), but lexical filehandles still improve the robustness of your code even when you forget.

Localizing Filehandles

If you have to use a package filehandle, localize it first.

Very occasionally, you simply have to use a package filehandle, rather than a lexical. For example, you might have existing code that relies on hard-wired bareword filehandle names.

---

* Of course, it would be even better if you gave the variable a lucid, lyric, imaginative, informative name (see Chapter 2). But that may not be your forte: "Dammit, Jim, I'm a Perl hacker, not Walt Whitman!"

In such cases, make sure that the symbol table entry involved is always referred to explicitly, with a leading asterisk. And, more importantly, always localize that typeglob within the smallest possible scope. For example:

```
# Wrap the Bozo::get_data( ) subroutine cleanly.
# (Apparently this subroutine is hard-wired to only read from a filehandle
#  named DATA::SRC. And it's used in hundreds of places throughout our
#  buffoon-monitoring system, so we can't change it. At least we fired the
#  clown that wrote this, didn't we???)...
sub get_fool_stats {
    my ($filename) = @_;

    # Create a temporary version of the hardwired filehandle...
    local *DATA::SRC;

    # Open it to the specified file...
    open *DATA::SRC, '<', $filename
        or croak "Can't open '$filename': $OS_ERROR";

    # Call the legacy subroutine...
    return Bozo::get_data( );
}
```

Applying local to the *DATA::SRC typeglob temporarily replaces that entry in the symbol table. Thereafter, the filehandle that is opened is stored in the temporary replacement typeglob, not in the original. And it's the temporary *DATA::SRC that Bozo::get_data( ) sees when it's called. Then, when the results of that call are returned, control passes back out of the body of get_fool_stats( ), at which point any localization within that scope is undone, and any pre-existing *DATA::SRC filehandle is restored.

Localization prevents most of the usual problems with bareword filehandles, because it ensures that the original *DATA::SRC is unaffected by the non-lexical open inside the call to get_fool_stats( ). It also guarantees that the filehandle is automatically closed at the end of the subroutine call. And using explicitly asterisked typeglobs instead of barewords avoids any confusion if there's also a DATA::SRC( ) subroutine.

Nonetheless, if you have a choice, lexical filehandles are still a better alternative. Unlike localized typeglobs, lexicals are strictly limited to the scope in which they are created. In contrast, localized package filehandles are available not only in their own scope, but—as the previous example illustrates—they can also be seen in any deeper scope that is called from their own scope. So a localized package filehandle can still potentially be pre-empted (i.e., broken) by another careless open in some nested scope.

Opening Cleanly

Use either the `IO::File` module
or the three-argument form of `open`.

You may have noticed that all of the examples so far use the three-argument form of open. This variant was introduced in Perl 5.6 and is more robust that the older two-argument version, which is susceptible to very rare, but subtle, failures:

```
# Log system uses a weird but distinctive naming scheme...
Readonly my $ACTIVE_LOG => '>temp.log<';
Readonly my $STATIC_LOG => '>perm.log<';

# and later...

open my $active,  "$ACTIVE_LOG"  or croak "Can't open '$$ACTIVE_LOG': $OS_ERROR";
open my $static, ">$STATIC_LOG"  or croak "Can't open '$STATIC_LOG': $OS_ERROR";
```

This code executes successfully, but it doesn't do what it appears to. The $active filehandle is opened for output to a file named *temp.log<*, not for input from a file named *>temp.log<*. And the $static filehandle is opened for appending to a file named *perm.log<*, rather than overwriting a file named *>perm.log<*. That's because the two open statements are equivalent to:

```
open my $active, '>temp.log<'   or croak "Can't open '>temp.log<': $OS_ERROR";
open my $static, '>>perm.log<'  or croak "Can't open '>perm.log<': $OS_ERROR";
```

and the '>' and '>>' prefixes on the second arguments tell open to open the files whose names appear after the prefixes in the corresponding output modes.

Using a three-argument open instead ensures that the specified opening mode can never be subverted by bizarre filenames, since the second argument now specifies only the opening mode, and the filename is supplied separately and doesn't have to be decoded at all:

```
# Log system uses a weird but distinctive naming scheme...
Readonly my $ACTIVE_LOG => '>temp.log<';
Readonly my $STATIC_LOG => '>perm.log<';

# and later...

open my $active, '<', $ACTIVE_LOG  or croak "Can't open '$ACTIVE_LOG': $OS_ERROR";
open my $static, '>', $STATIC_LOG  or croak "Can't open '$STATIC_LOG': $OS_ERROR";
```

And, as a small side-benefit, each open becomes visually more explicit about the intended mode of the resulting filehandle, which improves the readability of the resulting code slightly.

The only time you should use the two-argument form of open is if you need to open a stream to or from the standard I/O streams:

```
open my $stdin,  '<-' or croak "Can't open stdin: $OS_ERROR";
open my $stdout, '>-' or croak "Can't open stdout: $OS_ERROR";
```

The three-argument forms:

```
open my $stdin,  '<', '-' or croak "Can't open '-': $OS_ERROR";
open my $stdout, '>', '-' or croak "Can't open '-': $OS_ERROR";
```

don't have the same special magic; they simply attempt to open a file named "-" for reading or writing.

As an alternative to using open at all, you can also use Perl's object-oriented I/O interface to open files via the standard IO::File module. For example, the earlier log system example could also be written:

```
# Log system uses a weird but distinctive naming scheme...
Readonly my $ACTIVE_LOG => '>temp.log<';
Readonly my $STATIC_LOG => '>perm.log<';

# and later...
use IO::File;

my $active = IO::File->new($ACTIVE_LOG, '<')
    or croak "Can't open '$ACTIVE_LOG': $OS_ERROR";
my $static = IO::File->new($STATIC_LOG, '>')
    or croak "Can't open '$STATIC_LOG': $OS_ERROR";
```

The resulting filehandles in $active and $static can still be used like any other file-handle. In fact, the only significant difference between using IO::File->new() and using open is that the OO version blesses the resulting filehandle into the IO::File class, whereas open produces raw filehandles that act like objects of the IO::Handle class (even though they're not actually blessed).

Error Checking

Never open, close, **or** print **to a file**
without checking the outcome.

These three I/O functions are probably the ones that fail most often. They can fail because a path is bad, or a file is missing, or inaccessible, or has the wrong permissions, or a disk crashes, or the network fails, or the process runs out of file descriptors or memory, or the filesystem is read-only, or any of a dozen other problems.

So writing unguarded I/O statements like this:

```
open my $out,  '>', $out_file;
print {$out} @results;
close $out;
```

is sheer optimism, especially when it's not significantly harder to check that everything went to plan:

```
open my $out,  '>', $out_file  or croak "Couldn't open '$out_file': $OS_ERROR";
print {$out} @results          or croak "Couldn't write '$out_file': $OS_ERROR";
close $out                     or croak "Couldn't close '$out_file': $OS_ERROR";
```

Or, more forgivingly, as part of a larger interactive process:

```
SAVE:
while (my $save_file = prompt 'Save to which file? ') {
    # Open specified file and save results...
    open my $out, '>', $save_file  or next SAVE;
    print {$out} @results          or next SAVE;
    close $out                     or next SAVE;

    # Save succeeded, so we're done...
    last SAVE;
}
```

Also see the "Builtin Failures" guideline in Chapter 13 for a less intrusive way to ensure that every open, print, and close is properly checked.

Checking every print to a terminal device is also laudable, but not essential. Failure in such cases is much rarer, and usually self-evident. Besides, if your print statements can't reach the terminal, it's unlikely that your warnings or exceptions will either.

Cleanup

Close filehandles explicitly, and as soon as possible.

Lexical filehandles, and even localized package filehandles, automatically close as soon as their variable or localization goes out of scope. But, depending on the structure of your code, that can still be suboptimal:

```
sub get_config {
    my ($config_file) = @_;

    # Access config file or signal failure...
    open my $fh, '<', $config_file
        or croak "Can't open config file: $config_file";

    # Load file contents...
    my @lines = <$fh>;

    # Storage for config data...
    my %config;
    my $curr_section = $EMPTY_STR;
```

```
        # Decode config data...
        CONFIG:
        for my $line (@lines) {
            # Section markers change the second-level hash destination...
            if (my ($section_name) = $line =~ m/ \A \[ ([^]]+) \] /xms) {
                $curr_section = $section_name;
                next CONFIG;
            }

            # Key/value pairs are stored in the current second-level hash...
            if (my ($key, $val) = $line =~ m/\A \s* (.*?) \s* : \s* (.*?) \s* \z/xms) {
                $config{$curr_section}{$key} = $val;
                next CONFIG;
            }

            # Ignore everything else
        }

        return \%config;
    }
```

The problem here is that the input file remains open after it's used, and stays open for however long the decoding of the data takes.

The sooner a filehandle is closed, the sooner the internal and external resources it controls are freed up. The sooner it's closed, the less chance there is for accidental reuse or misuse. The sooner an output filehandle is closed, the sooner the written file is in a stable state.

The previous example would be more robust if it didn't rely on the scope boundary to close the lexical filehandle when the subroutine returns. It should have been written:

```
    sub get_config {
        my ($config_file) = @_;

        # Access config file or signal failure...
        open my $fh, '<', $config_file
            or croak "Can't open '$config_file': $OS_ERROR";

        # Load file contents and close file...
        my @lines = <$fh>;
        close $fh
            or croak "Can't close '$config_file' after reading: $OS_ERROR";

        # [Decode config data and return, as before]

    }
```

Input Loops

Use while (<>), **not** for (<>).

Programmers are occasionally tempted to write input loops using a for, like this:

```
use Regexp::Common;
Readonly my $EXPLETIVE => $RE{profanity};

for my $line (<>) {
    $line =~ s/$EXPLETIVE/[DELETED]/gxms;
    print $line;
}
```

That's presumably because for loops are inherently finite in their number of iterations, and hence intrinsically more robust. Or perhaps it's just that the keyword is two characters shorter.

Whatever the reason, using a for loop to iterate input is a very inefficient and brittle solution. The iteration list of a for loop is (obviously) a list context. So in the example, the <> operator is called in a list context. Evaluating <> in list context causes it to read in every line it can, building a temporary list as it does. Once the input is complete, that list becomes the list to be iterated by the for.

There are several problems with that approach. For a start, it means the for loop won't start to iterate until the entire input stream has been read and an end-of-file encountered. This means that the previous code can't be used interactively. Moreover, constructing a (potentially very long) list of the input lines is expensive, both in terms of the memory required to store the entire list and in terms of the time required to allocate that memory and to actually build the list.

Worst of all, the for input loop doesn't scale well. Its memory requirements are linearly proportional to the total size of the input, with something like a 200% overhead[*]. That means that a sufficiently large input might actually break the input loop with a memory allocation failure (Out of memory!), or at least slow it down intolerably with excessive memory allocation and swapping overheads.

In contrast, an equivalent while loop:

```
while (my $line = <>) {
    $line =~ s/$EXPLETIVE/[DELETED]/gxms;
    print $line;
}
```

---

[*] Under Perl 5.8, for example, to read in 100,000 lines of 30 characters each (i.e., 3 MB of data) in a for loop requires just under 6 MB of allocated memory for the initial list. Reading in a file of one million such lines requires 59 MB of allocated memory, before the loop even starts. In contrast, the equivalent while loop never uses more than 55 bytes for either file.

reads and processes only one line at a time. This version can be used interactively, and never allocates more memory than is needed to accommodate the longest individual line. So use a while instead of a for when reading input.

By the way, the same problems don't arise when iterating large ranges:

```
for my $n (2..1_000_000_000) {
    my @factors = factors_of($n);

    if (@factors == 2) {
        print "$n is prime\n";
    }
    else {
        print "$n is composite with factors: @factors\n";
    }
}
```

In modern versions of Perl, ranges are lazily evaluated, so the previous code doesn't first have to build a list of 999,999,999 consecutive integers before the for can start iterating.

Line-Based Input

Prefer line-based I/O to slurping.

Reading in an entire file in a single <> operation is colloquially known as "slurping". But the considerations of memory allocation discussed in the previous section mean that slurping the contents of a file and then manipulating those contents monolithically, like so:

```
# Slurp the entire file (see the next guideline)...
my $text = do { local $/; <> };

# Wash its mouth out...
$text =~ s/$EXPLETIVE/[DELETED]/gxms;

# Print it all back out...
print $text;
```

is generally slower, less robust, and less scalable than processing the contents a line at a time:

```
while (my $line = <>) {
    $line =~ s/$expletive/[DELETED]/gxms;
    print $line;
}
```

Reading an entire file into memory makes sense only when the file is unstable in some way, or is being updated asynchronously and you need a "snapshot", or if your planned text processing is likely to cross line boundaries:

```
sub get_C_code {
    my ($filename) = @_;

    # Get a handle on the code...
    open my $in, '<', $filename
        or croak "Can't open C file '$filename': $OS_ERROR";

    # Read it all in...
    my $code = do { local $/; <$in> };

    # Convert any C-style comment to a single space...
    use Regexp::Common;    # See Chapter 12
    $code =~ s{ $RE{comment}{C} }{$SPACE}gxms;

    return $code;
}
```

Because C comments can span multiple lines, it's necessary to load the entire file into memory at once so the pattern can detect such cases.

Simple Slurping

Slurp a filehandle with a do block for purity.

Whenever you do need to read in an entire file at once, the syntax shown in the final example of the previous guideline is the right way to do it:

```
my $code = do { local $/; <$in> };
```

Localizing the global $/ variable (a.k.a. $RS or $INPUT_RECORD_SEPARATOR, under use English) temporarily replaces it with a version whose value is undef. But, if the input record separator is undefined, there is effectively *no* input record separator, so Perl treats the input as a single, unseparated record, and the single <> (or readline) reads in the entire input stream as a single "line".

Reading in a complete file or stream this way is much more efficient than "concatenative" approaches such as:

```
my $code;
while (my $line = <$in>) {
    $code .= $line;
}
```

or:

```
my $code = join $EMPTY_STR, <$in>;
```

That second alternative is particularly bad because, like the for (<>) discussed earlier, the join evaluates the read operation in a list context, constructs a list of individual lines, and then joins them back together to create a single string. This process requires about three times as much memory as:

```
my $code = do { local $/; <$in> };
```

It's also appreciably slower, and doesn't scale nearly as well as the size of the input text increases[*].

Note that it's important to put that localization-and-read inside a do {...} or in some other small block. A common mistake is to write this instead:

```
$/ = undef;
my $text = <$in>;
```

That works perfectly well, in itself, but it also undefines the *global* input record separator, rather than its temporary localized replacement. But the global input record separator controls the read behaviour of every filehandle—even those that are lexically scoped, or in other packages. So, if you don't localize the change in $/ to some small scope, you're dooming every subsequent read everywhere in your program to vile slurpitude.

Power Slurping

Slurp a stream with Perl6::Slurp for power and simplicity.

Reading in an entire input stream is common enough, and the do {...} idiom is ugly enough, that the next major version of Perl (Perl 6) will provide a built-in function to handle it directly. Appropriately, that builtin will be called slurp.

Perl 5 doesn't have an equivalent builtin, and there are no plans to add one, but the future functionality *is* available in Perl 5 today, via the Perl6::Slurp CPAN module. Instead of:

```
my $text = do { local $/; <$file_handle> };
```

you can just write:

---

[*] By the way, for all its virtues, the do {...} approach *isn't* the fastest way to slurp a file of known (and very large) length. The very quickest way to do that is with a low-level system read:

```
sysread $fh, $text, -s $fh;
```

But then, of course, you have to live with the cryptic syntax, and with any idiosyncrasies that low-level I/O might be subject to on your particular platform. If you do need to use this highest-speed approach to slurping files, at least consider using the File::Slurp CPAN module, which encapsulates that messy sysread in a tidy read_file() subroutine.

```
use Perl6::Slurp;

my $text = slurp $file_handle;
```

which is cleaner, clearer, more concise, and consequently less error-prone.

The slurp( ) subroutine is also much more powerful. For example, if you have only the file's name, you would have to write:

```
my $text = do {
    open my $fh, '<', $filename or croak "$filename: $OS_ERROR";
    local $/;
    <$fh>;
};
```

which almost seems more trouble than it's worth. Or you can just give slurp( ) the filename directly:

```
my $text = slurp $filename;
```

and it will open the file and then read in its full contents for you.

In a list context, slurp( ) acts like a regular <> or readline, reading in every line separately and returning them all in a list:

```
my @lines = slurp $filename;
```

The slurp( ) subroutine also has a few useful features that <> and readline lack. For example, you can ask it to automatically chomp each line before it returns:

```
my @lines = slurp $filename, {chomp => 1};
```

or, instead of removing the line-endings, it can convert each one to some other character sequence (say, '[EOL]'):

```
my @lines = slurp $filename, {chomp => '[EOL]'};
```

or you can change the input record separator—just for that particular call to slurp( )—without having to monkey with the $/ variable:

```
# Slurp chunks...
my @paragraphs = slurp $filename, {irs => $EMPTY_STR};
```

Setting the input record separator to an empty string causes <> or slurp to read "paragraphs" instead of lines, where each "paragraph" is a chunk of text ending in two or more newlines.

You can even use a regular expression to specify the input record separator, instead of the plain string that Perl's standard $/ variable restricts you to:

```
# Read "human" paragraphs (separated by two or more whitespace-only lines)...
my @paragraphs = slurp $filename, {irs => qr/\n \s* \n/xms};
```

Standard Input

Avoid using `*STDIN`, **unless you really mean it.**

The `*STDIN` stream doesn't always mean "...from the tty". And it never means "...from the files specified on the command line", unless you go out of your way to arrange for it to mean that:

```
close *STDIN or croak "Can't close STDIN: $OS_ERROR";
for my $filename (@ARGV) {
    open *STDIN, '<', $filename or croak "Can't open STDIN: $OS_ERROR";
    while (<STDIN>) {
        print substr($_,2);
    }
}
```

which is, of course, so complicated and ugly that it constitutes its own punishment.

`*STDIN` is always attached to the zero[th] file descriptor of your process. By default, that's bound to the terminal (if any), but you certainly can't rely on that default. For example, if data is being piped into your process, then `*STDIN` will be bound to file descriptor number 1 of the previous process in the pipeline. Or if your input to your process is being redirected from a file, then `*STDIN` will be connected to that file.

To cope with these diverse possibilities *and* the possibility that the user just typed the desired input file(s) on the command line without bothering with any redirection arrows, it's much safer to use Perl's vastly cleverer alternative: `*ARGV`. The `*ARGV` stream is connected to wherever `*STDIN` is connected, unless there are filenames on the command line, in which case it's connected to the concatenation of those files.

So you can allow your program to cope with interactive input, shell-level pipes, file redirections, and command-line file lists by writing this instead:

```
while (my $line = <ARGV>) {
    print substr($line, 2);
}
```

In fact, you use this magic filehandle all the time, possibly without even realizing it. `*ARGV` is the filehandle that's used when you don't specify any other:

```
while (my $line = <>) {
    print substr($line, 2);
}
```

It's perfectly good practice to use that shorter—and more familiar—form. This guideline is intended mainly to prevent you from unintentionally "fixing it": trying to be explicit, but then using the wrong filehandle:

```
while (my $line = <STDIN>) {
    print substr($line, 2);
}
```

Printing to Filehandles

Always put filehandles in braces within any `print` statement.

It's easy to lose a lexical filehandle that's being used in the argument list of a `print`:

```
print $file $name, $rank, $serial_num, "\n";
```

Putting braces around the filehandle helps it stand out clearly:

```
print {$file} $name, $rank, $serial_num, "\n";
```

The braces also convey your intentions regarding that variable; namely, that you really did mean it to be treated as a filehandle, and didn't just forget a comma.

You should also use the braces if you need to `print` to a package-scoped filehandle:

```
print {*STDERR} $name, $rank, $serial_num, "\n";
```

Another acceptable alternative is to load the `IO::Handle` module and then use Perl's object-oriented I/O interface:

```
use IO::Handle;

$file->print( $name, $rank, $serial_num, "\n" );

*STDERR->print( $name, $rank, $serial_num, "\n" );
```

Simple Prompting

Always prompt for interactive input.

There are few things more frustrating than firing up a program and then sitting there waiting for it to complete its task, only to realize after a few minutes that it's actually been just sitting there too, silently waiting for you to start interacting with it:

```
# The quit command is case-insensitive and may be abbreviated...
Readonly my $QUIT => qr/\A q(?:uit)? \z/ixms;

# No command entered yet...
my $cmd = $EMPTY_STR;

# Until the q[uit] command is entered...
CMD:
while ($cmd !~ $QUIT) {
    # Get the next command...
    $cmd = <>;
    last CMD if not defined $cmd;
```

```
        # Clean it up and run it...
        chomp $cmd;
        execute($cmd)
            or carp "Unknown command: $cmd";
    }
```

Interactive programs should *always* prompt for interaction whenever they're being run interactively:

```
    # Until the q[uit] command is entered...
    CMD:
    while ($cmd !~ $QUIT) {
        # Prompt if we're running interactively...
        if (is_interactive()) {
            print get_prompt_str();
        }

        # Get the next command...
        $cmd = <>;
        last CMD if not defined $cmd;

        # Clean it up and run it...
        chomp $cmd;
        execute($cmd)
            or carp "Unknown command: $cmd";
    }
```

Interactivity

Don't reinvent the standard test for interactivity.

The is_interactive() subroutine used in the previous guideline is surprisingly difficult to implement. It sounds simple enough: just confirm that both input and output filehandles are connected to the terminal. If the input isn't, there's no need to prompt, as the user won't be entering the data directly. And if the output isn't, there's no need to prompt, because the user wouldn't see the prompt message anyway.

So most people just write:

```
    sub is_interactive {
        return -t *ARGV && -t *STDOUT;
    }

    # and later...

    if (is_interactive()) {
        print $PROMPT;
    }
```

Unfortunately, even with the use of *ARGV instead of *STDIN (in accordance with the earlier "Standard Input" guideline), that implementation of is_interactive( ) doesn't work.

For a start, the *ARGV filehandle has the special property that it only opens the files in @ARGV when the filehandle is actually first read. So you can't just use the -t builtin on *ARGV:

```
-t *ARGV
```

*ARGV won't be opened until you read from it, and you can't read from it until you know whether to prompt; and to know whether to prompt, you have to check where *ARGV was opened to, but *ARGV won't be opened until you read from it.

Several other magical properties of *ARGV can also prevent simple -t tests on the filehandle from providing the correct answer, even if the input stream *is* already open. In order to cope with all the special cases, you have to write:

```
use Scalar::Util qw( openhandle );

sub is_interactive {
    # Not interactive if output is not to terminal...
    return 0 if not -t *STDOUT;

    # If *ARGV is opened, we're interactive if...
    if (openhandle *ARGV) {
        # ...it's currently opened to the magic '-' file
        return -t *STDIN if $ARGV eq '-';

        # ...it's at end-of-file and the next file is the magic '-' file
        return @ARGV>0 && $ARGV[0] eq '-' && -t *STDIN if eof *ARGV;

        # ...it's directly attached to the terminal
        return -t *ARGV;
    }

    # If *ARGV isn't opened, it will be interactive if *STDIN is attached
    # to a terminal and either there are no files specified on the command line
    # or if there are one or more files and the first is the magic '-' file
    return -t *STDIN && (@ARGV==0 || $ARGV[0] eq '-');
}
```

That is not something you want to have to (re)write yourself for each interactive program you create. Nor something you're ever going to want to maintain yourself. Fortunately, it's already written for you and available from the CPAN, in the IO::Interactive module. Instead of the horrendous subroutine definition shown earlier, you can just write:

```
use IO::Interactive qw( is_interactive );

# and later...
```

```
if (is_interactive()) {
    print $PROMPT;
}
```

Alternatively, you could use the module's interactive( ) subroutine, which provides a special filehandle that sends output to *STDOUT only if the terminal is interactive (and just discards it otherwise):

```
use IO::Interactive qw( interactive );

# and later...

print {interactive} $PROMPT;
```

Power Prompting

Use the IO::Prompt **module for prompting.**

Because programs so often need to prompt for interactive input and then read that input, it's probably not surprising that there would be a CPAN module to make that process easier. It's called IO::Prompt and it exports only a single subroutine: prompt( ). At its simplest, you can just write:

```
use IO::Prompt;

my $line = prompt 'Enter a line: ';
```

The specified string will be printed (but only if the program is interactive), and then a single line will be read in. That line will also be automatically chomped*, unless you specifically request it not be.

The prompt( ) subroutine can also control the echoing of characters. For example:

```
my $password = prompt 'Password: ', -echo => '*';
```

which echoes an asterisk for each character typed in:

```
> Password: **********
```

You can even prevent echoing entirely (by echoing an empty string in place of each character):

```
my $password = prompt 'Password: ', -echo => $EMPTY_STR;
```

prompt( ) can return a single key-press (without requiring the Return key to be pressed as well):

```
my $choice = prompt 'Enter your choice [a-e]: ', -onechar;
```

---

* How many times have you read in a line, then immediately had to chomp it? That sequence seems to be the rule, rather than the exception, so prompt makes chomping the default. This particular design is discussed further in Chapter 17.

It can ignore inputs that are not acceptable:

```
my $choice = prompt 'Enter your choice [a-e]: ', -onechar,
                    -require=>{ 'Must be a, b, c, d, or e: ' => qr/[a-e]/xms };
```

It can be restricted to certain kinds of common inputs (e.g., only integers, only valid filenames, only 'y' or 'n'):

```
CODE:
while (my $ord = prompt -integer, 'Enter a code (zero to quit): ') {
    if ($ord == 0) {
        exit if prompt -yn, 'Really quit? ';
        next CODE;
    }
    print qq{Character $ord is: }, chr($ord), qq{'\n};
}
```

It has many more features, but the real power of prompt( ) is that it *abstracts* the ask-answer-verify sequence of operations into a single higher-level command, which can significantly reduce the amount of code you need to write. For example, the command-processing loop shown earlier in the "Simple Prompting" guideline:

```
# No command entered yet...
my $cmd = $EMPTY_STR;

# Until the q[uit] command is entered...
CMD:
while ($cmd !~ $QUIT) {
    # Prompt if we're running interactively...
    if (is_interactive()) {
        print get_prompt_str();
    }

    # Get the next command...
    $cmd = <>;
    last CMD if not defined $cmd;

    # Clean it up and run it...
    chomp $cmd;
    execute($cmd)
        or carp "Unknown command: $cmd";
}
```

can be reduced to:

```
# Until the q[uit] command is entered...
while ( my $cmd = prompt(get_prompt_str(), -fail_if => $QUIT) ) {
    # Run whatever else was...
    execute($cmd) or carp "Unknown command: $cmd";
}
```

Note especially that the $cmd variable no longer has to be defined outside the loop and can be more appropriately restricted in scope to the loop block itself.

Progress Indicators

Always convey the progress of long non-interactive operations within interactive applications.

As annoying as it is to sit like a mushroom whilst some mute program waits for your unprompted input, it's even more frustrating to tentatively start typing something into an interactive program, only to discover that the program is still busy initializing, or calculating, or connecting to a remote device:

```
# Initialize from any config files...
for my $possible_config ( @CONFIG_PATHS ) {
    init_from($possible_config);
}

# Connect to remote server...
my $connection;
TRY:
for my $try (1..$MAX_TRIES) {
    # Retry connection with increasingly tolerant timeout intervals...
    $connection = connect_to($REMOTE_SERVER, { timeout => fibonacci($try) });
    last TRY if $connection;
}
croak "Can't contact server ($REMOTE_SERVER)"
    if !$connection;

# Interactive portion of the program starts here...
while (my $cmd = prompt($prompt_str, -fail_if=>$QUIT)) {
    remote_execute($connection, $cmd)
        or carp "Unknown command: $cmd";
}
```

It's much better—and not much more onerous—to give an active indication that an interactive program is busy doing something non-interactive:

```
# Initialize from any config files...
print {*STDERR} 'Initializing...';
for my $possible_config ( @CONFIG_PATHS ) {
    print {*STDERR} '.';
    init_from($possible_config);
}
print {*STDERR} "done\n";

# Connect to remote server...
print {*STDERR} 'Connecting to server...';
my $connection;
```

```
TRY:
for my $try (1..$MAX_TRIES) {
    print {*STDERR} '.';
    $connection = connect_to($REMOTE_SERVER, { timeout => fibonacci($try) });
    last TRY if $connection;
}
croak "Can't contact server ($REMOTE_SERVER)"
    if not $connection;
print {*STDERR} "done\n";

# Interactive portion of the program starts here...
```

Better still, factor those messages out into a set of utility subroutines:

```
# Utility subs to provide progress reporting...
sub _begin_phase {
    my ($phase) = @_;
    print {*STDERR} "$phase...";
    return;
}
sub _continue_phase {
    print {*STDERR} '.';
    return;
}
sub _end_phase {
    print {*STDERR} "done\n";
    return;
}

_begin_phase('Initializing');
for my $possible_config ( @CONFIG_PATHS ) {
    _continue_phase();
    init_from($possible_config);
}
_end_phase();

_begin_phase('Connecting to server');
my $connection;
TRY:
for my $try (1..$MAX_TRIES) {
    _continue_phase();
    $connection = connect_to($REMOTE_SERVER, { timeout => fibonacci($try) });
    last TRY if $connection;
}
croak "Can't contact server ($REMOTE_SERVER)"
    if not $connection;
_end_phase();

# Interactive portion of the program starts here...
```

Note that some of the comments have been dispensed with, as the _begin_phase( )
calls adequately document each non-interactive code paragraph.

Automatic Progress Indicators

Consider using the `Smart::Comments` **module to automate your progress indicators.**

As an alternative to coding the inline progress indicators or writing utility subroutines (as suggested in the previous guideline), you might prefer to use the `Smart::Comments` CPAN module, which keeps the comments about phases, and dispenses with the indicator code instead:

```
use Smart::Comments;

for my $possible_config ( @CONFIG_PATHS ) {  ### Initializing...  done
    init_from($possible_config);
}

my $connection;
TRY:
for my $try (1..$MAX_TRIES) {                 ### Connecting to server...  done
    $connection = connect_to($REMOTE_SERVER, {timeout=>$TIMEOUT});
    last TRY if $connection;
}
croak "Can't contact server ($REMOTE_SERVER)"
    if not $connection;

# Interactive portion of the program starts here...
```

`Smart::Comments` allows you to put a specially marked comment (###) on the same line as any for or while loop. It then uses that comment as a template, from which it builds an automatic progress indicator for the loop. Other useful features of the `Smart::Comments` module are described under "Semi-Automatic Debugging" in Chapter 18.

Autoflushing

Avoid a raw `select` **when setting autoflushes.**

When it comes to maintainable code, it doesn't get much worse than this commonly used Perl idiom:

```
select((select($fh), $|=1)[0]);
```

The evil one-argument form of select[*] takes a filehandle and makes it the (global!) default destination for print statements from that point onwards. That is, after a

---

[*] As opposed to the evil four-argument select (see Chapter 8).

select, instead of writing to *STDOUT, any print statement that isn't given an explicit filehandle will now write to the filehandle that was select'd.

This change of default happens even if the newly selected filehandle was formerly confined to a lexical scope:

```
for my $filename (@files) {
    # Open a lexical handle (will be automatically closed at end of iteration)
    open my $fh, '>', $filename
        or next;

    # Make it the default print target...
    select $fh;

    # Print to it...
    print "[This file intentionally left blank]\n";
}
```

In actual applications, that last print statement would probably be replaced by a long series of separate print statements, controlled by some complex text-generation algorithm. Hence the desire to make the current $fh the default output filehandle, so as to avoid having to explicitly specify the filehandle in every print statement.

Unfortunately, because select makes its argument the *global* default for print, when the final iteration of the loop is finished, the last file that was successfully opened will *remain* the global print default. That filehandle won't be garbage-collected and auto-closed like all the other filehandles were, because the global default still refers to it. And for the remainder of your program, every print that isn't given an explicit file-handle will print to that final iterated filehandle, rather than to *STDOUT.

So don't use one-argument select. Ever.

And that appalling select statement shown at the start of this guideline?

```
select((select($fh), $|=1)[0]);
```

Well, that's the "classic" way to make the filehandle in $fh autoflush; that is, to write out its buffer on every print, not just when it sees a newline. First, you select the file-handle you want to autoflush (select($fh)). Then you set the punctuation variable that controls autoflushing of the currently selected filehandle ($|=1). The sneaky bit is that you do those two things in a list ((select($fh), $|=1)), so their return values become the two values of that list. Because select returns the previous default file-handle—the one that you just replaced—that previous filehandle must now be the first element of the list. So if you index back into the list, requesting the first element ((select($fh), $|=1)[0]), you'll get back the previously selected filehandle. Then all you need to do is pass that filehandle to select again (select((select($fh), $|=1)[0])) to restore the original default, and your journey to the Dark Side will be complete*.

---

* Once you start down that path, forever will it dominate your maintenance…confuse you, it will!

Fortunately, if you're using lexical filehandles, there's no need for this kind of necro-selectomancy. Lexical filehandles act like fully-fledged objects of the IO::Handle class so, if you're willing to load the IO::Handle module, there's a much simpler method for setting their autoflush behaviour:

```
use IO::Handle;

# and later...

$fh->autoflush( );
```

You can even use this same approach on the standard package-scoped filehandles:

```
use IO::Handle;

# and later...

*STDOUT->autoflush( );
```

## CHAPTER 11

References

*Pointers are like jumps, leading wildly from one part of
the data structure to another. Their introduction into
high-level languages has been a step backwards
from which we may never recover.*

—Charles Hoare

References in Perl are much safer than raw pointers (such as those available in C or
C++). Perl references cannot be left dangling towards a scalar that has been garbage-
collected, and they cannot be coerced into pretending that a hash is an array.

Semantically they're very robust, but sometimes their syntax lets them down, making code that uses references confusing or misleading. In certain configurations, they
can also interfere with the garbage collector.

Symbolic references have far more problems. It's entirely possible for them to dan-
gle, and they can easily be used to access the wrong type of referent. They also sub-
vert the pre-eminence of lexically scoped variables. All in all, they're more trouble
than they're worth.

Fortunately, every one of these problems can be avoided by following a small number of simple guidelines...

Dereferencing

Wherever possible, dereference with arrows.

Use the -> notation in preference to "circumfix" dereferencing. In other words, when
you're accessing references to containers, use the arrow syntax:

```
print 'Searching from ', $list_ref->[0] , "\n",
      '            to ', $list_ref->[-1] , "\n";
```

This style results in much cleaner code than explicit wrap-and-prefix dereferencing:

```
print 'Searching from ', ${$list_ref}[0],  "\n",
     '             to ', ${$list_ref}[-1], "\n";
```

Note that the arrow syntax also interpolates correctly into strings, so the previous example would be better written:

```
print "Searching from $list_ref->[0]\n",
     "             to $list_ref->[-1]\n";
```

Explicit dereferencing is prone to two specific mistakes, which can be hard to detect if use strict is not in effect. The first error is simply forgetting to wrap-and-prefix at all:

```
print 'Searching from ', $list_ref[0],  "\n",
     '             to ', $list_ref[-1], "\n";
```

The second mistake is wrapping-and-prefixing correctly, but accidentally leaving off the reference variable's own sigil (i.e., the one inside the braces):

```
print 'Searching from ', ${list_ref}[0],  "\n",
     '             to ', ${list_ref}[-1], "\n";
```

In both cases, the array accesses are accessing the variable @list_ref instead of the array referred to by the reference in $list_ref.

Of course, if you need to access more than one element of a container (i.e., to slice it) via a reference to that container, there's no choice except to use the wrap-and-prefix syntax:

```
my ($from, $to) = @{$list_ref}[0, -1];
```

Attempting to use the arrow notation to achieve the same effect doesn't work:

```
my ($from, $to) = $list_ref->[0, -1];
```

Because the access expression ($list_ref->[0, -1]) begins with a $ sigil, the square brackets are treated as a scalar context, so the list of indices is evaluated in scalar context, and the result is just the final index. So the previous example is equivalent to:

```
my ($from, $to) = ($list_ref->[-1], undef);
```

Braced References

**Where prefix dereferencing is unavoidable,
put braces around the reference.**

You can dereference a reference without first putting it in braces:

```
push @$list_ref, @results;

print substr($$str_ref, 0, $max_cols);

my $first = $$list_ref[0];
my @rest  = @$list_ref[1..$MAX];
```

```
my $first_name = $$name_ref{$first};
my ($initial, $last_name) = @$name_ref{$middle, $last};

print @$$ref_to_list_ref[1..$MAX];
```

All of these work correctly, but they may also produce intense uncertainty and anxiety on the part of future readers of your code, who will fret about the relative precedences of the multiple sigils, and of the indexing brackets and braces. Or they will misread the leading $$... sequence as being related to the $$ (a.k.a. $PID) variable—especially in string interpolations:

```
print "Your current ID is: JAPH_$$_ID_REF\n";
```

Braced references are always visually unambiguous:

```
print "Your current ID is: JAPH_${$_ID_REF}\n";
```

And they give the reader better clues as to the internal structure of dereference:

```
push @{$list_ref}, @results;

print substr(${$str_ref}, 0, $max_cols);

my $first = ${$list_ref}[0];
my @rest  = @{$list_ref}[1..$MAX];

my $first_name = ${$name_ref}{$first};
my ($initial, $last_name) = @{$name_ref}{$middle, $last};

print @{${$ref_to_list_ref}}[1..$MAX];
```

In some cases, bracketing can prevent subtle errors caused by the ambiguity of human expectations:

```
my $result = $$$stack_ref[0];
```

By which the programmer may have intended:

```
my $result = ${${$stack_ref[0]}};
```

or:

```
my $result = ${${$stack_ref}[0]};
```

or:

```
my $result = ${${$stack_ref}}[0];
```

If you're not entirely sure which of those three alternatives the unbracketed $$$stack_ref[0] is actually equivalent to*, that illustrates precisely how important it is to use the explicit braces. Or, better still, to unpack the reference in stages:

```
my $direct_stack_ref = ${$stack_ref};
my $result = $direct_stack_ref->[0];
```

---

* $$$stack_ref[0] is the same as ${${$stack_ref}}[0]. Indexing brackets are of lower precedence than sigils.

Symbolic References

Never use symbolic references.

If use `strict 'refs'` isn't in effect, a string containing the name of a variable can be used to access that variable:

```
my $hash_name = 'tag';

${$hash_name}{nick}   = ${nick};
${$hash_name}{rank}   = ${'rank'}[-1];      # Most recent rank
${$hash_name}{serial} = ${'serial_num'};
```

You can even use the arrow notation on a plain string to get the same effect:

```
my $hash_name = 'tag';

$hash_name->{nick}   = ${nick};
$hash_name->{rank}   = 'rank'->[-1];
$hash_name->{serial} = ${'serial_num'};
```

A string used in this way is known as a *symbolic reference*. It's called that because when Perl encounters a string where it was expecting a reference, it uses the string to look up the local symbol table and find an entry for the relevant variable of the same name.

Hence the previous examples (assuming they are in package `main`) are both equivalent to:

```
(*{$main::{$hash_name}}{HASH})->{nick}   = ${*{$main::{'nick'}}{SCALAR}};
(*{$main::{$hash_name}}{HASH})->{rank}   = *{$main::{'rank'}}{ARRAY}->[-1];
(*{$main::{$hash_name}}{HASH})->{serial} = ${*{$main::{'serial_num'}}{SCALAR}};
```

(For the viewers at home, the breakdown of that first line is shown in Figure 11-1. "Breakdown" being the operative word here.)

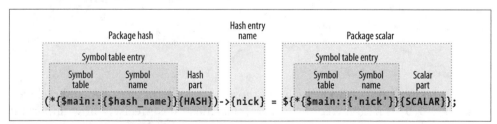

Figure 11-1. Symbolic reference breakdown

You'd never willingly write complex, unreadable code like that. So don't write code that's surreptitiously equivalent to it.

The example deconstruction illustrates that a symbolic reference looks up the name of a variable in the current package's symbol table. That means that a symbol reference can only ever refer to a package variable. And since you won't be using package variables in your own development (see Chapter 5), that will only lead to confusion. For example:

```
# Create help texts...
Readonly my $HELP_CD  => 'change directory';
Readonly my $HELP_LS  => 'list directory';
Readonly my $HELP_RM  => 'delete file';
Readonly my $NO_HELP  => 'No help available';

# Request and read in next topic...
while (my $topic = prompt 'help> ') {
    # Prepend "HELP_", find the corresponding variable (symbolically),
    # and display the help text it contains...
    if (defined ${"HELP_\U$topic"}) {
        print ${"HELP_\U$topic"}, "\n";
    }
    # Otherwise, display an unhelpful message...
    else {
        print "$NO_HELP\n";
    }
}
```

The `${"HELP_\U$topic"}` variable interpolates the requested topic (`$topic`) into a string, capitalizing the topic as it does so (`\U$topic`). It then uses the resulting string as the name of a variable and looks up the variable in the current symbol table.

Unfortunately, the desired help text won't *ever* be in the current symbol table; all the help texts were assigned to lexical variables, which don't live in symbol table entries.

The use of symbolic references almost always indicates a misdesign of the program's data structures. Rather than package variables located via symbolic references, what is almost always needed is a simple, lexical hash:

```
# Create table of help texts and default text...
Readonly my %HELP => (
    CD => 'change directory',
    LS => 'list directory',
    RM => 'delete file',
);

Readonly my $NO_HELP => 'No help available';

# Request and read in next topic...
while (my $topic = prompt 'help> ') {
    # Look up requested topic in help table and display it...
    if (exists $HELP{uc $topic}) {
        print $HELP{uc $topic}, "\n";
    }
    # Otherwise, be helpless...
    else {
        print "$NO_HELP\n";
    }
}
```

Cyclic References

Use weaken to prevent circular data structures from leaking memory.

Actual circular linked lists are quite rare in most Perl applications, mainly because they're generally not an efficient solution. Nor are they particularly easy to implement. Generally speaking, a standard Perl array with a little added "modulo length" logic is a cleaner, simpler, and more robust solution. For example:

```
{
    # Make variables "private" by declaring them in a limited scope
    my @buffer;
    my $next = -1;

    # Get the next element stored in our cyclic buffer...
    sub get_next_cyclic {
        $next++;                    # ...increment cursor
        $next %= @buffer;           # ...wrap around if at end of array
        return $buffer[$next];      # ...return next element
    }

    # Grow the cyclic buffer by inserting new element(s)...
    sub insert_cyclic {
        # At next pos (or start): remove zero elems, then insert args...
        splice @buffer, max(0,$next), 0, @_;

        return;
    }

    # etc.
}
```

However, circular data structures are still surprisingly easy to create. The commonest way is to have "owner" back-links in a hierarchical data structure. That is, if container nodes have references to the data nodes they own, and each data node has a reference back to the node that owns it, then you have cyclic references.

Non-hierarchical data can also easily develop circularities. Many kinds of bidirectional data relationships (such as peer/peer, supplier/consumer, client/server, or event callbacks) are modeled with links in both directions, to provide convenient and efficient navigation within the data structure.

Sometimes the cycle may not even be explicitly set up (or even intentional); sometimes it may just "fall out" of a natural arrangement of data*. For example:

---

* So it's something you need to watch for whenever you're setting up complex data structures.

```perl
# Create a new bank account...
sub new_account {
    my ($customer, $id, $type) = @_;

    # Account details are stored in anonymous hashes...
    my $new_account = {
        customer  => $customer,
        id        => generate_account_num( ),
        type      => $type,
        user_id   => $id,
        passwd    => generate_initial_passwd( ),
    };

    # The new account is then added to the customer's list of accounts...
    push @{$customer->{accounts}}, $new_account;

    return $new_account;
}
```

In the resulting data structure, each customer ($customer) is really a reference to a hash, in which the "accounts" entry ($customer->{accounts}) is a reference to an array, in which the most recently added element ($customer->{accounts}[-1]) is a reference to a hash, in which the value for the "customer" entry ($customer->{accounts}[-1]{customer}) is a reference back to the original customer hash. The great and mystical Circle Of Banking.

But even if it's stored in a lexical $customer variable, the allocated memory for this data structure will not be reclaimed when that variable goes out of scope. When $customer ceases to exist, the customer's hash will still be referred to by an entry in the hash that is referred to by an element of the array that is referred to by an entry in the customer's hash itself. The reference count of each of these variables is still (at least) one, so none of them is garbage collected.

Fortunately, in Perl 5.6 and later, it's easy to "weaken" references in order to break this chain of mutual dependency:

```perl
use Scalar::Util qw( weaken );

# Create a new bank account...
sub new_account {
    my ($customer, $id, $type) = @_;

    # Account details are stored in anonymous hashes...
    my $new_account = {
        customer  => $customer,
        id        => generate_account_num( ),
        type      => $type,
        user_id   => $id,
        passwd    => generate_initial_passwd( ),
    };
```

```
    # The new account is then added to the customer's list of accounts...
    push @{$customer->{accounts}},
        $new_account;

    # Make the backlink in the customer's newest account
    # invisible to the garbage collector...
    weaken $customer->{accounts}[-1]{customer};

    return $new_account;
}
```

The weaken function can be exported from Scalar::Util under Perl 5.8 and later (or from the WeakRef CPAN module if you're running under Perl 5.6). You pass weaken one argument, which must be a reference. It marks that reference as no longer contributing to the garbage collector's reference count for whatever referent the reference refers to. In other words, weaken artificially reduces the reference count of a referent by one, but without removing the reference itself.

In the second version of the example, the customer hash originally had a reference count of 2 (one reference to it in the $customer variable itself, and another reference in the nested hash entry $customer->{accounts}[-1]{customer}). Executing the line:

```
    weaken $customer->{accounts}[-1]{customer};
```

reduces that reference count from two to one, but leaves the second reference still in the nested hash. It's now as if only $customer referred to the hash, with $customer->{accounts}[-1]{customer} being a kind of "stealth reference", cruising along undetected below the garbage collector's radar.

That means that when $customer goes out of scope, the reference count of the customer hash will be decremented as normal, but now it will decrement to zero, at which point the garbage collector will immediately reclaim the hash. Whereupon each hash reference stored in the array in $customer->{accounts} will also cease to exist, so the reference counts of those hashes will also be decremented, once again, to zero. So they're cleaned up too.

Note also that a weakened reference automatically converts itself to an undef when its referent is garbage-collected, so there is no chance of creating a nasty "dangling pointer" if the weakened reference happens to be in some external variable that isn't garbage-collected along with the data structure.

By weakening any backlinks in your data structures, you keep the advantages of bidirectional navigation, but also retain the benefits of proper garbage collection.

## CHAPTER 12

Regular Expressions

> *Some people, when confronted with a problem, think:*
> *"I know, I'll use regular expressions".*
> *Now they have two problems.*
> —Jamie Zawinski

Regular expressions are one of the signature features of Perl, providing it with most of the practical extraction facilities for which it is famous. Many of those who are new to Perl (and many who aren't so new) approach regexes with mistrust, trepidation, or outright fear.

And with some justification. Regexes are specified in a compact and sometimes baroque syntax that is, all by itself, responsible for much of Perl's "executable line noise" reputation. Moreover, in the right hands, patterns are capable of performing mystifying feats of text recognition, analysis, transformation, and computation*.

It's no wonder they scare so many otherwise stalwart Perl hackers.

And no surprise that they also figure heavily in many suboptimal programming practices, especially of the "cut-and-paste" variety. Or, more often, of the "cut-and-paste-and-modify-slightly-and-oh-now-it-doesn't-work-at-all-so-let's-modify-it-some-more-and-see-if-that-helps-no-it-didn't-but-we're-committed-now-so-maybe-if-we-change-that-bit-instead-hmmmm-that's-closer-but-still-not-quite-right-maybe-if-I-made-that-third-repetition-non-greedy-instead-oops-now-it's-back-to-not-matching-at-all-perhaps-I-should-just-post-it-to-PerlMonks.org-and-see-if-they-know-what's-wrong" variety.

Yet the secret to taming regular expressions is remarkably simple. You merely have to recognize them for what they really are, and treat them accordingly.

---

* As anyone who has seen Abigail's virtuoso "prime number identifier" must surely agree:

```
sub is_prime {
    my ($number) = @_;
    return (1 x $number) !~ m/\A (?: 1? | (11+?) (?> \1+ ) ) \Z/xms;
}
```

(Working out precisely how this regex works its wonders is left as a punishment for the reader.)

And what are regular expressions really? They're subroutines. Text-matching subroutines. Text-matching subroutines that are coded in an embedded programming language that's nearly entirely unrelated to Perl.

Once you realize that regexes are just code, it becomes obvious that regex best practices will, for the most part, simply be adaptations of the universal coding best practices described in other chapters: consistent and readable layout, sensible naming conventions, decomposition of complex code, refactoring of commonly used constructs, choosing robust defaults, table-based techniques, code reuse, and test-driven development.

This chapter illustrates how those approaches can be applied to improving the readability, robustness, and efficiency of your regular expressions.

Extended Formatting

Always use the /x flag.

Because regular expressions are really just programs, all the arguments in favour of careful code layout that were advanced in Chapter 2 must apply equally to regexes. And possibly more than equally, since regexes are written in a language much "denser" than Perl itself.

At very least, it's essential to use whitespace to make the code more readable, and comments to record your intent[*]. Writing a pattern like this:

```
m{'[^\\']*(?:\\.[^\\']*)*'}
```

is no more acceptable than writing a program like this:

```
sub'x{local$_=pop;sub'_{$_>=$_[0
]?$_[1]:$"}_(1,'*')._(5,'-')._(4
,'*').$/._(6,'|').($_>9?'X':$_>8
?'/':$")._(8,'|').$/._(2,'*')._(
7,'-')._(3,'*').$/}print$/x($=).
x(10)x(++$x/10).x($x%10)while<>;
```

And no more readable, or maintainable.

The /x mode allows regular expressions to be laid out and annotated in a maintainable manner. Under /x mode, whitespace in your regex is ignored (i.e., it no longer matches the corresponding whitespace character), so you're free to use spaces and newlines for indentation and layout, as you do in regular Perl code. The # character is also special under /x. Instead of matching a literal '#', it introduces a normal Perl comment.

---

[*] Particularly as regular expressions so often fail precisely because the coder's intent is not accurately translated into their patterns.

For example, the pattern shown previously could be rewritten like so:

```
# Match a single-quoted string efficiently...

m{ '               # an opening single quote
   [^\\']*         # any non-special chars (i.e., not backslash or single quote)
   (?:             # then all of...
       \\ .        #    any explicitly backslashed char
      [^\\']*      #    followed by any non-special chars
   )*              # ...repeated zero or more times
   '               # a closing single quote
}x
```

That may still not be pretty, but at least it's now survivable.

Some people argue that the /x flag should be used only when a regular expression exceeds some particular threshold of complexity, such as only when it won't fit on a single line. But, as with all forms of code, regular expressions tend to grow in complexity over time. So even "simple" regexes will eventually need a /x, which will most likely *not* be retrofitted when the pattern reaches the particular complexity threshold you are using.

Besides, setting some arbitrary threshold of complexity makes both coding and maintenance harder. If you always use /x, then you can train your fingers to type it automatically for you, and you never need to think about it again. That's much more efficient and reliable than having to consciously[*] assess each regex you write to determine whether it merits the flag. And when you're maintaining the code, if you can rely on every regex having a /x flag, then you never have to check whether a particular regex is or isn't using the flag, and you never have to mentally switch regex "dialects".

In other words, it's perfectly okay to use the /x flag only when a regular expression exceeds some particular threshold of complexity…so long as you set that particular threshold at zero.

Line Boundaries

Always use the /m flag.

In addition to always using the /x flag, always use the /m flag. In every regular expression you ever write.

The normal behaviour of the ^ and $ metacharacters is unintuitive to most programmers, especially if they're coming from a Unix background. Almost all of the Unix utilities that feature regular expressions (e.g., *sed*, *grep*, *awk*) are intrinsically

---

[*] Or, worse still, *un*consciously.

line-oriented. So in those utilities, ^ and $ naturally mean "match at the start of any line" and "match at the end of any line", respectively.

But they don't mean that in Perl.

In Perl, ^ and $ mean "match at the start of the entire *string*" and "match at the end of the entire *string*". That's a crucial difference, and one that leads to a very common type of mistake:

```
# Find the end of a Perl program...

$text =~ m{ [^\0]*?        # match the minimal number of non-null chars
            ^__END__$      # until a line containing only an end-marker
          }x;
```

In fact, what that code really does is:

```
$text =~ m{ [^\0]*?        # match the minimal number of non-null chars
            ^              # until the start of the string
            __END__        # then match the end-marker
            $              # then match the end of the string
          }x;
```

The minimal number of characters until the start of the string is, of course, zero[*]. Then the regex has to match '__END__'. And then it has to be at the end of the string. So the only strings that this pattern matches are those that consist of '__END__'. That is clearly not what was intended.

The /m mode makes ^ and $ work "naturally"[†]. Under /m, ^ no longer means "match at the start of the string"; it means "match at the start of any line". Likewise, $ no longer means "at end of string"; it means "at end of any line".

The previous example could be fixed by making those two metacharacters actually mean what the original developer thought they meant, simply by adding a /m:

```
# Find the end of a Perl program...

$text =~ m{ [^\0]*?        # any non-nulls
            ^__END__$      # until an end-marker line
          }xm;
```

Which now really means:

```
$text =~ m{ [^\0]*?        # match the minimal number of chars
            ^              # until the start of any line (/m mode)
            __END__        # then match the end-marker
            $              # then match the end of a line (/m mode)
          }xm;
```

----

[*] "What part of 'the start' don't you understand???"

[†] That is, it makes them work in the unnatural way in which most programmers think they work.

Consistently using the /m on every regex makes Perl's behaviour consistently conform to your unreasonable expectations. So you don't have to unreasonably change your expectations to conform to Perl's behaviour[*].

String Boundaries

Use \A and \z as string boundary anchors.

Even if you don't adopt the previous practice of always using /m, using ^ and $ with their default meanings is a bad idea. Sure, *you* know what ^ and $ actually mean in a Perl regex. But will those who read or maintain your code know? Or is it more likely that they will misinterpret those metacharacters in the ways described earlier?

Perl provides markers that always—and unambiguously—mean "start of string" and "end of string": \A and \z (capital A, but lowercase z). They mean "start/end of string" regardless of whether /m is active. They mean "start/end of string" regardless of what the reader thinks ^ and $ mean.

They also stand out well. They're unusual. They're likely to be unfamiliar to the readers of your code, in which case those readers will have to look them up, rather than blithely misunderstanding them.

So rather than:

```
# Remove leading and trailing whitespace...
$text =~ s{^ \s* | \s* $}{}gx;
```

use:

```
# Remove leading and trailing whitespace...
$text =~ s{\A \s* | \s* \z}{}gxm;
```

And when you later need to match line boundaries as well, you can just use ^ and $ "naturally":

```
# Remove leading and trailing whitespace, and any -- line...
$text =~ s{\A \s* | ^-- [^\n]* $ | \s* \z}{}gxm;
```

The alternative (in which ^ and $ each have three distinct meanings in different contexts) is unnecessarily cruel:

```
# Remove leading and trailing whitespace, and any -- line...
$text =~ s{^ \s* | (?m: ^-- [^\n]* $) | \s* $}{}gx;
```

---

[*] In *Maxims for Revolutionists* (1903), George Bernard Shaw observed: "The reasonable man adapts himself to the world; the unreasonable one persists in trying to adapt the world to himself. Therefore all progress depends on the unreasonable man." That is an equally deep and powerful approach to programming.

End of String

Use \z, not \Z, to indicate "end of string".

Perl provides a variant of the \z marker: \Z. Whereas lowercase \z means "match at end of string", capital \Z means "match an optional newline, then at end of string". This variant can occasionally be convenient, if you're working with line-based input, as you don't have to worry about chomping the lines first:

```
# Print contents of lines starting with --...
LINE:
while (my $line = <>) {
    next LINE if $line !~ m/ \A -- ([^\n]+) \Z/xm;
    print $1;
}
```

But using \Z introduces a subtle distinction that can be hard to detect when displayed in some fonts. It's safer to be more explicit: to stick with using \z, and say precisely what you mean:

```
# Print contents of lines starting with --...
LINE:
while (my $line = <>) {
    next LINE if $line !~ m/ \A -- ([^\n]+) \n? \z/xm;   # Might be newline at end
    print $1;
}
```

especially if what you actually meant was:

```
# Print contents of lines starting with -- (including any trailing newline!)...
LINE:
while (my $line = <>) {
    next LINE if $line !~ m/ \A -- ([^\n]* \n?) \z/xm;
    print $1;
}
```

Using \n? \z instead of \Z forces you to decide whether the newline is part of the output or merely part of the scenery.

Matching Anything

Always use the /s flag.

At this point, you might be starting to detect a pattern. Once again, the problem is that the dot metacharacter (.) doesn't mean what most people think it means. Most

---

people—even those who actually know better—habitually think of it as meaning: "match any character".

It's easy to forget that it doesn't really mean that, and accidentally write something like:

```
# Capture the source of a Perl program...

$text =~ m{\A          # From start of string...
           (.*?)       # ...match and capture any characters
           ^__END__$   # ...until the first __END__ line
         }xm;
```

But the dot metacharacter doesn't match newlines, so the only strings this regex will match are those that start with '__END__'. That's because the ^ (start-of-line) metacharacter can match only at the start of the string or after a newline. But the preceding dot metacharacter can never match a newline, so the only way the ^ can match is if the preceding dot matches a start-of-string. But the dot metacharacter never matches start-of-string, because dot always matches exactly one character and start-of-string isn't a character.

In other words, as with ^ and $, the default behaviour of the dot metacharacter fails to be *un*reasonable (i.e., to be what most people expect). Fortunately, however, dot can be made to conform to the typical programmer's unreasonable expectations, simply by adding the /s flag. Under /s mode, a dot really does match every character, including newline:

```
# Capture the source of a Perl program...

$text =~ m{\A          # From start of string...
           (.*?)       # ...match and capture any characters (including newlines!)
           ^__END__$   # ...until the first __END__ line
         }xms;
```

Of course, the question then becomes: if you always use /s, how do you get the normal "any char but newline" meaning of dot when you actually need it? As with many of these guidelines, you do it by saying explicitly what you mean. If you need to match any character that isn't a newline, that's just the complemented character class [^\n]:

```
# Delete comments....

$source_code =~ s{            # Substitute...
                   \#         # ...a literal octothorpe
                   [^\n]*     # ...followed by any number of non-newlines
                 }
                 {$SPACE}gxms; # Replacing it with a single space
```

Lazy Flags

Consider mandating the `Regexp::Autoflags` **module.**

It takes about a week to accustom your fingers to automatically typing /xms at the end of every regex. But, realistically, some programmers will still not have the discipline required to develop and foster that good habit.

An alternative is to allow (that is, require) them to use the Regexp::Autoflags CPAN module instead, at the start of every source file they create. That module will then automatically turn on /xms mode in every regex they write.

That is, if they put:

```
use Regexp::Autoflags;
```

at the start of their file, from that point on they can write regexes like:

```
$text =~ m{\A            # From start of string...
          (.*?)          # ...match and capture any characters (including newlines!)
          ^__END__$  # ...until the first __END__ line
         };
```

and:

```
$source_code =~ s{            # Substitute...
                  \#          # ...a literal octothorpe
                  [^\n]*      # ...followed by any number of non-newlines
                 }
                 {$SPACE}g;   # Replacing it with a single space
```

They won't have to remember to append the all-important /xms flags, because the Regexp::Autoflags module will have automatically applied them.

Of course, this merely replaces the need for one kind of discipline (always use /xms) with the requirement for another (always use Regexp::Autoflags). However, it's much easier to check whether a single module has been loaded at least once, than it is to verify that the right regex flags have been used everywhere.

Brace Delimiters

Use m{ . . . } **in preference to** / . . . / **in multiline regexes.**

You might have noticed that every regex in this book that spans more than a single line is delimited with braces rather than slashes. That's because it's much easier to identify the boundaries of the brace-delimited form, both by eye and from within an editor[*].

That ability is especially important in regexes where you need to match a literal slash, or in regexes which use many escape characters. For example, this:

```
Readonly my $C_COMMENT => qr{
    / \*    # Opening C comment delimiter
    .*?     # Smallest number of characters (C comments don't nest)
    \* /    # Closing delimiter
}xms;
```

is a little easier to read than the more heavily backslashed:

```
Readonly my $C_COMMENT => qr/
    \/ \*  # Opening C comment delimiter
    .*?     # Smallest number of characters (delims don't nest)
    \* \/  # Closing delimiter
/xms;
```

Using braces as delimiters can also be advantageous in single-line regexes that are heavily laden with slash characters. For example:

```
$source_code =~ s/ \/ \* (.*?) \* \/ //gxms;
```

is considerably harder to unravel than:

```
$source_code =~ s{ / \* (.*?) \* / }{}gxms;
```

In particular, a final empty {} as the replacement text is much easier to detect and decipher than a final empty //. Though, of course, it would be better still to write that substitution as:

```
$source_code =~ s{$C_COMMENT}{$EMPTY_STR}gxms;
```

to ensure maximum maintainability.

Using braces as regex delimiters has two other advantages. Firstly, in a substitution, the two "halves" of the operation can be placed on separate lines, to further distinguish them from each other. For example:

```
$source_code =~ s{$C_COMMENT}
                 {$EMPTY_STR}xms;
```

The second advantage is that raw braces "nest" correctly within brace delimiters, whereas raw slashes don't nest at all within slash-delimited patterns. This is a particular problem under the /x flag, because it means that a seemingly straightforward regex like:

```
# Parse a 'set' command in our mini-language...

m/
    set      \s+  # Keyword
```

---

[*] Most editors can be configured to jump to a matching brace (in *vi* it's %; in *Emacs* it's a little more complicated—see Appendix C). You can also set most editors to autohighlight matching braces as you type (set the blink-matching-paren variable in *Emacs*, or the showmatch option in *vi*).

```
        ($IDENT) \s*  # Name of file/option/mode
        =         \s*  # literal =
        ([^\n]*)       # Value of file/option/mode
    /xms;
```

is seriously (and subtly) broken. It's broken because the compiler first determines that the regex delimiter is a slash, so it looks ahead to locate the next unescaped slash in the source, and treats the intervening characters as the pattern. Then it looks for any trailing regex flags, after which it continues parsing the next part of the current expression.

Unfortunately, in the previous example, the next unescaped slash in the source is the first unescaped slash in the line:

```
        ($IDENT) \s*  # Name of file/option/mode
```

which means that the regex finishes at that point, causing the code to be parsed as if it were something like:

```
    m/
        set       \s+ # Keyword
        ($IDENT) \s* # Name of file/o

    ption( ) / mode( ) = \s*          # literal =
                         ([^\n( )]*)    # Value of file/option/mode
                         /xms( )
                    );
```

whereupon it complains bitterly about the illegal call to the (probably non-existent) ption( ) subroutine, when it was expecting an operator or semicolon after the end of that nice m/.../o pattern. It probably won't be too pleased about the incomplete s*. ..*...* substitution with the weird asterisk delimiters either, or the dodgy assignment to mode( ).

The problem is that programmers expect comments to have no compile-time semantics[*]. But, within a regex, a comment *becomes* a comment only *after* the parser has decided where the surrounding regex finishes. So a slash character that seems to be within a regex comment may actually be a slash delimiter in your code.

Using braces as delimiters significantly reduces the likelihood of encountering this problem:

```
    m{
        set       \s+  # Keyword
        ($IDENT) \s*  # Name of file/option/mode
        =         \s*  # literal =
        ([^\n]*)       # Value of file/option/mode
    }xms;
```

---

[*] That sentence originally read: *The problem is that programmers are used to ignoring the specific content of comments.* Which is depressingly true, but not the relevant observation here.

because the slashes are no longer special to the parser, which consequently parses the entire regex correctly. Furthermore, as matching braces may be nested inside a brace-delimited regex, this variation is okay too:

```
m{
    set         \s+  # Keyword
    ($IDENT)    \s*  # Name of file/option/mode
    =           \s*  # literal =
    \{               # literal {
    ([^\n]*)         # Value of file/option/mode
    \}               # literal }
}xms;
```

Of course, *unbalanced* raw braces still cause problems within regex comments:

```
m{
    set         \s+  # Keyword
    ($IDENT)    \s*  # Name of file/option/mode
    =           \s*  # literal =
    ([^\n]*)         # Value of file/option/mode
    \}               # literal }
}xms;
```

However, unlike /, unbalanced raw braces are not a valid English punctuation form, and hence they're far rarer within comments than slashes. Besides which, the error message that's generated by that particular mistake:

```
Unmatched right curly bracket at demo.pl line 49, at end of line
(Might be a runaway multi-line {} string starting on line 42)
```

is much clearer than the sundry lamentations the equivalent slash-delimited version would produce:

```
Bareword found where operator expected at demo.pl line 46,
near "($IDENT)     # File/option"
    (Might be a runaway multi-line // string starting on line 42)
    (Missing operator before ption?)
Backslash found where operator expected at demo.pl line 49,
near ")     # File/option/mode value \"
    (Missing operator before \?)
syntax error at demo.pl line 46, near "($IDENT)     # File/option"
Unmatched right curly bracket at demo.pl line 7, at end of line
```

So use m{...}xms in preference to /.../xms wherever possible. Indeed, the only reason to ever use slashes to delimit regexes is to improve the comprehensibility of short, embedded patterns. For example, within the blocks of list operations:

```
my @counts = map { m/(\d{4,8})/xms } @count_reports;
```

slashes are better than braces. A brace-delimited version of the same regex would be using braces to denote "code block", "regex boundary", *and* "repetition count", all within the space of 20 characters:

```
my @counts = map { m{(\d{4,8})}xms } @count_reports;
```

Using the slashes as the regex delimiters in this case increases the visual distinctiveness of the regex and thereby improves the overall readability of the code.

Other Delimiters

Don't use any delimiters other than / . . . / or m{ . . . }.

Although Perl allows you to use *any* non-whitespace character you like as a regex delimiter, don't. Because leaving some poor maintenance programmer to take care of (valid) code like this:

```
last TRY if !$!!~m!/pattern/!;
```

or this:

```
$same=m={===m=}=;
```

or this:

```
harry s truman was the 33rd u.s. president;
```

is just cruel.

Even with more reasonable delimiter choices:

```
last TRY if !$OS_ERROR !~ m!/pattern/!;

$same = m#{# == m#}#;

harry s|ruman was |he 33rd u.s. presiden|;
```

the boundaries of the regexes don't stand out well.

By sticking with the two recommended delimiters (and other best practices), you make your code more predictable, so it is easier for future readers to identify and understand your regexes:

```
last TRY if !$OS_ERROR !~ m{ /pattern/ }xms;

$same = ($str =~ m/{/xms  ==  $str =~ m/}/xms);

harry( $str =~ s{ruman was }{he 33rd u.s. presiden}xms );
```

Note that the same advice also applies to substitutions and transliterations: stick to s/.../.../xms or s{...}{...}xms, and tr/.../.../ or tr{...}{...}.

Metacharacters

Prefer singular character classes to escaped metacharacters.

Escaped metacharacters are harder to decipher, and harder to distinguish from their unescaped originals:

```
m/ \{ . \. \d{2} \} /xms;
```

The alternative is to put each metacharacter in its own tiny, one-character character class, like so:

```
m/ [{] . [.] \d{2} [}] /xms;
```

Once you're familiar with this convention, it's very much easier to see the literal metacharacters when they're square-bracketed. That's particularly true for spaces under the /x flag. For example, the literal spaces to be matched in:

```
$name =~ m{ harry [ ] s [ ] truman
          | harry [ ] j [ ] potter
          }ixms;
```

stand out much better than those in:

```
$name =~ m{ harry \ s \ truman
          | harry \ j \ potter
          }ixms;
```

Note, however, that this approach can reduce the optimizer's ability to accelerate pattern matching under some versions of Perl. If benchmarking (see Chapter 19) indicates that this may be a problem for you, try the alternative approach suggested in the next guideline.

Named Characters

Prefer named characters to escaped metacharacters.

As an alternative to the previous guideline, Perl 5.6 (and later) supports named characters in regexes. As previously discussed*, this mechanism is much better for "unprintable" components of a regex. For example, instead of:

```
if ($escape_seq =~ /\177 \006 \030 Z/xms) {   # Octal DEL-ACK-CAN-Z
    blink(182);
}
```

---

* "Escaped Characters" in Chapter 4.

use:

```
use charnames qw( :full );

if ($escape_seq =~ m/\N{DELETE} \N{ACKNOWLEDGE} \N{CANCEL} Z/xms) {
    blink(182);
}
```

Note, however that named whitespace characters are treated like ordinary whitespace (i.e., they're ignored) under the /x flag:

```
use charnames qw( :full );

# and later...

$name =~ m{ harry \N{SPACE} s \N{SPACE} truman       # harrystruman
         | harry \N{SPACE} j \N{SPACE} potter        # harryjpotter
         }ixms;
```

You would still need to put them in characters classes to make them match:

```
use charnames qw( :full );

# and later...

$name =~ m{ harry [\N{SPACE}] s [\N{SPACE}] truman     # harry s truman
         | harry [\N{SPACE}] j [\N{SPACE}] potter      # harry j potter
         }ixms;
```

Properties

Prefer properties to enumerated character classes.

Explicit character classes are frequently used to match character ranges, especially alphabetics. For example:

```
# Alphabetics-only identifier...
Readonly my $ALPHA_IDENT => qr/ [A-Z] [A-Za-z]* /xms;
```

However, a character class like that doesn't actually match all possible alphabetics. It matches only ASCII alphabetics. It won't recognize the common Latin-1 variants, let alone the full gamut of Unicode alphabetics.

That result might be okay, if you're sure your data will never be other than parochial, but in today's post-modern, multicultural, outsourced world it's rather déclassé for an überhacking rō nin to create identifier regexes that won't even match 'déclassé' or 'überhacking' or 'rōnin'.

Regular expressions in Perl 5.6 and later* support the use of the \p{...} escape, which allows you to use full Unicode *properties*. Properties are Unicode-compliant named character classes and are both more general and more self-documenting than explicit ASCII character classes. The *perlunicode* manpage explains the mechanism in detail and lists the available properties.

So, if you're ready to concede that ASCII-centrism is a naïve façade that's gradually fading into Götterdämmerung, you might choose to bid it adiós and open your regexes to the full Unicode smörgåsbord, by changing the previous identifier regex to:

```
Readonly my $ALPHA_IDENT => qr/ \p{Uppercase}  \p{Alphabetic}* /xms;
```

There are even properties to help create identifiers that follow the normal Perl conventions but are still language-independent. Instead of:

```
Readonly my $PERL_IDENT => qr/ [A-Za-z_] \w*/xms;
```

you can use:

```
Readonly my $PERL_IDENT => qr/ \p{ID_Start} \p{ID_Continue}* /xms;
```

One other particularly useful property is \p{Any}, which provides a more readable alternative to the normal dot (.) metacharacter. For example, instead of:

```
m/ [{] . [.] \d{2} [}] /xms;
```

you could write:

```
m/ [{] \p{Any} [.] \d{2} [}] /xms;
```

and leave the reader in no doubt that the second character to be matched really can be anything at all—an ASCII alphabetic, a Latin-1 superscript, an Extended Latin diacritical, a Devanagari number, an Ogham rune, or even a Bopomofo symbol.

Whitespace

**Consider matching arbitrary whitespace,
rather than specific whitespace characters.**

Unless you're matching regular expressions against fixed-format machine-generated data, avoid matching specific whitespace characters exactly. Because if humans were directly involved anywhere in the data acquisition, then the notion of "fixed" will probably have been more honoured in the breach than in the observance.

---

* Perl's Unicode support was still highly experimental in the 5.6 releases, and has improved considerably since then. If you're intending to make serious use of Unicode in production code, you really need to be running the latest 5.8.X release you can, and at very least Perl 5.8.1.

If, for example, the input is supposed to consist of a label, followed by a single space, followed by an equals sign, followed by a single space, followed by an value…don't bet on it. Most users nowadays will—quite reasonably—assume that whitespace is negotiable; nothing more than an elastic formatting medium. So, in a configuration file, you're just as likely to get something like:

```
name        = Yossarian, J
rank        = Captain
serial_num = 3192304
```

The whitespaces in that data might be single tabs, multiple tabs, multiple spaces, single spaces, or any combination thereof. So matching that data with a pattern that insists on exactly one space character at the relevant points is unlikely to be uniformly successful:

```
$config_line =~ m{ ($IDENT)  [\N{SPACE}]  =  [\N{SPACE}]  (.*) }xms
```

Worse still, it's also unlikely to be uniformly unsuccessful. For instance, in the example data, it might only match the serial number. And that kind of intermittent success will make your program *much* harder to debug. It might also make it difficult to realize that any debugging is required.

Unless you're specifically vetting data to verify that it conforms to a required fixed format, it's much better to be very liberal in what you accept when it comes to whitespace. Use \s+ for any required whitespace and \s* for any optional whitespace. For example, it would be far more robust to match the example data against:

```
$config_line =~ m{ ($IDENT)  \s*  =  \s*  (.*) }xms
```

Unconstrained Repetitions

Be specific when matching "as much as possible".

The .* construct is a particularly blunt and ponderous weapon, especially under /s. For example, consider the following parser for some very simple language, in which source code, data, and configuration information are separated by % and & characters (which are otherwise illegal):

```
# Format is: <statements> % <data> & <config>...

if ($source =~ m/\A  (.*)  %  (.*)  &  (.*) /xms) {
    my ($statements, $data, $config) = ($1, $2, $3);

    my $prog = compile($statements, {config=>$config});
    my $res  = execute($prog, {data=>$data, config=>$config});
}
else {
    croak 'Invalid program';
}
```

Under /s, the first .* will successfully match the entire string in $source. Then it will attempt to match a %, and immediately fail (because there's none of the string left to match). At that point the regex engine will backtrack one character from the end of the string and try to match a % again, which will probably also fail. So it will backtrack one more character, try again, backtrack once more, try again, et cetera, et cetera, et cetera.

Eventually it will backtrack far enough to successfully match %, whereupon the second .* will match the remainder of the string, then fail to match &, backtrack one character, try again, fail again, and the entire "one-step-forward-two-steps-back" sequence will be played out again. Sequences of unconstrained matches like this can easily cause regular expression matches to become unacceptably slow.

Using a .*? can help in such cases:

```
if ($source =~ m/\A  (.*?)  %  (.*?)  &  (.*) /xms) {
    my ($statements, $data, $config) = ($1, $2, $3);

    my $prog = compile($statements, {config=>$config});
    my $res  = execute($prog, {data=>$data, config=>$config});
}
else {
    croak 'Invalid program';
}
```

since the "parsimonious repetitions" will then consume as little of the string as possible. But, to do this, they effectively have to do a look-ahead at every character they match, which can also become expensive if the terminator is more complicated than just a single character.

More importantly, both .* and .*? can also mask logical errors in the parsing process. For example, if the program incorrectly had an extra % or & in it, that would simply be consumed by one of the .* or .*? constructs, and therefore treated as part of the code or data, rather than as an error.

If you know precisely what character (or characters) the terminator of a "match anything" sequence will be, then it's very much more efficient—and clearer—to use a complemented character class instead:

```
# Format is: <source> % <data> & <config>...

if ($source =~ m/\A  ([^%]*)  %  ([^&]*)  &  (.*) /xms) {
    my ($statements, $data, $config) = ($1, $2, $3);

    my $prog = compile($statements, {config=>$config});
    my $res  = execute($prog, {data=>$data, config=>$config});
}
else {
    croak 'Invalid program';
}
```

This version matches every non-% (using [^%]*), followed by a %, followed by every non-& (via [^&]*), followed by a &, followed by the rest of the string (.*). The principal advantage is that the complemented character classes don't have to do per-character look-ahead like .*?, nor per-character backtracking like .*. Nor will this version allow an extra % in the source or & in the data. Once again, you're encoding your exact intentions.

Note that the .* at the end of the regex is still perfectly okay. When it finally gets its chance and gobbles up the rest of the source, the match will then be finished, so no backtracking will ever occur. On the other hand, putting a.*? at the end of a regular expression is *always* a mistake, as it will always successfully match nothing, at which point the pattern match will succeed and then terminate. A final .*? is either redundant, or it's not doing what you intended, or you forgot a \z anchor.

Capturing Parentheses

Use capturing parentheses only when you intend to capture.

It's a waste of processor cycles to capture a substring you don't need. More importantly, it's misleading to do so. When the unfortunates who have to maintain the following code see:

```
if ( $cmd =~ m/\A (q | quit | bye | exit) \n? \z/xms ) {
    perform_cleanup();
    exit;
}
```

they will almost certainly start casting around to determine where $1 is used (perhaps for an exit confirmation request, or inside perform_cleanup()).

They'll be rightly annoyed when they eventually discover that $1 isn't used anywhere. Because now they can't be sure whether that indicates a bug, or was just laziness on the part of the original coder. Hence, they'll probably have to re-examine the logic of perform_cleanup() to determine whether that unused capture is actually A.W.O.L. And that's a waste of maintainer cycles.

Perl provides a form of regex parentheses that deliberately don't capture: the (?:...) parentheses. If the previous example had been written:

```
if ( $cmd =~ m/\A (?:q | quit | bye | exit) \n? \z/xms ) {
    perform_cleanup();
    exit;
}
```

then there would be no doubt that the parentheses were being used simply to group the four alternative "exit" commands, rather than to capture the particular "exit" command used.

Use non-capturing parentheses by default, and reserve capturing parentheses for when you need to make use of some part of a matched string. That way, your coded instructions will also encode your intentions, which is a much more robust and effective style of programming.

Captured Values

Use the numeric capture variables only when you're sure that the preceding match succeeded.

Pattern matches that fail never assign anything to $1, $2, etc., nor do they leave those variables undefined. After an unsuccessful pattern match, the numeric capture variables remain exactly as they were before the match was attempted. Often, that means that they retain whatever values some *earlier* successful pattern match gave them.

So you can't test whether a pattern has matched by testing the numeric capture variables directly. A common mistake along those lines is to write something like:

```
$full_name =~ m/\A (Mrs?|Ms|Dr) \s+ (\S+) \s+ (\S+) \z/xms;

if (defined $1) {
    ($title, $first_name, $last_name) = ($1, $2, $3);
}
```

The problem is that, if the match fails, $1 may still have been set by some earlier successful match in the same scope, in which case the three variables would be assigned capture values left over from that previous match.

Captured values should be used only when it's certain they actually were captured. The easiest way to ensure that is to always put capturing matches inside some kind of preliminary boolean test. For example:

```
if ($full_name =~ m/\A (Mrs?|Ms|Dr) \s+ (\S+) \s+ (\S+) \z/xms) {
    ($title, $first_name, $last_name) = ($1, $2, $3);
}
```

or:

```
next NAME if $full_name !~ m/\A (Mrs?|Ms|Dr) \s+ (\S+) \s+ (\S+) \z/xms;

($title, $first_name, $last_name) = ($1, $2, $3);
```

Capture Variables

Always give captured substrings proper names.

$1, $2, etc. are dreadful names for variables. Like the parameter variables $_[0], $_[1], etc. (see "Named Arguments" in Chapter 9), they convey absolutely nothing about the values they store, except the order in which they occurred. They produce unreadable code like this:

```
CONFIG_LINE:
while (my $config = <>) {
    # Ignore lines that are unrecognisable...
    next CONFIG_LINE
        if $config !~ m/ \A  (\S+)  \s* = \s*  ([^;]+) ;  \s* \# (.*)/xms;

    # Verify the option makes sense...
    debug($3);
    croak "Unknown option ($1)"
        if not exists $option{$2};

    # Record the configuration option...
    $option{$2} = $1;
}
```

As the capture variables don't have meaningful names, it's much harder to work out what this code is actually doing, and to verify that it's correct. (It's not.)

Because numbered variables suffer from the same drawbacks as numbered arguments, it's not surprising that the solution is the same, too: simply unpack $1, $2, etc. into sensibly named variables immediately after a successful match. Doing that makes the purpose—and the errors—much more obvious:

```
CONFIG_LINE:
while (my $config = <>) {
    # Ignore lines that are unrecognisable...
    next CONFIG_LINE
        if $config !~ m/ \A  (\S+)  \s* = \s*  ([^;]+) ;  \s* \# (.*)/xms;

    # Name captured components...
    my ($opt_name, $opt_val, $comment) = ($1, $2, $3);

    # Verify the option makes sense...
    debug($comment);
    croak "Unknown option ($opt_name)"
        if not exists $option{$opt_val};   # Oops: value used as key

    # Record the configuration option...
    $option{$opt_val} = $opt_name;         # Oops*2: value as key; name as value
}
```

That, in turn, makes the code far easier to correct:

```
CONFIG_LINE:
while (my $config = <>) {
    # Ignore lines that are unrecognisable...
    next CONFIG_LINE
        if $config !~ m/ \A  (\S+)  \s* = \s*  ([^;]+) ;  \s* \# (.*)/xms;

    # Name captured components...
    my ($opt_name, $opt_val, $comment) = ($1, $2, $3);

    # Verify that the option makes sense...
    debug($comment);
    croak "Unknown option ($opt_name)"
        if not exists $option{$opt_name};  # Name used as key

    # Record the configuration option...
    $option{$opt_name} = $opt_val;          # Names as key; value as value
}
```

Naming the captures improves maintainability in another way too. If it later became necessary to capture some other piece of the match, some of the numbered variables might change number. For example, suppose you needed to support appending to an option as well as assigning. Then you'd need to capture the operator as well. The original code would have become:

```
CONFIG_LINE:
while (my $config = <>) {
    # Ignore lines that are unrecognisuble...
    next CONFIG_LINE
        if $config !~ m/\A (\S+) \s* (=|[+]=) \s* ([^;]+) ; \s* \# (.*)/xms;

    # Verify that the option makes sense...
    debug($4);
    croak "Unknown option ($1)"
        if not exists $option{$1};

    # Replace or append value depending on specified operator...
    if ($2 eq '=') {
        $option{$1} = $3;
    }
    else {
        $option{$1}.= $3;
    }
}
```

The Variable Formerly Known As $2 is now $3, and the old $3 is now $4. The odds of correctly managing that code change diminish rapidly as the size of the if block—or the number of captures—increases. But, if the captures are unpacked into named variables, then *none* of the previous names needs to change when a new capture is added:

```
CONFIG_LINE:
while (my $config = <>) {
```

```perl
        # Ignore lines that are unrecognisable...
        next CONFIG_LINE
            if $config !~ m/\A (\S+) \s* (=|[+]=) \s* ([^;]+) ; \s* \# (.*)/xms;

        # Unpack the components of the config line...
        my ($opt_name, $operator, $opt_val, $comment) = ($1, $2, $3, $4);

        # Verify that the option makes sense...
        debug($comment);
        croak "Unknown option ($opt_name)"
            if not exists $option{$opt_name};

        # Replace or append value depending on specified operator...
        if ($operator eq '=') {
            $option{$opt_name} = $opt_val;
        }
        else {
            $option{$opt_name}.= $opt_val;
        }
    }
```

Better still, Perl provides a way to assign captured substrings directly to named variables, without ever mentioning the numbered variables explicitly. If a regex match is performed in a list context, the list it returns is the list of captures that it made. That is, a match in a list context returns the list ($1, $2, $3, *etc.*). Those captures can then be unpacked directly, like so:

```perl
CONFIG_LINE:
while (my $config = <>) {
    # Match config line in list context, capturing components into named vars...
    my ($opt_name, $operator, $opt_val, $comment)
        = $config =~ m/\A (\S+) \s* (=|[+]=) \s* ([^;]+) ; \s* \# (.*)/xms;

    # Process line only if it was recognizable...
    next CONFIG_LINE if !defined $opt_name;

    # Verify that the option makes sense...
    debug($comment);
    croak "Unknown option ($opt_name)"
        if not exists $option{$opt_name};

    # Replace or append value depending on specified operator...
    if ($operator eq '=') {
        $option{$opt_name} = $opt_val;
    }
    else {
        $option{$opt_name}.= $opt_val;
    }
}
```

Capturing directly to named variables in this way avoids the possibility of introducing subtle unpacking mistakes such as:

```
    # Ignore lines that are unrecognisable...
    next CONFIG_LINE
        if $config !~ m/ \A  (\S+)  \s* (=|[+]=) \s*  ([^;]+) ;  \s* \# (.*)/xms;

    # Unpack the components of the config line...
    my ($opt_name, $operator, $opt_val, $comment) = ($1, $2, $3);    # Missing $4!
```

because a match in a list context always returns all of its captures, not just the ones you remembered to specify explicitly.

List-context captures are the least error-prone way of extracting information from pattern matches and, hence, strongly recommended. Note, however, that list-context captures aren't appropriate for regexes that use the /gc modifier (see the following guideline, "Piecewise Matching").

Piecewise Matching

Tokenize input using the /gc flag.

The typical approach to breaking an input string into individual tokens is to "nibble" at it, repeatedly biting off the start of the input string with successive substitutions:

```
while (length $input > 0) {
    if ($input =~ s{\A ($KEYWORD)}{}xms) {
        my $keyword = $1;
        push @tokens, start_cmd($keyword);
    }
    elsif ($input =~ s{\A ($IDENT)}{}xms) {
        my $ident = $1;
        push @tokens, make_ident($ident);
    }
    elsif ($input =~ s{\A ($BLOCK)}{}xms) {
        my $block = $1;
        push @tokens, make_block($block);
    }
    else {
        my ($context) = $input =~ m/ \A ([^\n]*) /xms;
        croak "Error near: $context";
    }
}
```

But this approach requires a modification to the $input string on every successful match, which makes it expensive to start with, and then causes it to scale badly as well. Nibbling away at strings is slow and gets slower as the strings get bigger.

In Perl 5.004 and later, there's a much better way to use regexes for tokenizing an input: you can just "walk" the string, using the /gc flag. The /gc flag tells a regex to track where each successful match finishes matching. You can then access that "end-of-the-last-match" position via the built-in pos() function. There is also a \G metacharacter, which is a positional *anchor*, just like \A is. However, whereas \A tells the regex to match only at the start of the string, \G tells it to match only where the previous successful /gc match finished. If no previous /gc match was successful, \G acts like a \A and matches only at the start of the string.

All of which means that, instead of using a regex substitution to lop each token off the start of the string (s{\A...}{}), you can simply use a regex match to start looking for the next token at the point where the previous token match finished (m{\G...}gc).

So the previous tokenizer could be rewritten more efficiently as:

```
# Reset the matching position of $input to the beginning of the string...
pos $input = 0;

# ...and continue until the matching position is past the last character...
while (pos $input < length $input) {
    if ($input =~ m{ \G ($KEYWORD) }gcxms) {
        my $keyword = $1;
        push @tokens, start_cmd($keyword);
    }
    elsif ($input =~ m{ \G ( $IDENT) }gcxms) {
        my $ident = $1;
        push @tokens, make_ident($ident);
    }
    elsif ($input =~ m{ \G ($BLOCK) }gcxms) {
        my $block = $1;
        push @tokens, make_block($block);
    }
    else {
        $input =~ m/ \G ([^\n]*) /gcxms;
        my $context = $1;
        croak "Error near: $context";
    }
}
```

Of course, because this style of parsing inevitably spawns a series of cascaded if statements that all feed the same @tokens array, it's even better practice to use the ternary operator and create a "parsing table" (see "Tabular Ternaries" in Chapter 6):

```
while (pos $input < length $input) {
    push @tokens, (
                            # For token type...      # Build token...
          $input =~ m{ \G ($KEYWORD) }gcxms ? start_cmd($1)
        : $input =~ m{ \G ( $IDENT ) }gcxms ? make_ident($1)
        : $input =~ m{ \G ( $BLOCK ) }gcxms ? make_block($1)
        : $input =~ m{ \G ( [^\n]* ) }gcxms ? croak "Error near:$1"
        :                                     die 'Internal error'
    );
}
```

Note that these examples don't use direct list capturing to rename the capture variables (as recommended in the preceding guideline). Instead they pass $1 into a token-constructing subroutine immediately after the match. That's because a list capture

---

would cause the regex to match in list context, which would force the /g component of the flag to incorrectly match every occurrence of the pattern, rather than just the next one.

Tabular Regexes

Build regular expressions from tables.

Tables like the one shown at the end of the previous guideline are a cleaner way of structuring regex matches, but they can also be a cleaner way of building a regex in the first place—especially when the resulting regex will be used to extract keys for the table.

Don't duplicate existing table information as part of a regular expression:

```perl
# Table of irregular plurals...
my %irregular_plural_of = (
    'child'       => 'children',
    'brother'     => 'brethren',
    'money'       => 'monies',
    'mongoose'    => 'mongooses',
    'ox'          => 'oxen',
    'cow'         => 'kine',
    'soliloquy'   => 'soliloquies',
    'prima donna' => 'prime donne',
    'octopus'     => 'octopodes',
    'tooth'       => 'teeth',
    'toothfish'   => 'toothfish',
);

# Pattern matching any of those irregular plurals...
my $has_irregular_plural = qr{
    child     | brother    | mongoose
  | ox        | cow        | monkey
  | soliloquy | prima donna | octopus
  | tooth(?:fish)?
}xms;

# Form plurals...
while (my $word = <>) {
    chomp $word;

    if ($word =~ m/ ($has_irregular_plural) /xms) {
        print $irregular_plural_of{$word}, "\n";
    }
    else {
        print form_regular_plural_of($word), "\n";
    }
}
```

Apart from the annoying redundancy of specifying each key twice, this kind of duplication is a prime opportunity for mistakes to creep in. As they did—twice—in the previous example*.

It's much easier to ensure consistency between a look-up table and the regex that feeds it if the regex is automatically constructed from the table itself. That's relatively easy to achieve, by replacing the regex definition with:

```
# Build a pattern matching any of those irregular plurals...
my $has_irregular_plural
    = join '|', map {quotemeta $_} reverse sort keys %irregular_plural_of;
```

The assignment statement starts by extracting the keys from the table (keys %irregular_plural_of), then sorts them in reverse order (reverse sort keys %irregular_plural_of). Sorting them is critical because the order in which hash keys are returned is unpredictable, so there's a 50/50 chance that the key 'tooth' will appear in the key list before the key 'toothfish'. That would be unfortunate, because the list of keys is about to be converted to a list of alternatives, and regexes always match the left-most alternative first. In that case, the word "toothfish" would always be matched by the alternative 'tooth', rather than by the later alternative 'toothfish'.

Once the keys are in a reliable order, the map operation escapes any metacharacters within the keys (map {quotemeta $_} keys %irregular_plural_of). This step ensures, for example, that 'prima donna' becomes 'prima\ donna', and so behaves correctly under the /x flag. The various alternatives are then joined together with standard "or" markers to produce the full pattern.

Setting up this automated process takes a little extra effort, but it significantly improves the robustness of the resulting code. Not only does it eliminate the possibility of mismatches between the table keys and the regex alternatives, it also makes extending the table a one-step operation: just add the new singular/plural pair to the initialization of %irregular_plural_of; the pattern in $has_irregular_plural will automatically reconfigure itself accordingly.

About the only way the code could be further improved would be to factor out the hairy regex-building statements into a subroutine:

```
# Build a pattern matching any of the arguments given...
sub regex_that_matches {
    return join '|', map {quotemeta $_} reverse sort @_;
}

# and later...
```

---

* The regular expression shown matches 'monkey', but the particular irregular noun it's supposed to match in that case is 'money'. The regex also matches 'primadonna' instead of 'prima donna', because the /x flag makes the intervening space non-significant within the regex.

```
my $has_irregular_plural
    = regex_that_matches(keys %irregular_plural_of);
```

Note that—as is so often the case—refactoring shaggy code in this way not only cleans up the source in which the statements were formerly used, but also makes the refactored statements themselves a little less hirsute.

Note that if you're in some strange locale where strings with common prefixes don't sort shortest-to-longest, then you may need to be more specific (but less efficient) about your sorting order, by including an explicit length comparison in your sort block:

```
# Build a pattern matching any of the arguments given...
sub regex_that_matches {
    return join '|',
                map {quotemeta $_}
                    # longest strings first, otherwise alphabetically...
                    sort { length($b) <=> length($a) or $a cmp $b }
                        @_;
}

# and later...

my $has_irregular_plural
    = regex_that_matches(keys %irregular_plural_of);
```

Constructing Regexes

Build complex regular expressions from simpler pieces.

Building a regular expression from the keys of a hash is a special case of a much more general best practice. Most worthwhile regexes—even those for simple tasks—are still too tedious or too complicated to code directly. For example, to extract the components of a number, you could write:

```
my ($number, $sign, $digits, $exponent)
    = $input =~ m{ (                         # Capture entire number
                    ( [+-]? )                # Capture leading sign (if any)
                    ( \d+ (?: [.] \d*)?      # Capture mantissa: NNN.NNN
                    | [.] \d+                #                or:    .NNN
                    )
                    ( (?:[Ee] [+-]? \d+)? )  # Capture exponent (if any)
                  )
                }xms;
```

Even with the comments, that pattern is bordering on unreadable. And checking that it works as advertised is highly non-trivial.

But a regular expression is really just a program, so all the arguments in favour of program decomposition (see Chapter 9) apply to regexes too. In particular, it's often better to decompose a complex regular expression into manageable (named) fragments, like so:

```
# Build a regex that matches floating point representations...
Readonly my $DIGITS    => qr{ \d+ (?: [.] \d*)? | [.] \d+        }xms;
Readonly my $SIGN      => qr{ [+-]                               }xms;
Readonly my $EXPONENT  => qr{ [Ee] $SIGN? \d+                    }xms;
Readonly my $NUMBER    => qr{ ( ($SIGN?) ($DIGITS) ($EXPONENT?) ) }xms;

# and later...

my ($number, $sign, $digits, $exponent)
    = $input =~ $NUMBER;
```

Here, the full $NUMBER regex is built up from simpler components ($DIGITS, $SIGN, and $EXPONENT), much in the same way that a full Perl program is built from simpler subroutines. Notice that, once again, refactoring cleans up both the refactored code itself and the place that code is later used.

Note, however, that interpolating qr'd regexes inside other qr'd regexes (as in the previous example) may impose a performance penalty in some cases. That's because when the component regexes are interpolated, they are first decompiled back to strings, then interpolated, and finally recompiled. Unfortunately, the conversion of the individual components back to strings is not optimized, and will sometimes produce less efficient patterns, which are then recompiled into less efficient regexes.

The alternative is to use q{} or qq{} strings to specify the components. Using strings ensures that what you write in a component is exactly what's later interpolated from it:

```
# Build a regex that matches floating-point representations...
Readonly my $DIGITS    =>  q{ (?: \d+ (?: [.] \d*)? | [.] \d+   ) };
Readonly my $SIGN      =>  q{ (?: [+-]                          ) };
Readonly my $EXPONENT  => qq{ (?: [Ee] $SIGN? \\d+              ) };
Readonly my $NUMBER    => qr{ ( ($SIGN?) ($DIGITS) ($EXPONENT?) ) }xms;
```

However, using qr{} instead of strings is still the recommended practice here. Specifying subpatterns in a q{} or qq{} requires very careful attention to the use of escape characters (such as writing \\d in some, but not all, of the components). You must also remember to add an extra (?:...) around each subpattern, to ensure that the final interpolated string is treated as a single item (for example, so the ? in $EXPONENT? applies to the entire exponent subpattern). In contrast, the inside of a qr{} always behaves exactly like the inside of an m{} match, so no arcane metaquoting is required.

If you need to build very complicated regular expressions, you should also look at the Regexp::Assemble CPAN module, which allows you to build regexes in an OO style, and then optimizes the resulting patterns to minimize backtracking. The module can also optionally insert debugging information into the regular expressions it builds, which can be invaluable for highly complex regexes.

Canned Regexes

Consider using Regexp::Common
instead of writing your own regexes.

Regular expressions are wonderfully easy to code wrongly: to miss edge-cases, to include unexpected (and incorrect) matches, or to create a pattern that's correct but hopelessly inefficient. And even when you get your regex right, you still have to maintain the code that you used to build it.

It's a drag. Worse, it's *everybody's* drag. All around the world there are thousands of Perl programmers continually reinventing the same regexes: to match numbers, and URLs, and quoted strings, and programming language comments, and IP addresses, and Roman numerals, and zip codes, and Social Security numbers, and balanced brackets, and credit card numbers, and email addresses.

Fortunately there's a CPAN module named Regexp::Common, whose entire purpose is to generate these kinds of everyday regular expressions for you. The module installs a single hash (%RE), through which you can create thousands of commonly needed regexes.

For example, instead of building yourself a number-matcher:

```
# Build a regex that matches floating point representations...
Readonly my $DIGITS    => qr{ \d+ (?: [.] \d*)? | [.] \d+          }xms;
Readonly my $SIGN      => qr{ [+-]                                 }xms;
Readonly my $EXPONENT  => qr{ [Ee] $SIGN? \d+                      }xms;
Readonly my $NUMBER    => qr{ ( ($SIGN?) ($DIGITS) ($EXPONENT?) )  }xms;

# and later...

my ($number)
    = $input =~ $NUMBER;
```

you can ask Regexp::Common to do it for you:

```
use Regexp::Common;

# Build a regex that matches floating point representations...
Readonly my $NUMBER => $RE{num}{real}{-keep};

# and later...

my ($number)
    = $input =~ $NUMBER;
```

And instead of beating your head against the appalling regex needed to match formal HTTP-style URIs:

```
# Build a regex that matches HTTP addresses...
Readonly my $HTTP => qr{
    (?:(?:http)://(?:(?:(?:(?:(?:(?:[a-zA-Z0-9][-a-zA-Z0-9]*)?[a-zA-Z0-9])[.])*
```

```
    (?:[a-zA-Z][-a-zA-Z0-9]*[a-zA-Z0-9]|[a-zA-Z])[.]?)|(?:[0-9]+[.][0-9]+[.]
    [0-9]+[.][0-9]+[.][0-9]+)))(?::(?:(?:[0-9]*)))?(?:/(?:(?:(?:(?:(?:(?:[a-zA-Z0-9
    \-_.!~*'():@&=+\$,]+|(?:%[a-fA-F0-9][a-fA-F0-9]))*)(?:;(?:(?:[a-zA-Z0-9
    \-_.!~*'():@&=+\$,]+|(?:%[a-fA-F0-9][a-fA-F0-9]))*))*)(?:/(?:(?:(?:[a-zA-Z0-9
    \-_.!~*'():@&=+\$,]+|(?:%[a-fA-F0-9][a-fA-F0-9]))*)(?:;(?:(?:[a-zA-Z0-9
    \-_.!~*'():@&=+\$,]+|(?:%[a-fA-F0-9][a-fA-F0-9]))*))*))*))*))(?:[?]
    (?:(?:(?:[;/?:@&=+\$,a-zA-Z0-9\-_.!~*'()]+|(?:%[a-fA-F0-9][a-fA-F0-9
    ]))*)))?))?)
}xms;

# Find web pages...
URI:
while (my $uri = <>) {
    next URI if $uri !~ m/ $HTTP /xms;
    print $uri;
}
```

You can just use:

```
use Regexp::Common;

# Find web pages...
URI:
while (my $uri = <>) {
    next URI if $uri !~ m/ $RE{URI}{HTTP} /xms;
    print $uri;
}
```

The benefits are perhaps most noticeable when you need a slight variation on a common regex, such as one that matches numbers in base 12, with between six and nine duodecimal places:

```
use Regexp::Common;

# The alien hardware device requires duodecimal floating-point numbers...
Readonly my $NUMBER => $RE{num}{real}{-base=>12}{-places=>'6,9'}{-keep};

# and later...

my ($number)
    = $input =~ m/$NUMBER/xms;
```

or a regular expression to help expurgate potentially rude words:

```
use Regexp::Common;

# Clean up their [DELETED] language...
$text =~ s{ $RE{profanity}{contextual} }{[DELETED]}gxms;
```

or a pattern that checks Australian postcodes:

```
use Regexp::Common;
use IO::Prompt;
```

```
# Strewth, better find out where this bloke lives...
my $postcode
    = prompt 'Giz ya postcode, mate: ',
             -require=>{'Try again, cobber: ' => qr/\A $RE{zip}{Australia} \Z/xms};
```

The regexes produced by Regexp::Common are reliable, robust, and efficient, because they're in wide and continual use (i.e., endlessly crash-tested), and they're regularly maintained and enhanced by some of the most competent developers in the Perl community. The module also has the most extensive test suite on the entire CPAN, with more than 175,000 tests.

Alternations

Always use character classes instead of single-character alternations.

Individually testing for single character alternatives:

```
if ($cmd !~ m{\A (?: a | d | i | q | r | w | x ) \z}xms) {
    carp "Unknown command: $cmd";
    next COMMAND;
}
```

may make your regex slightly more readable. But that gain isn't sufficient to compensate for the heavy performance penalty this approach imposes. Furthermore, the cost of testing separate alternatives this way increases linearly with the number of alternatives to be tested.

The equivalent character class:

```
if ($cmd !~ m{\A [adiqrwx] \z}xms) {
    carp "Unknown command: $cmd";
    next COMMAND;
}
```

does exactly the same job, but 10 times faster. And it costs the same no matter how many characters are later added to the set.

Sometimes a set of alternatives will contain both single- and multicharacter alternatives:

```
if ($quotelike !~ m{\A (?: qq | qr | qx | q | s | y | tr ) \z}xms) {
    carp "Unknown quotelike: $quotelike";
    next QUOTELIKE;
}
```

In that case, you can still improve the regex by aggregating the single characters:

```
if ($quotelike !~ m{\A (?: qq | qr | qx | [qsy] | tr ) \z}xms) {
    carp "Unknown quotelike: $quotelike";
    next QUOTELIKE;
}
```

Sometimes you can then factor out the commonalities of the remaining multicharacter alternatives into an additional character class:

```
if ($quotelike !~ m{\A (?: q[qrx] | [qsy] | tr ) \z}xms) {
    carp "Unknown quotelike: $quotelike";
    next QUOTELIKE;
}
```

Factoring Alternations

Factor out common affixes from alternations.

It's not just single character alternatives that are slow. Any alternation of subpatterns can be expensive. Especially if the resulting set of alternatives involves a repetition.

Every alternative that has to be tried requires the regex engine to backtrack up the string and re-examine the same sequence of characters it just rejected. And, if the alternatives are inside a repeated subpattern, the repetition itself may have to backtrack and retry every alternative from a different starting point. That kind of nested backtracking can easily produce an exponential increase in the time the complete match requires.

As if those problems weren't bad enough, alternations aren't very smart either. If one alternative fails, the matching engine just backs up and tries the next possibility, with absolutely no forethought as to whether that next alternative can possibly match.

For example, when a regular expression like:

```
m{
    with \s+ each \s+ $EXPR \s* $BLOCK
  | with \s+ each \s+ $VAR  \s* in \s* [(] $LIST [)] \s* $BLOCK
  | with \s+ [(] $LIST [)] \s* $BLOCK
}xms
```

is matching a string, it obviously tries the first alternative first. Suppose the string begins 'with er go est...'. In that case, the first alternative will successfully match with, then successfully match \s+, then successfully match e, but will then fail to match r (since it expected ach at that point). So the regex engine will backtrack to the start of the string and try the second alternative instead. Once again, it will successfully match with and \s+ and e, but then once again fail to match r. So it will backtrack to the start of the string once more and try the third alternative. Yet again it will successfully match with, then \s+, before failing to match the [(].

That's much less efficient than it could be. The engine had to backtrack twice and, in doing so, it had to retest and rematch the same with \s+ subpattern three times, and the longer with \s+ e subpattern twice.

A human in the same situation would notice that all three alternatives start the same way, remember that the first four characters of the string matched the first time, and simply skip that part of the rematch on the rest of the alternatives.

But Perl doesn't optimize regexes in that way. There's no theoretical reason why it couldn't do so, but there *is* an important practical reason: it's prohibitively expensive to analyze every regex every time it's compiled, just to identify these kinds of occasional opportunities for optimization. The extra time required to be that clever almost always far outweighs any performance gain that might be derived. So Perl sticks with a "dumb but fast" approach instead.

So if you want Perl to be smarter about matching regexes of this kind, you have to do the thinking for it; analyze and optimize the regex yourself. That's not particularly difficult. You just put the set of alternatives in non-capturing parentheses:

```
m{
    (?: with \s+ each \s+ $EXPR \s* $BLOCK
    |   with \s+ each \s+ $VAR  \s* in \s* [(] $LIST [)] \s* $BLOCK
    |   with \s+ [(] $LIST [)] \s* $BLOCK
    )
}xms
```

then grab the common prefix shared by every alternative and factor it out, placing it in front of the parentheses:

```
m{
    with \s+
    (?: each \s+ $EXPR \s* $BLOCK
    |   each \s+ $VAR  \s* in \s* [(] $LIST [)] \s* $BLOCK
    |   [(] $LIST [)] \s* $BLOCK
    )
}xms
```

This version of the regex does exactly what a human (or programmer) would do: it matches the with \s+ once only, then tries the three alternative "completions", without stupidly backtracking to the very start of the string to recheck that the initial 'with ' is still there.

Of course, having made that optimization, you might well find it opens up other opportunities to avoid backtracking and rechecking. For example, the first two alternations in the non-capturing parentheses now both start with each \s+, so you could repeat the factoring-out on just those two alternatives, by first wrapping them in another set of parentheses:

```
m{
    with \s+
    (?:
        (?: each \s+ $EXPR \s* $BLOCK
        |   each \s+ $VAR  \s* in \s* [(] $LIST [)] \s* $BLOCK
        )
    | [(] $LIST [)] \s* $BLOCK
    )
}xms
```

and then extracting the common prefix:

```
m{
    with \s+
    (?: each \s+
        (?: $EXPR \s* $BLOCK
        |   $VAR  \s* in \s* [(] $LIST [)] \s* $BLOCK
        )
    |   [(] $LIST [)] \s* $BLOCK
    )
}xms
```

Likewise, if every alternative *ends* in the same sequence—in this case, \s* $BLOCK—
then that common sequence can be factored out and placed after the alternatives:

```
m{
    with \s+
    (?: each \s+
        (?:$EXPR
        |   $VAR  \s* in \s* [(] $LIST [)]
        )
    |   [(] $LIST [)]
    )
    \s* $BLOCK
}xms
```

Note, however, that there is a significant price to be paid for these optimizations.
Compared to the original:

```
m{
      with \s+ each \s+ $EXPR \s* $BLOCK
    | with \s+ each \s+ $VAR  \s* in \s* [(] $LIST [)] \s* $BLOCK
    | with \s+ [(] $LIST [)] \s* $BLOCK
}xms
```

the final version of the regex is considerably more efficient, but also considerably less
readable. Of course, the original is no great beauty either, so that may not be a critical issue, especially if the refactored regex is appropriately commented and perhaps
turned into a constant:

```
Readonly my $WITH_BLOCK => qr{
    with \s+                              # Always a 'with' keyword
    (?: each \s+                          # If followed by 'each'
        (?:$EXPR                          #   Then expect an expression
        |   $VAR  \s* in \s* [(] $LIST [)] #   or a variable and list
        )
    |   [(] $LIST [)]                     # Otherwise, no 'each' and just a list
    )
    \s* $BLOCK                            # And the loop block always at the end
}xms;
```

Backtracking

Prevent useless backtracking.

In the final example of the previous guideline:

```
qr{
    with \s+
    (?: each \s+
        (?:$EXPR
          | $VAR  \s* in \s* [(] $LIST [)]
        )
      | [(] $LIST [)]
    )
    \s* $BLOCK
}xms
```

if the match successfully reaches the shared \s* $BLOCK suffix but subsequently fails to match the trailing block, then the regex engine will immediately backtrack. That backtracking will cause it to reconsider the various (nested) alternatives: first by backtracking within the previous successful alternative, and then by trying any remaining unexamined alternatives. That's potentially a lot of expensive matching, all of which is utterly useless. For a start, the syntaxes of the various options are mutually exclusive, so if one of them already matched, none of the subsequent candidates ever will.

Even if that weren't the case, the regex is backtracking only because there wasn't a valid block at the end of the loop specification. But backtracking and messing around with the other alternatives won't change that fact. Even if the regex *does* find another way to match the first part of the loop specification, there still won't be a valid block at the end of the string when matching reaches that point again.

This particular situation arises every time an alternation consists of mutually exclusive alternatives. The "dumb but fast" behaviour of the regex engine forces it to go back and mindlessly try every other possibility, even when—to an outside observer—that's provably a complete waste of time and the engine would do much better to just forget about backtracking into the alternation.

As before, you have to explicitly point that optimization out to Perl. In this case, that's done by enclosing the alternation in a special form of parentheses: (?>...). These are Perl's "don't-ever-backtrack-into-me" markers. They tell the regex engine that the enclosed subpattern can safely be skipped over during backtracking, because you're confident that re-matching the contents either won't succeed or, if it does succeed, won't help the overall match.

In practical terms, you just need to replace the (?:...) parentheses of any mutually exclusive set of alternatives with (?>...) parentheses. For example, like this:

```
m{
    with \s+
    (?> each \s+                            # (?> means:
        (?: $EXPR                           #     There can be only
          | $VAR  \s* in \s* [(] $LIST [)]  #     one way to match
        )                                   #     the enclosed set
      | [(] $LIST [)]                       #     of alternatives
    )                                       # )
    \s* $BLOCK
}xms;
```

This kind of optimization is even more important for repeated subpatterns (especially those containing alternations).

Suppose you wanted to write a regular expression to match a parenthesized list of comma-separated items. You might write:

```
$str =~ m{ [(]           # A literal opening paren
           $ITEM         # At least one item
           (?:           # Followed by...
               ,         #     a comma
               $ITEM     #     and another item
           )*            #   as many times as possible (but none is okay too)
           [)]           # A literal closing paren
         }xms;
```

That pattern works fine: it matches every parenthesized list you give it and fails to match everything else. But consider what actually happens when you give it *nearly* the right input. If, for example, $str contains a list of items that's missing its final closing parenthesis, then the regex engine would have to backtrack into the (?: , $ITEM)* and try to match one fewer comma-item sequence. But doing that will leave the matching position at the now-relinquished comma, which certainly won't match the required closing parenthesis. So the regex engine will backtrack again, giving back another comma-item sequence, leaving the matching position at the comma, where it will again fail to find a closing parenthesis. And so on and so on until every other possibility has failed.

There's no point in backtracking the repeated comma-item subpattern at all. Either it must succeed "all the way", or it can never succeed at all. So this is another ideal place to add a pair of non-backtracking parentheses. Like so:

```
m{ [(] $ITEM (?> (?: , $ITEM )* ) [)] }xms;
```

Note that the (?>...) have to go around the entire repeated grouping; don't use them simply to replace the existing parentheses:

```
m{ [(] $ITEM      (?> , $ITEM )*    [)] }xms;    # A common mistake
```

This version is wrong because the repetition marker is still outside the (?>...) and hence it will still be allowed to backtrack (uselessly).

In summary, whenever two subpatterns *X* and *Y* are mutually exclusive in terms of the strings they match, then rewrite any instance of:

```
X | Y
```

as:

```
(?> X | Y )
```

and rewrite:

```
X* Y
```

as:

```
(?> X* ) Y
```

String Comparisons

Prefer fixed-string eq comparisons to fixed-pattern regex matches.

If you're trying to compare a string against a fixed number of fixed keywords, the temptation is to put them all inside a single regex, as anchored alternatives:

```
# Quit command has several variants...
last COMMAND if $cmd =~ m{\A (?: q | quit | bye ) \z}xms;
```

The usual rationale for this is that a single, highly optimized regex match must *surely* be quicker than three separate eq tests:

```
# Quit command has several variants...
last COMMAND if $cmd eq 'q'
            || $cmd eq 'quit'
            || $cmd eq 'bye';
```

Unfortunately, that's not the case. Regex-matching against a series of fixed alternations is at least 20% slower than individually eq-matching the same strings—not to mention the fact that the eq-based version is significantly more readable.

Likewise, if you're doing a pattern match merely to get case insensitivity:

```
# Quit command is case-insensitive...
last COMMAND if $cmd =~ m{\A quit \z}ixms;
```

then it's more efficient, and arguably more readable, to write:

```
# Quit command is case-insensitive...
last COMMAND if lc($cmd) eq 'quit';
```

Sometimes, if there are a large number of possibilities to test:

```
Readonly my @EXIT_WORDS => qw(
    q  quit  bye  exit  stop  done  last  finish  aurevoir
);
```

or the number of possibilities is indeterminate at compile time:

```
Readonly my @EXIT_WORDS
    => slurp $EXIT_WORDS_FILE, {chomp=>1};
```

then a regex might seem like a better alternative, because it can easily be built on the fly:

```
Readonly my $EXIT_WORDS => join '|', @EXIT_WORDS;

# Quit command has several variants...
last COMMAND if $cmd =~ m{\A (?: $EXIT_WORDS ) \z}xms;
```

But, even in these cases, eq offers a cleaner (though now slower) solution:

```
use List::MoreUtils  qw( any );

# Quit command has several variants...
last COMMAND if any { $cmd eq $_ } @EXIT_WORDS;
```

Of course, in this particular case, an even better solution would be to use table look-up instead:

```
Readonly my %IS_EXIT_WORD
    => map { ($_ => 1) } qw(
            q  quit  bye  exit  stop  done  last  finish  aurevoir
        );

# and later...

# Quit command has several variants...
last COMMAND if $IS_EXIT_WORD{$cmd};
```

## CHAPTER 13

Error Handling

*Several recent languages have adopted an
Intercal-like, asynchronous, computed
COME-FROM concept. Only they
refer to it with funny terms like
"exception handling".*
—Hans Mulder

The two central difficulties of programming are the same as the two central difficulties of road safety: like cars, programs are built by humans; and, like cars, programs are driven by humans.

Debugging (see Chapter 18) is the art of overcoming the fallibility of those who create software systems. Error handling is the art of surviving the fallibility of those who drive such systems.

Effective and maintainable error handling is one of the keys to creating software that can be considered robust. Even a program with no internal bugs* must still interact with the environment in which it executes: at very least, the operating system, filesystem, terminal I/O, hardware devices, and network connections.

That environment must be treated as hostile, because any or all of its components may fail in some unpredictable manner. Robust software must allow for that possibility, detect when it occurs, and either overcome the problem, if possible, or report it and fail gracefully. All of which comes under the mantle of error handling.

This chapter suggests several coding practices that can help. Those practices are all based on two fundamental principles. The first is that all detectable run-time errors must be detected, classified, and reported. The second is that it should not be possible to ignore any detected error without a conscious and visible effort.

* Yeah. Right.

The important—though perhaps not obvious—consequence of these two principles is that detectable errors must be allowed to propagate only upwards (to callers), not laterally (to other statements within the same scope), and certainly never downwards (into subsequent subroutine calls).

Exceptions

Throw exceptions instead of returning special values or setting flags.

Returning a special error value on failure, or setting a special error flag, is a very common error-handling technique. Collectively, they're the basis for virtually all error notification from Perl's own built-in functions[*].

Error notification via flags and return values has a serious flaw: flags and return values can be silently ignored. And ignoring them requires absolutely no effort on the part of the programmer. In fact, in a void context, ignoring return values is Perl's default behaviour. Ignoring an error flag that has suddenly appeared in a special variable is just as easy: you simply don't bother to check the variable.

Moreover, because ignoring a return value is the void-context default, there's no syntactic marker for it. So there's no way to look at a program and immediately see where a return value is deliberately being ignored, which means there's also no way to be sure that it's not being ignored *accidentally*.

The bottom line: regardless of the programmer's (lack of) intention, an error indicator is being ignored. That's not good programming.

Ignoring error indicators frequently causes programs to propagate errors in entirely the wrong direction, as happens in Example 13-1.

Example 13-1. Returning special error values

```
# Find and open a file by name, returning the filehandle
# or undef on failure...
sub locate_and_open {
    my ($filename) = @_;

    # Check acceptable directories in order...
    for my $dir (@DATA_DIRS) {
        my $path = "$dir/$filename";
```

---

[*] For example, the builtins eval, exec, flock, open, print, stat, and system all return special values on error. Unfortunately, they don't all use the same special value. Some of them also set a flag on failure. Sadly, it's not always the same flag. See the *perlfunc* manpage for the gory details.

Example 13-1. Returning special error values (continued)

```
        # If file exists in an acceptable directory, open and return it...
        if (-r $path) {
            open my $fh, '<', $path;
            return $fh;
        }
    }

    # Fail if all possible locations tried without success...
    return;
}

# Load file contents up to the first <DATA/> marker...
sub load_header_from {
    my ($fh) = @_;

    # Use DATA tag as end-of-"line"...
    local $/ = '<DATA/>';

    $ Read to end-of-"line"...
    return <$fh>;
}

# and later...

for my $filename (@source_files) {
    my $fh = locate_and_open($filename);
    my $head = load_header_from($fh);
    print $head;
}
```

Within the locate_and_open( ) subroutine, the call to open is simply assumed to work, and the filehandle ($fh) is then immediately returned, whatever the actual outcome of the open. Presumably, the expectation is that whoever calls locate_and_open( ) will check whether the return value was a valid filehandle.

Except, of course, "whoever" doesn't. Instead of testing for failure, the main for loop takes the failure value and immediately propagates it "across" the block, to the rest of the statements in the loop. That causes the call to loader_header_from( ) to propagate the error value "downwards". And it's in that subroutine that the attempt to treat the failure value as a filehandle eventually kills the program:

```
    readline( ) on unopened filehandle at demo.pl line 28.
```

Code like that—where an error is reported in an entirely different part of the program from where it actually occurred—is particularly onerous to debug.

Of course, you could argue that the fault lies squarely with whoever wrote the loop, for using locate_and_open( ) without checking its return value. And, in the narrowest sense, that's entirely correct. But the deeper fault lies with whoever actually wrote locate_and_open( ) in the first place. Or, at least, whoever assumed that the caller *would* always check its return value.

Humans simply aren't like that. Rocks almost never fall out of the sky, so humans soon conclude that they never do, and stop looking up for them. The rains almost always come in Spring, so humans assume that they always will, and stop sacrificing unbelievers to Tlaloc to make it happen. Fires rarely break out in their homes, so humans soon forget that they might, and stop testing their smoke detectors every month. In the same way, programmers inevitably abbreviate "almost never fails" to "never fails", and then simply stop checking.

That's why so very few people bother to verify their print statements:

```
if (!print 'Enter your name: ') {
    print {*STDLOG} warning => 'Terminal went missing!'
}
```

It's human nature to "trust but *not* verify".

And human nature is why returning an error indicator is not best practice. Errors are (supposed to be) unusual occurrences, so error markers will almost never be returned. Those tedious and ungainly checks for them will almost never do anything useful, so eventually they'll be quietly omitted. After all, leaving the tests off almost always works just fine. It's so much easier not to bother. Especially when not bothering is the default!

The second shortcoming of return values as failure markers is the implicit assumption that the caller of a subroutine will be in a position to do anything about a failure that's reported. That's not always the case, especially when a complex procedure has been carefully factored into several nested levels of subroutine calls. If the immediate caller can't recover from the error, it will have to return a failure value itself, which *its* caller will then have to test for. And if that caller can't resolve the problem, it too will have to return a failure value, and so on. Every subroutine in the call chain will have to explicitly check for a returned failure value, and then explicitly pass it back up the call tree. That explicit propagation of errors increases the amount of unproductive infrastructure code required around any subroutine call that might fail, which, in turn, reduces the overall readability for the code and offers new opportunities for subtle flow-of-control errors to creep in.

Don't return special error values when something goes wrong; throw an exception instead. The great advantage of exceptions is that they reverse the usual default behaviours, bringing untrapped errors to immediate and urgent attention[*]. On the other hand, ignoring an exception requires a deliberate and conspicuous effort: you have to provide an explicit eval block to neutralize it.

Exceptions also avoid the need to explicitly test-and-return failure values. Instead, error indicators are automatically propagated upwards, bypassing any callers who are unable to cope with them.

---

[*] The imminent prospect of program termination concentrates the programmer's mind wonderfully.

The locate_and_open( ) subroutine would be much cleaner and more robust if the errors within it threw exceptions:

```
# Find and open a file by name, returning the filehandle
# or throwing an exception on failure...
sub locate_and_open {
    my ($filename) = @_;

    # Check acceptable directories in order...
    for my $dir (@DATA_DIRS) {
        my $path = "$dir/$filename";

        # If file exists in an acceptable directory, open and return it...
        if (-r $path) {
            open my $fh, '<', $path
                or croak( "Located $filename at $path, but could not open" );
            return $fh;
        }
    }

    # Fail if all possible locations tried without success...
    croak( "Could not locate $filename" );
}

# and later...

for my $filename (@source_files) {
    my $fh = locate_and_open($filename);
    my $head = load_header_from($fh);
    print $head;
}
```

Notice that the main for loop didn't change at all. The developer using locate_and_open( ) still assumes that nothing can go wrong. But now there's some justification for that expectation, because if anything *does* go wrong, the loop code will be automatically terminated by the exception that's thrown.

If the maintainers of the for loop wanted it to survive a failure, they could easily—and explicitly—ensure that with an eval block:

```
for my $filename  (@source_files) {
    if (my $fh = eval { locate_and_open($filename) }) {
        my $head = load_header_from($fh);
        print $head;
    }
    else {
        carp "Couldn't access $filename. Skipping it\n";
    }
}
```

Exceptions are a better choice even if you *are* the careful type who religiously checks every return value for failure:

```
SOURCE_FILE:
for my $filename (@source_files) {
```

```
    my $fh = locate_and_open($filename);
    next SOURCE_FILE if !defined $fh;

    my $head = load_header_from($fh);
    next SOURCE_FILE if !defined $head;

    print $head;
}
```

Constantly checking return values for failure clutters your code with validation statements, often greatly decreasing its readability. In contrast, exceptions allow an algorithm to be implemented without having to intersperse any error-handling infrastructure at all. The error-handling code can be completely factored out of the code and either relegated to after the surrounding eval (see "OO Exceptions" later in this chapter) or else dispensed with entirely:

```
for my $filename (@directory_path) {
    # Just ignore any source files that don't load...
    eval {
        my $fh = locate_and_open($filename);
        my $head = load_header_from($fh);
        print $head;
    }
}
```

Builtin Failures

Make failed builtins throw exceptions too.

Given that exceptions are the recommended way of signaling and handling errors, Perl's own builtins pose something of a problem: they rely on special return values or flag variables instead.

Ignoring the return values of builtins makes for prettier, but much less robust, code:

```
open my $fh, '>', $filename;
print {$fh} $results;
close $fh;
```

As it turns out, though, it's much easier to change how Perl's builtins fail than it is to change how Perl programmers code. You just need to use the standard Fatal module:

```
use Fatal qw( open close );

open my $fh, '>', $filename;
print {$fh} $results;
close $fh;
```

The Fatal module is passed a list of builtins and, by the use of dark and terrible magics*, it transforms those functions so that they no longer return false on failure; they now throw an exception instead. This means that the last three untested lines of the previous example are now perfectly acceptable. Either each builtin will succeed, or one will fail, at which point that builtin will throw an exception.

use Fatal can also be applied to subroutines, to convert them from return-false-on-failure to throw-exception-on-failure. For example, in the previous guideline, instead of rewriting locate_and_open( ), you could have Fatal'd it:

```
# Load subroutine to find and open a file by name
# (Unfortunately, we're stuck with using the original version,
#  which returns false on failure.)
use Our::Corporate::File::Utilities qw( locate_and_open );

# So change that unacceptable failure behaviour to throw exceptions instead...
use Fatal qw( locate_and_open );

# and later...

for my $filename  (@source_files) {
    my $fh = locate_and_open($filename);    # Now throws exception on failure
    my $head = load_header_from($fh);
    print $head;
}
```

Contextual Failure

Make failures fatal in all contexts.

The Fatal pragma can also be invoked with the special marker :void. Loading Fatal with this extra marker causes it to rewrite builtins and subroutines in a slightly different way, such that they throw a failure exception only if they were called in a void context. Under :void, they continue to silently return false in non-void contexts. That is:

```
use Fatal qw( :void open close );

if (open my $out, '>', $filename) {     # Call to open() in non-void context so
                                        #     open() returns false on failure

    open my $in, '<', '$filename.dat';  # Call to open() in void context so
                                        #     open() throws exception on failure
```

---

* These are well worth studying if you're brave enough to delve into the source of *Fatal.pm*.

```
        print {$out} <$in>;

        close $out                          # Call close() in non-void context so
            or carp "close failed: $OS_ERROR";   #    close() returns false on failure

        close $in;                          # Call close() in void context so
                                            #    close() throws exception on failure
    }
```

While this may seem like an improvement (more flexible, more Perlish), it's actually a step backwards in terms of code reliability. The problem is that it's far too easy to call a subroutine or function in a non-void context and still not actually test it. For example:

```
    # Change unacceptable failure behaviour to throw exceptions instead...
    use Fatal qw( :void locate_and_open );

    # and later...

    for my $filename  (@source_files) {
        my $fh = locate_and_open($filename);
        my $head = load_header_from($fh);
        print $head;
    }
```

Here, locate_and_open( ) is upgraded to throw exceptions on void-context failure. Unfortunately, it isn't called in a void context. It's called in scalar context, so it still returns its usual undef-on-failure. But, once again, the return value isn't subsequently checked.

Non-void context doesn't always imply a test, so a use Fatal qw(:void *funcname*) may make your code appear to be more robust, without actually making that code more robust…which makes that code *less* robust.

Systemic Failure

Be careful when testing for failure of the system builtin.

The system command is a particularly nasty case. Unlike most other Perl builtins, it returns false on success and true on failure. Fatal doesn't work on it either, so most people give up and write something like:

```
    system $cmd
        and croak "Couldn't run: $cmd ($OS_ERROR)";
```

The flow-of-control there is highly counterintuitive unless you're familiar with system's unusual failure return value.

A cleaner approach is to use the WIFEXITED ("if-exited") subroutine from the standard POSIX module:

```
use POSIX qw( WIFEXITED );

# And later...

WIFEXITED(system $cmd)
    or croak "Couldn't run: $cmd ($OS_ERROR)";
```

Note that this particular return value anomaly will be fixed in Perl 6. The revised system function will still return an integer status value as in Perl 5, but the boolean value of that status will be "reversed": true if the status is zero and false otherwise. Those new semantics are already available in Perl 5, via the Perl6::Builtins CPAN module:

```
use Perl6::Builtins qw( system );

# and later...

system $cmd
    or croak "Couldn't run: $cmd ($OS_ERROR)";
```

Recoverable Failure

Throw exceptions on all failures, including recoverable ones.

All of the examples so far in this chapter have dealt with *unrecoverable errors*. If a file doesn't exist, can't be found, or can't be created, then there's not much more that a program can do except give up and throw an exception.

However, there are other kinds of resource acquisition failures—such as failing to open a file that's currently locked by someone else, or being unable to fork a new process when your process limit has been reached—that are not always hanging offenses. If the resource is likely to become available later, your application might choose to idle for a short period and try to acquire it again. It might even try that several times before giving up.

In such cases, it's tempting to report failure by returning undef:

```
TRY:
for my $try (1..$MAX_TRIES) {
    # Take care of locking of, and connection to, resource...
    $resource = acquire_resource($resource_id);

    # Got it...
    last TRY if defined $resource;
```

```
    # Report non-recoverable failure if no more tries
    croak 'Could not acquire resource' if $try == $MAX_TRIES;

    # Else wait for increasing random intervals to help resolve contention...
    nap( rand fibonacci($try) );
}

do_something_using($resource);
```

But, even when the expected failures are *recoverable* like this, it's still better to throw exceptions:

```
TRY:
for my $try (1..$MAX_TRIES) {
    # If resource successfully acquired, we're done...
    eval {
        $resource = acquire_resource($resource_id);
        last TRY;
    };

    # Report non-recoverable failure if no more tries
    croak( $EVAL_ERROR ) if $try == $MAX_TRIES;

    # Otherwise, try again after an increasing randomized interval...
    nap( rand fibonacci($try) );
}

do_something_using($resource);
```

In this second version, acquire_resource( ) throws an exception on failure. That exception immediately terminates the execution of the eval block, so the last statement is skipped. The eval then captures the exception and neutralizes it, and the for loop continues on to take a nap. On the other hand, if acquire_resource( ) succeeds, it returns the appropriate resource descriptor, the assignment statement completes, the last statement is executed, and the for loop terminates.

So why use exceptions here? Especially since the code in the undef-on-failure version was slightly simpler.

The reason is precisely the same as in the previous three guidelines: because developers don't always check for failure. Instead of the careful retry strategies implemented in the previous example, they're just as likely to write:

```
$resource = acquire_resource($resource_id);
do_something_using($resource);
```

If acquire_resource( ) doesn't throw exceptions on failure, that code is broken, because it's going to propagate any failure down into do_something_using( ). So *always* throw exceptions on failure, even when that failure is potentially survivable.

Reporting Failure

**Have exceptions report from the caller's location,
not from the place where they were thrown.**

If someone is using a subroutine you wrote:

```
use Data::Checker qw( check_in_range );

for my $measurement ( @remote_samples ) {
    check_in_range($measurement, {min => 0, max => $INSTRUMENT_MAX_VAL});
}
```

they're not going to want to encounter an exception like this:

```
Value 24536526 is out of range (0..99) at /usr/lib/perl/Data/Checker.pm line 1345
```

The message itself is fine, but the location information is close to useless. Developers who are using your code don't care where your code *detected* a problem; all they care about is where their code *caused* the problem. They want to see something like:

```
Value 24536526 is out of range (0..99) at reactor_check.pl line 23
```

That is, they want to be told the location where the fatal subroutine was called, not the internal location where it actually threw the exception.

And, of course, that's the whole purpose of the standard Carp module: to report exceptions from the caller's point of view. So never use die to throw an exception:

```
die "Value $val is out of range ($min..$max)"
    if $val < $min || $val > $max;
```

Always use croak( ) instead:

```
use Carp;

# and later...

croak( "Value $val is out of range ($min..$max)" )
    if $val < $min || $val > $max;
```

The only situation when die could reasonably be used instead of croak( ) is if the error is a purely internal problem within your code, and not the caller's fault in any way. For example, if your subroutine is supposed to generate a result within a certain range using a very complicated process, you might choose to test whether the result was valid before returning it, like so:

```
die "Internal error: somehow generated an inconsistent result ($result)"
    if $result < $min || $result > $max;

return $result;
```

The simple rule of thumb here is that any exception message thrown with a die should always start with the words: 'Internal error:...'.

However, even in the case of internal errors, it can still better to use croak( ):

```
croak "Internal error: somehow generated an inconsistent result ($result)"
    if $result < $min || $result > $max;

return $result;
```

For a start, reporting the internal error from the caller's point of view allows developers to work out where their code is affected by your bug (in other words, where they'll have to devise a workaround).

More importantly, the Carp module provides a special 'verbose' option, which can be activated from the command line:

```
> perl -MCarp=verbose bug_example.pl
```

Running a program with this mode enabled causes every call to croak( ) to provide a full stack back-trace after the error message. For example, instead of a message like:

```
Internal error: inconsistent data format at 'bug_example.pl' line 33
```

under the "verbose" option, you would be given the full context of the failed call, including subroutine arguments:

```
Internal error: inconsistent data format at /usr/lib/perl/Data/Loader.pm line 58
        Data::Loader::get('income.stats') called at ./Stats/Demography.pm line 2346
        Stats::Demography::get_stats_from('income.stats','CODE(0x80ec54)')
        called at 'bug_example.pl' line 33
```

By always reporting internal errors via croak( ), you make it easier for developers to cope with them at the time, and easier for you to debug them later (without having to modify your module's code to do so).

All the preceding arguments apply to warning messages, too. So always report warning messages using the carp( ) subroutine, instead of the built-in warn.

Error Messages

Compose error messages in the recipient's dialect.

An error message is nearly useless if it's unintelligible to those who encounter it. For example, someone who uses a subroutine to load DAXML data[*]:

---

[*] Sorry...no idea what kind of XML variant DAXML is. The acronym is entirely made up. Still, you'll probably see someone patenting it in the near future.

```
use XML::Parser::DAXML qw( load_DAXML );

my $DAXML_root = load_DAXML($source_file);
```

will want to see an error message like this:

```
File 'index.html' is not valid DAXML.
Missing "</BLINK>" tag
Problem detected near "</BLINK</HEAD>".
Failed at 'DAXML_to_PDF.pl', line 3
```

An error message like that indicates what the overall problem is (not valid DAXML), why it was considered a problem (Missing "</BLINK>" tag), where the problem occurred (File 'index.html', near "<BLINK</HEAD>"), and which line in the caller's source failed ('DAXML_to_PDF.pl', line 3).

Collectively this information—what's wrong, why it's wrong, where in the data, and whence in the code—makes it easy for those who are using your utility to locate and correct their own problems.

Unfortunately, most exception messages are written by developers, and for developers (i.e., themselves). Most often, they're written during the testing or debugging process, so they tend to be written in the language of the developers, using the vocabulary of the implementation. So someone who is using your utility is likely to be confronted with an error message like:

```
Invalid token ('<') at 'Acquisition.pm', line 2637
```

This is very concise (one-fifth the size of the error message suggested earlier) and completely accurate (the problem is indeed the unexpected < of the </HEAD> tag buried in the incomplete </BLINK tag). But it's likely to be of very little help to those who are using your module. They may have no idea what a parser token is, they're faced with thousands of angle-brackets in their data, and they certainly don't want to look through several thousand lines of your module source to try and work out what they did wrong.

So, don't throw exceptions with curt messages that are expressed in the terminology of the implementation:

```
# Otherwise parsing has failed...
else {
    # So report the guilty token...
    die qq{Unmatched token ('$start_token')};
}
```

Instead, always croak with a detailed message. And phrase it in the vocabulary of the problem space, using concepts that will be familiar to the caller:

```
# Otherwise parsing has failed...
else {
    # So grab up to $REPORT_CONTEXT_LEN characters on the same line,
    # from the point in the data where things went wrong...
    my ($context)
        = $source =~ m/ \G [^\n]{0,$REPORT_CONTEXT_LEN} /gcxms;
```

```
    # And throw an exception explaining what/why/where/whence...
    croak(
        qq{File '$filename' is not valid DAXML.\n},
        qq{Missing "$tag_stack[-1]" tag.\n},
        qq{Problem detected near "$context".\n},
        qq{Failed},
    );
}
```

Documenting Errors

Document every error message in the recipient's dialect.

It's important to document every exception (or warning) your code may ever generate (see Chapter 7), but it's vital to do so in a way that will be comprehensible to the likely recipient of these messages.

For example, suppose someone uses your new Random::Utils module:

```
use Random::Utils qw( pick_from );

# and later...

$random_item = pick_from(@items);
```

And suppose that call to pick_from( ) causes their program to terminate unexpectedly with the message:

```
Can't pick a random element from an empty list at monte_carlo.pl line 42
```

If they're not familiar with your module, they may be unsure what the problem is, or what caused it, or what to do about it. In which case, you'd hope that they'll try and work out what to do by reading the fine Random::Utils manual*.

That kind of self-help will be far more likely to happen if your documentation actually does help readers solve their problems. To achieve that goal, you first need to explain the problem more fully, in one or more complete sentences; sentences that are longer—and written in less dense language—than the error message itself. You should then describe the most common causes of the problem, and finally suggest how the offending code might be fixed. For example:

```
=head1 DIAGNOSTICS

=over
```

---

* Rather than, say, sending you the usual mail message entitled "YOUR RANDOM LIBRARY IS B0RKEN!!!!", that consists of a single sentence "Please fix this Perl bug *ASAP*", followed by a 20MB file attachment (*problem.gz.tar.zip.uu.Z*) containing a recent—though not current—version of their entire source tree.

```
=item Can't pick an element from an empty list

The C<pick_from( )> subroutine was called without any arguments, which
meant it had no values to choose amongst. Perhaps you forgot to supply
an argument to C<pick_from( )>. Alternatively, maybe you passed an
array to the subroutine, but that array was empty at the time.
If you need to pass C<pick_from( )> an array that might sometimes have no
elements, try using the C<pick_with_default_from( )>  subroutine instead
(see L<Picking randomly with a fall-back value>).
```

The standard *perldiag* documentation is a superb example of this user-friendly
approach to documenting exceptions and warnings. For example, it explains the
mysteriously Zen-like Attempt to join self error message like so:

```
=item Attempt to join self

(F) You tried to join a thread from within itself, which is an
impossible task.  You may be joining the wrong thread, or you may
need to move the C<join( )> to some other thread.
```

OO Exceptions

**Use exception objects whenever
failure data needs to be conveyed to a handler.**

Since Perl 5.005 it has been possible to pass a single blessed reference to die or croak.
Suppose, for example, you've created an exception class[*] named X::TooBig. Then you
can create an X::TooBig object and pass it straight to die or croak:

```
croak( X::TooBig->new( {value=>$num, range=>[0,$MAX_ALLOWED_VALUE]} ) )
    if $num > $MAX_ALLOWED_VALUE;
```

Using objects as an exception has two important advantages: exception objects can
be detected by type (using the exception classes' caught( ) methods), and they can
ferry complex data structures back to an exception handler, carrying them inside the
exception objects. For example:

```
# Get the next number...
my $value = eval { get_number() };

# If the attempt fails...
if ($EVAL_ERROR) {
    # If the candidate was considered too big, go with the maximum allowed...
    if ( X::TooBig->caught( ) ) {
        my @range = $EVAL_ERROR->get_range( );
        $value = $range[-1];
    }
```

---

[*] The "Exception Classes" guideline later in this chapter shows how to implement these types of classes.

```
    # If the candidate was deemed too small, try it anyway...
    elsif ( X::TooSmall->caught() ) {
        $value = $EVAL_ERROR->get_value();
    }
    # Otherwise, rethrow the exception...
    else {
        croak( $EVAL_ERROR );
    }
}
```

Here, the exception coming back from get_number( ) is an object, so you can check it
against each exception class to which it might belong:

```
if ( X::TooBig->caught() ) {
    # [Handle "Too Big" problem]
}
elsif ( X::TooSmall->caught() ) {
    # [Handle "Too Small" problem]
}
```

When it's identified, you can then call methods on it:

```
my @range = $EVAL_ERROR->get_range();
```

to recover information about the problem.

If that exception had been string-based:

```
croak( "Numeric value $num too big (must be $MAX_ALLOWED_VALUE or less)" )
    if $num > $MAX_ALLOWED_VALUE;
```

then you'd need to use regular expressions to recognize the exception, identify the
necessary information in the string, and extract it:

```
# Get the next number...
my $value = eval { get_number() };

# If the attempt fails...
if (defined $EVAL_ERROR) {
    # If the candidate was considered too big, go with the maximum allowed...
    if ($EVAL_ERROR =~ m{ \A Numeric [ ] value [ ] \S+ [ ] too [ ] big }xms) {
        ($value) = $EVAL_ERROR =~ m{ must [ ] be [ ] (\S+) [ ] or [ ] less }xms;
    }
    # If the candidate was deemed too small, try it anyway...
    elsif ($EVAL_ERROR =~ m{ \A Numeric [ ] value [ ] (\S+) [ ] too [ ] small }xms) {
        $value = $1;
    }
    # Otherwise, rethrow the exception...
    else {
        croak( $EVAL_ERROR );
    }
}
```

This is clearly an inferior solution to object-based exceptions. Most obviously, it produces code that's more cumbersome and less readable. More importantly, it requires

the code to stringify important data that might help with recovery, then re-extract that data to actually perform the recovery. That, in turn, restricts exceptions to passing data that can be serialized and deserialized.

In contrast, exception objects can channel *any* type of Perl data type back to an exception handler. For example:

```
croak( X::EOF->new( {handle=>$fh} ) )
    if $fh->eof( );
```

Because the resulting exception object carries the actual filehandle with it, a handler in some outer scope has the possibility of rewinding that handle and trying again:

```
sub try_next_line {
    # Give get_next_line( ) two chances...
    for my $already_retried (0..1) {

        # Return immediately on success, but catch any failure...
        eval {
            return get_next_line( )
        };

        # Rethrow the caught exception if it isn't an EOF problem...
        croak( $EVAL_ERROR )
            if !X::EOF->caught( );

        # Also rethrow the caught exception
        # if we've already tried rewinding the filehandle...
        croak( $EVAL_ERROR )
            if $already_retried;

        # Otherwise, try rewinding the filehandle...
        seek $EVAL_ERROR->handle( ), 0, 0;
    }
}
```

In this example, try_next_line( ) gives get_next_line( ) two tries to return some data, by putting the call to get_next_line( ) in a for loop that iterates twice. It first attempts to call get_next_line( ) and return the result. If that attempt succeeds, then the call to try_next_line( ) is done*. But if get_next_line( ) throws an exception, then the return will not be executed, the eval will catch the exception, and the rest of the for loop will proceed.

The second statement in the loop will check whether the failure was due to an X::EOF exception (which the remainder of the loop may be able to handle) or if some unknown exception was thrown, in which case that exception will simply be rethrown (croak $EVAL_ERROR).

---

* And, more importantly, no error-handling overheads were incurred. This is yet another advantage of using exceptions: they allow you to optimize for successful behaviour.

The loop then checks whether this is the second time an exception has been encountered in this call to try_next_line( ) and, if the subroutine has already retried get_next_line( ), it immediately gives up and repropagates the exception.

Finally, the loop grabs the offending filehandle that was passed back in the exception object ($EVAL_ERROR->get_handle( )) and seeks it back to its start-of-file position. The loop then reiterates, to give get_next_line( ) its second, and final, chance.

Of course, this is possible only because the exception was an object, and able to carry the filehandle in question back to try_next_line( ). Using a string-based exception:

```
croak( "Filehandle $fh at EOF" )
    if $fh->eof( );
```

would have made that impossible, since the exception that try_next_line( ) received back would have been something like:

```
Filehandle GLOB(0x800368) at EOF at demo.pl line 420
```

in which case try_next_line( ) would have no way to access the original filehandle, and hence no way to "fix" it and try again.

Volatile Error Messages

Use exception objects when error messages may change.

In a string-based exception, the error message *is* the exception. That can lead to problems during development or maintenance, because it means that any exception handler's ability to recognize a string-based exception is inextricably tied to the structure of the error message itself.

If you ever need to change an exception message in any way, you're going to have to check and update every place that error might ever be caught. In practice, that means that you can never change the text of any exception once the code that throws it is in production[*].

In contrast, the error message of an object-oriented exception is merely one attribute of that object. More importantly, that message no longer defines the identity and type of the exception. That defining role is now played by the class into which the exception is blessed, or more particularly, by the caught( ) method that the class provides.

So the error message of an exception object can be rewritten whenever necessary. Provided the class of the exception remains the same, any exception handlers that catch it will be unaffected by the change of message.

---

[*] Which is why Perl's own built-in exceptions nowadays find themselves in a maze of twisty grammatical forms, variant spellings, and inconsistent capitalizations…none alike.

Exception Hierarchies

Use exception objects when two or more exceptions are related.

Another problem with using raw strings as exceptions is that string-based exceptions offer no easy way to create new and specialized forms of existing exceptions that existing code can still catch and handle.

Consider the string-based exception for reporting integers outside a given range, as shown previously in the "OO Exceptions" guideline:

```
croak( "Numeric value $num too big (must be $MAX_ALLOWED_VALUE or less)" )
    if $num > $MAX_ALLOWED_VALUE;
```

Suppose you also need to provide a special version of that exception for reporting integers that are so big that they're outside the range that Perl can represent exactly:

```
croak( "Numeric value $num waaaaay too big (must be $MAX_INT or less)" )
    if $num > $MAX_INT;
```

The original test for catching the string-based "big number" exception was:

```
# If the candidate was considered too big, go with the maximum allowed...
if ($EVAL_ERROR =~ m{\A Numeric [ ] value [ ] \S+ [ ] too [ ] big}xms) {
```

Unfortunately, that regex won't match the error message of this new exception, so the handler will completely ignore it. Unless, of course, it was changed to:

```
# If the candidate was considered too big, go with the maximum allowed...
if ($EVAL_ERROR =~ m{\A Numeric [ ] value [ ] \S+ [ ] (wa+y [ ])? too [ ] big}xms) {
```

But that change makes the code that catches these exceptions more complex, harder to read, and less maintainable. Worse still, you're also going to have to change every other similar regex anywhere else that the original exception was being caught.

In contrast, suppose you had originally used an object-oriented exception:

```
croak( X::TooBig->new( {num=>$num, limit=>$MAX_ALLOWED_VALUE} )
    if $num > $MAX_ALLOWED_VALUE;
```

with a correspondingly object-oriented test in the exception handler:

```
if ( X::TooBig->caught() ) {
```

If you subsequently needed to also use exceptions of a more-specific (i.e., derived) class:

```
package X::WaaaaayTooBig;
use base qw( X::TooBig );
# [Implement variant behaviour here]

# and later...

croak( X::WaaaaayTooBig->new( {num=>$num} ) )
    if $num > $MAX_INT;
```

---

then your exception handler would have to become:

```
if ( X::TooBig->caught() ) {
```

That is, it would stay exactly the same and continue to work just fine with no modification whatsoever. And it would continue to work no matter how many other exception types you subsequently derived from X::TooBig.

This ability to decouple exception-handling code from the particulars of the exceptions it handles is probably the single most compelling reason to use object-oriented exceptions.

Processing Exceptions

Catch exception objects in most-derived-first order.

The only drawback to using method calls to detect particular types of exceptions:

```
if ( X::TooBig->caught() ) {
```

is that you have to be careful about the order in which you try your alternatives. For example, if X::WaaaaayTooBig inherits from X:TooBig, the following code won't work correctly:

```
# If the attempt fails...
if ($EVAL_ERROR) {
    # If the candidate was considered too big, go with the maximum allowed...
    if ( X::TooBig->caught() ) {
        my @range = $EVAL_ERROR->get_range();
        $value = $range[-1];
    }
    # If the candidate was considered waaaaay too big, rethrow the exception...
    elsif ( X::WaaaaayTooBig->caught() ) {
        $EVAL_ERROR->rethrow();
    }
    # etc.
}
```

The problem is that if an X::WaaaaayTooBig exception is thrown, $EVAL_ERROR will refer to an X::WaaaaayTooBig object. But the X::WaaaaayTooBig class inherits from the X::TooBig class, so an X::WaaaaayTooBig object *is* an X::TooBig object. That means the first if test will succeed, and the specialized derived-class exception will be treated like a generic base-class exception instead.

The solution is simple: whenever you're determining the type of an exception you just caught, test for the most-derived classes first.

Exception Classes

Build exception classes automatically.

As the preceding guidelines illustrate, using objects as exceptions can significantly improve the robustness and future maintainability of your error-handling code. There is, however, a downside: you have to build the exception classes to instantiate those exceptions. And those exception classes need to be reasonably sophisticated in order to work correctly.

For example, they need to provide for throwing, rethrowing, and identifying exceptions; they need to provide the appropriate internal storage for preserving the error information and context; and they need some kind of stringification overloading (see Chapter 16) to ensure that they still produce sensible error messages in string contexts: for example, when they're printed out as they terminate a program. A minimal hash-based implementation of the X::EOF class used in the previous guidelines of this chapter is shown in Example 13-2.

Example 13-2. Minimal X::EOF exception class

```perl
# Define the class representing end-of-file exceptions...
package X::EOF;
use Carp;

# Make X::EOF objects stringify to the same message used previously...
use overload (
    q{""} => sub {
        my ($self) = @_;
        return "Filehandle $self->{handle} at EOF $self->{caller_location}";
    },
    fallback => 1,
);

# Create a X::EOF exception...
sub new {
    my ($class, $args_ref) = @_;

    # Allocate memory for the object and initialize it...
    my %self = %{$args_ref};

    # If no filehandle is passed, indicate that it's unknown...
    if (! exists $self{handle}) {
        $self{handle} = '(unknown)';
    }

    # Ask Carp::shortmess() where croak() would report the error occurring...
    if (!exists $self{caller_location}) {
        $self{caller_location} = Carp::shortmess();
```

Example 13-2. Minimal X::EOF exception class (continued)

```perl
    }

    # Add it to the class and send it on its way...
    return bless \%self, $class;
}

# Give access to the handle that was passed into the constructor...
sub get_handle {
    my ($self) = @_;
    return $self->{handle};
}

# Test whether the currently propagating exception is of this type...
sub caught {
    my ($this_class) = @_;

    use Scalar::Util qw( blessed );
    return if !blessed $EVAL_ERROR;
    return $EVAL_ERROR->isa($this_class);
}
```

Of course, the processes of creating exception objects, overloading their stringification behaviours, and helping them work out where they were created, are essentially identical for all exception classes, so those methods could be factored out into a common base class, as shown in Example 13-3.

Example 13-3. Refactoring the X::EOF exception class

```perl
# Abstract the common behaviours of all exception classes...
package X::Base;

# Make exception objects stringify to an appropriate string...
use overload (
    q{""} => sub {
        my ($self) = @_;
        return "$self->{message} $self->{caller_location}";
    },
    fallback => 1,
);

# Create the base object underlying any exception...
sub new {
    my ($class, $args_ref) = @_;

    # Allocate memory for the object and initialize it...
    my %self = %{$args_ref};

    # Make sure it has an error message, building one if necessary...
    if (! exists $self{message}) {
        $self{message} = "$class exception thrown";
    }
```

Example 13-3. Refactoring the X::EOF exception class (continued)

```
    # Ask Carp::shortmess()where croak() would report the error occurring
    # (but make sure Carp ignores whatever derived class called this
    #  constructor, by temporarily  marking that class as being "internal"
    #  and hence invisible to Carp)...
    local $Carp::Internal{caller()} = 1;
    if (!exists $self{caller_location}) {
        $self{caller_location} = Carp::shortmess();
    }

    # Add it to the class and send it on its way...
    return bless \%self, $class;
}


# Test whether the currently propagating exception is of this type...
sub caught {
    my ($this_class) = @_;

    use Scalar::Util qw( blessed );
    return if !blessed $EVAL_ERROR;
    return $EVAL_ERROR->isa($this_class);
}

# Define the X::EOF class, inheriting useful behaviours from X::Base...
package X::EOF;
use base qw( X::Base );

# Create a X::EOF exception...
sub new {
    my ($class, $args_ref) = @_;
    if (! exists $args_ref->{handle}) {
        $args_ref->{handle} = '(unknown)';
    }

    return $class->SUPER::new({
        handle   => $args_ref->{handle },
        message  => "Filehandle $args_ref->{handle} at EOF",
    });
}

# Give access to the handle that was passed into the constructor...
sub get_handle {
    my ($self) = @_;
    return $self->{handle};
}
```

As you can see, even with some of the effort being amortized into a common base class, there's still a considerable amount of tedious work required to create any exception class.

A much cleaner solution is to use the Exception::Class CPAN module instead. This module provides a powerful predefined base class for exceptions. It also offers an easy way to create new exception classes that are derived from that base class, allowing you to quickly add in any extra attributes and methods that those new classes might require.

For example, using Exception::Class, you could build the complete X::EOF class in under 10 lines of code:

```
# Define the X::EOF class, inheriting useful behaviours
# from Exception::Class::Base...
use Exception::Class (
    X::EOF => {
        # Specify that X::EOF objects have a 'handle' attribute
        # and a corresponding handle() method...
        fields => [ 'handle' ],
    },
);

# Redefine the message to which an X::EOF object stringifies...
sub X::EOF::full_message {
    my ($self) = @_;
    return 'Filehandle ' . $self->handle() . ' at EOF';
}
```

Throwing the exception using this version of X::EOF would remain essentially the same, with only the slight syntactic difference that Exception::Class constructors pass their arguments as raw pairs, rather than in hashes. That is, you would now write:

```
croak( X::EOF->new( handle => $fh ) );
```

Better still, classes built with Exception::Class provide an even easier way to create and throw their exception:

```
X::EOF->throw( handle => $fh );
```

Exception::Class has many other features that help with handling fatal errors. Exceptions built with the module can produce full call-stack traces; can rethrow themselves in a very simple and clean way; can report user, group, and process IDs; and can create and export "alias subroutines", which can further simplify exception throwing. The module is highly recommended.

Unpacking Exceptions

Unpack the exception variable in extended exception handlers.

If an exception handler becomes long or complex, you may need to refactor parts of it. For example, consider the X::EOF handler inside try_next_line() from the "OO Exceptions" guideline:

```
sub try_next_line {
    # Give get_next_line() two chances...
    for my $already_retried (0..1) {
```

```
        # Return immediately on success, but catch any failure...
        eval {
            return get_next_line()
        };

        # Rethrow the caught exception if it isn't an EOF problem...
        croak $EVAL_ERROR
            if !X::EOF->caught();

        # Also rethrow the caught exception
        # if we've already tried rewinding the filehandle...
        croak $EVAL_ERROR
            if $already_retried;

        # Otherwise, try rewinding the filehandle...
        seek $EVAL_ERROR->handle(), 0, 0;
    }
}
```

This code would seem to be cleaner and easier to extend if the separate rethrows were refactored like this:

```
sub try_next_line {
    # Give get_next_line() two chances...
    for my $already_retried (0..1) {

        # Return immediately on success, but catch any failure...
        eval {
            return get_next_line()
        };

        # If we can handle this exception...
        if (X::EOF->caught() ) {
            # Fail on irremedially bad cases...
            fail_if_incorrigible($EVAL_ERROR, $already_retried);

            # Otherwise, try rewinding the filehandle...
            seek $EVAL_ERROR->handle(), 0, 0;
        }
        # Otherwise, let some caller handle it...
        else {
            $EVAL_ERROR->rethrow();
        }
    }
}
```

Refactoring in this way is usually a highly recommended practice, but in this case it has the potential to introduce a subtle bug. The problem is that the $EVAL_ERROR exception variable (a.k.a. $@) is a global variable. So if fail_if_incorrigible() happens to throw—and then internally catch—some other exception during its execution, that nested exception will overwrite $EVAL_ERROR.

So, after the call to fail_if_incorrigible(), the exception variable might still have the original X::EOF exception, or it might contain some other totally unrelated exception, left over from the internal machinations of fail_if_incorrigible( ). That uncertainty makes the seek statement after the call to fail_if_incorrigible( ) problematic. It tries to seek the handle that was sent back inside the original exception, but there's now no guarantee that $EVAL_ERROR still contains that exception.

Fortunately, it's comparatively simple to solve this problem: just copy the exception into a lexical variable before attempting to handle it:

```
if (X::EOF->caught( ) ) {
    my $exception = $EVAL_ERROR;

    # Fail on irremediably bad cases...
    fail_if_incorrigible($exception, $already_retried);

    # Otherwise, try rewinding the filehandle...
    seek $exception->handle( ), 0, 0;
}
```

Using the Exception::Class module makes this practice even easier to follow, because its version of the caught( ) method always returns a copy of $EVAL_ERROR on success. So you can just write:

```
if (my $exception = X::EOF->caught( ) ) {
    # Fail on irremediably bad cases...
    fail_if_incorrigible($exception, $already_retried);

    # Otherwise, try rewinding the filehandle...
    seek $exception->fh( ), 0, 0;
}
```

## CHAPTER 14

Command-Line Processing

> *The demiurge sits at his teletype, pounding out one command line after another,*
> *specifying the values of fundamental constants of physics:*
> universe -G 6.672e-11 -e 1.602e-19 -h 6.626e-34....
> *and when he's finished typing out the command line,*
> *his right pinky hesitates above the ENTER key for an aeon or two,*
> *wondering what's going to happen; then down it comes—*
> *and the WHACK you hear is another Big Bang.*
>
> —Neal Stephenson
> *In the Beginning was the Command Line*

Perl started out as a language that was "also good for many system administration tasks"[*]. In the beginning, Larry created it to help him write utility programs for data mining, report generation, text munging, stream filtering, and pattern matching; as an easy way to build new command-line tools, without the constraints of shell scripting or the burdens of C programming.

Nearly two decades on, Perl is still beloved by sysadmins, toolsmiths, and other denizens of the shell, as a fast and powerful way to create new testaceous utilities. And for most of these utility programs, the command line is still the primary user interface.

If you're designing a new tool, script, utility, application, or suite, chances are it will need some kind of command-line interface. If it does, make sure that interface is convenient, powerful, flexible, mnemonic, consistent, and predictable.

Sounds difficult? It is. In fact, it's even more difficult than it sounds. But this chapter provides some guidelines that can help.

[*] *perl.man.1*, 18 December 1987.

Command-Line Structure

Enforce a single consistent command-line structure.

Command-line interfaces have a strong tendency to grow over time, accreting new options as features are added to the application. Unfortunately, the evolution of such interfaces is rarely designed, managed, or controlled, so the set of flags, options, and arguments that a given application accepts are likely to be ad hoc and unique.

This also means they're likely to be inconsistent with the unique, ad hoc sets of flags, options, and arguments that other related applications provide. The result is inevitably a suite of programs, each of which is driven in a distinct and idiosyncratic way. For example:

```
> orchestrate source.txt -to interim.orc

> remonstrate +interim.rem -interim.orc

> fenestrate  --src=interim.rem --dest=final.wdw
Invalid input format

> fenestrate --help
Unknown option: --help.
Type 'fenestrate -hmo' for help
```

Here, the *orchestrate* utility expects its input file as its first argument, while its output file is specified using the -to flag. But the related *remonstrate* tool uses *–infile* and *+outfile* options instead, with the output file coming first. And the *fenestrate* program seems to require GNU-style "long options": --src=*infile* and --dest=*outfile*. Except, apparently, for its oddly named help flag. All in all, it's a mess.

When you're providing a suite of programs, all of them should appear to work the same way, using the same flags and options for the same features across all applications. This enables your users to take advantage of existing knowledge[*] instead of asking you.

Those three programs should work like this:

```
> orchestrate -i source.txt -o dest.orc

> remonstrate -i source.orc -o dest.rem

> fenestrate  -i source.rem -o dest.wdw
Input file ('source.rem') not a valid Remora file
```

---

[*] Or, as your pointy-haired boss would prefer you to say: "…proactively maximizes quality client-level cross-semantic uptake synergies by leveraging in-house cognitive investment transfer from pre-assimilated complexity-enabled environments".

```
(type "fenestrate --help" for help)

> fenestrate --help
fenestrate - convert Remora .rem files to Windows .wdw format

Usage: fenestrate [-i <infile>] [-o <outfile>] [-cstq] [-h|-v]

Options:
    -i <infile>     Specify input source       [default: STDIN]
    -o <outfile>    Specify output destination [default: STDOUT]
    -c              Attempt to produce a more compact representation
    -h              Use horizontal (landscape) layout
    -v              Use vertical (portrait) layout
    -s              Be strict regarding input
    -t              Be extra tolerant regarding input
    -q              Run silent

    --version       Print version information
    --usage         Print the usage line of this summary
    --help          Print this summary
    --man           Print the complete manpage
```

Here, every application that takes input and output files uses the same two flags to do so. So a user who wants to use the *substrate* utility (to convert that final *.wdw* file to a subroutine) is likely to be able to guess correctly the required syntax:

```
> substrate  -i dest.wdw -o dest.sub
```

And, anyone who can't guess that probably *can* guess that:

```
> substrate  --help
```

is likely to render aid and comfort.

Command-Line Conventions

Adhere to a standard set of conventions in your command-line syntax.

A large part of making interfaces consistent is being consistent in the way individual components of those interfaces are specified. Some conventions that may help to design consistent and predictable interfaces include:

Require a flag preceding every piece of command-line data, except filenames

The arguments advanced in Chapter 9 against passing subroutine arguments positionally apply equally well to entire applications. Users don't want to have to remember that your application requires "input file, output file, block size, operation, fallback strategy"...and requires them in that precise order:

```
> lustrate sample_data proc_data 1000 normalize log
```

They want to be able to say explicitly what they mean, in any order that suits them:

```
> lustrate sample_data proc_data -op=normalize -b1000 --fallback=log
```

Provide a flag for each filename, too, especially when a program can be given files for different purposes

Users might also not want to remember the order of the two positional file-names, so let them label those arguments as well, and specify them in whatever order they prefer:

```
> lustrate -i sample_data -op normalize -b1000 --fallback log -o proc_data
```

Use a single - prefix for short-form flags, up to three letters (-v, -i, -rw, -in, -out)

Short-form flags are appreciated by experienced users, as a way of reducing typing and limiting command-line clutter. So don't make them type two dashes in these shortcuts.

Use a double -- prefix for longer flags (--verbose, --interactive, --readwrite, --input, --output)

Flags that are complete words improve the readability of a command line (in a shell script, for example). The double dash also helps to distinguish between the longer flag name and any nearby file names.

If a flag expects an associated value, allow an optional = between the flag and the value

Some people prefer to visually associate a value with its preceding flag:

```
> lustrate -i=sample_data -op=normalize -b=1000 --fallback=log -o=proc_data
```

Others don't:

```
> lustrate -i sample_data -op normalize -b1000 --fallback log -o proc_data
```

Still others want it both ways:

```
> lustrate -i sample_data -o proc_data -op=normalize -b=1000 --fallback=log
```

Let the user choose.

Allow single-letter options to be "bundled" after a single dash

It's irritating to have to type repeated dashes for a series of flags:

```
> lustrate -i sample_data -v -l -x
```

So allow experienced users to also write:

```
> lustrate -i sample_data -vlx
```

Provide a multiletter version of every single-letter flag

Short-form flags may be appreciated by experienced users, but they can be troublesome for new users: hard to remember and even harder to recognize. Don't force people to do either. Give them a verbose alternative to every concise flag—full words that are easier to remember, and also more self-documenting in shell scripts.

Always allow - as a special filename
> A widely used convention is that a dash (-) where an input file is expected means "read from standard input", and a dash where an output file is expected means "write to standard output".

Always allow -- as a file list marker
> Another widely used convention is that the appearance of a double-dash (--) on the command line marks the end of any flagged options, and indicates that the remaining arguments are a list of filenames, even if some of them look like flags.

Meta-options

Standardize your meta-options.

Meta-options are those command-line flags that tell the user how to use the application, rather than telling the application how to behave. They're the "What are my options?" options.

Every program you write should provide (at least) four of these, all of which print to standard output and then terminate the program immediately. Those four meta-options are:

`--usage`
> This option should print a concise usage line.

`--help`
> This option should print the `--usage` line, followed by a one-line summary of each available option.

`--version`
> This option should print the program's version number.

`--man`
> This option[*] should print the complete documentation for the program, paging it out if necessary.

Note that the names of the four options are *not* negotiable. That's what "standardized" means.

And, yes, those standardized names are much longer than -u, -h, -v, and -m. That's also intentional. Meta-options should need to be called only relatively infrequently, especially if your other options have been designed carefully and consistently, so

---

[*] The flag ought to have been single-dashed (-man) under the "Command-Line Conventions" guidelines, but the double dash is used instead, to keep all four meta-options structurally consistent.

they're easy to remember. And, because they'll be infrequent choices, meta-options ought to have longer invocations, leaving the shorter names available for things that users type all the time.

For example, -h and -v are far more useful as flags to specify horizontality or verticality, or height and velocity, or hairiness and verbosity. But if all your applications already use them to summon help and version information, you'll be stuck with -hor/-ver, or -hgt/-vel, or -hair/-verb.

Don't make up other names for these standard flags*. For example, using -hmo as the "help me, Obi-Wan" flag is cute. For about five seconds. After which, it becomes just another counter-intuitive, hard-to-remember, have-to-look-it-up-every-time obstacle to the user.

In-situ Arguments

Allow the same filename to be specified for both input and output.

When users want to do in-situ processing on a file, they often specify it as both the input and output file:

```
> lustrate -i sample_data -o sample_data -op=normalize
```

But if the -i and -o flags are processed independently, the program will usually open the file for input, open it again for output (at which point the file will be truncated to zero length), and then attempt to read in the first line of the now-empty file:

```
# Open both filehandles...
use Fatal qw( open );
open my $src,  '<', $source_file;
open my $dest, '>', $destination_file;

# Read, process, and output data, line-by-line...
while (my $line = <$src>) {
    print {$dest} transform($line);
}
```

Not only does this *not* perform the requested transformation on the file, it also destroys the original data, which conveniently prevents users from feeling frustrated, by making them irate instead.

Clobbering data files in this way during an in-situ update is perhaps the single commonest command-line interface design error. Fortunately, it's extremely easy to avoid—just make sure that you unlink the output file before you open it:

---

* Not unless you have the clout to make your choices the universal standards throughout your project. And your entire client base.

```
# Open both filehandles...
use Fatal qw( open );
open my $src,  '<', $source_file;
unlink $destination_file;
open my $dest, '>', $destination_file;

# Read, process, and output data, line-by-line...
while (my $line = <$src>) {
    print {$dest} transform($line);
}
```

If the input and output files are different, unlinking the output file merely removes a file that was about to be rewritten anyway. Then the second open simply recreates the output file, ready for writing.

If the two filenames actually refer to a single in-situ file, unlinking the output file-name removes that filename from its directory, but doesn't remove the file itself from the filesystem. The file is already open through the filehandle in $input, so the filesystem will preserve the unlinked file until that input filehandle is closed. The second open then creates a new version of the in-situ file, ready for writing.

The only limitation of this technique is that it changes the inode of any in-situ file*. That can be a problem if the file has any hard-linked aliases, or if other applications are identifying the file by its inode number. If either of those situations is possible, you can preserve the in-situ file's inode by using the IO::InSitu CPAN module instead:

```
# Open both filehandles...
use IO::InSitu;
my ($src, $dest) = open_rw($source_file, $destination_file);

# Read, process, and output data, line-by-line...
while (my $line = <$src>) {
    print {$dest} transform($line);
}
```

The open_rw( ) subroutine takes the names of two files: one to be opened for reading, the other for writing. It returns a list of two filehandles, opened to those two files. However, if the two filenames refer to the same file, open_rw( ) first makes a temporary copy of the file, which it opens for input. It then opens the original file for output. In such cases, when the input filehandle is eventually closed, IO::InSitu arranges for the temporary file to be automatically deleted.

This approach preserves the original file's inode, but at the cost of making a temporary copy of the file. The name of the temporary copy is usually formed by appending '.bak' to the original filename, but this can be altered, by passing an option to open_rw( ).

---

* The *inode* of a file is the internal data structure that a Unix file system uses to represent and access that file. Within a particular storage device, every file is uniquely identified by the index of its inode: its *inode number*.

Command-Line Processing

Standardize on a single approach to command-line processing.

Providing a consistent set of command-line arguments across all applications helps the users of the suite, but it can also help the implementers and the maintainers. If a collection of programs all use consistent command-line arguments, then each program can use the same approach to parsing those arguments.

Defining a consistent command-line interface makes the programs easier to write in the first place, because once the command-line processing has been set up for the first application, the universal components of it can be refactored into a separate module and reused by subsequent programs (as described under "Interapplication Consistency" later in this chapter). This approach also makes the suite much more maintainable, as debugging or enhancing that one module automatically fixes or extends the command-line processing of perhaps dozens of individual applications.

There are plenty of inappropriate ways to parse command lines. For example, Perl has a built-in –s option (as documented in the *perlrun* manpage) that will happily unpack your command line for you, as Example 14-1 demonstrates.

Example 14-1. Command-line parsing via perl -s

```
#!/usr/bin/perl -s
# Use the -s shebang line option to handle command lines of the form:
#
#       > orchestrate -in=source.txt -out=dest.orc -v

# The -s automatically parses the command line into these package variables...
use vars qw( $in $out $verbose $len );

# Handle meta-options (which will appear in package variables whose names
# start with a dash. Oh, the humanity!!!)...
no strict qw( refs );
X::Version->throw( ) if ${-version};
X::Usage->throw( )   if ${-usage};
X::Help->throw( )    if ${-help};
X::Man->throw( )     if ${-man};

# Report intended behaviour...
if ($verbose) {
    print "Loading first $len chunks of file: $in\n"
}
# etc.
```

Under -s, every command-line argument of the form *–argname* is converted to a package variable ${*argname*}. The use of a package variable is a problem in itself, but it gets worse. The interpreter names each of these variables by simply removing the

---

leading dash of the corresponding command-line flag. So the leading dash of -h is removed to create ${h}, and the leading dash of -help is removed to generate ${help}. Unfortunately, when a mandatory meta-option like --help appears on the command line, its *single* leading dash is removed too, producing the variable ${-help}, which is legal only under no strict 'refs'.

A better solution, though much more complex, would be to define a regular expression for each valid option, in whatever form you wished them to take. Then you would test any matches against the command line using iterated /gc pattern matches (see Chapter 12). An argument that doesn't match any of your regexes could be caught at the end of the outer loop and reported as an error. Example 14-2 illustrates exactly that approach.

Example 14-2. Command-line parsing via a hand-coded parser

```
# Handle command lines of the form:
#
#       > orchestrate -in=source.txt -out dest.orc -v

# Create table describing argument flags, default values,
# and how to match the remainder of each argument...
my @options = (
    { flag=>'-in',      val=>'-', pat=>qr/ \s* =? \s* (\S*) /xms },
    { flag=>'-out',     val=>'-', pat=>qr/ \s* =? \s* (\S*) /xms },
    { flag=>'-len',     val=>24,  pat=>qr/ \s* =? \s* (\d+) /xms },
    { flag=>'--verbose', val=>0,   pat=>qr/                 /xms },
);

# Initialize hash for arguments...
my %arg = map { $_->{flag} => $_->{val} } @options;

# Create table of meta-options and associated regex...
my %meta_option = (
    '--version' => sub { X::Version->throw() },
    '--usage'   => sub { X::Usage->throw()   },
    '--help'    => sub { X::Help->throw()    },
    '--man'     => sub { X::Man->throw()     },
);
my $meta_option = join '|', reverse sort keys %meta_option;

# Reconstruct full command line, and start matching at the start...
my $cmdline = join $SPACE, @ARGV;
pos $cmdline = 0;

# Step through cmdline...
ARG:
while (pos $cmdline < length $cmdline) {
    # Checking for a meta-option each time...
    if (my ($meta) = $cmdline =~ m/ \s* ($meta_option) \b /gcxms ) {
        $meta_option{$meta}->();
    }
```

Example 14-2. Command-line parsing via a hand-coded parser (continued)

```
    # Then trying each option...
    for my $opt_ref ( @options ) {
        # Seeing whether that option matches at this point in the cmdline...
        if (my ($val)
                = $cmdline =~ m/\G \s* $opt_ref->{flag} $opt_ref->{pat} /gcxms) {
            # And, if so, storing the value and moving on...
            $arg{$opt_ref->{flag}} = $val;
            next ARG;
        }
    }

    # Otherwise, extract the next chunk of text
    # and report it as an unknown flag...
    my ($unknown) = $cmdline =~ m/ (\S*) /xms;
    croak "Unknown cmdline flag: $unknown";
}

# Report intended behaviour...
if ($arg{'--verbose'}) {
    print "Loading first $arg{-len} chunks of file: $arg{-in}\n"
}
# etc.
```

Using a table-drive approach here is important—both because it would make it easier to add extra options as the program develops, and because data-driven solutions are much easier to factor out into a separate module that can later be shared by your entire application suite.

And, of course, many people already have done exactly that: factored out their table-driven command-line processors into modules. Such modules are traditionally created within the Getopt:: namespace, and Perl's standard library comes with two of them: Getopt::Std and Getopt::Long. The Getopt::Std module can recognize only single-character flags (except for --help and --version) and so is not recommended.

Getopt::Long, on the other hand, is a much cleaner and more powerful tool. For example, the earlier command-line processing examples could be simplified to the version shown in Example 14-3.

Example 14-3. Command-line parsing via Getopt::Long

```
# Handle command lines of the form:
#
#     > orchestrate --i source.txt --o=dest.orc -v

# Use the standard Perl module...
use Getopt::Long;

# Variables that will be set in response to command-line arguments
# (with defaults values, in case those arguments are not provided)...
my $infile   = '-';
my $outfile  = '-';
```

Example 14-3. Command-line parsing via Getopt::Long (continued)

```perl
my $length  = 24;
my $width   = 78;
my $verbose = 0;

# Specify cmdline options and process command line...
my $options_okay = GetOptions (
    # Application-specific options...
    'in=s'     => \$infile,    # --in option expects a string
    'out=s'    => \$outfile,   # --out option expects a string
    'length=i' => \$length,    # --length option expects an integer
    'width=i'  => \$width,     # --width option expects an integer
    'verbose'  => \$verbose,   # --verbose flag is boolean

    # Standard meta-options
    # (the subroutines are executed immediately the flag is encountered
    #  and are used here to throw suitable exceptions - see Chapter 13)...
    'version' => sub { X::Version->throw(); },
    'usage'   => sub { X::Usage->throw();   },
    'help'    => sub { X::Help->throw();    },
    'man'     => sub { X::Man->throw();     },
);

# Fail if unknown arguments encountered...
X::Usage->throw() if !$options_okay;

# Report intended behaviour...
if ($verbose) {
    print "Loading first $length chunks of file: $infile\n"
}

# etc.
```

That's noticeably shorter than the regex-based version in Example 14-2, and much more robust than the version in Example 14-1. It's also neatly table-driven, so you could refactor it out into your own module, to be re-used across all your applications. And it uses a core module, so your program will be portable to any Perl platform.

Getopt::Long is probably more than adequate for most developers' command-line processing needs. And while its feature set is still limited, those very limitations may actually be an advantage, as they tend to discourage the creation of "adventurous" interfaces.

However, if your applications *do* have more advanced requirements—such as mutually exclusive options (--verbose vs --taciturn), or options that can be used only with other options (-bak being valid only if --insitu is in effect), or options that imply other options (--garrulous implying --verbose)—then there are dozens of other Getopt:: modules on the CPAN to choose from*.

---

* Literally. At last count there were at least 30 distinct Getopt:: modules on CPAN. Perl's secret shame!

One of the most powerful and adaptable of these is `Getopt::Clade`. With it, the command-line processing implemented in the previous examples could be implemented as in Example 14-4.

Example 14-4. Command-line parsing via Getopt::Clade

```
# Handle command lines of the form:
#
#     > orchestrate -in source.txt -o=dest.orc --verbose

# Specify and parse valid command-line arguments...
use Getopt::Clade q{
    -i[n]  [=] <file:in>    Specify input file  [default: '-']
    -o[ut] [=] <file:out>   Specify output file [default: '-']

    -l[en] [=] <l:+int>     Display length [default: 24 ]
    -w[id] [=] <w:+int>     Display width  [default: 78 ]

    -v                      Print all warnings
    --verbose               [ditto]
};

# Report intended behaviour...
if ($ARGV{-v}) {
    print "Loading first $ARGV{'-l'} chunks of file: $ARGV{'-i'}\n"
}
# etc.
```

To create an interface using `Getopt::Clade`, you simply load the module and pass it the usage message you'd like to see. It then extracts the various options you've specified, builds a parser for them, parses the command line, and then does any appropriate type-checking on what it finds. For example, the –i flag's `<file>` slot is specified with the suffix :in, indicating that it's supposed to be an input file. So `Getopt::Clade` checks whether any string in that slot is the name of a readable file. Likewise, the :+int marker in –l `<l:+int>` causes the module to accept only a positive integer in that slot.

Once the command line has been parsed and verified, the module fills in any missing defaults, and puts results in the standard %ARGV hash[*].

Notice that there are no specifications for --help, --usage, --version, or --man flags; they're always generated automatically. Likewise, there's no need for explicit error-handling code: if command-line parsing fails, `Getopt::Clade` generates the appropriate error message automatically, piecing together a full usage line from the options you specified. The module has many other features, and is definitely worth considering when implementing complex command-line interfaces.

---

[*] Yes, that's a non-lexical variable. However, like its more famous siblings @ARGV and $ARGV, it has special status in a Perl program. Like the %ENV hash, it represents part of the external environment of the program, so the use of this global variable is acceptable under these guidelines. It doesn't even create problems under use strict.

Interface Consistency

**Ensure that your interface, run-time messages,
and documentation remain consistent.**

Making sure that a program's documentation matches its actual behaviour is a universal problem. And that problem is even tougher for command-line interface code, where the functionality and documentation must also stay consistent with the messages provided by the --usage, --help, and --man flags, as well as with any diagnostics produced by the command-line processor.

The best solutions to this challenge all rely on defining the desired command-line semantics in a single place, then using some tool to generate the actual parsing code, the meta-option responses, the error diagnostics, and the documentation.

For example, a feature of the Getopt::Clade module is that its --man meta-option is context-sensitive. Normally, a call like:

```
> illustrate --man
```

extracts any POD documentation from the *illustrate* source file, replaces the SYNOPSIS, REQUIRED ARGUMENTS, and OPTIONS sections of that documentation with a description of the actual interface that was defined, feeds the modified POD though a pod-to-text formatter, and displays it. However, if --man is specified when the program's standard output stream is not attached to a terminal:

```
> illustrate --man  > illustrate.pod
```

then Getopt::Clade still extracts and modifies the program's documentation, but doesn't format or page it in any way. The resulting file of raw POD can then be pasted back into the source file to ensure that the documentation is consistent with the interface.

Getopt::Clade even allows this process to be fully automated. If you type:

```
> illustrate --man=update
```

then the module will generate its own SYNOPSIS, REQUIRED ARGUMENTS, and OPTIONS sections as usual, but then edit that POD directly into the source file[*].

Another CPAN module, Getopt::Euclid, takes exactly the opposite approach. Instead of generating documentation directly from the program's specification of the interface, this module generates the interface directly from the program's documentation.

Using Getopt::Euclid, you can set up a command-line interface without writing any command-line processing code[†] whatsoever. All you need to do is document the

---

[*] Provided, of course, the user has write permission on that file, and can flock it.

[†] Except for the use Getopt::Euclid line, of course. The module is clever, but it's not psychic.

---

interface you'd like, and the module will read that description at run time and automatically create the equivalent command-line parser. Example 14-5 shows how you
could reproduce the same command-line interface that was repeatedly implemented
in Examples 14-1 through 14-4.

Example 14-5. Command-line parsing via Getopt::Euclid

```
# Handle command lines of the form:
#
#     > orchestrate -in source.txt -o=dest.orc --verbose

# Create a command-line parser that implements the documentation below...
use Getopt::Euclid;

# Report intended behaviour...
if ($ARGV{-v}) {
    print "Loading first $ARGV{-l} chunks of file: $ARGV{-i}\n"
}

# etc.

__END__

=head1 NAME

orchestrate - Convert a file to Melkor's .orc format

=head1 VERSION

This documentation refers to orchestrate version 1.9.4

=head1 USAGE

    orchestrate  -in source.txt  -out dest.orc  [options]

=head1 OPTIONS

=over

=item  -i[n] [=] <file>

Specify input file

=for Euclid:
    file.type:     readable
    file.default:  '-'

=item  -o[ut] [=] <file>

Specify output file
```

Example 14-5. Command-line parsing via Getopt::Euclid (continued)

```
=for Euclid:
    file.type:    writable
    file.default: '-'

=item  -l[en] [=] <l>

Display length (default is 24 lines)

=for Euclid:
    l.type:    integer > 0
    l.default: 24

=item  -w[id] [=] <w>

Display width (default is 78 columns)

=for Euclid:
    w.type:    integer > 0
    w.default: 78

=item -v

=item --verbose

Print all warnings

=item --version

=item --usage

=item --help

=item --man

Print the usual program information

=back

=begin remainder of documentation here...
```

At first glance, this approach looks like it requires far more effort than, say, Getopt::
Clade did in Example 14-4. But that's not actually the case. The previous versions of
this command-line parser didn't include the POD that the application would still
require (see Chapter 7). If the length of that necessary documentation is taken into
account, the Getopt::Euclid version is by far the quickest and easiest solution. It
requires only a single line of code, and a small number of =for Euclid annotations in
the POD itself.

Happily, it's also the most robust and maintainable approach. Using this module, it's
simply impossible for the documentation, command-line processing behaviour, or

diagnostic messages ever to differ in any way. And maintainers don't even have to type –man=update to ensure proper synchronization when the command-line specification changes.

The only significant limitation of the POD-based approach used by Getopt::Euclid is that the resulting interface must be explicit in the documentation and is fixed at the time that documentation is written. Procedural specifications, like those used by Getopt::Long or Getopt::Clade, allow the interface to be defined at run time. Such situations are comparatively rare, but may arise if your interface depends on external resources.

Interapplication Consistency

Factor out common command-line interface components into a shared module.

Tools such as Getopt::Long, Getopt::Clade, and Getopt::Euclid make it easy to follow the advice of the "Command-Line Structure" guideline to enforce a single consistent command-line structure across all of your applications.

If you're using Getopt::Long or Getopt::Clade, you can simply create a module that provides a suitable description of the standard interface. For example, if you're using Getopt::Clade, you might create a module (such as in Example 14-6) that provides the standard interface features that every application is expected to provide:

Example 14-6. Standard interface components for Getopt::Clade

```
package Corporate::Std::Cmdline;
use strict;
use warnings;

use Getopt::Clade q{

    -i[n]  [=] <file:in>     Specify input file  [default: '-']
    -o[ut] [=] <file:out>    Specify output file [default: '-']

    -v                       Print all warnings
    --verbose                [ditto]

};

1;  # Magic true value required at the end of every module
```

You could then reuse it in each program you created. For example, you could refactor Example 14-4 to Example 14-7.

Example 14-7. Standardized command-line parsing via Getopt::Clade

```
# Specify and parse valid command-line arguments...
use Corporate::Std::Cmdline plus => q{

    -l[en] [=] <l:+int>     Display length [default: 24 ]
    -w[id] [=] <w:+int>     Display width  [default: 78 ]

};

# Report intended behaviour...
if ($ARGV{-v}) {
    print "Loading first $ARGV{'-l'} chunks of file: $ARGV{'-i'}\n"
}
# etc.
```

Getopt::Euclid allows you to construct interface specification modules in a similar way. The main difference is that those modules mainly contain POD (see Example 14-8).

Example 14-8. Standard interface components for Getopt::Euclid

```
package Corporate::Std::Cmdline;
use Getopt::Euclid;

1;  # POD-only modules still need a magic true value at the end

=head1 STANDARD OPTIONS

=over

=item  -i[nfile] [=] <file>

Specify input file

=for Euclid:
    file.type:    readable
    file.default: '-'

=item  -o[utfile] [=] <file>

Specify output file

=for Euclid:
    file.type:    writable
    file.default: '-'

=item -v[erbose]

Print all warnings

=item --version
```

Example 14-8. Standard interface components for Getopt::Euclid (continued)

```
=item --usage

=item --help

=item --man

Print the usual program information

=back
```

Once that module was installed in the normal way, you could refactor Example 14-5 to the implementation shown in Example 14-9. Note that, once again, only the application-specific arguments need to be specified within the application itself.

Example 14-9. Standardized command-line parsing via Getopt::Euclid

```
# Handle command lines of the form:
#
#    > orchestrate -in source.txt -o=dest.orc -verbose

# Create a command-line parser that implements the documentation below...
use Corporate::Std::Cmdline;

# Report intended behaviour...
if ($ARGV{-v}) {
    print "Loading first $ARGV{-l} chunks of file: $ARGV{-i}\n"
}

# etc.

__END__

=head1 NAME

orchestrate - Convert a file to Melkor's .orc format

=head1 VERSION

This documentation refers to orchestrate version 1.9.4

=head1 USAGE

    orchestrate  -in source.txt  -out dest.orc  -verbose  -len=24

=head1 OPTIONS

=over

=item  -l[en] [=] <l>

Display length (default is 24 lines)
```

Example 14-9. Standardized command-line parsing via Getopt::Euclid (continued)

```
=for Euclid:
    l.type:    integer > 0
    l.default: 24

=item  -w[id] [=] <w>

Display width (default is 78 columns)

=for Euclid:
    w.type:    integer > 0
    w.default: 78

=back

=head1 STANDARD INTERFACE

See L<Corporate::Std::Cmdline> for a description of the standard
command-line arguments available for all applications in the Strate suite.

=begin remainder of documentation here...
```

CHAPTER 15
Objects

Object-oriented programming offers a sustainable
way to write spaghetti code. It lets you accrete
programs as a series of patches.
—Paul Graham
  The Hundred-Year Language

Perl's approach to object orientation is almost excessively Perlish: there are *far* too many ways to do it.

There are at least a dozen different ways to build an object (from a hash, from an array, from a subroutine, from a string, from a database, from a memory-mapped file, from an empty scalar variable, etc., etc.). Then there are scores of ways to implement the behaviour of the associated class. On top of that, there are also hundreds of different techniques for access control, inheritance, method dispatch, operator overloading, delegation, metaclasses, generics, and object persistence[*]. And, of course, many developers also make use of one or more of the over 400 "helper" modules from the CPAN's `Class::` and `Object::` namespaces.

There are just so many possible combinations of implementation, structure, and semantics that it's quite rare to find two unrelated class hierarchies that use precisely the same style of Perl OO.

That diversity creates a huge problem. The dizzying number of possible OO implementations makes it very much harder to comprehend any particular implementation, because the reader might not encounter a single familiar code structure by which to navigate the class definitions.

---

[*] *Object Oriented Perl* (Manning, 1999) gives a comprehensive overview of the main techniques.

There is no guarantee of what a class declaration will look like, nor how it will specify its attributes and methods, nor where it will store its data, nor how its methods will mediate access to that data, nor what the class constructor will be called, nor what a method call will look like, nor how inheritance relationships will be declared, nor just about anything else.

You can't even assume that there will *be* a class declaration (see the `Class::Classless` module, for example), or that the attributes or methods are specified at all (as in `Class::Tables`), or that object data isn't stored outside the program completely (like `Cache::Mmap` does), or that methods don't magically redefine themselves in derived classes when called a certain special way (as happens under `Class::Data::Inheritable`).

This cornucopia of alternatives rarely results in robust or efficient code. Of the several dozen OO approaches most frequently used in Perl development, none of them scales well to the demands of large systems. That includes the consensus first choice: hash-based classes.

This chapter summarizes a better approach; one that produces concise readable classes, ensures reliable object behaviour, prevents several common errors, and still manages to maintain near-optimal performance.

Using OO

Make object orientation a choice, not a default.

There are plenty of excellent reasons to use object orientation: to achieve cleaner encapsulation of data; to better decouple the components of a system; to take advantage of hierarchical type relationships using polymorphism; or to ensure better long-term maintainability.

There are also plenty of reasons *not* to use object orientation: because it tends to result in poorer overall performance; because large numbers of method calls can reduce syntactic diversity and make your code less readable; or just because object orientation is simply a poor fit for your particular problem, which might be better solved using a procedural, functional, data flow, or constraint-based approach[*].

Make sure you choose to use OO because of the pros and despite the cons, not just because it's the big, familiar, comfortable hammer in your toolset.

---

[*] An excellent starting point for exploring these alternatives in Perl is the book *Higher-Order Perl*, by Mark Jason Dominus (Morgan Kaufmann, 2005).

Criteria

Choose object orientation using appropriate criteria.

When deciding whether to use object orientation, look for features of the problem—
or of the proposed solution—that suggest that OO might be a good fit. For example, object orientation might be the right approach in any of the following situations:

The system being designed is large, or is likely to become large
> Object orientation helps in large systems, because it breaks them down into
> smaller decoupled systems (called "classes"), which are generally still simple
> enough to fit in a single brain—unlike the large system as a whole.

The data can be aggregated into obvious structures, especially if there's a large amount
of data in each aggregate
> Object orientation is about classifying data into coherent chunks (called
> "objects") and then specifying how those chunks can interact and change over
> time. If there are natural clusterings in the data to be handled by your system,
> then the natural place for those clusterings is probably inside an object. And the
> larger the amount of data in each chunk, the more likely it is that you're going to
> need to think of those chunks at some higher, more abstract level. It's also more
> likely that you'll need to control access to that data more tightly to ensure it
> remains consistent.

The various types of data aggregate form a natural hierarchy that facilitates the use of
inheritance and polymorphism
> Object orientation provides a way to capture, express, and take advantage of the
> abstract relationships between chunks of data in your code. If one kind of data is
> a special form of another kind of data (a restriction, or elaboration, or some
> other variation), then organizing that data into class hierarchies can minimize
> the amount of nearly identical code that has to be written.

You have a piece of data on which many different operations are applied
> You're going to be calling many different subroutines on the same data. But Perl
> subroutines don't type-check their arguments in any way, so it's very easy to
> send the wrong type of data to the wrong subroutine. If that happens, Perl's oth-
> erwise helpful implicit behaviours[*] can conspire to mask the mistake, making it
> vastly harder to detect and correct. In contrast, if the data is an object, then only
> those subroutines that are methods of the appropriate class can ever be called on
> that data.

---

[*] Such as the automatic interconversion of strings and numbers, and the autovivification of non-existent hash
and array elements.

You need to perform the same general operations on related types of data, but with slight variations depending on the specific type of data the operations are applied to

For example, if every piece of equipment needs to have check( ), register( ), deploy( ), and activate( ) applied to it, but the process of checking, registration, deployment, and activation differs for each type of equipment, then you have the textbook conditions for using polymorphic method calls.

It's likely you'll have to add new data types later

New data types will usually be related in some way to existing data types. If those existing data types are in class hierarchies, you'll be able to use inheritance to create the new type with minimal extra effort, and little or no duplication of code. Better still, the new data type will then be usable in existing code, without the need to modify that code in any way.

The typical interactions between pieces of data are best represented by operators

Perl operators can be overloaded only when at least one of their operands is an object.

The implementation of individual components of the system is likely to change over time

Proper encapsulation of objects can ensure that any code that uses those objects is isolated from the details of how the objects' data is stored and manipulated. This means that no source code outside your control will ever rely on those details, so you're free to change how the object is implemented whenever necessary, without having to rewrite huge amounts of client code.

The system design is already object-oriented

If the designers have designed a huge, complex, awkward nail, then the big, familiar, comfortable hammer of OO will almost certainly be the best tool for the job.

Large numbers of other programmers will be using your code modules

Object-oriented modules tend to have interfaces that are more clearly defined, which often makes them easier to understand and use correctly. Unlike procedural APIs that export subroutines into the caller's symbol table, classes never pollute client namespaces, and therefore are much less likely to clash with other modules. And the need to use object constructors and accessors can often improve the integrity of data as well, because it's easy to embed vetting procedures into the initialization or access methods.

Pseudohashes

Don't use pseudohashes.

Pseudohashes were a mistake. Their goal—better compile-time type-checking, leading to comparatively faster run-time access—was entirely laudable. But they achieved that goal by actually slowing down all normal hash and array accesses.

They can also double both the memory footprint and the access-time for objects, unless they're used in exactly the right way. They're particularly inefficient if you ever forget to give their container variables a type (which is pretty much guaranteed, since you never have to give any other Perl variable a type, so you're not in the habit). Pseudohashes are also prone to very hard-to-fathom errors when used in inheritance hierarchies*.

Don't use them. If you're currently using them, plan to remove them from your code. They don't work with Perl releases prior to Perl 5.005, they're deprecated in Perl 5.8, and will be removed from the language entirely in 5.10.

Restricted Hashes

Don't use restricted hashes.

Restricted hashes were developed as a mechanism to partially replace pseudohashes. An ordinary hash can be converted into a restricted hash simply by calling one or more of the lock_keys( ), lock_value( ), or lock_hash( ) subroutines provided by the Hash::Util module, which is standard in Perl 5.8 and later.

If the keys of a hash are locked with lock_keys( ), that hash is prevented from creating entries for keys other than the keys that existed at the time the hash keys were locked. If a hash value is locked with lock_value( ), the value for that particular hash entry is made constant. And if the entire hash is locked with lock_hash( ), neither its keys nor their associated values can be altered.

If you build a hash-based object and then lock its keys, no-one can accidentally access $self->{Name} when the object's attribute is supposed to be in $self->{name} instead. That's a valuable form of consistency checking. If you also lock the values before the constructor returns the object, then no-one outside the class can mess

---

* For details of the numerous problems with the pseudohash construct, see Chapters 4 and 6 of *Object Oriented Perl* (Manning, 1999).

---

with the contents of your object, so you also get encapsulation. And as they're still just regular hashes, you don't lose any appreciable performance.

The problem is that like the now-deprecated pseudohashes, restricted hashes still offer only voluntary security[*]. The Hash::Util module also provides unlock_keys( ), unlock_value( ), and unlock_hash( ) subroutines, with which all that pesky consistency checking and annoying attribute encapsulation can be instantly circumvented.

Encapsulation

Always use fully encapsulated objects.

The voluntary nature of the security that restricted hashes offer is a genuine problem. Lack of encapsulation is one of the reasons why plain, unrestricted hashes aren't a suitable basis for objects either. Objects without effective encapsulation are vulnerable. Instead of politely respecting their public interface, like so:

```
# Use our company's proprietary OO file system interface...
use File::Hierarchy;

# Make an object representing the user's home directory...
my $fs = File::Hierarchy->new('~');

# Ask for the list of files in it...
for my $file ( $fs->get_files() ) {
    # ...then ask for the name of each file, and print it...
    print $file->get_name(), "\n";
}
```

some clever client coder inevitably will realize that it's marginally faster to interact directly with the underlying implementation:

```
# Use our company's proprietary OO file system interface...
use File::Hierarchy;

# Make an object representing the user's home directory...
my $fs = File::Hierarchy->new('~');

# Then poke around inside the (array-based) object
# and pull out its embedded file objects...
for my $file (@{$fs->{files}}) {
    # Then poke around inside each (hash-based) file object,
    # pull out its name, and print it...
    print $file->{name}, "\n";
}
```

---

[*] You know, the type of safety measures that are effective only against well-meaning, law-abiding folk, for whom they're not actually needed. Like airport security.

From the moment someone does that, your class is no longer cleanly decoupled from the code that uses it. You can't be sure that any bugs in your class are actually caused by the internals of your class, and are not the result of some kind of monkeying by the client code. And to make matters worse, now you can't ever change those internals without the risk of breaking some other part of the system.

Of course, if the client programmers *have* deliberately flouted the (unenforced) encapsulation of your objects, and your subsequent essential class modifications unavoidably and necessarily break several thousands of errant lines of their malignant code, surely that's just instant justice, isn't it? Unfortunately, your pointy-haired boss will probably only hear that "your sub…essential class modifications un…necessarily break…thousands of…lines of…code". Now, guess who's going to have to fix it all.

So you have to be aggressively pre-emptive about enforcing object encapsulation. If the first attempt to circumvent your interface fails, there won't be a second. Or a thousandth. From the very start, you need to enforce the encapsulation of your class rigorously; fatally, if possible. Fortunately, that's not difficult in Perl.

There is a simple, convenient, and utterly secure way to prevent client code from accessing the internals of the objects you provide. Happily, that approach guards against misspelling attribute names, as well as being just as fast as—and often more memory-efficient than—ordinary hash-based objects.

That approach is referred to by various names—*flyweight scalars, warehoused attributes, inverted indices*—but is most commonly known as: *inside-out objects*.

They're aptly named, too, because they reverse all of Perl's standard object-oriented conventions. For example, instead of storing the collected attributes of an object in an individual hash, inside-out objects store the individual attributes of an object in a collection of hashes. And, rather than using the object's attributes as separate keys into an object hash, they use each object as a key into separate attribute hashes.

That description might sound horribly convoluted, but the technique itself certainly isn't. For example, consider the two typical hash-based Perl classes shown in Example 15-1. Each declares a constructor named new( ), which blesses an anonymous hash to produce a new object. The constructor then initializes the attributes of the nascent object by assigning values to appropriate keys within the blessed hash. The other methods defined in the classes (get_files( ) and get_name( )) then access the state of the object using the standard hash look-up syntax: $self->{attribute}.

Example 15-1. Typical hash-based Perl classes

```perl
package File::Hierarchy;


# Objects of this class have the following attributes...
#     'root'   - The root directory of the file hierarchy
#     'files'  - An array storing an object for each file in the root directory

# Constructor takes path of file system root directory...
sub new {
    my ($class, $root) = @_;

    # Bless a hash to instantiate the new object...
    my $new_object = bless {}, $class;

    # Initialize the object's "root" attribute...
    $new_object->{root} = $root;

    return $new_object;
}

# Retrieve files from root directory...
sub get_files {
    my ($self) = @_;

    # Load up the "files" attribute, if necessary...
    if (!exists $self->{files}) {
        $self->{files}
            = File::System->list_files($self->{root});
    }

    # Flatten the "files" attribute's array to produce a file list...
    return @{$self->{files}};
}


package File::Hierarchy::File;


# Objects of this class have the following attributes...
#     'name' - the name of the file

# Constructor takes name of file...
sub new {
    my ($class, $filename) = @_;
```

Example 15-1. Typical hash-based Perl classes (continued)

```
    # Bless a hash to instantiate the new object...
    my $new_object = bless {}, $class;

    # Initialize the object's "name" attribute...
    $new_object->{name} = $filename;

    return $new_object;
}

# Retrieve name of file...
sub get_name {
    my ($self) = @_;

    return $self->{name};
}
```

Example 15-2 shows the same two classes, reimplemented using inside-out objects. The first thing to note is that the inside-out version of each class requires exactly the same number of lines of code as the hash-based version*. Moreover, the *structure* of each class is line-by-line identical to that of its previous version, with only minor syntactic differences on a few corresponding lines.

---

* Okay, so there's a small fudge there: the hash-based versions *could* each save three lines by leaving out the comments describing the class attributes. Of course, in that case the two versions, although still functionally identical, would no longer be identically maintainable.

Example 15-2. Atypical inside-out Perl classes

```perl
package File::Hierarchy;
use Class::Std::Utils;
{
    # Objects of this class have the following attributes...
    my %root_of;   # The root directory of the file hierarchy
    my %files_of;  # An array storing an object for each file in the root directory

    # Constructor takes path of file system root directory...
    sub new {
        my ($class, $root) = @_;

        # Bless a scalar to instantiate the new object...
        my $new_object = bless \do{my $anon_scalar}, $class;

        # Initialize the object's "root" attribute...
        $root_of{ident $new_object} = $root;

        return $new_object;
    }

    # Retrieve files from root directory...
    sub get_files {
        my ($self) = @_;

        # Load up the "files" attribute, if necessary...
        if (!exists $files_of{ident $self}) {
            $files_of{ident $self}
                = File::System->list_files($root_of{ident $self});
        }

        # Flatten the "files" attribute's array to produce a file list...
        return @{ $files_of{ident $self} };
    }
}

package File::Hierarchy::File;
use Class::Std::Utils;
{
    # Objects of this class have the following attributes...
    my %name_of;  # the name of the file

    # Constructor takes name of file...
    sub new {
        my ($class, $filename) = @_;
```

Example 15-2. Atypical inside-out Perl classes (continued)

```perl
        # Bless a scalar to instantiate the new object...
        my $new_object = bless \do{my $anon_scalar}, $class;

        # Initialize the object's "name" attribute...
        $name_of{ident $new_object} = $filename;

        return $new_object;
    }

    # Retrieve name of file...
    sub get_name {
        my ($self) = @_;

        return $name_of{ident $self};
    }
}
```

But although those few differences are minor and syntactic, their combined effect is enormous, because they make the resulting classes significantly more robust, completely encapsulated, and considerably more maintainable[*].

The first difference between the two approaches is that, unlike the hash-based classes, each inside-out class is specified inside a surrounding code block:

```perl
package File::Hierarchy;
{
    # [Class specification here]
}

package File::Hierarchy::File;
{
    # [Class specification here]
}
```

That block is vital, because it creates a limited scope, to which any lexical variables that are declared as part of the class will automatically be restricted. The benefits of that constraint will be made apparent shortly.

Speaking of lexical variables, the next difference between the two versions of the classes is that the *descriptions* of attributes in Example 15-1:

```perl
# Objects of this class have the following attributes...
#     'root'  - The root directory of the file hierarchy
#     'files' - An array storing an object for each file in the root directory
```

---

[*] They can be made thread-safe, too, provided each attribute hash is declared as being :shared and the attribute entries themselves are consistently passed to lock( ) before each attribute access. See the *perlthrtut* documentation for more details.

have become *declarations* of attributes in Example 15-2:

```
# Objects of this class have the following attributes...
my %root_of;   # The root directory of the file hierarchy
my %files_of;  # An array storing an object for each file in the root directory
```

This is an enormous improvement. By telling Perl what attributes you expect to use, you enable the compiler to check—via use strict—that you do indeed use only those attributes.

That's possible because of the third difference in the two approaches. Each attribute of a hash-based object is stored in an entry in the object's hash: $self->{name}. In other words, the name of a hash-based attribute is *symbolic*: specified by the string value of a hash key. In contrast, each attribute of an inside-out object is stored in an entry of the attribute's hash: $name_of{ident $self}. So the name of an inside-out attribute isn't symbolic; it's a hard-coded variable name.

With hash-based objects, if an attribute name is accidentally misspelled in some method:

```
sub set_name {
    my ($self, $new_name) = @_;

    $self->{naem} = $new_name;           # Oops!

    return;
}
```

then the $self hash will obligingly—and silently!—create a new entry in the hash, with the key 'naem', then assign the new name to it. But since every other method in the class correctly refers to the attribute as $self->{name}, assigning the new value to $self->{naem} effectively makes that assigned value "vanish".

With inside-out objects, however, an object's "name" attribute is stored as an entry in the class's lexical %name_of hash. If the attribute name is misspelled, then you're attempting to refer to an entirely different hash: %naem_of. Like so:

```
sub set_name {
    my ($self, $new_name) = @_;

    $naem_of{ident $self} = $new_name;      # Kaboom!

    return;
}
```

But, because there's no such hash declared in the scope, use strict will complain (with extreme prejudice):

```
Global symbol "%naem_of" requires explicit package name at Hierarchy.pm line 86
```

Not only is that consistency check now automatic, it's also performed at compile time.

The next difference is even more important and beneficial. Instead of blessing an empty anonymous hash as the new object:

```
my $new_object = bless {}, $class;
```

the inside-out constructor blesses an empty anonymous scalar:

```
my $new_object = bless \do{my $anon_scalar}, $class;
```

That odd-looking \do{my $anon_scalar} construct is needed because there's no built-in syntax in Perl for creating a reference to an anonymous scalar; you have to roll-your-own (see the upcoming "Nameless Scalars" sidebar for details). Alternatively, you may prefer to avoid the oddity and just use the anon_scalar() function that's provided by the Class::Std::Utils CPAN module:

```
use Class::Std::Utils;

# and later...

my $new_object = bless anon_scalar(), $class;
```

Whichever way the anonymous scalar is created, it's immediately passed to bless, which anoints it as an object of the appropriate class. The resulting object reference is then stored in $new_object.

Once the object exists, it's used to create a unique key (ident $new_object) under which each attribute that belongs to the object will be stored (e.g., $root_of{ident $new_object} or $name_of{ident $self}). The ident() utility that produces this unique key is provided by the Class::Std::Utils module and is identical in effect to the refaddr() function in the standard Scalar::Util module. That is, ident($obj) simply returns the memory address of the object as an integer. That integer is guaranteed to be unique to the object, because only one object can be stored at any given memory address. You could use refaddr() directly to get the address if you prefer, but the Class::Std::Utils gives it a shorter, less obtrusive name, which makes the resulting code more readable.

To recap: every inside-out object is a blessed scalar, and has—intrinsic to it—a unique identifying integer. That integer can be obtained from the object reference itself, and then used to access a unique entry for the object in each of the class's attribute hashes.

But why is that so much better than just using hashes as objects? Because it means that every inside-out object is nothing more than an uninitialized scalar. When your constructor passes a new inside-out object back to the client code, all that comes back is an empty scalar, which makes it *impossible* for that client code to gain direct access to the object's internal state.

Oh, sure, the client code *could* pass an object reference to refaddr() or ident() to obtain the unique identifier under which that object's state is stored. But that won't

Nameless Scalars

Perl has special language constructs that make it easy to create references to anonymous hashes and arrays:

```
my $hash_ref  = {};
my $array_ref = [];
```

But there's no equivalent shorthand for creating anonymous scalars. Instead, there's a "longhand":

```
my $scalar_ref  = \do{ my $anon_scalar };
```

The trick to creating an anonymous scalar is to declare it as a (named) lexical scalar instead (such as my $anon_scalar), but declare it in a very limited scope. And the most limited scope possible is the inside of a single-statement do{} block: as soon as the variable is created, bang! It reaches the end of its scope.

That might seem like a complete waste of time; everybody knows that lexical variables in Perl cease to exist as soon as they hit the end of their declaration scope. Except, of course, that's not entirely correct. It's actually only the lexical's *name* that always ceases to exist at the end of its scope.

The variable itself may also be garbage-collected at the same point, but that's merely an epiphenomenon; it happens only because the sole reference to the variable (its name) is being removed at that point, so the variable's reference count goes to zero and its allocated memory is reclaimed.

However, if a named lexical variable is also referred to by some other reference, then the lexical destruction of the variable's name will still decrement its reference count, but not to zero, in which case the variable will *not* be destroyed, and will therefore outlast its own name (i.e., become anonymous).

That's exactly what the \do{my $anon_scalar} is doing. Because the declaration of $anon_scalar is the last thing in the do{} block, the block itself will evaluate to that variable and then the backslash will take a reference to it. So there'll be a second reference to it—temporarily, at least—as the do{} block finishes. The scalar variable's name will disappear, but the variable itself will continue to exist. Anonymously.

Incidentally, just like anonymous hashes and arrays, anonymous scalars can be initialized as they're being created. Like so:

```
my $scalar_ref = \do{ my $anon_scalar = 'initial value' };
```

help. The client code is outside the block that surrounds the object's class. So, by the time the client code gets hold of an object, the lexical attribute hashes inside the class block (such as %names_of and %files_of) will be out of scope. The client code won't even be able to see them, let alone access them.

At this point you might be wondering: *if those attribute hashes are out of scope, why didn't they cease to exist?* As explained in the "Nameless Scalars" sidebar, variables are garbage-collected only when nothing refers to them anymore. But the attribute hashes in each class are permanently referred to—by name—in the code of the various methods of the class. It's those references that keep the hashes "alive" even after their scope ends. Interestingly, that also means that if you declare an attribute hash and then don't actually refer to it in any of the class's methods, that hash *will* be garbage-collected as soon as the declaration scope finishes. So you don't even pay a storage penalty for attributes you mistakenly declare but never use.

With a hash-based object, object state is protected only by the client coder's self-discipline and sense of honour (that is, not at all):

```
# Find the user's videos...
$vid_lib = File::Hierarchy->new('~/videos');

# Replace the first three with titles that aren't
# actually in the directory (bwah-ha-ha-hah!!!!)...
$vid_lib->{files}[0]  = q{Phantom Menace};
$vid_lib->{files}[1]  = q{The Man Who Wasn't There};
$vid_lib->{files}[2]  = q{Ghost};
```

But if the File::Hierarchy constructor returns an inside-out object instead, then the client code gets nothing but an empty scalar, and any attempt to mess with the object's internal state by treating the object as a raw hash will now produce immediate and fatal results:

```
Not a HASH reference at client_code.pl line 6
```

By implementing all your classes using inside-out objects from the very beginning, you can ensure that client code never has the opportunity to rely on the internals of your class—as it will never be given access to those internals. That guaranteed isolation of internals from interface makes inside-out objects intrinsically more maintainable, because it leaves you free to make changes to the class's implementation whenever you need to.

Of the several popular methods of reliably enforcing encapsulation in Perl*, inside-out objects are also by far the cheapest. The run-time performance of inside-out classes is effectively identical to that of regular hash-based classes. In particular, in both schemes, every attribute access requires only a single hash look-up. The only appreciable difference in speed occurs when an inside-out object is destroyed (see the "Destructors" guideline later in this chapter).

The relative memory overheads of the two schemes are a little more complex to analyze. Hash-based classes require one hash per object (obviously). On the other hand, inside-out classes require one (empty) scalar per object, plus one hash per declared attribute (i.e., %name_of, %files_of, and so on). Both schemes also need one scalar per

---

* Including subroutine-based objects, "flyweight" objects, and the Class::Securehash module—see Chapter 11 of *Object Oriented Perl* (Manning, 1999).

attribute per object (the actual storage for their data inside the various hashes), but that cancels out in the comparison and can be ignored. All of which means that, given the relative sizes of an empty hash and an empty scalar (about 7.7 to 1), inside-out objects are more space-efficient than hash-based objects whenever the number of objects to be created is at least 15% higher than the number of attributes per object. In practical terms, inside-out classes scale better than hash-based classes as the total number of objects increases.

The only serious drawback of inside-out objects stems directly from their greatest benefit: encapsulation. Because their internals cannot be accessed outside their class, you can't use Data::Dumper (or any other serialization tool) to help you debug the structure of your objects. "Automating Class Hierarchies" in Chapter 16 describes a simple means of overcoming this limitation.

Constructors

Give every constructor the same standard name.

Specifically, name the constructor of every class you write: new( ). It's short, accurate, and standard across many OO languages.

If every constructor uses the same name, the developers using your classes will always be able to guess correctly what method they should call to create an object, which will save them time and frustration looking up the fine manual—yet again—to remind themselves which obscurely named method call is required to instantiate objects of each particular class.

More importantly, using a standard constructor will make it easier for the maintainers of your code to understand what a particular method call is doing. Specifically, if the call is to new( ), then it will definitely be creating an object.

Constructors with clever names are cute and may sometimes even improve readability:

```
my $port = Port->named($url);

my $connection = Socket->connected_to($port);
```

But constructors with standard names make the resulting code easier to write correctly, and possible to comprehend in six months time:

```
my $port = Port->new({ name => $url });

my $connection = Socket->new({ connect_to => $port });
```

Cloning

Don't let a constructor clone objects.

If you overload your constructors to also clone objects, it's too hard to tell the difference between construction and copying in client code:

```
$next_obj = $requested->new(\%args);      # New object or copy?
```

Methods that create new objects and methods that clone existing objects have a large amount of overlap in their behaviour. They both have to create a new data structure, bless it into an object, locate and verify the data to initialize its attributes, initialize its attributes, and finally return the new object. The only significant difference between construction and cloning is where the attribute data originates: externally in the case of a constructor, and internally in the case of a clone method.

The natural temptation is to combine the two methods into a single method. And the usual mental leap at that point is that Perl methods can always be called either as class methods or as instance methods. So, hey, why not simply have new( ) act like a constructor if it's called as a class method:

```
$new_queue = Queue::Priority->new({ selector => \&most_urgent });
```

and then act like a cloning method if it's called on an existing object:

```
$new_queue = $curr_queue->new( );
```

Because that can be achieved by adding only a single "paragraph" at the start of the existing constructor, as Example 15-3 illustrates. Cool!

Example 15-3. A constructor that also clones

```
sub new {
    my ($invocant, $arg_ref) = @_;

    # If method called on an object (i.e., a blessed reference)...
    if (ref $invocant) {
        # ...then build the argument list by copying the data from the object...
        $arg_ref = {
            selector => $selector_of{ident $invocant},
            data     => [ @{$data_of{ident $invocant} } ],
        }
    }

    # Work out the actual class name...
    my $class = ref($invocant)||$invocant;

    # Build the object...
    my $new_object = bless anon_scalar(), $class;

    # And initialize its attributes...
    $selector_of{ident $new_object} = $arg_ref->{selector};
```

Example 15-3. A constructor that also clones (continued)

```
    $data_of{ident $new_object}      = $arg_ref->{data};

    return $new_object;
}
```

A variation on this idea is to allow constructor calls on objects, but have them still act like ordinary constructors, creating a new object of the same class as the object on which they're called:

```
sub new {
    my ($invocant, $arg_ref) = @_;

    # Work out the actual class name...
    my $class = ref($invocant)||$invocant;

    # Build the object...
    my $new_object = bless anon_scalar(), $class;

    # And initialize its attributes...
    $selector_of{ident $new_object} = $arg_ref->{selector};
    $data_of{ident $new_object}      = $arg_ref->{data};

    return $new_object;
}
```

Unfortunately, there are several flaws in either of these approaches. The most obvious is that it suddenly becomes impossible to be sure what a given call to new() is actually doing. That is, there's no way to tell whether a statement like:

```
$next_possibility->new( \%defaults );
```

is creating a new object or copying an existing one. At least, no way to tell without first determining what's in $next_possibility. If, for example, the call to new() is part of a processing loop like:

```
# Investigate alternative storage mechanisms...
for my $next_possibility ( @possible_container_classes ) {
    push @active_queues, $next_possibility->new( \%defaults );
    # etc.
}
```

then it's (probably) a constructor, but if it's part of a loop like:

```
# Examine possible data sources...
for my $next_possibility ( @active_queues ) {
    push @phantom_queues, $next_possibility->new( \%defaults );
    # etc.
}
```

then it's likely to be cloning. The point is, you can no longer tell what's happening just by looking at the code where it's happening. You can't even really tell by looking at the array that's being iterated, until you trace back further and work out what kind of values that array is actually storing.

In contrast, if new( ) only ever constructs, and cloning is always done with a method called clone( ), then the very same method call:

```
$next_possibility->new( \%defaults );
```

is now clearly and unambiguously a constructor, regardless of context. Had it been intended to be a cloning operation, it would—equally unambiguously—have been written:

```
$next_possibility->clone( \%defaults );
```

Apart from not being able to say precisely what you mean, multipurpose constructors create a second maintenance problem: as Example 15-3 illustrates, adding cloning support needlessly complicates the constructor code itself. Especially when a separate clone( ) method can often be implemented far more cleanly in fewer lines of code, without modifying new( ) at all:

```
sub clone {
    my ($self) = @_;

    # Work out the object's class (and verify that it actually has one)...
    my $class = ref $self
        or croak( qq{Can't clone non-object: $self} );

    # Construct a new object,
    # copying the current object's state into the constructor's argument list...
    return $class->new({
        selector => $selector_of{ident $self},
        data     => [ @{ $data_of{ident $self} } ],
    });
}
```

Separating your new( ) and clone( ) methods makes it possible to accurately encode your intentions in any code that creates new objects. That, in turn, makes understanding and debugging that code very much easier. Separate creation methods also make your class's own code cleaner and more maintainable.

Note that the same reasoning and advice applies in *any* situation where you're tempted to overload the behaviour of a single method or subroutine to provide two or more related functions. Resist that urge.

Destructors

Always provide a destructor for every inside-out class.

The many advantages of inside-out classes described earlier come at almost no performance cost. Almost. The one respect in which they are marginally less efficient is their destructor requirements.

Hash-based classes often don't even *have* a destructor requirement. When the object's reference count decrements to zero, the hash is automatically reclaimed, and any data structures stored inside the hash are likewise cleaned up. This technique works so well that many OO Perl programmers find that they never need to write a DESTROY( ) method; Perl's built-in garbage collection handles everything just fine.

The only time that hash-based classes do need a destructor is when their objects are managing resources that are external to the objects themselves: databases, files, system processes, hardware devices, and so on. Because the resources aren't inside the objects (or inside the program, for that matter), they aren't affected by the object's garbage collection. Their "owner" has ceased to exist, but they remain: still reserved for the use of the program in question, but now completely unbeknownst to it.

So the general rule for Perl classes is: always provide a destructor for any object that manages allocated resources that are not actually located inside the object.

But the whole *point* of an inside-out object is that its attributes are stored in allocated hashes that are not actually located inside the object. That's precisely how it achieves secure encapsulation: by not sending the attributes out into the client code.

Unfortunately, that means when an inside-out object is eventually garbage-collected, the only storage that is reclaimed is the single blessed scalar implementing the object. The object's attributes are entirely unaffected by the object's deallocation, because the attributes are not inside the object, nor are they referred to by it in any way.

Instead, the attributes are referred to by the various attribute hashes in which they're stored. And because those hashes will continue to exist until the end of the program, the defunct object's orphaned attributes will likewise continue to exist, safely nestled inside their respective hashes, but now untended by any object. In other words, when an inside-out object dies, its associated attribute hashes leak memory.

The solution is simple. Every inside-out class has to provide a destructor that "manually" cleans up the attributes of the object being destructed. Example 15-4 shows the necessary addition to the File::Hierarchy class from Example 15-2.

Example 15-4. An inside-out class with its necessary destructor

```
package File::Hierarchy;
use Class::Std::Utils;
{
    # Objects of this class have the following attributes...
    my %root_of;   # The root directory of the file hierarchy
    my %files_of;  # An array storing an object for each file in the root directory

    # Constructor takes path of file system root directory...
    sub new {
        # [As in Example 15-2]
    }
```

Example 15-4. An inside-out class with its necessary destructor (continued)

```
    # Retrieve files from root directory...
    sub get_files {
        # [As in Example 15-2]
    }

    # Clean up attributes when object is destroyed...
    sub DESTROY {
        my ($self) = @_;

        delete $root_of{ident $self};
        delete $files_of{ident $self};

        return;
    }
}
```

The obligation to provide a destructor like this in every inside-out class can be mildly irritating, but it is still a very small price to pay for the considerable benefits that the inside-out approach otherwise provides for free. And the irritation can easily be eliminated by using the appropriate class construction tools, as explained under "Automating Class Hierarchies" in Chapter 16.

Methods

When creating methods, follow the general guidelines for subroutines.

Despite their obvious differences in dispatch semantics, methods and subroutines are similar in most respects. From a coding point of view, about the only significant difference between the two is that methods tend to have fewer parameters[*].

When you're writing methods, use the same approach to layout (Chapter 2), and the same naming conventions (Chapter 3), and the same argument-passing mechanisms and return behaviours (Chapter 9), and the same error-handling techniques (Chapter 13) as for subroutines.

The only exception to that advice concerns naming. Specifically, the "Homonyms" guideline in Chapter 9 doesn't apply to methods. Unlike subroutines, it's acceptable for a method to have the same name of a built-in function. That's because methods are always called with a distinctive syntax, so there's no possible ambiguity between:

```
    $size = length $target;     # Stringify target object; take length of string
```

---

[*] If that proves not to be the case, you should probably re-evaluate your design. Do certain combinations of arguments regularly appear together? Perhaps they ought to be encapsulated in an object of their own that's then passed to the method. Or maybe they ought to be attributes of the invocant itself.

and:

```
$size = $target->length( );   # Call length( ) method on target object
```

It's important to be able to use builtin names for methods, because one of the commonest uses of object-oriented Perl is to create new data types, which often need to provide the same kinds of behaviours as Perl's built-in data types. If that's the case, then those behaviours ought to be named the same as well. For instance, the class in Example 15-5 is a kind of queue, so code that uses that class will be easier to write, and later comprehend, if the queue objects push and shift data using push( ) and shift( ) methods:

```
my $waiting_list = FuzzyQueue->new( );

# Load client names...
while (my $client = prompt 'Client: ') {
    $waiting_list->push($client);
}

# Then rotate the contents of the queue (approximately) one notch...
$waiting_list->push(  $waiting_list->shift( ) );
```

Naming those same methods append( ) and next( ) makes it slightly harder to work out what's going on (as you can't reason by analogy to Perl's builtins):

```
my $waiting_list = FuzzyQueue->new( );

# Load client names...
while (my $client = prompt('Client: ')) {
    $waiting_list->append($client);
}

# Then rotate the contents of the queue (approximately) one notch...
$waiting_list->append(  $waiting_list->next( ) );
```

Example 15-5. A mildly stochastic queue

```
# Implement a queue that's slightly blurry about where it adds new elements...
package FuzzyQueue;
use Class::Std::Utils;
use List::Util qw( max );
{
    # Attributes...
    my %contents_of;     # The array storing each fuzzy queue's data
    my %vagueness_of;    # How fuzzy should the queue be?

    # The usual inside-out constructor...
    sub new {
        my ($class, $arg_ref) = @_;

        my $new_object = bless anon_scalar( ), $class;

        $contents_of{ident $new_object} = [];
        $vagueness_of{ident $new_object}
            = exists $arg_ref=>{vagueness} ? $arg_ref=>{vagueness} : 1;
```

Example 15-5. A mildly stochastic queue (continued)

```perl
        return $new_object;
    }

    # Push each element somewhere near the end of queue...
    sub push {
        my ($self) = shift;

        # Unpack contents of queue...
        my $queue_ref = $contents_of{ident $self};

        # Grab each datum...
        for my $datum (@_) {
            # Scale the random fuzziness to the amount specified for this queue...
            my $fuzziness = rand $vagueness_of{ident $self};

            # Squeeze the datum into the array, using a negative number
            # to count (fuzzily) back from the end, but making sure not
            # to run off the front...
            splice @{$queue_ref}, max(-@{$queue_ref}, -$fuzziness), 0, $datum;
        }

        return;
    }

    Grab the object's data and shift off the first datum (in a non-fuzzy way)...
    sub shift {
        my ($self) = @_;
        return shift @{ $data_of{ident $self} };
    }
}
```

Accessors

Provide separate read and write accessors.

Most developers who write classes in Perl provide access to an object's attributes in the way that's demonstrated in Example 15-6.

That is, they write a single method[*] for each attribute, giving that method the same name as the attribute. Each accessor method always returns the current value of its corresponding attribute, and each can be called with an extra argument, in which case it also updates the attribute to that new value. For example:

```perl
# Create the new military record...
my $dogtag = Dogtag->new({ serial_num => 'AGC10178B' });
```

---

[*] Sometimes referred to as a *mutator*.

```
$dogtag->name( 'MacArthur', 'Dee' );      # Called with args, so store name attr
$dogtag->rank( 'General' );               # Called with arg, so store rank attr

# Called without arg, so just retrieve attribute values...
print 'Your new commander is: ',
      $dogtag->rank(), $SPACE, $dogtag->name( )->{surname},
      "\n";

print 'Her serial number is:  ', $dogtag->serial_num( ), "\n";
```

This approach has the advantage of requiring only a single, obviously named method per attribute, which means less code to maintain. It also has the advantage that it's a widely known convention, used both throughout Perl's OO-related manpages and in numerous books.

However, despite those features, it's clearly not the best way to write accessor methods.

Example 15-6. The usual way accessor methods are implemented

```
package Dogtag;
use Class::Std::Utils;
{
    # Attributes...
    my %name_of;
    my %rank_of;
    my %serial_num_of;

    # The usual inside-out constructor...
    sub new {
        my ($class, $arg_ref) = @_;

        my $new_object = bless anon_scalar(), $class;

        $serial_num_of{ident $new_object} =  $arg_ref->{serial_num},

        return $new_object;
    }

    # Control access to the name attribute...
    sub name {
        my ($self, $new_surname, $new_first_name) = @_;
        my $ident = ident($self);          # Factor out repeated calls to ident()

        # No argument means return the current value...
        return $name_of{$ident} if @_ == 1;

        # Otherwise, store the two components of the new value...
        $name_of{$ident}{surname}    = $new_surname;
        $name_of{$ident}{first_name} = $new_first_name;

        return;
    }
```

Example 15-6. The usual way accessor methods are implemented (continued)

```
    # Same deal for accessing the rank attribute...
    sub rank {
        my ($self, $new_rank) = @_;

        return $rank_of{ident $self} if @_ == 1;

        $rank_of{ident $self} = $new_rank;

        return;
    }

    # Serial numbers are read-only, so this accessor is much simpler...
    sub serial_num {
        my ($self) = @_;

        return $serial_num_of{ident $self};
    }

    # [Other methods of the class here]

    sub DESTROY {
        my ($self) = @_;
        my $ident = ident($self);      # Factor out repeated calls to ident()

        for my $attr_ref (\%name_of, \%rank_of, \%serial_num_of) {
            delete $attr_ref->{$ident};
        };

        return;
    }
}
```

For a start, these dual-purpose methods suffer from some of the same drawbacks as the dual-purpose constructors that were advised against earlier (see the "Cloning" guideline). For example, this might or might not change the dogtag's name:

```
    $dogtag->name(@curr_soldier);
```

depending on whether @curr_soldier is empty. That *might* sometimes be very desirable behaviour, but it can also mask some very subtle bugs if it's not what was intended. Either way, a dual-purpose accessor doesn't always give you the ability to encode your intentions unambiguously.

The combined store/retrieve methods are also marginally less efficient than they could be, as they have to perform an extra conditional test every time they're called, in order to work out what they're supposed to do. Comparisons of this kind are very cheap, so it's not a big deal—at least, not until your system scales to the point where you're doing a very large number of accesses.

The final problem with this approach is subtler and more profound; in fact, it's psychological. There's actually a nasty flaw in the code of one of the accessors shown in Example 15-6. It's comparatively hard to see because it's a sin of *omission*. It bites developers because of the way they naturally think.

The problem is in the serial_num( ) method: unlike the other two accessors, it isn't dual-purpose. The consistent get/set behaviour of the name( ) and rank( ) methods* sets up and then reinforces a particular expectation: pass an argument, update the attribute.

So it's natural to expect that the following will also work as intended:

```
# convert from old serial numbers to the new prefixed scheme...
for my $dogtag (@division_personnel) {
    my $old_serial_num = $dogtag->serial_num( );
    $dogtag->serial_num( $division_code . $old_serial_num );
}
```

But, of course, it doesn't work at all. Worse, it fails silently. The call to serial_num( ) completely ignores any arguments passed to it, and quietly goes about its sole task of returning the existing serial number, which is then silently thrown away. Debugging these kinds of problems can be exceptionally difficult, because your brain gets in the way. Having subliminally recognized the "pass argument; set attribute" pattern, your brain will have filed that belief away as one of the axioms of the class, and when it later sees:

```
$dogtag->serial_num( $division_code . $old_serial_num );
```

it automatically excludes the possibility that that statement could possibly be the cause of the program's misbehaviour. You're passing an argument, so it *must* be updating the attribute. That's a given. The problem must be somewhere else.

Of course, none of this happens at a conscious level. You just automatically ignore the offending line and start debugging the hard way, tracing the data back to see where it "got corrupted" and then forward to see where it "gets erased". Finally, after a couple of fruitless, frustrating hours some weedy intern on his very first day, being shown around by your boss, will glance over your shoulder, look straight at the serial_num( ) call, and point out your "obvious" error.

The real problem here isn't your brain's psychological blind-spot; the real problem is that the rest of the dual-purpose accessors are *guessing* your intention from the data sent to them. But the single-purpose serial_num( ) doesn't need to guess; it always knows exactly what to do. The natural, human response is to rejoice in that certainty and simply code for what you know the method should always do, rather than catering for what others might potentially think it could do.

---

* And of the future billet( ) and company( ) and platoon( ) and assignment( ) and service_history( ) and fitrep( ) and medical_record( ) and citations( ) and shoesize( ) methods.

The problem isn't hard to solve, of course. You simply rewrite serial_num( ) to anticipate and avoid the inevitable psychological trap:

```
# Serial numbers are read-only, so this accessor is much simpler...
sub serial_num {
    my ($self) = @_;

    croak q{Can't update serial number} if @_ > 1;

    return $serial_num_of{ident $self};
}
```

Unfortunately, very few developers ever do that. It's easier not to write the extra line. And it's *much* easier not to have to ponder the *gestalt* psychodynamic ramifications of the class on the collective developer consciousness in order to work out that you needed to write that extra line in the first place.

Under the dual-purpose accessor idiom, the natural inclination to omit that "unnecessary" code leaves the interpreter unable to diagnose a common mistake. Fortunately, it isn't difficult to turn those consequences around, so that leaving unnecessary code out *causes* the interpreter to diagnose the mistake. All you need to do is split the two distinct access tasks into two distinct methods, as shown in Example 15-7.

Example 15-7. A better way to implement class accessors

```
# Control access to the name attribute...
sub set_name {
    my ($self, $new_surname, $new_first_name) = @_;

    # Check that all arguments are present and accounted for...
    croak( 'Usage: $obj->set_name($new_surname, $new_first_name)' )
        if @_ < 3;

    # Store components of new value in a hash...
    $name_of{ident $self}{surname}    = $new_surname;
    $name_of{ident $self}{first_name} = $new_first_name;

    return;
}

sub get_name {
    my ($self) = @_;
    return $name_of{ident $self};
}

# Same deal for accessing the rank attribute...
sub set_rank {
    my ($self, $new_rank) = @_;

    $rank_of{ident $self} = $new_rank;
```

Example 15-7. A better way to implement class accessors (continued)

```
    return;
}

sub get_rank {
    my ($self) = @_;
    return $rank_of{ident $self};
}

# Serial numbers are read-only, so there's no set_serial_num( ) accessor...
sub get_serial_num {
    my ($self) = @_;
    return $serial_num_of{ident $self};
}
```

Here, each accessor that returns a value just returns that value, whereas each accessor that stores a value expects a second argument (the new value), uses it to update the attribute, and then returns nothing.

Any code that uses these accessors will now explicitly record the developer's intention for each accessor call:

```
# Create the new military record...
my $dogtag = Dogtag->new( {serial_num => 'AGC10178B'} );

$dogtag->set_name( 'MacArthur', 'Dee' );
$dogtag->set_rank( 'General' );

# Retrieve attribute values...
print 'Your new commander is: ',
        $dogtag->get_rank(), $SPACE, $dogtag->get_name( )->{surname}, "\n";

print 'Her serial number is: ',
        $dogtag->get_serial_num( ), "\n";
```

The code is also now slightly easier to read, because you can tell at a glance whether a particular accessor call is updating or retrieving an attribute value. So the former "reminder" comments (# Called with arg, so store name attr) are no longer necessary; the code is now self-documenting in that respect.

More importantly, no-one is ever going to mistakenly write:

```
$dogtag->get_serial_num( $division_code . $old_serial_num );
```

Human brains don't misbehave that particular way—which means you don't have to remember to have get_serial_number( ) test for that possibility.

That's not to say that developers who use the class won't still misgeneralize the getting-vs-storing axiom. They will. But now, having successfully called set_name( ) and set_rank( )*, the rule they'll mistakenly devise is: "call set_*whatever*( ); update

---

* And set_billet( ) and set_company( ) and set_platoon( ) and...aw, you get the idea.

an attribute". Hence when they erroneously try to update the serial number, what they'll write is:

```
$dogtag->set_serial_num( $division_code . $old_serial_num );
```

At which point the interpreter will immediately shoot to kill:

```
Can't locate object method "set_serial_num" via package "Dogtag"
at rollcall.pl line 99
```

Now the natural programmer tendency to leave out extraneous code is actually working in your favour. By *not* implementing set_serial_num( ), you've ensured that any erroneous attempts to use it are automatically detected, and loudly reported.

Implementing separate "get" and "set" accessors for attributes offers a significant improvement in readability and self-documentation, and even a marginal boost in performance. By using distinct method names for distinct operations, you can better encode your intentions in your source code, use one human frailty (under-exertion) to guard against another (overgeneralization) and—best of all—convince the compiler to debug your colleagues' miswired brains for you.

Lvalue Accessors

Don't use lvalue accessors.

Since Perl 5.6, it has been possible to specify a subroutine that returns a scalar result as an lvalue, which can then be assigned to. So another popular approach to implementing attribute accessor methods has arisen: using lvalue subroutines, as in Example 15-8.

Example 15-8. Another way to implement accessor methods

```
# Provide access to the name attribute...
sub name :lvalue {
    my ($self) = @_;
    return $name_of{ident $self};
}

sub rank :lvalue {
    my ($self) = @_;
    return $rank_of{ident $self};
}

# Serial numbers are read-only, so not lvalue...
sub serial_num {
    my ($self) = @_;
    return $serial_num_of{ident $self};
}
```

The resulting code is certainly much more concise. And, perhaps surprisingly, the return to a single accessor per attribute doesn't reinstate the problems of uncertain intention leading to invisible errors, because the accessors would now be used differently, with a clear syntactic distinction between storing and retrieving:

```
# Create the new military record...
my $dogtag = Dogtag->new( {serial_num => 'AGC10178B'} );

# Store attribute values...
$dogtag->name = {surname=>'MacArthur', first_name=>'Dee'};
$dogtag->rank = 'General' ;

# Retrieve attribute values...
print 'Your new commander is: ',
      $dogtag->rank(), $SPACE, $dogtag->name()->{surname}, "\n";

print 'Her serial number is: ',
      $dogtag->serial_num(), "\n";
```

And, now, if overgeneralization again leads to a misguided attempt to update the serial number:

```
$dogtag->serial_num() = $division_code . $old_serial_num;
```

the compiler will again detect and report the problem:

```
Can't modify non-lvalue subroutine call at rollcall.pl line 99
```

This certainly looks like a viable alternative to separate getting and storing. It requires less code and handles the psychology just as well. Unfortunately, lvalue methods are less reliable and less maintainable.

They're unreliable because they remove all your carefully crafted encapsulation from around the object, by granting direct and unrestricted access to its attributes. That is, a call such as $obj->name() is now identical to a direct access like $name_of{$obj}. So you can no longer guarantee that your Dogtag objects store their name information under the correct keys, or even in a hash at all.

For example, the set_name() method in Example 15-7 ensures that both names are passed and then stored in a hash in the appropriate attribute entry, so a misuse like this:

```
$dogtag->set_name('Dee MacArthur');
```

throws an immediate exception:

```
Usage: $obj->set_name($new_surname, $new_first_name) at 'promote.pl' line 33
```

But using the equivalent lvalue name() accessor from Example 15-8 doesn't do any data validation; it just returns the attribute storage, with which client code can then have its wicked way:

```
$dogtag->name = 'Dee MacArthur';
```

That string is assigned directly to the internal $name_of{ident $dogtag} attribute, which is supposed to store only a hash reference. So any other methods that rely on $name_of{ident $self} being a hash reference:

```
# much later...

$dogtag->log_orders($orders);
```

are going to produce unexpected and hard-to-debug errors, because the object's internal state is no longer as expected:

```
Can't use string ("Dee MacArthur") as a HASH ref
while "strict refs" in use at 'promote.pl' line 702
```

Lvalue accessors also make it very much harder to extend or improve your class. Get/ set accessors retain control over how attributes are accessed, so if you need to add some sanity checking when military ranks are updated, that's relatively easy to accommodate. For example, you might create a look-up table of known military ranks and a utility subroutine to verify that its argument is a known rank (or die trying):

```
# Create look-up table of known ranks...
Readonly my @KNOWN_RANKS => (
#    Enlisted...         Commissioned...
     'Private',          'Lieutenant',
     'PFC',              'Captain',
     'Corporal',         'Colonel',
     'Sergeant',         'General',
     # etc.              etc.
);
Readonly my %IS_KNOWN_RANK => map { $_ => 1 } @KNOWN_RANKS;

# Utility subroutine to vet new "rank" values....
sub _check_rank {
    my ($rank) = @_;

    return $rank if $IS_KNOWN_RANK{$rank};

    croak "Can't set unknown rank ('$rank')";
}
```

It would then be trivial to modify the set_rank( ) accessor from Example 15-7 to apply that check every time a dogtag's rank attribute is updated:

```
sub set_rank {
    my ($self, $new_rank) = @_;

    # New rank now checked first...
    $rank_of{ident $self} = _check_rank($new_rank);

    return;
}
```

On the other hand, there's no way to add this same check to the lvalue rank( ) accessor from Example 15-8, except by resorting to a tied variable (which is not an acceptable solution—see Chapter 19).

Indirect Objects

Don't use the indirect object syntax.

Quite simply: indirect object syntax is ambiguous. Whereas an "arrowed" method call is certain to call the corresponding method:

```
my $female_parent = $family->mom( );
my $male_parent   = $family->pop( );
```

with an indirect object call, the outcome is not at all certain:

```
my $female_parent = mom $family;    # Sometimes the same as: $family->mom( )
my $male_parent   = pop $family;    # Never the same as: $family->pop( )
```

The pop( ) case is fairly obvious: Perl assumes you're calling the built-in pop function... and then complains that it's not being applied to an array*. The potential problem in the mom( ) case is a little more subtle: if there's a mom( ) subroutine declared in the package in which mom $family is called, then Perl will interpret that call as mom($family) instead (that is, as a subroutine call, rather than as a method call).

Unfortunately, that particular problem often bites under the most common use of the indirect object syntax: constructor calls. Many programmers who would otherwise never write indirect object method calls will happily call their constructors that way:

```
my $uniq_id = new Unique::ID;
```

The problem is that they often do this kind of thing in the method of some other class. For example, they might decide to improve the Dogtag class by using Unique:: ID objects as serial numbers:

```
package Dogtag;
use Class::Std::Utils;
{
    # Attributes...
    my %name_of;
    my %rank_of;
    my %serial_num_of;
```

---

* Even that helpful message can be confusing when you're working in a method-call mindset: "I thought methods could be called only on scalars? And why would the Family::pop( ) method require a polygamous array of families anyway?"

```
    # The usual inside-out constructor...
    sub new {
        my ($class, $arg_ref) = @_;

        my $new_object = bless anon_scalar(), $class;

        # Now using special objects to ensure serial numbers are unique...
        $serial_num_of{ident $new_object} = new Unique::ID;

        return $new_object;
    }
```

That approach works fine, until they decide they need to factor it out into a separate class method:

```
    # The usual inside-out constructor...
    sub new {
        my ($class, $arg_ref) = @_;

        my $new_object = bless anon_scalar(), $class;

        # Now allocating serial numbers polymorphically...
        $serial_num_of{ident $new_object} = $class->_allocate_serial_num();

        return $new_object;
    }

    # Override this method in any derived class that needs a
    # different serial number allocation mechanism...
    sub _allocate_serial_num {
        return new Unique::ID;
    }
```

As soon as they make this change, the first call to Dogtag->new( ) produces the exception:

```
Can't locate object method "_allocate_serial_num" via package "Unique::ID"
at Dogtag.pm line 17.
```

where line 17 is (mysteriously) the assignment:

```
        $serial_num_of{ident $new_object} = $class->_allocate_serial_num();
```

What happened? Previously, when the new Unique::ID call was still directly inside new( ), that call had to be compiled before new( ) itself could be completely defined. Thus, when the compiler looked at the call, there was—as yet—no subroutine named new( ) defined in the current package, so Perl interpreted new Unique::ID as an indirect method call.

But once the new Unique::ID call has been factored out into a method that's defined *after* new( ), then the call will be compiled *after* the compilation of new( ) is complete. So, this time, when the compiler looks at that call, there *is* a subroutine named new( ) already defined in the current package. So Perl interprets new Unique:: ID as a direct unparenthesized subroutine call (to the subroutine Dogtag::new( ))

instead. Which means that it immediately calls DogTag::new( ) again, this time passing the string 'Unique::ID' as the sole argument. And when that recursive call to new( ) reaches line 17 again, $class will now contain the 'Unique::ID' string, so the $class->_allocate_serial_num( ) call will attempt to call the non-existent method Unique::ID::_allocate_serial_num( ), and the mysterious exception will be thrown.

That code is hard enough to debug, but it could also have gone wrong in a much more subtle and silent way. Suppose the Unique::ID class actually did happen to have its own _allocate_serial_num( ) method. In that case, the recursive call from Dogtag::_allocate_serial_num back into to the Dogtag constructor *wouldn't* fail; it would instead put whatever value was returned by the call to Unique::ID->_allocate_serial_num( ) into the $serial_num{ident $self} attribute of the object being created by the recursive Dogtag constructor call, and then return that object. Back in the original constructor call, that Dogtag object would then be assigned to yet another $serial_num{ident $self} attribute: this time the one for the object created in the non-recursive constructor call. The outermost constructor would also succeed and return its own Dogtag object.

But, now, instead of having a Unique::ID object for its serial number, that final Dogtag object would possess a serial number that consisted of a (nested) Dogtag object, whose own serial number attribute would contain whatever kind of value Unique::ID::_allocate_serial_num( ) happened to return: perhaps a Unique::ID object, or possibly a raw string, or maybe even just undef (if Unique::ID::_allocate_serial_num( ) happened to be a *mutator method* that merely updates its own object and doesn't return a value at all).

Pity the poor maintenance programmer who has to unravel that mess[*].

Indirect object method calls are ambiguous, brittle, fickle, and extremely context-sensitive. They can be broken simply by moving them about within a file, or by declaring an entirely unrelated subroutine somewhere else in the current package. They can lead to complex and subtle bugs. Don't use them.

Class Interfaces

Provide an optimal interface, rather than a minimal one.

When it comes to designing the interface of a class, developers are often advised to follow Occam's Razor and avoid multiplying their methods unnecessarily. The result is all too often a class that offers only the absolute minimal set of functionality, as in Example 15-9.

---

[*] If you got lost reading the explanation of this problem, you can no doubt imagine how hard it would be to debug the error in live code.

Example 15-9. A bit-string class with the smallest possible interface

```
package Bit::String;
use Class::Std::Utils;
{
    Readonly my $BIT_PACKING => 'b*';     # i.e. vec() compatible binary
    Readonly my $BIT_DENSITY => 1;        # i.e. 1 bit/bit

    # Attributes...
    my %bitset_of;

    # Internally, bits are packed eight-to-the-character...
    sub new {
        my ($class, $arg_ref) = @_;

        my $new_object = bless anon_scalar(), $class;

        $bitset_of{ident $new_object}
            = pack $BIT_PACKING, map {$_ ? 1 : 0} @{$arg_ref->{bits}};

        return $new_object;
    }

    # Retrieve a specified bit...
    sub get_bit {
        my ($self, $bitnum) = @_;

        return vec($bitset_of{ident $self}, $bitnum, $BIT_DENSITY);
    }

    # Update a specified bit...
    sub set_bit {
        my ($self, $bitnum, $newbit) = @_;

        vec($bitset_of{ident $self}, $bitnum, $BIT_DENSITY) = $newbit ? 1 : 0;

        return 1;
    }
}
```

Rather than enhancing maintainability, classes like that often reduce it, because they force developers who are using the class to invent their own sets of utility subroutines for frequent tasks:

```
# Convenience subroutine to flip individual bits...
sub flip_bit_in {
    my ($bitset_obj, $bitnum) = @_;

    my $bit_val = $bitset_obj->get_bit($bitnum);
    $bitset_obj->set_bit( $bitnum, !$bit_val );

    return;
}
```

```
    # Convenience subroutine to provide a string representation of the bits...
    sub stringify {
        my ($bitset_obj) = @_;

        my $bitstring = $EMPTY_STR;
        my $next_bitnum = 0;

        RETRIEVAL :
        while (1) {
            my $nextbit = $bitset_obj->get_bit($next_bitnum++);
            last RETRIEVAL if !defined $nextbit;

            $bitstring .= $nextbit;
        }

        return $bitstring;
    }
```

And that's definitely "sets" (plural), because it's highly likely that every developer—or at least every project team—will develop a *separate* set of these utility subroutines. And it's also likely—because of the strong encapsulation provided by inside-out objects—that every one of those sets of utility subroutines will be just as inefficient as the ones shown earlier.

Don't be afraid to provide optimized methods for the common usages. Implementing frequently used procedures internally, as in Example 15-10, often makes those utilities far more efficient, as well as making the class itself more useful and user-friendly.

Example 15-10. A bit-string class with a more useful interface

```
package Bit::String;
use Class::Std::Utils;
{
    Readonly my $BIT_PACKING => 'b*';    # i.e. vec( ) compatible binary
    Readonly my $BIT_DENSITY => 1;       # i.e. 1 bit/bit

    # Attributes...
    my %bitset_of;

    sub new {
        # [As in Example 15-9]
    }

    sub get_bit {
        # [As in Example 15-9]
    }

    sub set_bit {
        # [As in Example 15-9]
    }

    # Convenience method to flip individual bits...
    sub flip_bit {
        my ($self, $bitnum) = @_;
```

Example 15-10. A bit-string class with a more useful interface (continued)

```
        vec($bitset_of{ident $self}, $bitnum, $BIT_DENSITY)
            = !vec($bitset_of{ident $self}, $bitnum, $BIT_DENSITY);

        return;
    }

    # Convenience method to provide a string representation of the bits...
    sub as_string {
        my ($self) = @_;

        return join $EMPTY_STR, unpack $BIT_PACKING, $bitset_of{ident $self};
    }
}
```

Convenience methods can also dramatically improve the readability and self-documentation of the resulting client code:

```
$curr_state->flip_bit($VERBOSITY_BIT);

print 'The current state is: ', $curr_state->as_string(), "\n";
```

Because, if they aren't provided, the developers may *not* choose to devise their own utility subroutines, preferring instead to cut and paste nasty, incomprehensible fragments like:

```
$curr_state->set_bit($_, !$curr_state->get_bit($_)) for $VERBOSITY_BIT;

print 'The current state is: ',
    do {
        my @bits;
        while (defined(my $bit = $curr_state->get_bit(scalar @bits))) {
            push @bits, $bit;
        }
        @bits;
    },
    "\n";
```

Operator Overloading

Overload only the isomorphic operators of algebraic classes.

Operator overloading is very tempting. It offers the prospect of being able to express operations of your new data type in a compact and syntactically distinctive way. Unfortunately, overloading operators more often produces code that is both hard to comprehend and vastly less maintainable. For example:

```
# Special string class with useful operators...
package OpString;
{
```

```
    use overload (
        '+'    => 'concatenate',
        '-'    => 'up_to',
        '/'    => 'either_or',
        '<=>'  => 'swap_with',
        '~'    => 'optional',

        # Use Perl standard behaviours for other operations...
        fallback => 1,
    );
}

# And later...

$search_for = $MR/$MRS + ~$first_name + $family_name;

$allowed_pet_range = $CAT-$DOG;

$home_phone <=> $work_phone;
```

Though the resulting client code *is* compact, the non-standard usages of the various operators make it much harder to understand and maintain, compared to:

```
package OpString;
{
    use overload (
        '.'    => 'concatenate',

        # Use Perl standard behaviours for other operations...
        fallback => 1,
    );
}

# And later...

$search_for = $MR->either_or($MRS) . first_name->optional( ) . $family_name;

$allowed_pet_range = $CAT->up_to($DOG);

$home_phone->swap_with($work_phone);
```

Note that overloading the "dot" operator was perfectly acceptable here, as it (presumably) works just like Perl's built-in string concatenator.

Overloading other operators can make good sense (and good code), provided two conditions are met. First, the operators you choose to overload must match the standard *algebraic notation* within the problem's native domain: the set of operators that the domain experts routinely use. Second, the standard domain-specific notation you're recreating in your Perl class must conform to the Perlish precedences and associativities of the operators you're overloading.

Together, those two conditions ensure that the appearance of the selected Perl operator mirrors that of the desired problem domain operator, and that the algebraic properties (precedence and associativity) of the problem domain operator mirror those of the selected Perl operator. In other words, there must be a one-to-one correspondence of form and function: the two notations must be *isomorphic*.

For example, if your domain experts use the operators +, ., and ! on certain types of values, then it may be appropriate to overload those Perl operators for the corresponding class. However, if those domain experts treat . as being of higher precedence than + (as many mathematicians do), then overloading the corresponding Perl operators *isn't* appropriate, because . and + have the same precedence in Perl. That kind of mismatch between expectation and reality always leads to hard-to-find bugs.

On the other hand, if the domain experts use ±, •, and ¬, it's definitely inappropriate to overload the Perl operators +, ., and ! to represent them. The notation isn't the same, so it won't help those who understand the domain to understand your code. In fact, the mismatch of algebraic syntax is far more likely to get in the way.

Coercions

Always consider overloading the boolean, numeric, and string coercions of objects.

When an object reference is used as a boolean, it always evaluates to true by default, so:

```
croak( q{Can't use non-zero value} ) if $fuzzynum;
```

always throws an exception, even when $fuzzynum contains 0±0.

An even more serious problem arises when object references are treated as numbers: by default, they numerify to the integer value of their memory address. That means that a statement like:

```
$constants[$fuzzynum] = 42;
```

is really something like:

```
$constants[0x256ad1f3] = 42;
```

which is:

```
$constants[627757555] = 42;
```

which will almost certainly segfault when it tries to allocate six hundred million elements in the @constants array.

A similar problem arises if an object is used where a string is expected:

```
my $fuzzy_pi = Num::Fuzzy->new({val => 3.1, plus_or_minus => 0.0416});

# And later...

print "Pi is $fuzzy_pi\n";    # $fuzzy_pi expected to interpolate a string
```

In a string context, the object's reference is converted to a debugging value that specifies the class of the object, its underlying data type, and its hexadecimal memory address. So the previous print statement would print something like:

```
Pi is Num::Fuzzy=SCALAR[0x256ad1f3]
```

The developer was probably hoping for something more like:

Pi is 3.1 ± 0.0416

All of these problems occur because objects in Perl are almost always accessed via references. And those references behave like objects only when they're specifically used like objects (i.e., when methods are called on them). When they're used like values (as in the examples), they behave like reference values. The resulting bugs can be particularly hard to discover, and even harder to diagnose once they're noticed.

It's good practice to overload the boolean, numeric, and string coercion behaviour of objects to do something useful and expected. For example:

```perl
package Num::Fuzzy;
use charnames qw( :full );
{
    use overload (
        # Ignore the error range when converting to a number...
        q{0+} => sub {
            my ($self) = @_;
            return $self->get_value();
        },

        # Only true if the range of possible values doesn't include zero...
        q{bool} => sub {
            my ($self) = @_;
            return ! $self->range_includes(0);
        },

        # Convert to string using the as_str() method...
        q{""} => sub {
            my ($self) = @_;
            return $self->get_value()
                . "\N{PLUS-MINUS SIGN}"
                . $self->get_fuzziness();
        },

        # Use Perl standard behaviours for other operations...
        fallback => 1,
    );

    # etc.
}
```

In many classes, the most useful thing to do is simply to signal that attempting the coercion was a bad idea:

```perl
package Process::Queue;
use Carp;
{
    use overload (
        # Type coercions don't make sense for process queues...
        q{0+} => sub {
            croak( q{Can't numerify a Process::Queue } );
        },

        q{bool} => sub {
            croak( q{Can't get the boolean value of a Process::Queue } );
        },

        q{""} => sub {
            croak( q{Can't get the string value of a Process::Queue } );
        },

        # Use Perl standard behaviours for other operations...
        fallback => 1,
    );

    # etc.
}
```

This last example, suitably adapted, makes an excellent default for any class.

## CHAPTER 16

Class Hierarchies

> *The ham and cheese omelet class is worth special attention*
> *because it must inherit characteristics from the pork, dairy,*
> *and poultry classes. Thus, we see that the problem cannot be*
> *properly solved without multiple inheritance. At run time, the*
> *program must create the proper object and send a message to*
> *the object that says, "Cook yourself". The semantics of this*
> *message depend, of course, on the kind of object, so they have*
> *a different meaning to a piece of toast than to scrambled eggs.*
> *Reviewing the process so far, we see that the analysis phase*
> *has revealed that the primary requirement is to cook any kind*
> *of breakfast food. In the design phase, we have discovered*
> *some derived requirements. Specifically, we need an object-*
> *oriented language with multiple inheritance. Of course, users*
> *don't want the eggs to get cold while the bacon is frying, so*
> *concurrent processing is required, too.*
>
> —Do-While Jones
> *The Breakfast Food Cooker*

The disadvantages of implementing classes via blessed hashes become even more pronounced when those classes are used as the bases of inheritance hierarchies. For example, the lack of encapsulation makes it almost inevitable that base-class attributes will be accessed directly in derived-class methods, thereby strongly coupling the two classes.

This notion that derived classes should have some kind of exemption to the encapsulation of their base class—usually known as "protected access"—certainly seemed like a good idea at the time. But long and bitter experience now strongly suggests that this practice is just as detrimental to the maintainability of class hierarchies as full "public access" is.

Worse still, in a hash-based object, the attributes live in a single namespace (the keys of the hash), so derived classes have to contend with their base classes, and with each other, for ownership of particular attributes.

Other serious problems can also arise in Perl class hierarchies, regardless of their underlying implementation type. Constructor and destructor methods have no privileged status, and constructors usually intermix the creation and initialization of objects. These two factors make it easy for subclasses—especially those inheriting from multiple base classes—to misconstruct, incompletely initialize, or only partially clean up their derived objects.

This chapter describes a set of design and coding practices that avoid all these problems.

Inheritance

Don't manipulate the list of base classes directly.

One of the most unusual, and least robust, aspects of Perl's OO mechanism is that each class keeps its inheritance hierarchy information in an ordinary package variable: @ISA. Apart from bringing along all the problems of package variables (see Chapter 5), this approach also means that Perl class hierarchies are typically set up by run-time assignments:

```
package Superman;
our @ISA = qw( Avian Agrarian Alien );
```

instead of by compile-time declarations.

That arrangement can lead to very obscure compile-time bugs when objects are created and used before the run-time components of their class's code have been executed (for example, in a BEGIN block).

So always define a class's hierarchy declaratively at compile time, using the standard use base pragma:

```
package Superman;
use base qw( Avian Agrarian Alien );
```

This ensures that the inheritance relationship is set up as early as possible, and also ensures that the necessary modules (e.g., *Avian.pm*, *Agrarian.pm*, *Alien.pm*) are automatically loaded for you.

Better still, this approach discourages messing about with class hierarchies at run time, by reassigning @ISA. The temptation to modify @ISA at run time is usually a sign that your class might be better implemented as a factory, a façade, or with some other meta-object technique.

Objects

Use distributed encapsulated objects.

Inside-out classes generalize very cleanly to class hierarchies, even multiple-inheritance hierarchies.

In particular, the inside-out structure neatly avoids the problem of "attribute collisions", in which both the base and derived class wish to use an attribute of the same name, but cannot successfully do so because there's only one key of that name in the object's hash.

Example 16-1 illustrates the problems of using a single, publicly accessible, collision-prone hash as your derived object. The Object class and the Psyche class each think they own the $self->{id} entry in each object's hash*. But, because that attribute isn't encapsulated, neither of them can be assured of its contents. Both classes are able to alter it at will, and the attribute is also susceptible to external tampering, as the final line of the example demonstrates.

The describe( ) method is a particularly disturbing piece of code in this respect. Transcribed from a genuine real-world example, it illustrates how the powerful human ability to recognize intent by context can work against a developer. Within four lines, the programmer has used $self->{id} both as the Object's ID number, and as the Psyche's *id*...apparently, without the slightest awareness of the fundamental contradiction that represents.

Example 16-1. Making a hash of your psyche

```
# Generic base class confers an ID number and description attribute
# on all derived classes...
package Object;

# Class attribute...
my $next_id = 1;

# Constructor expects description as argument,
# and automatically allocates ID number...
sub new {
    my ($class, $arg_ref) = @_;

    # Create object representation...
    my $new_object = bless {}, $class;
```

---

* Psyche thinks the hash entry stores a complex representation of the object's primitive instincts and psychic energies, but Object reduces the same attribute to a simple integer. Orwellian programming at its double-plus-ungoodest.

Example 16-1. Making a hash of your psyche (continued)

```perl
    # Initialize attributes...
    $new_object->{ id } = $next_id++;
    $new_object->{desc} = $arg_ref->{desc};

    return $new_object;
}

# and later...

# Derived class for psychological modelling...
package Psyche;

# All instances need ID and description...
use base qw( Object );

# Constructor expects to be passed an ego representation,
# but generates other psychological layer automatically...
sub new {
    my ($class, $arg_ref) = @_;

    # Call base-class constructor to create object representation
    # and initialize identity attributes...
    my $new_object = $class->SUPER::new($arg_ref);

    # Initialize psyche-specific attributes...
    $new_object->{super_ego} = Ego::Superstructure->new();
    $new_object->{   ego   } = Ego->new($arg_ref->{ego});
    $new_object->{   id    } = Ego::Substrate->new();    # Oops! Reused 'id' entry

    return $new_object;
}

# Summarize a particular psyche...
sub describe {
    my ($self) = @_;

    # List case number...
    print "Case $self->{id}...\n";

    # Describe psychological layers...
    $self->{super_ego}->describe();
    $self->{   ego   }->describe();
    $self->{   id    }->describe();

    return;
}

# and later still...

my $psyche = Psyche->new({ desc=>'me!', ego=>'sum' });

$psyche->{id} = 'est';
```

Example 16-2 shows the same class hierarchy, but with each class implemented using the inside-out approach. Note that now the $id_of{ident $self} attributes of the base and derived classes no longer share a single hash entry. They're now separate entries in separate lexical hashes in separate scopes. The fact that they have the same name is now irrelevant: the methods of each class can see only the attribute that belongs to their own class.

The describe() method has also now been sanitized. As the Object class's $id_of{ident $self} is not in scope within the Psyche class, the only way to access it is via the public get_id() accessor method that Psyche inherits from the Object class. Apart from making the two "id" attributes syntactically distinct, restricting the accessibility of base case attributes in this way has the added advantage of decoupling the two classes. Psyche no longer relies on the implementation details of Object, so any aspect of the implementation of the base class could be changed without needing to modify its derived class* to compensate.

Example 16-2. Turning your psyche inside-out

```
# Generic base class confers an ID number and description attribute
# on all derived classes...
package Object;
use Class::Std::Utils;
{
    # Class attribute...
    my $next_id = 1;

    # Object attributes...
    my %id_of;    # ID number
    my %desc_of;  # Description

    # Constructor expects description as argument,
    # and automatically allocates ID number...
    sub new {
        my ($class, $arg_ref) = @_;

        # Create object representation...
        my $new_object = bless anon_scalar(), $class;

        # Initialize attributes...
        $id_of{ident $new_object}   = $next_id++;
        $desc_of{ident $new_object} = $arg_ref->{desc};

        return $new_object;
    }

    # Read-only access to ID number...
    sub get_id {
```

---

* Or, more usually, modifying all of its *many* derived classes.

Example 16-2. Turning your psyche inside-out (continued)

```perl
        my ($self) = @_;
        return $id_of{ident $self};
    }
}

# and  later...

# Derived class for psychological modelling...
package Psyche;
use Class::Std::Utils;
{
    # All instances need ID and description...
    use base qw( Object );

    # Attributes...
    my %super_ego_of;
    my %ego_of;
    my %id_of;

    # Constructor expects to be passed an ego representation,
    # but generates other psychological layers automatically...
    sub new {
        my ($class, $arg_ref) = @_;

        # Call base-class constructor to create object representation
        # and initialize identity attributes...
        my $new_object = $class->SUPER::new($arg_ref);

        # Initialize psyche-specific attributes...
        $super_ego_of{ident $new_object} = Ego::Superstructure->new( );
        $ego_of{ident $new_object}       = Ego->new($arg_ref->{ego});
        $id_of{ident $new_object}        = Ego::Substrate->new( );

        return $new_object;
    }

    # Summarize a particular psyche...
    sub describe {
        my ($self) = @_;

        # List case number...
        print 'Case ', $self->SUPER::get_id( ), "...\n";

        # Describe pschological layers...
        $super_ego_of{ident $self}->describe( );
        $ego_of{ident $self}->describe( );
        $id_of{ident $self}->describe( );

        return;
    }
}
```

Example 16-2. Turning your psyche inside-out (continued)

```
# and later still...

my $psyche = Psyche->new({ desc=>'me!', ego=>'sum' });

$psyche->{id} = 'est';     # Exception thrown: Not a HASH reference...
```

Blessing Objects

Never use the one-argument form of bless.

The built-in bless function associates a referent of some kind (typically a hash, an array, or a scalar) with a particular class, thereby converting the raw data type into an object. Normally, bless takes two arguments: a reference to the referent that is to become the object, and a string naming the desired class of that object. However, the second argument is actually optional, and defaults to the current package name.

Developers will occasionally attempt to save a miniscule amount of effort by writing a constructor like so:

```
package Client;
use Class::Std::Utils;
{
    my %client_num_of;

    sub new {
        my ($class, $arg_ref) = @_;

        my $new_object = bless anon_scalar();
        # (One-arg bless saves typing!)

        $client_num_of{ident $new_object} = $arg_ref->{client_num};

        return $new_object;
    }

    # etc.
}
```

Unfortunately, the half a second they save that way can lead to much more substantial amounts of time lost when they have to work out why objects of the following derived class don't work correctly:

```
package Client::Corporate;
use base qw( Client );
use Class::Std::Utils;
{
    # Attribute...
    my %corporation_of;
```

```
    sub new {
        my ($class, $arg_ref) = @_;

        # Call base class constructor to allocate and initialize object...
        my $new_object = $class->SUPER::new($arg_ref);

        # Initialize derived classes own attributes...
        $corporation_of{ident $new_object} = $arg_ref->{corp};

        return $new_object;
    }

    # etc.
}
```

What they will eventually discover is that calls like:

```
Client::Corporate->new(\%client_data);
```

are actually producing objects of class Client, rather than of the requested subclass.
That's because Client::Corporate::new() calls the Client::new(), which does a one-
argument bless, which blesses into the current package. And, inside Client::new(),
the current package is always Client.

Using the two-argument form of bless prevents the problem, as you're always telling the function explicitly which class the object belongs to:

```
package Client;
use Class::Std::Utils;
{
    my %client_num_of;

    sub new {
        my ($class, $arg_ref) = @_;

        my $new_object = bless anon_scalar(), $class;
        # (Two-arg bless saves debugging!)

        $client_num_of{ident $new_object} = $arg_ref->{client_num};

        return $new_object;
    }

    # etc.
}
```

However, when using the two-argument form of bless, it's important to avoid
explicitly stringifying the class name:

```
my $new_object = bless anon_scalar(), "$class";
```

Always call bless with a copy of the actual first argument the constructor was
passed, like so:

```
my $new_object = bless anon_scalar(), $class;
```

Under Perl 5.8 and later, bless is able to detect when an object reference is mistakenly used as a class name. That usually happens when a constructor is being called as an object method, rather than a class method:

```
my $back_up = $existing_client->new();    # The benefits of human cloning
```

If bless always just quietly stringified its second argument (as it used to do, prior to Perl 5.8), then inside the constructor the object reference in $class would be stringified to something nasty like 'Client::Corporate=SCALAR[0x12b37ca]', which would then be used as the name of the class into which the new object was actually blessed. That is unlikely to be what the client code expects or wants*.

Recent versions of Perl (5.8 and later) prevent such calamities by checking whether the second argument to bless is already a string, and complaining (fatally) if it isn't. Explicitly stringifying that second argument before it's passed will thwart that important sanity check.

Of course, the problem still exists under earlier versions of Perl. To avoid it, you can add a statement at the start of the destructor to explicitly detect when the "class" is actually a reference to an object:

```
sub new {
    my ($class, $arg_ref) = @_;

    croak 'Constructor called on existing object instead of class'
        if ref $class;

    my $new_object = bless anon_scalar(), $class;

    $client_num_of{ident $new_object} = $arg_ref->{client_num};

    return $new_object;
}
```

Constructor Arguments

Pass constructor arguments as labeled values, using a hash reference.

As the examples in the earlier guidelines show, when creating an object of a derived class, the initialization phase of each constructor in the class hierarchy needs to pick out the appropriate initial values for that class's attributes.

---

* Although it's not *impossible* that that was the desired effect: several advanced OO techniques make use of a similar trick to generate unique class names for singleton objects at run time. The gruesome details of such techniques are left to the reader's imagination.

This requirement makes positional arguments problematical at best, as the order in which arguments will then need to be passed to the derived constructor will depend on the order in which it inherits from its ancestral classes, as demonstrated in Example 16-3.

Example 16-3. Positional arguments to constructors

```
package Client;
use Class::Std::Utils;
{
    my %client_num_of;

    sub new {
        my ($class, $client_num) = @_;

        my $new_object = bless anon_scalar(), $class;

        $client_num_of{ident $new_object} = $client_num;

        return $new_object;
    }

    # etc.
}

package Client::Corporate;
use base qw( Client );
use Class::Std::Utils;
{
    my %corporation_of;

    sub new {
        my ($class, $client_num, $corp_name) = @_;

        my $new_object = $class->SUPER::new($client_num);

        $corporation_of{ident $new_object} = $corp_name;

        return $new_object;
    }

    # etc.
}

# and later...

my $new_client
    = Client::Corporate->new( '124C1', 'Florin' );
```

The real problem with this approach is that any subsequent change in argument ordering (for example, adding an extra argument to either of the classes) will then

require that every constructor call be rewritten, or else every derived-class constructor will have to do some sly slicing-and-dicing of the original argument list before
passing it on to a base class (as in Example 16-4).

Example 16-4. Adding extra positional arguments to constructors

```perl
package Client;
use Class::Std::Utils;
{
    my %client_num_of;
    my %name_of;            # New attribute in base class

    sub new {
        # Expect extra positional argument to constructor...
        my ($class, $client_num, $client_name) = @_;

        my $new_object = bless anon_scalar(), $class;

        $client_num_of{ident $new_object} = $client_num;
        $name_of{ident $new_object}       = $client_name;

        return $new_object;
    }

    # etc.
}

package Client::Corporate;
use base qw( Client );
use Class::Std::Utils;
{
    my %corporation_of;
    my %position_of;        # New attribute in derived class
    sub new {
        # Expect extra positional arguments to constructor...
        my ($class, $client_num, $corp_name, $client_name, $position) = @_;

        # Pass extra positional argument to base class constructor...
        my $new_object = $class->SUPER::new($client_num, $client_name);

        $corporation_of{ident $new_object} = $corp_name;
        $position_of{ident $new_object}    = $position;

        return $new_object;
    }

    # etc.
}

# and later...

my $new_client
    = Client::Corporate->new( '124C1', 'Florin', 'Humperdinck',  'CEO' );
```

Note too that it's essential to preserve the original ordering of the original positional arguments, regardless of subsequent additions to the argument list. Otherwise, you'll have to reorder the arguments in every existing constructor call in any source code that uses your class. But keeping the original arguments in their original order means that the new constructor argument lists end up with a somewhat counterintuitive interleaving of arguments for the base and derived classes. Those calls are also becoming hard to read because of the sheer number of arguments in a row[*].

Hashes, on the other hand, don't care what order their entries are specified in, so passing constructor arguments in a single hash is much simpler and far more change-tolerant. As Example 16-5 demonstrates, if initialization data is always passed in a hash, then each class's constructor can simply pull out of that hash those arguments it cares about, without worrying about the sequence in which the arguments were specified. Moreover, in the constructor call itself, the arguments can be specified in any convenient order. They're clearly labeled as well, which makes the code more comprehensible.

Example 16-5. Avoiding positional arguments to constructors

```perl
package Client;
use Class::Std::Utils;
{
    my %client_num_of;
    my %name_of;

    sub new {
        my ($class, $arg_ref) = @_;

        my $new_object = bless anon_scalar(), $class;

        $client_num_of{ident $new_object} = $arg_ref->{client_num};
        $name_of{ident $new_object}       = $arg_ref->{client_name};

        return $new_object;
    }

    # etc.
}

package Client::Corporate;
use base qw( Client );
use Class::Std::Utils;
{
    my %corporation_of;
    my %position_of;
    sub new {
        my ($class, $arg_ref) = @_;
```

---

[*] Is that Mr Humperdinck of Florin Corp, or Mr Florin of Humperdinck Inc???

Example 16-5. Avoiding positional arguments to constructors (continued)

```
        my $new_object = $class->SUPER::new($arg_ref);

        $corporation_of{ident $new_object} = $arg_ref->{corp_name};
        $position_of{ident $new_object}    = $arg_ref->{position};

        return $new_object;
    }

    # etc.
}

# and later...

my $new_client
    = Client::Corporate->new( {
        client_num  => '124C1',
        client_name => 'Humperdinck',
        corp_name   => 'Florin',
        position    => 'CEO',
    });
```

Base Class Initialization

Distinguish arguments for base classes by class name as well.

As explained earlier, one of the great advantages of using inside-out classes instead of hashes is that a base class and a derived class can then each have an attribute of exactly the same name. In a single-level hash, that's impossible.

But that very fact also presents something of a problem when constructor arguments are themselves passed by hash. If two or more classes in the name hierarchy do happen to have attributes of the same name, the constructor will need two or more initializers with the name key—which a single hash can't provide.

The solution is to allow initializer values to be partitioned into distinct sets, each uniquely named, which are then passed to the appropriate base class. The easiest way to accomplish that is to pass in a hash of hashes, where each top-level key is the name of one of the base classes, and the corresponding value is a hash of initializers specifically for that base class. Example 16-6 shows how this can be achieved.

Example 16-6. Avoiding name collisions in constructor arguments

```
package Client;
use Class::Std::Utils;
{
    my %client_num_of;    # Every client has an ID number
    my %name_of;
```

Example 16-6. Avoiding name collisions in constructor arguments (continued)

```perl
    sub new {
        my ($class, $arg_ref) = @_;

        my $new_object = bless anon_scalar(), $class;

        # Initialize this class's attributes with the appropriate argument set...
        $client_num_of{ident $new_object} = $arg_ref->{'Client'}{client_num};
        $name_of{ident $new_object}        = $arg_ref->{'Client'}{client_name};

        return $new_object;
    }

}

package Client::Corporate;
use base qw( Client );
use Class::Std::Utils;
{
    my %client_num_of;        # Corporate clients have an additional ID number
    my %corporation_of;
    my %position_of;

    sub new {
        my ($class, $arg_ref) = @_;

        my $new_object = $class->SUPER::new($arg_ref);
        my $ident = ident($new_object);

        # Initialize this class's attributes with the appropriate argument set...
        $client_num_of{$ident}   = $arg_ref->{'Client::Corporate'}{client_num};
        $corporation_of{$ident}  = $arg_ref->{'Client::Corporate'}{corp_name};
        $position_of{$ident}     = $arg_ref->{'Client::Corporate'}{position};

        return $new_object;
    }

}

# and later...

my $new_client
    = Client::Corporate->new( {
        'Client' => {
            client_num   => '124C1',
            client_name  => 'Humperdinck',
        },
        'Client::Corporate' => {
            client_num   => 'F_1692',
            corp_name    => 'Florin',
            position     => 'CEO',
        },
    });
```

Now each class's constructor picks out the initializer subhash whose key is that class's own name. Because every class name is different, the top-level keys of this multilevel initializer hash are guaranteed to be unique. And because no single class can have two identically named attributes, the keys of each second-level hash will be unique as well. If two classes in the hierarchy both need an initializer of the same name (e.g., 'client_num'), those two hash entries will now be in separate subhashes, so they will never clash.

A more sophisticated variation—which is generally much more convenient for the users of your class—is to allow both general *and* class-specific initializers in your top-level hash, as demonstrated in Example 16-7.

Example 16-7. More flexible initializer sets

```
package Client;
use Class::Std::Utils;
{
    my %client_num_of;
    my %name_of;

    sub new {
        my ($class, $arg_ref) = @_;

        my $new_object = bless anon_scalar(), $class;

        # Initialize this class's attributes with the appropriate argument set...
        my %init = extract_initializers_from($arg_ref);

        $client_num_of{ident $new_object} = $init{client_num};
        $name_of{ident $new_object}       = $init{client_name};

        return $new_object;
    }

    # etc.
}

package Client::Corporate;
use base qw( Client );
use Class::Std::Utils;
{
    my %client_num_of;
    my %corporation_of;
    my %position_of;

    sub new {
        my ($class, $arg_ref) = @_;

        my $new_object = $class->SUPER::new($arg_ref);
        my $ident = ident($new_object);
```

Example 16-7. More flexible initializer sets (continued)

```
        # Initialize this class's attributes with the appropriate argument set...
        my %init = extract_initializers_from($arg_ref);
        $client_num_of{$ident}   = $init{client_num};
        $corporation_of{$ident} = $init{corp_name};
        $position_of{$ident}      = $init{position};

        return $new_object;
    }

    # etc.
}
```

In this version of the classes, clients don't need to specify classnames for initializers unless the names of those initializers actually are ambiguous:

```
my $new_client
    = Client::Corporate->new( {
            client_name => 'Humperdinck',
            corp_name   => 'Florin',
            position    => 'CEO',

            'Client'            => { client_num => '124C1'  },
            'Client::Corporate' => { client_num => 'F_1692' },
        });
```

Any other arguments can just be passed directly in the top-level hash. This convenience is provided by the extract_initializers_from( ) utility method (which is exported from the Class::Std::Util CPAN module):

```
sub extract_initializers_from {
    my ($arg_ref) = @_;

    # Which class are we extracting arguments for?
    my $class_name = caller;

    # Find the class-specific sub-hash (if any)...
    my $specific_inits_ref
        = first {defined $_} $arg_ref->{$class_name}, {};
    croak "$class_name initializer must be a nested hash"
        if ref $specific_inits_ref ne 'HASH';

    # Return initializers, overriding general initializers from the top level
    # with any second-level initializers that are specific to the class....
    return ( %{$arg_ref}, %{$specific_inits_ref} );
}
```

The subroutine is always called with the original multilevel argument set ($arg_ref) from the constructor. It then looks up the class's own name in the argument set hash, to see if an initializer with that key has been defined (i.e., $arg_ref->{$class_name}). If none has, an empty hash ({}) is used instead. Either way, the resulting set of class-specific initializers ($specific_inits_ref) is then checked, to make sure it's a genuine (sub)hash.

Finally, extract_initializers_from( ) returns the flattened set of key/value pairs for the class's initializer set, by appending the class-specific initializer set (%{$specific_inits_ref}) to the end of the original generic initializer set (%{$arg_ref}). Appending the specific initializers after the generic ones means that any key in the class-specific set will override any key in the generic set, thereby ensuring that the most relevant initializers are always selected, but that generic initializers are still available where no class-specific value has been passed in.

The only drawback of using hash-based initialization is that you re-introduce the possibility that misspelling an attribute name will result in mis-initialization. For example, the following constructor call would correctly initialize everything except the client name:

```perl
my $new_client
    = Client::Corporate->new( {
            calient_name => 'Humperdinck',           # Diantre!
            corp_name    => 'Florin',
            position     => 'CEO',

            'Client'              => { client_num => '124C1' },
            'Client::Corporate' => { client_num => 'F_1692' },
        });
```

There are two straightforward solutions to this problem. The first is radical: prohibit initialization completely. That is, every constructor is implemented as:

```perl
sub new {
        my ($class) = @_;
        croak q{Can't initialize in constructor (use accessors)} if @_ > 1;

        # [Set up purely internal state here]

        return bless anon_scalar( ), $class;
}
```

This style forces every object to be initialized through its standard accessor mechanisms:

```perl
my $new_client = Client::Corporate->new( );

$new_client->set_client_name('Humperdinck');
$new_client->set_corp_name ('Florin');
$new_client->set_position('CEO');

$new_client->Client::set_client_num ('124C1');
$new_client->Client::Corporate::set_client_num('F_1692');
```

Most people find this approach inconvenient, unless they set up each set_... accessor so that it returns its own $self value. For example:

```perl
sub set_client_name {
    my ($self, $new_name) = @_;

    $name_of{ident $self} = $new_name;
```

```
        return $self;
    }
```

If every set_... accessor is built that way, they can then be chained during
initializations:

```
my $new_client = Client::Corporate->new()
    -> set_client_name('Humperdinck')
    -> set_corp_name('Florin')
    -> set_position('CEO')
    -> Client::set_client_num('124C1')
    -> Client::Corporate::set_client_num('F_1692')
    ;
```

An alternative solution that does allow initializer values to be passed to the constructor, but still ensures that every attribute is correctly initialized, is described under
"Attribute Building" later in this chapter.

Construction and Destruction

Separate your construction, initialization, and destruction processes.

Classes that use a single new( ) method to both create and initialize objects usually
don't work well under multiple inheritance. When a class hierarchy offers two or
more new( ) methods (either at different inheritance levels, or in different base classes
at the same level), then there is automatically a conflict of control.

Only one of those new( ) methods can ultimately allocate and bless the storage for the
new object, and if there is multiple inheritance anywhere in the class hierarchy you're
using, the new( ) chosen may not be the new( ) you expected. Even if it *is* the one you
wanted, any constructors on other branches of the inheritance tree will have been
pre-empted and the object will not be completely initialized.

Likewise, when the object's destructors are called, only one of the two or more inheritance branches can be followed during destructor look-up, so only one of the several base-class destructors will ever be called. That's particularly bad, because it's
critical to call all the destructors of an inside-out object, to ensure that its attribute
hashes don't leak memory (see "Destructors" in Chapter 15).

For example, you could create a well-implemented inside-out class like this:

```
package Wax::Floor;
use Class::Std::Utils;
{
    # Attributes...
    my %name_of;
    my %patent_of;

    sub new {
        my ($class, $arg_ref) = @_;
```

```perl
        my %init = extract_initializers_from($arg_ref);

        my $new_object = bless anon_scalar( ), $class;

        $name_of{ident $new_object}   = $init{name};
        $patent_of{ident $new_object} = $init{patent};

        return $new_object;
    }

    sub DESTROY {
        my ($self) = @_;

        delete $name_of{ident $self};
        delete $patent_of{ident $self};

        return;
    }
}
```

and a second class such as:

```perl
package Topping::Dessert;
use Class::Std::Utils;
{
    # Attributes...
    my %name_of;
    my %flavour_of;

    sub new {
        my ($class, $arg_ref) = @_;

        my %init = extract_initializers_from($arg_ref);

        my $new_object = bless anon_scalar( ), $class;

        $name_of{ident $new_object}    = $init{name};
        $flavour_of{ident $new_object} = $init{flavour};

        return $new_object;
    }

    sub DESTROY {
        my ($self) = @_;

        delete $name_of{ident $self};
        delete $flavour_of{ident $self};

        return;
    }
}
```

But it's impossible to create a class that correctly inherits from both. The closest you
can get is the class shown in Example 16-8. And it still fails dismally.

Example 16-8. When multiple inheritance attacks

```
package Shimmer;
use base qw( Wax::Floor  Topping::Dessert );
use Class::Std::Utils;
{
    # Attributes...
    my %name_of;
    my %patent_of;

    sub new {
        my ($class, $arg_ref) = @_;

        my %init = extract_initializers_from($arg_ref);

        # Call base-class constructor to allocate and pre-initialize...
        my $new_object = $class->SUPER::new($arg_ref);

        $name_of{ident $new_object}   = $init{name};
        $patent_of{ident $new_object} = $init{patent};

        return $new_object;
    }

    sub DESTROY {
        my ($self) = @_;

        delete $name_of{ident $self};
        delete $patent_of{ident $self};

        # Call base-class destructor to continue clean-up...
        $self->SUPER::DESTROY();

        return;
    }
}
```

In the Shimmer constructor, the nested call to the ancestral constructor ($class->
SUPER::new($arg_ref)) will find only the left-most ancestral new( ). So Wax::Floor::
new( ) will be called, and will successfully create the object itself and initialize its
"waxy" attributes. But the second inherited constructor—Topping::Dessert::new( )—
will never be invoked, so the "edible" attributes of the object will never be initialized.
Likewise, in the Shimmer class's destructor, the nested call to $self->SUPER::DESTROY( )
will be dispatched to the left-most base class only. The Wax::Floor destructor will be
called, but not the destructor for Topping::Dessert.

Curiously, the real problem here is not that there aren't enough constructor and
destructor calls; it's that there are *too many*. The correct way to handle the problem
is to ensure that there is only ever one call to new( ) during each construction and
only one call to DESTROY( ) during each destruction. You then arrange for those single calls to correctly coordinate the initialization and cleanup for every class in the
object's hierarchy.

To achieve that, individual classes can no longer be responsible for their own memory allocation or object blessing, nor for their own destruction; they must not have their own new( ) or DESTROY( ) methods. Instead, they should inherit a suitable new( ) and DESTROY( ) from some standard base class. And, as every class must automatically inherit the same constructor and destructor for this scheme to work correctly, it makes sense to put that constructor and destructor in the one class that every other class automatically inherits: UNIVERSAL. The necessary code is shown in Example 16-9.

Example 16-9. Implementing a universal constructor and destructor

```perl
package UNIVERSAL;
use List::MoreUtils qw( uniq );

# Return a list of the base classes of the class passed as an argument...
sub _hierarchy_of {
    my ($class, $reversed) = @_;

    no strict 'refs';    # ...needed to make the '::ISA' look-ups run silent

    # Start with the class, and its parents...
    my @hierarchy = ( $class );
    my @parents   = $reversed ? reverse @{$class . '::ISA'}
                   :                    @{$class . '::ISA'}
                   ;

    # For each parent, add it to the hierarchy and remember the grandparents...
    while (defined (my $parent = shift @parents)) {
        push @hierarchy, $parent;
        push @parents, $reversed ? reverse @{$parent . '::ISA'}
                   :                       @{$parent . '::ISA'}
                   ;
    }

    # Sort the (unique) classes most-basic first...
    my @traversal_order = sort { $a->isa($b) ? -1
                               : $b->isa($a) ? +1
                               :                0
                               } uniq @hierarchy;

    # Return in appropriate traversal order...
    return reverse @traversal_order if $reversed;
    return @traversal_order;
}

use Memoize;
memoize '_hierarchy_of';

use Class::Std::Utils;

# Universal constructor is shared by every class. It allocates their objects
# and coordinates their initializations...
sub new {
    my ($class, $arg_ref) = @_;
```

```perl
    # Create an inside-out object of the desired class...
    my $new_obj = bless anon_scalar( ), $class;
    my $new_obj_ident = ident($new_obj);

    # Iterate all base classes, visiting the most basic classes first...
    for my $base_class (_hierarchy_of($class, 'reversed')) {
        no strict 'refs';   # ...needed for the '::BUILD' look-up

        # If this particular base class defines a BUILD() method...
        if (my $build_ref = *{$base_class.'::BUILD'}{CODE}) {
            # Extract the correct set of initializers...
            my %arg_set
                = extract_initializers_from($arg_ref, {class => $base_class} );

            # Then call the class's BUILD() method...
            $build_ref->($new_obj, $new_obj_ident, \%arg_set);
        }
    }

    return $new_obj;
}

sub DESTROY {
    my ($self) = @_;
    my $ident = ident($self);

    # Iterate all base classes, visiting the most derived classes first...
    for my $base_class (_hierarchy_of(ref $self)) {
        no strict 'refs';   # ...needed for the '::DEMOLISH' look-up

        # If this particular base class defines a DEMOLISH() method...
        if (my $demolish_ref = *{$base_class.'::DEMOLISH'}{CODE}) {
            # Then call the class's DEMOLISH() method...
            $demolish_ref->($self, $ident);
        }
    }

    return;
}
```

The _hierarchy_of( ) subroutine traverses the inheritance tree from a given class upwards, and returns a list of the classes it inherits from. Normally, that list is sorted so that every derived class appears before any base class that it inherits from, unless the $reversed argument is true, in which case the list is sorted base-before-any-derived[*].

---

[*] Note that neither of those orderings are the same as the class traversal order that Perl's normal method dispatch uses. That is: self, first ancestor, second ancestor, third ancestor, etc. If two or more ancestral classes inherit from a common base class (a situation known as "diamond" inheritance), it's possible for the shared base class to be visited before the second of its derived classes is seen. That sequence would create problems in destructors, because the second derived class may be relying on base class components that no longer exist. Hence the more sophisticated sorting order employed in _hierarchy_of( ).

The `UNIVERSAL::new( )` method starts out like any other constructor, creating an inside-out object in the usual way. Having created the object, `new( )` then walks down through the class hierarchy from most basic to most derived (hence the `'reversed'` flag on the call to `_hierarchy_of( )`). For each of these ancestral classes, it looks in the corresponding symbol table (`*{$base_class.'::BUILD'}`) to see whether that class has a `BUILD( )` method defined (`*{$base_class.'::BUILD'}{CODE}`). If so, the universal constructor will call that method, passing it the appropriate initializer values (as recommended in the earlier "Constructor Arguments" guideline).

As a result, every class everywhere inherits the same constructor, which creates an inside-out object and then calls every `BUILD( )` method it can find anywhere in the class's hierarchy. Each class-specific `BUILD( )` is passed the object, followed by its unique identifier (to avoid recomputing that value in every class), and finally a hash containing the appropriate constructor arguments.

Similarly, the `UNIVERSAL::DESTROY( )` method walks back up through the object's class hierarchy, most-derived classes first (so no `'reversed'` flag). Using the same kind of symbol-table inspections as the constructor, it looks for and calls any `DEMOLISH( )` method in any ancestral class, passing it the object and its unique identifying number.

All of which means that no class now has to define its own constructor or destructor. Instead, they can all just define an initializer (`BUILD( )`) and a clean-up method (`DEMOLISH( )`), which will be called in the appropriate sequence, taking into account multiple inheritance relationships of the class's inheritance hierarchy.

With this facility in place, you could rewrite the various wax and topping classes as shown in Example 16-10.

Example 16-10. Using the universal constructor and destructor

```
package Wax::Floor;
{
    # Attributes...
    my %name_of;
    my %patent_of;

    sub BUILD {
        my ($self, $ident, $arg_ref) = @_;

        $name_of{$ident}   = $arg_ref->{name};
        $patent_of{$ident} = $arg_ref->{patent};

        return;
    }

    sub DEMOLISH {
        my ($self, $ident) = @_;

        delete $name_of{$ident};
        delete $patent_of{$ident};
```

Example 16-10. Using the universal constructor and destructor (continued)

```
        return;
    }
}

package Topping::Dessert;
{
    # Attributes...
    my %name_of;
    my %flavour_of;

    sub BUILD {
        my ($self, $ident, $arg_ref) = @_;

        $name_of{$ident}    = $arg_ref->{name};
        $flavour_of{$ident} = $arg_ref->{flavour};

        return;
    }

    sub DEMOLISH {
        my ($self, $ident) = @_;

        delete $name_of{$ident};
        delete $flavour_of{$ident};

        return;
    }
}
```

Then the Shimmer class could (correctly!) inherit them both like so:

```
package Shimmer;
use base qw( Wax::Floor  Topping::Dessert );
{
    # Attributes...
    my %name_of;
    my %patent_of;

    sub BUILD {
        my ($class, $ident, $arg_ref) = @_;

        $name_of{$ident}   = $arg_ref->{name};
        $patent_of{$ident} = $arg_ref->{patent};

        return;
    }

    sub DEMOLISH {
        my ($self, $ident) = @_;

        delete $name_of{$ident};
        delete $patent_of{$ident};
```

```
        return;
    }
}
```

Having factored out the common construction and destruction tasks, notice how much less work is now required to implement individual classes. More importantly, the code implementing derived classes is now totally decoupled from its base classes: no more ancestral constructor calls via $class->SUPER::new( ).

This approach to implementing classes is cleaner, more robust, far more scalable, and easier to maintain. It also ensures that every class is implemented in a consistent fashion, and can interoperate (under multiple inheritance) with any other class that is implemented using the same techniques.

Note that it's still possible for individual classes to provide their own constructors and destructors when that's desirable, so this technique allows legacy or non-standard classes to be used as well—though not, of course, with the same guarantees of robustness.

Automating Class Hierarchies

Build the standard class infrastructure automatically.

The universal constructor and destructor demonstrated in the previous guideline are, by definition, supposed to be used for every class hierarchy, in every file of every program within every system you create. So it would make sense to factor them out into a separate module, from which they could then be supplied to every class that needs them.

There is already a CPAN module that does precisely that. It's called Class::Std, and it implements all of the class infrastructure* shown in Example 16-9. So classes like Wax::Floor, Topping::Dessert, and Shimmer (Example 16-10 and the code that immediately follows it) could be implemented without having to construct that infrastructure yourself, merely by using Class::Std inside each class:

```
package Wax::Floor;
use Class::Std;
{
    # [Class definition, exactly as in Example 16-10]
}
```

Loading Class::Std installs a generic constructor that creates and initializes inside-out objects using the approach explained in the preceding guidelines, but with some other convenient shortcuts (described later). The module also installs a destructor (see the next guideline, "Attribute Demolition") that greatly simplifies the cleanup of attributes. Class::Std also exports the ident( ) utility to your class's namespace.

---

* And many other useful features as well, as described in subsequent guidelines.

Class::Std provides all the benefits of inside-out objects, as well as all the benefits of decoupled initialization and cleanup (i.e., it provides full support for BUILD( ) and DEMOLISH( ) methods). It is strongly recommended for any object-oriented Perl development.

Attribute Demolition

Use Class::Std to automate the deallocation of attribute data.

As mentioned under "Destructors" in Chapter 15, one of the very few annoyances of using inside-out objects rather than blessed hashes is the inevitable need to write separate clean-up code for every attribute, as in Example 16-11.

Example 16-11. Cleaning up object attributes

```perl
package Book;
use Class::Std;
{
    # Attributes...
    my %title_of;
    my %author_of;
    my %publisher_of;
    my %year_of;
    my %topic_of;
    my %style_of;
    my %price_of;
    my %rating_of;

    # and then...

    sub DEMOLISH {
        my ($self, $ident) = @_;

        # Update library information...
        Library->remove($self);

        # Clean up attribute hashes...
        delete $title_of{$ident};
        delete $author_of{$ident};
        delete $publisher_of{$ident};
        delete $year_of{$ident};
        delete $topic_of{$ident};
        delete $style_of{$ident};
        delete $price_of{$ident};
        delete $rating_of{$ident};

        return;
    }
}
```

This kind of highly repetitive code structure is inherently error-prone to set up, unbearably tedious to read, and unnecessarily hard to maintain. For example, are you confident that the DEMOLISH() method shown in Example 16-11 actually *did* clean up every one of the object's attributes?

The goal here is always exactly the same: to iterate through every attribute hash in the class and delete the $ident entry inside it. It would be much better if there were some way for the class itself to keep track of its attribute hashes, so the class itself could automatically step through those attributes and remove the appropriate element from each.

Of course, you could do that "manually", by creating an array of references to the class's attribute hashes and then iterating that array with a for loop. For example:

```perl
package Book;
{
    # Declare attribute hashes, and construct a list of references to them
    # (the \(...) applies the \ operator to each element of the list)...
    my @attr_refs = \(
        my %title_of,
        my %author_of,
        my %publisher_of,
        my %year_of,
        my %topic_of,
        my %style_of,
        my %price_of,
        my %rating_of,
        my %sales_of,
    );

    # Clean up attributes when object is destroyed...
    sub DEMOLISH {
        my ($self, $ident) = @_;

        # Update library information...
        Library->remove($self);

        # Clean up attribute hashes...
        for my $attr_ref (@attr_refs) {
            delete $attr_ref->{$ident};
        }

        return;
    }
}
```

But then you'd need to write essentially the same DEMOLISH() in every class. The code for declaring and collecting the attributes is pretty scary, too.

The Class::Std module provides a simpler way to accomplish precisely the same goal. It provides a "marker" (:ATTR) that can be appended to the declaration of each attribute hash*. Whenever that marker is used, Class::Std stores a reference to the marked hash and then automatically applies the appropriate delete call after the class's DEMOLISH( ) method has been called. So the previous code could be rewritten—with exactly the same functionality—like so:

```
package Book;
use Class::Std;
{
    my %title_of        :ATTR;
    my %author_of       :ATTR;
    my %publisher_of    :ATTR;
    my %year_of         :ATTR;
    my %topic_of        :ATTR;
    my %style_of        :ATTR;
    my %price_of        :ATTR;
    my %rating_of       :ATTR;
    my %sales_of        :ATTR;

    # and then...

    sub DEMOLISH {
        my ($self) = @_;

        # Update library information...
        Library->remove($self);

        return;
    }
}
```

With this version, the necessary attribute-hash deletions would be performed automatically, immediately after the universal destructor's call to DEMOLISH( ) was finished. And if the class didn't define a DEMOLISH( ) method at all, the destructor would still perform the deletions at the appropriate time.

Note too that the # Attributes... comment has been omitted from this second version; the column of :ATTR markers is sufficient documentation.

As a final improvement to maintainability, a single :ATTR marker (or its synonym, :ATTRS) can also be applied to an entire list of attribute-hash definitions. So the previous code could be further reduced to:

```
package Book;
use Class::Std;
{
    my (
        %title_of,   %author_of,   %publisher_of,
        %year_of,    %topic_of,    %style_of,
        %price_of,   %rating_of ,  %sales_of,
    ) :ATTRS;
```

---

* Confusingly, these kinds of markers are also known as "attributes" in Perl (see the standard *perlsub* documentation), even though they have nothing to do with the data members of an object.

```
    # and then...

    sub DEMOLISH {
        my ($self) = @_;

        # Update library information...
        Library->remove($self);

        return;
    }
}
```

Attribute Building

Have attributes initialized and verified automatically.

Most of the BUILD( ) methods shown so far in this chapter do nothing except initialize attributes with values extracted from the constructor's initializer hash. For example:

```
package Topping::Dessert;
use Class::Std;
{
    # Attributes...
    my %name_of     :ATTR;
    my %flavour_of  :ATTR;

    sub BUILD {
        my ($self, $ident, $arg_ref) = @_;

        $name_of{$ident}    = $arg_ref->{name};
        $flavour_of{$ident} = $arg_ref->{flavour};

        return;
    }

    # etc.
```

Because this is such a common requirement, Class::Std provides a shortcut. When you declare an attribute using the :ATTR marker, you can specify the entry of the constructor's initialization hash that is to be used to initialize it. For example:

```
package Topping::Dessert;
use Class::Std;
{
    # Attributes...
    my %name_of     :ATTR( init_arg => 'name'    );
    my %flavour_of  :ATTR( init_arg => 'flavour' );

    # [No BUILD method required]

    # etc.
```

This extra specification causes the new( ) method provided by Class::Std to automatically initialize those attributes with the correspondingly labeled values from the initialization hash it is passed.

More importantly, the approach also solves the problem of misspelled initializer labels (see "Base Class Initialization" earlier). When attributes are declared with :ATTR and an init_arg is specified, the Class::Std constructor will automatically throw an exception if the initialization hash doesn't contain a suitably named initialization value. For example, given the previous definition, a call like:

```
my $syrup
    = Topping::Dessert->new({ taste => 'Cocolicious', naem => 'UltraChoc' });
```

will throw the exception:

```
Missing initializer label for Topping::Dessert: 'name'.
Missing initializer label for Topping::Dessert: 'flavour'.
(Did you mislabel one of the args you passed: 'taste' or 'naem'?)
Fatal error in constructor call at 'badnames.pl' line 22
```

Coercions

Specify coercions as :STRINGIFY, :NUMERIFY,
and :BOOLIFY **methods.**

In addition to the :ATTR markers for attribute hashes, Class::Std also supplies markers for subroutines that implement conversions to numbers, strings, and booleans:

```
sub count : NUMERIFY {    # Call count( ) method whenever object used as number
    my ($self, $ident) = @_;
    return scalar @{ $elements_of{$ident} };
}

sub as_str : STRINGIFY {  # Call as_str( ) method whenever object used as string
    my ($self, $ident) = @_;
    return sprintf '(%s)', join $COMMA, @{ $elements_of{$ident} };
}

sub is_okay : BOOLIFY {   # Call is_okay( ) method whenever object used as boolean
    my ($self) = @_;
    return !$self->Houston_We_Have_A_Problem( );
}
```

This provides a simpler, more convenient, and less repetitive interface than use overload:

```
sub count {
    my ($self) = @_;
    return scalar @{ $elements_of{ident $self} };
}
```

```
sub as_str {
    my ($self) = @_;
    return sprintf '(%s)', join $COMMA, @{ $elements_of{ident $self} };
}

sub is_okay {
    my ($self) = @_;
    return !$self->Houston_We_Have_A_Problem();
}

use overload (
    q{0+}   => 'count',
    q{""}   => 'as_str',
    q{bool} => 'is_okay',

    fallback => 1,
);
```

Cumulative Methods

Use : CUMULATIVE **methods instead of** SUPER:: **calls.**

One of the most important advantages of using the BUILD( ) and DEMOLISH( ) mechanisms supplied by Class::Std is that those methods don't require nested calls to their ancestral methods via the SUPER pseudoclass. The constructor and destructor provided by Class::Std take care of the necessary redispatching automatically. Each BUILD( ) method can focus solely on its own responsibilities; it doesn't have to also help orchestrate the cumulative constructor effects across the class hierarchy by remembering to call $self->SUPER::BUILD( ).

This approach produces far more reliable class implementations, because forgetting to include the SUPER call in a "chained" constructor or destructor will immediately terminate the chain of calls, disenfranchising all the remaining construction/destruction methods higher up in the class's hierarchy.

Moreover, calls via SUPER can only ever call the method of exactly one ancestral class, which is not sufficient under multiple inheritance. This second problem can be solved in various ways (for example, by using the standard NEXT module), but all those solutions still rely on developers remembering to add the necessary code to every method in every class in order to continue the chain of calls. So all those solutions are inherently fragile.

Class::Std provides a different way of creating methods whose effects accumulate through a class hierarchy, in the same way as those of BUILD( ) and DEMOLISH( ) do. Specifically, the module allows you to define your own *cumulative methods*. An ordinary non-cumulative method hides any method of the same name inherited from any base class, so when a non-cumulative method is called, only the most-derived version of it is ever invoked. In contrast, a cumulative method doesn't hide ancestral methods of the same name; it *assimilates* them. When a cumulative method is called, the most-derived version of it is invoked, then any parental versions, then any grandparental versions, and so on, until every cumulative method of the same name throughout the entire hierarchy has been called.

For example, you could add a cumulative describe( ) method to the various wax and topping classes from Example 16-10 as follows:

```perl
package Wax::Floor;
use Class::Std;
{
    my %name_of    :ATTR( init_arg => 'name'   );
    my %patent_of  :ATTR( init_arg => 'patent' );

    sub describe :CUMULATIVE {
        my ($self) = @_;

        print "The floor wax $name_of{ident $self} ",
              "(patent: $patent_of{ident $self})\n";

        return;
    }
}

package Topping::Dessert;
use Class::Std;
{
    my %name_of     :ATTR( init_arg => 'name'    );
    my %flavour_of  :ATTR( init_arg => 'flavour' );

    sub describe :CUMULATIVE {
        my ($self) = @_;

        print "The dessert topping $name_of{ident $self} ",
              "with that great $flavour_of{ident $self} taste!\n";

        return;
    }
}

package Shimmer;
use base qw( Wax::Floor  Topping::Dessert );
use Class::Std;
{
    my %name_of    :ATTR( init_arg => 'name'   );
    my %patent_of  :ATTR( init_arg => 'patent' );

    sub describe :CUMULATIVE {
        my ($self) = @_;

        print "New $name_of{ident $self} (patent: $patent_of{ident $self})\n",
              "Combining...\n";
```

```
            return;
        }
    }
```

Because the various describe( ) methods are marked as being cumulative, a subsequent call to:

```
my $product
    = Shimmer->new({ name=>'Shimmer', patent=>1562516251, flavour=>'Vanilla' });

$product->describe();
```

will work its way up through the classes of Shimmer's inheritance tree (in the same order as a destructor call would), calling each describe( ) method it finds along the way. So the single call to describe( ) would invoke the corresponding method in each class, producing:

```
New Shimmer (patent: 1562516251)
Combining...
The floor wax Shimmer (patent: 1562516251)
The dessert topping Shimmer with that great Vanilla taste!
```

Note that the accumulation of describe( ) methods is hierarchical, and dynamic in nature. That is, each class only sees those cumulative methods that are defined in its own package or in one of its ancestors. So calling the same describe( ) on a base class object:

```
my $wax
    = Wax::Floor->new({ name=>'Shimmer ', patent=>1562516251 });

$wax->describe();
```

invokes only the corresponding cumulative methods from that point on up the hierarchy, and hence prints only:

```
The floor wax Shimmer (patent: 1562516251)
```

Cumulative methods also accumulate their return values. In a list context, they return a (flattened) list that accumulates the lists returned by each individual method invoked. In a scalar context, a set of cumulative methods returns an object that, in a string context, concatenates individual scalar returns to produce a single string.

For example, if the classes each have a cumulative method that returns their list of sales features:

```
package Wax::Floor;
use Class::Std;
{
    sub feature_list :CUMULATIVE {
        return ('Long-lasting', 'Non-toxic', 'Polymer-based');
    }
}

package Topping::Dessert;
use Class::Std;
{
```

```
        sub feature_list :CUMULATIVE {
            return ('Low-carb', 'Non-dairy', 'Sugar-free');
        }
}

package Shimmer;
use Class::Std;
use base qw( Wax::Floor  Topping::Dessert );
{
    sub feature_list :CUMULATIVE {
        return ('Multi-purpose', 'Time-saving', 'Easy-to-use');
    }
}
```

then calling feature_list( ) in a list context:

```
my @features = Shimmer->feature_list();
print "Shimmer is the @features alternative!\n";
```

would produce a concatenated list of features, which could then be interpolated into a suitable sales pitch:

```
Shimmer is the Multi-purpose Time-saving Easy-to-use Long-lasting
Non-toxic Polymer-based Low-carb Non-dairy Sugar-free alternative!
```

Finally, it's also possible to specify a set of cumulative methods that start at the base class(es) of the hierarchy and work downwards, the way BUILD( ) does. To get that effect, mark each method with :CUMULATIVE(BASE FIRST), instead of just :CUMULATIVE. For example:

```
package Wax::Floor;
use Class::Std;
{
    sub active_ingredients :CUMULATIVE(BASE FIRST) {
        return "\tparadichlorobenzene, cyanoacrylate, peanuts (in wax)\n";
    }
}

package Topping::Dessert;
use Class::Std;
{
    sub active_ingredients :CUMULATIVE(BASE FIRST) {
        return "\tsodium hypochlorite, isobutyl ketone, ethylene glycol "
            . "(in topping)\n";
    }
}

package Shimmer;
use Class::Std;
use base qw( Wax::Floor  Topping::Dessert );

{
    sub active_ingredients :CUMULATIVE(BASE FIRST) {
        return "\taromatic hydrocarbons, xylene, methyl mercaptan (in binder)\n";
    }
}
```

So a scalar-context call to active_ingredients( ):

```
my $ingredients = Shimmer->active_ingredients( );
print "May contain trace amounts of:\n$ingredients";
```

would start in the base classes and work downwards, concatenating base-class ingredients *before* those of the derived class, to produce:

```
May contain trace amounts of:
    paradichlorobenzene, cyanoacrylate, peanuts (in wax)
    sodium hypochlorite, isobutyl ketone, ethylene glycol (in topping)
    aromatic hydrocarbons, xylene, methyl mercaptan (in binder)
```

Note that you can't specify both :CUMULATIVE and :CUMULATIVE(BASE FIRST) on methods of the same name in the same hierarchy. The resulting set of methods would have no well-defined invocation order, so Class::Std throws a compile-time exception instead.

Autoloading

Don't use AUTOLOAD( ).

Perl provides a mechanism by which you can capture and handle calls to methods that are not defined anywhere in your class hierarchy: the AUTOLOAD method.

Normally when you call a method, the interpreter starts at the class of the object on which the method was called. It then works its way upwards through the class hierarchy until it finds a package with a subroutine of the corresponding name, which it then invokes.

But if this hierarchical search fails to find a suitable method implementation anywhere in the inheritance tree, the interpreter returns to the most derived class and repeats the look-up process. On the second time through, it looks for a subroutine named AUTOLOAD( ) instead.

That means that the left-most-depth-first AUTOLOAD( ) that an object inherits will always be called to handle every unknown method call. And that's the problem. If the object's class hierarchy has two or more AUTOLOAD( ) definitions, it might be that the second one would have been the correct one to handle a particular missing method. But normally, that second one will never get the chance to do so.

There are various ways to circumvent that problem. For example, the standard NEXT module can be used to reject a particular AUTOLOAD( ) invocation and resume the original method look-up; or under Class::Std you can declare each AUTOLOAD( ) to be :CUMULATIVE and make sure only one of them ever returns a value; or you can dispense with AUTOLOAD( ) entirely and use Class::Std's AUTOMETHOD( ) mechanism instead[*].

However, none of these solutions uses the standard Perl AUTOLOAD( ) semantics, so all of them will be harder to maintain. And the first two suggestions also require additional vigilance to get right: either making certain that every AUTOLOAD( ) redispatches on failure via a call to $self->NEXT::AUTOLOAD( ); or ensuring that every AUTOLOAD( ) is marked :CUMULATIVE and that they're all mutually exclusive. So neither of them will be as robust as normal methods.

More importantly, a class that autoloads undefined methods effectively has an interface of unlimited size and complexity. That in itself is reason enough not to use the mechanism. But, worse still, the overwhelming majority of that interface will then rely on a single AUTOLOAD( ) subroutine. Such a subroutine is correspondingly much harder to write, as it has to identify all the method calls it can handle, then handle those calls correctly, whilst cleanly and accurately rejecting cases it can't handle. As a result, AUTOLOAD( ) methods tend to be large, complex, slow, and riddled with difficult corner cases.

By far the commonest mistakes are to forget to provide an explicit DESTROY( ) method for any class with an AUTOLOAD( ) or, alternatively, to forget to tell AUTOLOAD( ) how to handle a DESTROY( ) request. Either way, if there is no explicit destructor, every time an object of the class is destroyed, the AUTOLOAD( ) is called instead, usually with either comic or tragic results.

AUTOLOAD( ) doesn't promote efficiency, conciseness, robustness, or maintainability, and is best avoided entirely. Providing an arbitrary number of methods via autoloading can sometimes *appear* to be the right solution:

```
package Phonebook;
use Class::Std;
use Carp;
{
    my %entries_of : ATTR;

    # Any method call is someone's name: store their phone number or get it...
    sub AUTOLOAD {
        my ($self, $number) = @_;

        # Extract get/set mode and person's name from method name...
        our $AUTOLOAD;
        my ($mode, $name) = $AUTOLOAD =~ m/.* :: ([gs]et)_(.*)/xms
            or croak "Can't call $AUTOLOAD on object";

        # Update if it's a set_<name> operation...
        if ($mode eq 'set') {
            croak "Missing argument for set_$name" if @_ == 1;
            $entries_of{ident $self}->{$name} = $number;
        }
```

---

* For more details on these alternatives, with full examples, see the documentation of the NEXT and Class::Std modules.

```
        return $entries_of{ident $self}->{$name};
    }
}

# and later...

my $lbb = Phonebook->new( );

$lbb->set_Jenny(867_5309);
$lbb->set_Glenn(736_5000);

print $lbb->get_Jenny( ), "\n";
print $lbb->get_Glenn( ), "\n";
```

However, it's almost always cleaner, more maintainable, and more flexible to define a fixed number of predefined methods to provide the necessary functionality, passing them an extra argument that specifies the particular arbitrary behaviour desired. For example:

```
package Phonebook;
use Class::Std;
use Carp;
{
    my %entries_of : ATTR;

    # Set numbers...
    sub set_number_of {
        croak 'Missing argument for set_number_of( )' if @_ < 3;

        my ($self, $name, $number) = @_;

        $entries_of{ident $self}->{$name} = $number;

        return;
    }

    # Get numbers...
    sub get_number_of {
        croak 'Missing argument for get_number_of( )' if @_ < 2;

        my ($self, $name) = @_;

        return $entries_of{ident $self}->{$name};
    }
}

# and later...

my $lbb = Phonebook->new( );

$lbb->set_number_of(Jenny => 867_5309);
$lbb->set_number_of(Glenn => 736_5000);

print $lbb->get_number_of('Jenny'), "\n";
print $lbb->get_number_of('Glenn'), "\n";
```

If autoloading *still* seems like the right solution, then consider using the AUTOMETHOD( ) mechanism provided by Class::Std instead of Perl's standard AUTOLOAD( ). An AUTOMETHOD( ) is expected to return either a handler subroutine that implements the requested method functionality, or else an undef to indicate that it doesn't know how to handle the request. Class::Std then coordinates every AUTOMETHOD( ) in an object's hierarchy, trying each one in turn until one of them produces a suitable handler.

The advantage of this approach is that the first AUTOMETHOD( ) that's invoked doesn't have to disenfranchise every other AUTOMETHOD( ) in the hierarchy. If the first one can't handle a particular method call, it simply declines it and Class::Std tries the next candidate instead.

For example, the AUTOLOAD'd version of the Phonebook class could be made cleaner, more robust, and less disruptive in class hierarchies by rewriting it like so:

```
package Phonebook;
use Class::Std;
{
    my %entries_of : ATTR;

    # Any method call is someone's name: store their phone number or get it...
    sub AUTOMETHOD {
        my ($self, $ident, $number) = @_;

        my $subname = $_;    # Requested subroutine name is passed via $_

        # Return failure if not a get_<name> or set_<name>
        # (Next AUTOMETHOD( ) in hierarchy will then be tried instead)...
        my ($mode, $name) = $subname =~ m/\A ([gs]et)_(.*) \z/xms
            or return;

        # If get_<name>, return a handler that just returns the old number...
        return sub { return $entries_of{$ident}->{$name}; }
            if $mode eq 'get';

        # Otherwise, set_<name>, so return a handler that updates the entry
        # and then returns the old number...
        return sub {
            $entries_of{$ident}->{$name} = $number;
            return;
        };
    }
}

# and later...

my $lbb = Phonebook->new( );

$lbb->set_Jenny(867_5309);
$lbb->set_Glenn(736_5000);

print $lbb->get_Jenny( ), "\n";
print $lbb->get_Glenn( ), "\n";
```

## CHAPTER 17

Modules

Any fool can make things bigger, more complex, and more violent. It takes a touch of genius—and a lot of courage—to move in the opposite direction.
—Albert Einstein

Code reuse is a core best practice, and modules are Perl's principal large-scale mechanism for code reuse. They are also at the heart of Perl's greatest software asset: the CPAN.

Refactoring source code into modules will not only increase the reusability of that code, it is also likely to make the code cleaner* and easier to maintain. If nothing else, the programs from which the original code is removed will become shorter, better abstracted, and consequently more maintainable.

The keys to good module design and implementation are: designing the interface first, keeping that interface small and functional, using a standard implementation template, and not reinventing the wheel. The guidelines in this chapter explore these issues.

Interfaces

Design the module's interface first.

The most important aspect of any module is not how it implements the facilities it provides, but the way in which it provides those facilities in the first place. If the module's API is too awkward, or too complex, or too extensive, or too fragmented, or even just poorly named, developers will avoid using it. They'll write their own code instead.

---

* Because revisiting *any* existing piece of code is likely to make it cleaner, once you get over the involuntary twitching.

In that way, a poorly designed module can actually reduce the overall maintainability of a system.

Designing module interfaces requires both experience and creativity. The easiest way to work out how an interface should work is to "play test" it: to write examples of code that will use the module before the module itself is implemented[*]. The key is to write that code as if the module *were* already available, and write it the way you'd most like the module to work.

Once you have some idea of the interface you want to create, convert your "play tests" into actual tests (see Chapter 18). Then it's just a Simple Matter Of Programming to make the module work the way that the code examples and tests want it to.

Of course, it may not be *possible* for the module to work the way you'd most like, in which case attempting to implement it that way will help you determine what aspects of your API are not practical, and allow you to work out what might be an acceptable alternative.

For example, when the IO::Prompt module (see Chapter 10) was being designed, having potential clients write hypothetical code fragments quickly made it obvious that what was needed was a drop-in replacement for the <> input operator. That is, to replace:

```
CMD:
while (my $cmd = <>) {
    chomp $cmd;
    last CMD if $cmd =~ m/\A (?: q(?:uit)? | bye ) \z/xms;

    my $args;
    if ($takes_arg{$cmd}) {
        $args = <>;
        chomp $args;
    }

    exec_cmd($cmd, $args);
}
```

with:

```
CMD:
while (my $cmd = prompt 'Cmd: ') {
    chomp $cmd;
    last CMD if $cmd =~ m/\A (?: q(?:uit)? | bye ) \z/xms;

    my $args;
    if ($takes_arg{$cmd}) {
        $args = prompt 'Args: ';
        chomp $args;
    }
```

---

[*] These examples will not be wasted when the design is complete. They can usually be recycled into demos, documentation examples, or the core of a test suite.

```
        }
    exec_cmd($cmd, $args);
}
```

But to make this work, prompt( ) would have to reproduce the special test that a while (<>) performs on the result of the readline operation. That is, the result of a prompt( ) call had to automatically test for definedness in a boolean context, rather than for simple truth. Otherwise, a user typing in a zero or an empty line would cause the loop to terminate. This requirement constrained the prompt( ) subroutine to return an object with an overloaded boolean test method, rather than a simple string.

The module didn't exist at that point but, by programming with it anyway, the interface it would require had started to become clear.

Examining the code examples soon made it obvious that virtually every call to prompt( ) was going to be immediately followed by a chomp on the result. So it seemed obvious that prompted values should be automatically chomped. Except that there was one developer who submitted a sample code fragment that *didn't* chomp the input after prompting:

```
# Print only unique lines (retaining their order)...
INPUT:
while (my $line = prompt '> ') {
    next INPUT if $seen{$line};
    print $line;
    $seen{$line} = 1;
}
```

This result initially suggested that the IO::Prompt module's interface needed a separate prompt_line( ) subroutine as well:

```
# Print only unique lines (retaining their order)...
INPUT:
while (my $line = prompt_line '> ') {
    next INPUT if $seen{$line};
    print $line;
    $seen{$line} = 1;
}
```

However, in further play-testing, prompt_line( ) proved to have exactly the same set of options as prompt( ) and exactly the same behaviour in every respect except for autochomping. There seemed no justification for doubling the size of the interface, when the same effect could be achieved merely by adding an extra -line option to prompt( ):

```
# Print only unique lines (retaining their order)...
INPUT:
while (my $line = prompt -line, '> ') {
    next INPUT if $seen{$line};
    print $line;
```

```
        $seen{$line} = 1;
    }
```

This last decision was a consequence of a more general module design principle. If a module accomplishes a single "composable" task (e.g., prompt for input with some combination of echo-control, chomping, menu-generation, input constraints, default values), then it's better to provide that functionality through a single subroutine with multiple options, as IO::Prompt provides. On the other hand, if a module handles several related but distinct tasks (for example, find the unique elements in a list, find the maximum of a set of strings, sum a list of numbers), then those facilities are better supplied via separate functions, as List::Util does.

In one particular hypothetical program, the programmers had wanted to build a menu of items and then prompt for a choice. They had written a utility subroutine using prompt():

```
sub menu {
    my ($prompt_str, @choices) = @_;

    # Starting at a, list the options in a menu...
    my $letter = 'a';
    print "$prompt_str\n";
    for my $alternative (@choices) {
        print "\t", $letter++, ". $alternative\n";
    }

    CHOICE:
    while (1) {
        # Take the first key pressed...
        my $choice = prompt 'Choose: ';

        # Reject any choice outside the valid range...
        redo CHOICE if $choice lt 'a' || $choice ge $letter;

        # Translate choice back to an index; return the corresponding data...
        return $choices[ ord($choice)-ord('a') ];
    }
}

# and later...

my $answer = menu('Which is the most correct answer: ', @answers);
```

This seemed likely to be a common requirement, so a more sophisticated version of this menu() subroutine was added into the proposed IO::Prompt interface:

```
my $answer = prompt 'Choose the most correct answer: ',
                    -menu => \@answers;
```

All of these decisions, and many others, were reached before the first version of the module was implemented, and many of the interface requirements that were uncovered though this play-testing were not part of the original design.

Some of them made the implementation code more complex than it otherwise would have been, but the result was that the "natural" and "obvious" code submitted by the play-testers eventually worked exactly as they had imagined. That, in turn, makes it far more likely that they will use the actual module.

Refactoring

Place original code inline.
Place duplicated code in a subroutine.
Place duplicated subroutines in a module.

The first time you're tempted to copy-paste-and-modify a piece of code:

```
package Process::Queue;
use Carp;
{
    use overload (
        # Type coercions don't make sense for process queues...
        q{""}   => sub {
            croak q{Can't stringify a Process::Queue};
        },
        q{0+}   => sub {
            croak q{Can't numerify a Process::Queue };
        },
        q{bool} => sub {
            croak q{Can't get the boolean value of a Process::Queue };
        },
    );
}

# and later...

package Socket;
use Carp;
{
    use overload (
        # Type coercions don't make sense for sockets...
        q{""}   => sub {
            croak q{Can't convert a Socket to a string};
        },
        q{0+}   => sub {
            croak q{Can't convert a Socket to a number};
        },
        q{bool} => sub {
            croak q{Can't get the boolean value of a Socket };
        },
    );
}
```

…don't do it!

Instead, convert the code into a subroutine, parameterize the parts you would have modified, and then replace *both* the original and duplicated code with calls to that subroutine:

```
use Carp;

sub _Class::cannot {
    # What kind of coercion cannot be done?
    my ($coerce) = @_;

    # Build a subroutine with the corresponding error message...
    return sub {
        my ($self) = @_;
        croak sprintf qq{Can't $coerce}, ref $self;
    };
}

# and later...

package Process::Queue;
{
    use overload (
        # Type coercions don't make sense for process queues...
        q{""}   => _Class::cannot('stringify a %s'),
        q{0+}   => _Class::cannot('numerify a %s'),
        q{bool} => _Class::cannot('get the boolean value of a %s'),
    );
}

# and later still...

package Socket;
{
    use overload (
        # Type coercions don't make sense for sockets...
        q{""}   => _Class::cannot('stringify a %s'),
        q{0+}   => _Class::cannot('numerify a %s'),
        q{bool} => _Class::cannot('get the boolean value of a %s'),
    );
}
```

This refactoring might produce slightly more code, but that code will be cleaner, more self-documenting, and easier to maintain. And the next time you need the same functionality, the total amount of code will almost certainly be less than cutting and pasting would have produced.

Note that factoring out the messages still left a chunk of repeated code in each class. In such cases you should re-refactor the code:

```
use Carp;

sub _Class::cannot {
    # What kind of coercion cannot be done?
    my ($coerce) = @_;
```

```
    # Build a subroutine with the corresponding error message...
    return sub {
        my ($self) = @_;
        croak sprintf qq{Can't $coerce}, ref $self;
    };
}

sub _Class::allows_no_coercions {
    return (
        q{""}   => _Class::cannot('stringify a %s'),
        q{0+}   => _Class::cannot('numerify a %s'),
        q{bool} => _Class::cannot('get the boolean value of a %s'),
    );
}

# and later...

package Process::Queue;
{
    # Type coercions don't make sense for process queues...
    use overload  _Class::allows_no_coercions( );
}

# and later still...

package Socket;
{
    # Type coercions don't make sense for sockets...
    use overload  _Class::allows_no_coercions( );
}
```

The first time you're tempted to copy and paste a *subroutine definition* into some other file, program, or system…don't do that either! Instead, place the subroutine in a module and export it:

```
package Coding::Toolkit::Coercions;
use Carp;

sub _Class::cannot {
    # What kind of coercion cannot be done?
    my ($coerce) = @_;

    # Build a subroutine with the corresponding error message...
    return sub {
        my ($self) = @_;
        croak sprintf qq{Can't $coerce}, ref $self;
    };
}

sub _Class::allows_no_coercions {
    return (
        q{""}   => _Class::cannot('stringify a %s'),
        q{0+}   => _Class::cannot('numerify a %s'),
        q{bool} => _Class::cannot('get the boolean value of a %s'),
```

```
        );
    }

    1; # Magic true value required at the end of any module
```

Then import it wherever you need it:

```
    use Coding::Toolkit::Coercions;

    package Process::Queue;
    {
        # Type coercions don't make sense for process queues...
        use overload  _Class::allows_no_coercions();
    }
```

Version Numbers

Use three-part version numbers.

When specifying the version number of a module, don't use vstrings:

```
    our $VERSION = v1.0.3;
```

They will break your code when it's run under older (pre-5.8.1) versions of Perl. They will also break it under newer versions of Perl, as they're deprecated in the 5.9 development branch and will be removed in the 5.10 release.

They're being removed because they're error-prone; in particular, because they're actually just weirdly specified character strings. For example, v1.0.3 is just short-hand for the character string "\x{1}\x{0}\x{3}". So vstrings don't compare correctly under numeric comparison.

Don't use floating-point version numbers, either:

```
    our $VERSION = 1.000_03;
```

It's too easy to get them wrong, as the preceding example does: it's equivalent to 1.0.30, not 1.0.3.

Instead, use the version CPAN module and the qv(...) version-object constructor:

```
    use version; our $VERSION = qv('1.0.3');
```

The resulting version objects are much more robust. In particular, they compare correctly under either numeric or string comparisons.

Note that, in the previous example, the use version statement and the $VERSION assignment were written on the same line. Loading and using the module in a single line is important, because it's likely that many users of your module will install it using either the ExtUtils::MakeMaker module or the Module::Build module. Each of these modules will attempt to extract and then evaluate the $VERSION assignment line in your module's source code, in order to ascertain the module's version number. But neither of them supports qv'd version numbers directly[*]. By placing the $VERSION assignment on the same line as the use version, you ensure that when that line is extracted and executed, the qv( ) subroutine is correctly loaded from *version.pm*.

The module also supports the common CPAN practice of marking unstable development releases by appending an underscored alpha count to the version number of the previous stable release:

```
# This is the 12th alpha built on top of the 1.5 release...
use version; our $VERSION = qv('1.5_12');
```

These "alpha versions" will also compare correctly. That is, qv('1.5_12') compares greater than qv('1.5') but less than qv('1.6').

Version Requirements

Enforce your version requirements programmatically.

Telling future maintainers about a module's version requirements is certainly a good practice:

```
package Payload;
# Only works under 5.6.1 and later

use IO::Prompt;            # must be 0.2.0 or better, but not 0.3.1
use List::Util qw( max );  # must be 1.13 or better
use Benchmark qw( cmpthese );  # but no later than version 1.52

# etc.
```

But telling Perl itself about these constraints is an even better practice, as the compiler can then *enforce* those requirements.

Perl has a built-in mechanism to do (some of) that enforcement for you. If you call use with a decimal number instead of a module name, the compiler will throw an exception if Perl's own version number is less than you specified:

```
package Payload;
use 5.006001;        # Only works under 5.6.1 and later
```

Unfortunately, that version number has to be an old-style decimal version. You can't use the version module's qv( ) subroutine (as recommended in the previous

---

[*] At least, not as of the publication of this book. Patches correcting the problem have been submitted for both modules and the issue may have been resolved by now—in which case you should go back to putting each statement on a separate line (as recommended in Chapter 2).

guideline), because the compiler interprets the qv identifier as the name of a module
to be loaded:

```
package Payload;
use version;
use qv('5.6.1');          # Tries to load qv.pm
```

If you load a module with a normal use, but place a decimal version number after its
name and before any argument list, then the compiler calls the module's VERSION
method, which defaults to throwing an exception if the module's $VERSION variable is
less than the version number that was specified:

```
use IO::Prompt  0.002;                # must be 0.2.0 or better
use List::Util  1.13    qw( max );    # must be 1.13 or better
```

Note that there are no commas on either side of the version number; that's how the
compiler knows it's a version restriction, rather than just another argument to the
module's import( ) subroutine.

Once again, the version number has to be an old-style decimal version. A qv( ) isn't
recognized:

```
use IO::Prompt qv('0.2.0') qw( prompt );    # Syntax error
```

Perl doesn't provide a built-in way to specify "no later version than…" or "any version except…", apart from testing those conditions explicitly:

```
package Payload;
use version;
use Carp;

use IO::Prompt qw( prompt );
use Benchmark qw( cmpthese );

# Version compatibility...
BEGIN {
    # Test against compiler version in $]
    # (there's no nice use English name for it)
    croak 'Payload only works under 5.6.1 and later, but not 5.8.0'
        if $] < qv('5.6.1') || $] == qv('5.8.0');

    croak 'IO::Prompt must be 0.2.0 or better, but not 0.3.1 to 0.3.3'
        if $IO::Prompt::VERSION < qv('0.2.0')
        || $IO::Prompt::VERSION >= qv('0.3.1')
            && $IO::Prompt::VERSION <= qv('0.3.3');

    croak 'Benchmark must be no later than version 1.52'
        if $Benchmark::VERSION > qv('1.52') ;
}
```

This approach is tedious, repetitive, and error-prone, so naturally there's a module on the CPAN to simplify the process of loading a module and verifying that its
version number is acceptable. The module is named only and it can be used (under
Perl 5.6.1 and later) like so:

```
package Payload;
# Works only under Perl 5.6.1 and later, but not 5.8.0
use only q{ 5.6.1-  !5.8.0 };

# IO::Prompt must be 0.2.0 or better, but not 0.3.1 to 0.3.3
use only 'IO::Prompt' => q{ 0.2-  !0.3.1-0.3.3 },  qw( prompt );

# Benchmark must be no later than version 1.52
use only Benchmark => q{ -1.52 },  qw( cmpthese );
```

That is, you write use only, followed by the module name, followed by a single string that specifies the range of versions that are acceptable. The use only first loads the module you requested, then checks whether the version it loaded matches the range of versions you specified.

You can specify ranges of acceptable versions ('1.2.1-1.2.8'), or a minimum acceptable version ('2.7.3-'), or a maximum acceptable version ('-1.9.17'). You can negate any of these, to specify unacceptable versions ('!1.2.7', '!3.2-3.2.9'). Most importantly, you can combine these different types of specification to provide "ranges with holes". For example, in the previous example:

```
use only 'IO::Prompt' => '0.2-  !0.3.1-0.3.3',  qw( prompt );
```

this means "any version at or above 0.2, except those in the range 0.3.1 to 0.3.3".

The only module has other, even more powerful features. It provides exceptional support for legacy applications that may rely on outdated versions of particular modules. You can install multiple versions of the same module, and then use only will select the most appropriate available version of the module for each program.

Exporting

Export judiciously and, where possible, only by request.

As with classes (see Chapter 15), modules should aim for an optimal interface, rather than a minimal one. In particular, you should provide any non-fundamental utility subroutines that client coders will frequently need, and are therefore likely to (re-)write themselves.

On the other hand, it's also important to minimize the number of subroutines that are exported by default. Especially if those subroutines have common names. For example, if you're writing a module to support software testing, then you might want to provide subroutines like ok( ), skip( ), pass( ), and fail( ):

```
package Test::Utils;

use base qw( Exporter );
our @EXPORT = qw( ok skip pass fail );    # Will export these by default

# [subroutine definitions here]
```

But exporting those subroutines by default can make the module more difficult to use, because the names of those subroutines may collide with subroutine or method definitions in the software you're testing:

```
use Perl6::Rules;    # CPAN module implements a subset of Perl 6 regexes
use Test::Utils;     # Let's test it...

my ($matched)
    = 'abc' =~ m{ ab {ok 1} d      # Test nested code blocks in regexes
                | {ok 2; fail}     # Test explicit failure of alternatives
                | abc {ok 3}       # Test successful matches
                }xms;

if ($matched) {
    ok(4);
}
```

Unfortunately, both the Perl6::Rules and Test::Utils modules export a fail() subroutine by default. As a result, the example test is subtly broken, because the Test::Utils::fail() subroutine has been exported "over the top of" the previously exported Perl6::Rules::fail() subroutine. So the fail() call inside the regex isn't invoking the expected fail().

The point is that *both* modules are behaving badly. Neither of them ought to be exporting a subroutine with a name like fail() by default; they should be allowing those subroutines to be exported only by explicit request. For example:

```
package Test::Utils;

use base qw( Exporter );
our @EXPORT_OK = qw( ok skip pass fail );     # Can export these, on request

# [subroutine definitions here]
```

In that case, both of them would then have to be loaded like so:

```
use Perl6::Rules qw( fail );
use Test::Utils  qw( ok skip );
```

and there would no longer be a conflict. Or, if they *were* going to collide, then the conflict would be immediately obvious:

```
use Perl6::Rules qw( fail );
use Test::Utils  qw( ok skip fail );
```

So make the interface of a module exportable on request, rather than exported by default.

The only exception to this guideline would be a module whose central purpose is always to make certain subroutines available (as IO::Prompt does with the prompt() subroutine, or Perl6::Slurp does with slurp()—see Chapter 10). If a module will always be used because programmers definitely want one particular subroutine it provides, then it's cleaner to export that subroutine by default:

```
package Perl6::Slurp;

use base qw( Exporter );

our @EXPORT = qw( slurp );        # The whole point of loading this module
                                  # is to then call slurp()
```

Declarative Exporting

Consider exporting declaratively.

The Exporter module has served Perl well over many years, but it's not without its flaws.

For a start, its interface is ungainly and hard to remember, which leads to unsanitary cutting and pasting. That interface also relies on subroutine names stored as strings in package variables. This design imposes all the inherent problems of using package variables, as well as the problems of symbolic references (see Chapters 5 and 11).

It's also redundant: you have to name each subroutine at least twice—once in its declaration and again in one (or more) of the export lists. And if those disadvantages weren't enough, there's also the ever-present risk of *not* successfully naming a particular subroutine twice, by misspelling it in one of the export lists.

Exporter also allows you to export variables from a module. Using variables as part of your interface is a bad interface practice (see the following guideline, "Interface Variables"), but actually aliasing them into another package is even worse. For a start, exported variables are ignored by use `strict`, so they may mask other problems in your code. But more importantly, exporting a module's state variables exposes that module's internal state in such a way that it can be modified without the module's name even appearing in the assignment:

```
use Serialize ($depth);

# and much later...

$depth = -20;       # Change the internal state of the Serialize module
```

That's neither obvious, nor robust, nor comprehensible, nor easy to maintain.

To set up a module with a full range of export facilities, including default exports, exports-by-request, and tagged export sets, you have to write something like this:

```
package Test::Utils;

use base qw( Exporter );

our @EXPORT    = qw( ok );              # Default export
our @EXPORT_OK = qw( skip pass fail );  # By explicit request only
```

```
our %EXPORT_TAGS = (
    ALL  => [@EXPORT, @EXPORT_OK],      # Everything if :ALL tagset requested
    TEST => [qw( ok pass fail )],       # These if :TEST tagset requested
    PASS => [qw( ok pass )],            # These if :PASS tagset requested
);

sub ok   {...}
sub pass {...}
sub fail {...}
sub skip {...}
```

The large amount of infrastructure code required to set up this interface can obscure what's actually being accomplished, which makes it harder to know if what's been accomplished is what was supposed to be accomplished.

A cleaner alternative is to use the Perl6::Export::Attrs CPAN module. With this module there is no separate specification of the export list. Instead, you just annotate the subroutines that you want exported, saying how you want them exported: by default, by request, or as part of particular tagsets.

Using Perl6::Export::Attrs, the export behaviour set up in the previous example could be specified with just:

```
package Test::Utils;
use Perl6::Export::Attrs;

sub ok   :Export( :DEFAULT, :TEST, :PASS ) {...}
sub pass :Export(          :TEST, :PASS ) {...}
sub fail :Export(          :TEST        ) {...}
sub skip :Export                          {...}
```

These annotated definitions specify precisely the same behaviour as the earlier Exporter-based code. Namely that:

- ok( ) will be exported when requested by name, or when the :TEST or :PASS tagset is requested. It will also be exported by default when no exports are explicitly requested.

- pass( ) will be exported when requested by name, or when the :TEST or :PASS tagset is requested.

- fail( ) will be exported when requested by name, or when the :TEST tagset is requested.

- skip( ) will be exported only when specifically requested by name.

- Every subroutine marked :Export will automatically be exported if the :ALL tagset is requested

Interface Variables

Never make variables part of a module's interface.

Variables make highly unsatisfactory interface components. They offer no control over who accesses their values, or how those values are changed. They expose part of the module's internal state information to the client code, and they provide no easy way to later impose constraints on how that state is used or modified.

This, in turn, forces every component of the module to re-verify any interface variable whenever it's used. For example, consider the parts of a module for serializing Perl data structures* shown in Example 17-1.

Example 17-1. Variables as a module's interface

```
package Serialize;
use Carp;
use Readonly;
use Perl6::Export::Attrs;
use List::Util qw( max );

Readonly my $MAX_DEPTH => 100;

# Package variables that specify shared features of the module...
our $compaction = 'none';
our $depth      = $MAX_DEPTH;

# Table of compaction tools...
my %compactor = (
  # Value of       Subroutine returning
  # $compaction    compacted form of arg
      none    =>   sub { return shift },
      zip     =>   \&compact_with_zip,
      gzip    =>   \&compact_with_gzip,
      bz      =>   \&compact_with_bz,
      # etc.
);

# Subroutine to serialize a data structure, passed by reference...
sub freeze : Export {
    my ($data_structure_ref) = @_;

    # Check whether the $depth variable has a sensible value...
    $depth = max(0, $depth);
```

---

* There are several such modules on the CPAN: Data::Dumper, YAML, FreezeThaw, and Storable.

Example 17-1. Variables as a module's interface (continued)

```
    # Perform actual serialization...
    my $frozen = _serialize($data_structure_ref);

    # Check whether the $compact variable has a sensible value...
    croak "Unknown compaction type: $compaction"
        if ! exists $compactor{$compaction};

    # Return the compacted form...
    return $compactor{$compaction}->($frozen);
}

# and elsewhere...

use Serialize qw( freeze );

$Serialize::depth      = -20;        # oops!
$Serialize::compaction = 1;          # OOPS!!!

# and later...

my $frozen_data = freeze($data_ref);      # BOOM!!!
```

Because the serialization depth and compaction mode are set via variables, the freeze( ) subroutine has to check those variables every time it's called. Moreover, if the variables are incorrectly set (as they are in the previous example), that fact will not be detected until freeze( ) is actually called. That might be hundreds of lines later, or in a different subroutine, or even in a different module entirely. That's going to make tracking down the source of the error very much harder.

The cleaner, safer, more future-proof alternative is to provide subroutines via which the client code can set state information, as illustrated in Example 17-2. By verifying the new state as it's set, errors such as negative depths and invalid compaction schemes will be detected and reported where and when they occur. Better still, those errors can sometimes be corrected on the fly, as the set_depth( ) subroutine demonstrates.

Example 17-2. Accessor subroutines instead of interface variables

```
package Serialize;
use Carp;
use Readonly;
use Perl6::Export::Attrs;

Readonly my $MAX_DEPTH => 100;

# Lexical variables that specify shared features of the module...
my $compaction = 'none';
my $depth      = $MAX_DEPTH;

# Table of compaction tools...
my %compactor = (
```

```perl
    # Value of        Subroutine returning
    # $compaction     compacted form of arg
        none    =>   sub { return shift },
        zip     =>   \&compact_with_zip,
        gzip    =>   \&compact_with_gzip,
        bz      =>   \&compact_with_bz,
        # etc.
);

# Accessor subroutines for state variables...
sub set_compaction {
    my ($new_compaction) = @_;

    # Has to be a compaction type from the table...
    croak "Unknown compaction type ($new_compaction)"
        if !exists $compactor{$new_compaction};

    # If so, remember it...
    $compaction = $new_compaction;

    return;
}

sub set_depth {
    my ($new_depth) = @_;

    # Any non-negative depth is okay...
    if ($new_depth >= 0) {
        $depth = $new_depth;
    }
    # Any negative depth is an error, so fix it and report...
    else {
        $depth = 0;
        carp "Negative depth ($new_depth) interpreted as zero";
    }

    return;
}

# Subroutine to serialize a data structure, passed by reference...
sub freeze : Export {
    my ($data_structure_ref) = @_;

    return $compactor{$compaction}->( _serialize($data_structure_ref) );
}

# and elsewhere...

use Serialize qw( freeze );

Serialize::set_depth(-20);        # Warning issued and value normalized to zero
Serialize::set_compaction(1);     # Exception thrown here
```

```
# and later...

my $frozen_data = freeze($data_ref);
```

Note that although subroutines are undoubtedly safer than raw package variables, you are still modifying non-local state information through them. Any change you make to a package's internal state can potentially affect every user of that package, at any point in your program.

Often, a better solution is to recast the module as a class. Then any code that needs to alter some internal configuration or state can create its own object of the class, and modify that object's internal state instead. Using that approach, the package shown in Example 17-2 would be rewritten as shown in Example 17-3.

Example 17-3. Objects instead of accessor subroutines

```
package Serialize;
use Class::Std;
use Carp;
{
    my %compaction_of : ATTR( default => 'none' );
    my %depth_of      : ATTR( default => 100    );

    # Table of compaction tools...
    my %compactor = (
      # Value of         Subroutine returning
      # $compaction      compacted form of arg
          none    =>    sub { return shift },
          zip     =>    \&compact_with_zip,
          gzip    =>    \&compact_with_gzip,
          bz      =>    \&compact_with_bz,
          # etc.
    );

    # Accessor subroutines for state variables...
    sub set_compaction {
        my ($self, $new_compaction) = @_;

        # Has to be a compaction type from the table...
        croak "Unknown compaction type ($new_compaction)"
            if !exists $compactor{$new_compaction};

        # If so, remember it...
        $compaction_of{ident $self} = $new_compaction;

        return;
    }

    sub set_depth {
        my ($self, $new_depth) = @_;
```

Example 17-3. Objects instead of accessor subroutines (continued)

```perl
        # Any non-negative depth is okay...
        if ($new_depth >= 0) {
            $depth_of{ident $self} = $new_depth;
        }
        # Any negative depth is an error, so fix it and report...
        else {
            $depth_of{ident $self} = 0;
            carp "Negative depth ($new_depth) interpreted as zero";
        }

        return;
    }

    # Method to serialize a data structure, passed by reference...
    sub freeze {
        my ($self, $data_structure_ref) = @_;

        my $compactor = $compactor{$compaction_of{ident $self}};

        return $compactor->( _serialize($data_structure_ref) );
    }

    # etc.
}

# and elsewhere...

# Create a new interface to the class...
use Serialize;
my $serializer = Serialize->new( );

# Set up the state of that interface as required...
$serializer->set_depth(20);
$serializer->set_compaction('zip');

# and later...

my $frozen_data = $serializer->freeze($data_ref);
```

Creating Modules

Build new module frameworks automatically.

The "bones" of every new module are basically the same:

```perl
    package <MODULE NAME>;

    use version; our $VERSION = qv('0.0.1');
```

```
use warnings;
use strict;
use Carp;

# Module implementation here

1; # Magic true value required at end of module
__END__

=head1 NAME

<MODULE NAME> - [One line description of module's purpose here]

=head1 VERSION

This document describes <MODULE NAME> version 0.0.1

=head1 SYNOPSIS

    use <MODULE NAME>;

    # And the rest of the documentation template here
    # (as described in Chapter 7)
```

So it makes sense to create each new module automatically, reusing the same templates for each. This rule applies not just to the *.pm* file itself, but also to the other standard components of a module distribution: the *MANIFEST* file, the *Makefile.PL*, the *Build.PL*, the *README*, the *Changes* file, and the *lib/* and *t/* subdirectories.

The easiest way to create all those components consistently is to use the `Module::Starter` CPAN module. After installing `Module::Starter` and setting up a minimal *~/.module-starter/config* file:

```
author:   Yurnaam Heere
email:    YHEERE@cpan.org
```

you can then simply type:

```
> module-starter --module=New::Module::Name
```

on the command line. `Module::Starter` will immediately construct a new subdirectory named *New-Module-Name/* and populate it with the basic files that are needed to create a complete module.

Better still, `Module::Starter` has a simple plug-in architecture that allows you do specify how it creates each new module directory and its contents. For example, you can use the `Module::Starter::PBP` plugin (also on the CPAN) to cause `Module::Starter` to use the module templates, documentation proformas, and testing tools recommended in this book.

After installing the `Module::Starter::PBP` module, you can type:

```
> perl -MModule::Starter::PBP=setup
```

on the command line and the plug-in will automatically configure itself, prompting for any information it needs in order to do so. Once `Module::Starter::PBP` is set up, you can easily edit the standard templates it will have installed, to customize the boilerplate code to your own needs.

The Standard Library

Use core modules wherever possible.

It's definitely best practice to avoid unnecessary work, and code reuse is a primary example of that. Perl has two main software libraries of reusable code: the standard Perl library and the CPAN. It's almost always a serious mistake to start hacking on a solution without at least exploring whether your problem has already been solved.

The library of modules that come standard with every Perl distribution is the ideal place to start. There are no issues of availability: if a core module solves your problem, then that solution will already have been installed anywhere that Perl itself is available. There are no issues of authorization either: if Perl has been approved for production use in your organization, the library modules will almost certainly be acceptable too.

Another major advantage is that the standard library contains some of the most heavily used Perl modules available. Frequent use means they're also some of the most strenuously stress-tested—and therefore more likely to be both reliable and efficient.

Perl's standard library contains modules for creating declaration attributes; optimizing the loading of modules; using arbitrary precision numbers, complex numbers, and a full range of trigonometric functions; adding I/O layers to the standard streams; interfacing with flat-file and relational databases; verifying and debugging Perl code; benchmarking and profiling program performance; CGI scripting; accessing the CPAN; serializing and deserializing data structures; calculating message digests; dealing with different character encodings; accessing system error constants; imposing exception semantics on failure-returning functions and subroutines; processing filenames in a filesystem-independent manner; searching for, comparing, and copying files; filtering source code; command-line argument processing; performing common operations on scalars, arrays, and hashes; internationalizing and localizing programs; setting up and using pipes and sockets; interacting with network protocols (including FTP, NNTP, ping, POP3, and SMTP); encoding and decoding MIME; data caching and subroutine memoization; accessing the complete POSIX function library; processing POD documentation; building software test suites; text processing; thread programming; acquiring and manipulating time and date information; and using Unicode.

There is rarely a good reason to roll your own code for any of those common tasks. For example, if you need a temporary filename, it may be tempting to throw the necessary code together yourself:

```
# Range of acceptable replacements for placeholders in template...
my @letter = ('A'..'Z');

# Given a template, fill it in randomly, making sure the file doesn't exist...
sub tempfile {
    my ($template) = @_;
    my $filename;

    ATTEMPT:
    while (1) {
        $filename = $template;
        $filename =~ s{ X }{$letter[rand @letter]}gexms;
        last ATTEMPT if ! -e $filename;
    }

    return $filename;
}

my $filename = tempfile('.myapp_XXXXXX');
open my $fh, '>', $filename
    or croak "Couldn't open temp file: $filename";
```

But that's a waste of time and effort, when the necessary functionality is better implemented, more thoroughly tested, and already sitting there waiting on your system:

```
use File::Temp qw( tempfile );

my ($fh, $filename) = tempfile('.myapp_XXXXXX');
```

The *perlmodlib* documentation is a good place to start exploring the Perl Standard Library.

CPAN

Use CPAN modules where feasible.

The Comprehensive Perl Archive Network (CPAN) is often referred to as Perl's *killer app*, and rightly credited with much of Perl's success in recent years. It is a truly vast repository of code, providing solutions for just about every programming task you might commonly encounter.

As with Perl's standard library, many of the modules on the CPAN are heavily relied-upon—and severely stress-tested—by the global Perl community. This makes CPAN modules like DBI, DateTime, Device::SerialPort, HTML::Mason, POE, Parse::RecDescent, SpreadSheet::ParseExcel, Template::Toolkit, Text::Autoformat, and `XML::Parser` extremely reliable and powerful tools. Extremely reliable and powerful *free* tools.

Of course, not all the code archived on CPAN is equally reliable. There is no centralized quality control mechanism for the archive; that's not its purpose. There is an integrated ratings system for CPAN modules, but it is voluntary and many modules remain unrated. So it's important to carefully assess any modules you may be considering.

Nevertheless, if your organization allows it, always check the CPAN (*http://search. cpan.org*) before you try to solve a new problem yourself. An hour or so of searching, investigation, quality assessment, and prototyping will frequently save days or weeks of development effort. Even if you decide not to use an existing solution, those modules may give you ideas that will help you design and implement your own in-house version.

Of course, many organizations are wary of any external software, *especially* if it's open source. One way to encourage your organization to allow you to use the enormous resources of the CPAN is to explain it properly. In particular don't characterize your intent as "importing unknown software"; characterize it as "exporting known development delays, testing requirements, and maintenance costs".

Another resource that may help sway your local Powers That Be is the "Perl Success Stories" archive (*http://perl.oreilly.com/news/success_stories.html*). Companies like Hewlett Packard, Amazon.com, Barclays Bank, Oxford University Press, and NBC are leveraging the resources of CPAN to better compete in their respective markets. Exploring their successes may cast Perl's software archive in a new and attractive pecuniary light for your boss.

CHAPTER 18
Testing and Debugging

Debugging is twice as hard as writing the code in the first place.
Therefore, if you write the code as cleverly as possible, you are,
by definition, not smart enough to debug it.
—Brian Kernighan

Most people recognize that testing and debugging are somehow related; that debugging is the natural consequence of testing, and that testing is a natural tool during debugging.

But, when used correctly, testing and debugging are actually antagonistic: the better your testing, the *less* you'll need to debug. Better testing habits repay themselves many times over, by reducing the effort required to diagnose, locate, and fix bugs.

Testing and debugging are huge topics, and a single chapter like this can only outline the simplest and most universal practices. For much deeper explorations of the possibilities, see *Perl Testing: A Developer's Notebook* (O'Reilly, 2005), *Perl Debugged* (Addison Wesley, 2001), and *Perl Medic* (Addison Wesley, 2004).

Test Cases

Write the test cases first.

Probably the single best practice in all of software development is writing your test suite first.

A test suite is an executable, self-verifying *specification* of the behaviour of a piece of software. If you have a test suite, you can—at any point in the development process—verify that the code works as expected. If you have a test suite, you can—after any changes during the maintenance cycle—verify that the code is *still* working as expected.

So write the tests first. Write them as soon as you know what your interface will be (see "Interfaces" in Chapter 17). Write them *before* you start coding your application or module. Because unless you have tests, you have no unequivocal specification of what the software is supposed to do, and no way of knowing whether it does it.

Modular Testing

Standardize your tests with `Test::Simple` **or** `Test::More`.

Writing tests always seems like a chore, and an unproductive chore at that: you don't have anything to test yet, so why write tests? And yet, most developers will—almost automatically—write driver software to test their new module in an ad hoc way:

```
> cat try_inflections.pl

# Test my shiny new English inflections module...
use Lingua::EN::Inflect qw( inflect );

# Try some plurals (both standard and unusual inflections)...
my %plural_of = (
    'house'          => 'houses',
    'mouse'          => 'mice',
    'box'            => 'boxes',
    'ox'             => 'oxen',
    'goose'          => 'geese',
    'mongoose'       => 'mongooses',
    'law'            => 'laws',
    'mother-in-law'  => 'mothers-in-law',
);

# For each of them, print both the expected result and the actual inflection...
for my $word ( keys %plural_of ) {
    my $expected = $plural_of{$word};
    my $computed = inflect( "PL_N($word)" );

    print "For $word:\n",
          "\tExpected: $expected\n",
          "\tComputed: $computed\n";
}
```

A driver like that is actually *harder* to write than a test suite, because you have to worry about formatting the output in a way that is easy to read. And it's *much* harder to use the driver than it would be to use a test suite, because every time you run it you have to wade though that formatted output and verify "by eye" that everything is as it should be:

```
> perl try_inflections.pl

For house:
    Expected: houses
```

```
     Computed: houses
For law:
     Expected: laws
     Computed: laws
For mongoose:
     Expected: mongooses
     Computed: mongeese
For goose:
     Expected: geese
     Computed: geese
For ox:
     Expected: oxen
     Computed: oxen
For mother-in-law:
     Expected: mothers-in-law
     Computed: mothers-in-laws
For mouse:
     Expected: mice
     Computed: mice
For box:
     Expected: boxes
     Computed: boxes
```

That's also error-prone; eyes are not optimized for picking out small differences in the middle of large amounts of nearly identical text.

Rather than hacking together a driver program, it's easier to write a test program using the standard Test::Simple module. Instead of print statements showing what's being tested, you just write calls to the ok( ) subroutine, specifying as its first argument the condition under which things are okay, and as its second argument a description of what you're actually testing:

```
> cat inflections.t

use Lingua::EN::Inflect qw( inflect );
use Test::Simple qw( no_plan );

my %plural_of = (
    'mouse'         => 'mice',
    'house'         => 'houses',
    'ox'            => 'oxen',
    'box'           => 'boxes',
    'goose'         => 'geese',
    'mongoose'      => 'mongooses',
    'law'           => 'laws',
    'mother-in-law' => 'mothers-in-law',
);

for my $word ( keys %plural_of ) {
    my $expected = $plural_of{$word};
    my $computed = inflect( "PL_N($word)" );

    ok( $computed eq $expected, "$word -> $expected" );
}
```

Test programs like this should be kept in files with a *.t* suffix (*inflections.t*, *conjunctions.t*, *articles.t*,) and stored in a directory named *t/* within your development directory for the application or module. If you set up your development directory using `Module::Starter` or `Module::Starter::PBP` (see "Creating Modules" in Chapter 17), this test directory will be set up for you automatically, with some standard *.t* files already provided.

Note that `Test::Simple` is loaded with the argument `qw( no_plan )`. Normally that argument would be `tests => count`, indicating how many tests are expected, but here the tests are generated from the `%plural_of` table at run time, so the final count will depend on how many entries are in that table. Specifying a fixed number of tests when loading the module *is* useful if you happen know that number at compile time, because then the module can also "meta-test": verify that you carried out all the tests you expected to.

The `Test::Simple` program is slightly more concise and readable than the original driver code, and the output is *much* more compact and informative:

```
> perl inflections.t

ok 1 - house -> houses
ok 2 - law -> laws
not ok 3 - mongoose -> mongooses
#     Failed test (inflections.t at line 21)
ok 4 - goose -> geese
ok 5 - ox -> oxen
not ok 6 - mother-in-law -> mothers-in-law
#     Failed test (inflections.t at line 21)
ok 7 - mouse -> mice
ok 8 - box -> boxes
1..8
# Looks like you failed 2 tests of 8.
```

More importantly, this version requires far less effort to verify the correctness of each test. You just scan down the left margin looking for a "not" and a comment line.

You might prefer to use the `Test::More` module instead of `Test::Simple`. Then you can specify the actual and expected values separately, by using the `is( )` subroutine, rather than `ok( )`:

```perl
use Lingua::EN::Inflect qw( inflect );
use Test::More qw( no_plan );      # Now using more advanced testing tools

my %plural_of = (
    'mouse'           => 'mice',
    'house'           => 'houses',
    'ox'              => 'oxen',
    'box'             => 'boxes',
    'goose'           => 'geese',
    'mongoose'        => 'mongooses',
    'law'             => 'laws',
    'mother-in-law'   => 'mothers-in-law',
);
```

```
    for my $word ( keys %plural_of ) {
        my $expected = $plural_of{$word};
        my $computed = inflect( "PL_N($word)" );

        # Test expected and computed inflections for string equality...
        is( $computed, $expected, "$word -> $expected" );
    }
```

Apart from no longer having to type the eq yourself*, this version also produces more detailed error messages:

```
> perl inflections.t

ok 1 - house -> houses
ok 2 - law -> laws
not ok 3 - mongoose -> mongooses
#     Failed test (inflections.t at line 20)
#          got: 'mongeese'
#     expected: 'mongooses'
ok 4 - goose -> geese
ok 5 - ox -> oxen
not ok 6 - mother-in-law -> mothers-in-law
#     Failed test (inflections.t at line 20)
#          got: 'mothers-in-laws'
#     expected: 'mothers-in-law'
ok 7 - mouse -> mice
ok 8 - box -> boxes
1..8
# Looks like you failed 2 tests of 8.
```

The Test::Tutorial documentation that comes with Perl 5.8 provides a gentle introduction to both Test::Simple and Test::More.

Test Suites

Standardize your test suites with Test::Harness.

Once you've written your tests using one of the Test:: modules, in a series of *.t* files in the *t/* subdirectory (as described in the previous guideline, "Modular Testing"), you can use the Test::Harness module to make it easier to run all the test files in your test suite.

The module is specifically designed to understand and summarize the output format used by Test::Simple and Test::More. It comes with an invaluable utility program named *prove*, which makes it trivially easy to run all the tests in your */t* directory and have the results summarized for you:

---

* The ok subroutine is still available from Test::More if you do want to specify your own comparisons.

```
> prove -r

t/articles........ok
t/inflections.....NOK 3#        Failed test (inflections.t at line 21)
t/inflections.....NOK 6#        Failed test (inflections.t at line 21)
t/inflections.....ok 8/0# Looks like you failed 2 tests of 8.
t/inflections.....dubious
t/other/conjunctions....ok
t/verbs/participles.....ok

Failed 1/4 test scripts, 75.00% okay. 2/119 subtests failed, 98.32% okay.
```

The -r option tells *prove* to recursively search through subdirectories looking for *.t* files to test. You can also specify precisely where to look for tests by explicitly telling *prove* the directory or file:

```
> prove t/other

t/other/conjunctions....ok

All tests successful.
```

The utility has many other options that allow you to preview which tests will be run (without actually running them), change the file extension that is searched for, run tests in a random order (to catch any order dependencies), run tests in taint mode (see the *perlsec* manpage), or see the individual results of every test rather than just a summary.

Using a standard testing setup and a coordinating utility like this, it's trivial to regression test each modification you make to a module or application. Every time you modify the source of your module or application, you simply type **prove -r**. Instantly, you can see whether your modification fixed what it was supposed to, and whether that fix broke anything else.

Failure

Write test cases that fail.

Testing is not actually about ensuring correctness; it's about discovering mistakes. The only successful test is one that *fails*, and thereby reveals a bug.

To use testing effectively, it's vital to get into the right (i.e., slightly counterintuitive) mindset when writing tests. You need to get to the point where you're mildly disappointed if the test suite runs without reporting a problem.

The logic behind that disappointment is simple. All non-trivial software has bugs. Your test suite's job is to find those bugs. If your software passes your test suite, then your test suite isn't doing its job.

Of course, at some point in the development process you have to decide that the code is finally good enough to deploy (or ship). And, at that point, you definitely want that code to pass its test suite before you send it out. But always remember: it's passing the test suite because you decided you'd found all the bugs you cared to test for, *not* because there were no more bugs to find.

What to Test

Test both the likely and the unlikely.

Having a test suite that fails to fail might not be a major problem, so long as your tests cover the most common ways in which your software will actually be used. The single most important practice here is to run your tests on real-world cases.

That is, if you're building software to handle particular datasets or data streams, test it using actual samples of that data. And make sure those samples are of a similar size to the data on which the software will eventually need to operate.

Play-testing (see Chapter 17) can also come in handy here. If you (or other prospective users) have prototyped the kind of code you expect to write, then you should test the kinds of activities that your exploratory code implements, and the kinds of errors that you made when writing that code. Better yet, just write your hypothetical code as a test suite, using one of the Test:: modules. Then, when you're ready to implement, your test suite will already be in place.

Testing the most likely uses of your software is essential, but it's also vital to write tests that examine both edge-cases (i.e., one parameter with an extreme or unusual value) and corner-cases (i.e., several parameters with an extreme or unusual value).

Good places to hunt for bad behaviour include:

- The minimum and maximum possible values
- Slightly less than the minimum possible value and slightly more than the maximum possible value
- Negative values, positive values, and zero
- Very small positive and negative values
- Empty strings and multiline strings
- Strings with control characters (including "\0")
- Strings with non-ASCII characters (e.g., Latin-1 or Unicode)
- undef, and lists of undef
- '0', '0E0', '0.0', and '0 but true'
- Empty lists, arrays, and hashes

- Lists with duplicated and triplicated values
- Input values that "will *never* be entered" (but which are)
- Interactions with resources that "will *never* be missing" (but which are)
- Non-numeric input where a number is expected, and vice versa
- Non-references where a reference is expected, and vice versa
- Missing arguments to a subroutine or method
- Extra arguments to a subroutine or method
- Positional arguments that are out of order
- Key/value arguments that are mislabeled
- Loading the wrong version of a module, where multiple versions are installed on your system
- Every bug you ever actually encounter (see the following guideline, "Debugging and Testing")

Debugging and Testing

Add new test cases before you start debugging.

The first step in any debugging process is to isolate the incorrect behaviour of the system, by producing the shortest demonstration of it that you reasonably can. If you're lucky, this may even have been done for you:

```
To: DCONWAY@cpan.org
From: sascha@perlmonks.org
Subject: Bug in inflect module

Zdravstvuite,

I have been using your Lingua::EN::Inflect module to normalize terms in a
data-mining application I am developing, but there seems to be a bug in it,
as the following example demonstrates:

    use Lingua::EN::Inflect qw( PL_N );

    print PL_N('man'), "\n";        # Prints "men", as expected
    print PL_N('woman'), "\n";      # Incorrectly prints "womans"
```

Once you have distilled a short working example of the bug, convert it to a series of tests, such as:

```
    use Lingua::EN::Inflect qw( PL_N );
    use Test::More qw( no_plan );

    is(PL_N('man') ,  'men',   'man -> men'    );
    is(PL_N('woman'), 'women', 'woman -> women' );
```

Don't try to fix the problem straightaway. Instead, immediately add those tests to your test suite. If that testing has been well set up, that can often be as simple as adding a couple of entries to a table:

```
my %plural_of = (
    'mouse'         => 'mice',
    'house'         => 'houses',
    'ox'            => 'oxen',
    'box'           => 'boxes',
    'goose'         => 'geese',
    'mongoose'      => 'mongooses',
    'law'           => 'laws',
    'mother-in-law' => 'mothers-in-law',

    # Sascha's bug, reported 27 August 2004...
    'man'           => 'men',
    'woman'         => 'women',
);
```

The point is: if the original test suite didn't report this bug, then that test suite was *broken*. It simply didn't do its job (i.e., finding bugs) adequately. So fix the test suite first…by adding tests that cause it to fail:

```
> perl inflections.t

ok 1 - house -> houses
ok 2 - law -> laws
ok 3 - man -> men
ok 4 - mongoose -> mongooses
ok 5 - goose -> geese
ok 6 - ox -> oxen
not ok 7 - woman -> women
#     Failed test (inflections.t at line 20)
#           got: 'womans'
#      expected: 'women'
ok 8 - mother-in-law -> mothers-in-law
ok 9 - mouse -> mice
ok 10 - box -> boxes
1..10
# Looks like you failed 1 tests of 10.
```

Once the test suite is detecting the problem correctly, then you'll be able to tell when you've correctly fixed the actual bug, because the tests will once again stop failing.

This approach to debugging is most effective when the test suite covers the full range of manifestations of the problem. When adding test cases for a bug, don't just add a single test for the simplest case. Make sure you include the obvious variations as well:

```
my %plural_of = (
    'mouse'         => 'mice',
    'house'         => 'houses',
    'ox'            => 'oxen',
    'box'           => 'boxes',
    'goose'         => 'geese',
```

```
    'mongoose'      => 'mongooses',
    'law'           => 'laws',
    'mother-in-law' => 'mothers-in-law',

    # Sascha's bug, reported 27 August 2004...
    'man'           => 'men',
    'woman'         => 'women',
    'human'         => 'humans',
    'man-at-arms'   => 'men-at-arms',
    'lan'           => 'lans',
    'mane'          => 'manes',
    'moan'          => 'moans',
);
```

The more thoroughly you test the bug, the more completely you will fix it.

Strictures

Always use strict.

Making use strict your default will help *perl* (the interpreter) pick up a range of frequently made mistakes caused by Perl (the language) being overhelpful. For example, use strict detects and reports—at compile time—the common error of writing:

```
my $list = get_list();

# and later...

print $list[-1];                # Oops! Wrong variable
```

instead of:

```
my $list_ref = get_list();

# and later...

print $list_ref->[-1];
```

But it's also important not to rely too heavily on use strict, or to assume that it's infallible. For example, it won't pick up that incorrect array access in the following example:

```
my @list;

# and later in the same scope...

my $list = get_list();

# and later...

print $list[-1];
```

That's because now the problem with $list[-1] isn't just that someone forgot the arrow; it's that they're referring to the wrong (valid) variable.

Similarly, the following code contains both symbolic references and unqualified package variables, both of which use strict is supposed to prevent. Yet it compiles without even a warning:

```
use strict;
use warnings;
use Data::Dumper;

use Readonly;
Readonly my $DUMP => 'Data::Dumper::Dumper';
Readonly my $MAX  => 10;

# and later...

sub dump_a {
    my $dump = \&{$DUMP};                   # Symbolic reference

    my @a = (0..$MAX);

    for my $i (0..$#a) {
        $a->[$MAX-$i] = $a->[$i];           # Oops! Wrong variables
        print $dump->($a[$i]);
    }

    return;
}
```

The uncaught symbolic reference is in \&{$DUMP}, where $DUMP contains a string, not a subroutine reference. The symbolic access is ignored because dump_at( ) is never called, so use strict never gets the change to detect the symbolic reference.

The uncaught package variable is the scalar $a in $a->[$i] and $a->[$MAX-$i]. That's almost certainly supposed to be $a[$i], as it is in the print statement. Perhaps the:

```
my @a = (0..$MAX);
```

line was originally:

```
my $a = [0..$MAX];
```

and, when it was changed, the rest of the subroutine was incompletely updated. After all, use strict will point out any uses of $a that might have been missed, won't it?

In this particular case, it doesn't. The package variables $a and $b are exempt from use strict qw(vars), because they're frequently required in sort blocks, and no-one wants to have to write:

```
@ordered_results = sort { our ($a, $b); $b <=> $a } @results;
```

And they're not the only variables that are invulnerable to use strict. Other "stealth" package variables include $ARGV, @ARGV, @INC, %INC, %ENV, %SIG, and occasionally @F (in the main package under the -a flag). Moreover, because use strict exempts the entire symbol table entry for each of the previous variables, none of the following are caught either: %ARGV, $INC, @ENV, $ENV, @SIG, and $SIG.

This doesn't mean that using strict isn't a good practice; it most definitely *is*. But it's critical to think of it as a tool, not as a crutch.

Warnings

Always turn on warnings explicitly.

If you're developing under Perl 5.6 or later, always use warnings at the start of each file. Under earlier versions of Perl, always use the -w command-line flag, or set the $WARNING variable (available from use English) to a true value.

Perl's warning system is invaluable. It can detect more than 200 different questionable programming practices, including common errors like using the wrong sigil on an array access; trying to read an output stream (or vice versa); leaving parentheses off ambiguous declarations; runaway strings with no closing delimiter; dyslexic assignment operators (=-, =+, etc.); using non-numbers as numbers; using | instead of ||, or || instead of or; misspelling a package or class name; mixing up \1 and $1 in a regex; ambiguous subroutine/function calls; and improbable control flow (e.g., returning from a subroutine via a call to next).

Some of these warnings are enabled by default, but all of them are worth enabling.

Not taking advantage of these warnings can result in code like this, which compiles without complaint, even though it has (at least) nineteen distinct problems:

```perl
my $n = 9;
my $list = (1..$n);

my $n = <TTY>;

print ("\n" x 100, keys %$list), "\n";
print $list[$i];

sub keys ($list) {
    $list ||= $_[1], \@default_list;
    push digits, @{$list} =~ m/([A-Za-\d])/g;
    return uc \1;
}
```

Under use warnings the awful truth can be revealed:

```
"my" variable $n masks earlier declaration in same scope at caveat.pl line 4.
print (...) interpreted as function at caveat.pl line 6.
Illegal character in prototype for main::keys : $list at caveat.pl line 9.
Unquoted string "digits" may clash with future reserved word at caveat.pl line 11.
False [] range "a-\d" in regex; marked by <-- HERE in m/([A-Za-\d <-- HERE ])/
at caveat.pl line 11.
```

```
Applying pattern match (m//) to @array will act on scalar(@array) at
caveat.pl line 11.
Array @digits missing the @ in argument 1 of push() at caveat.pl line 11.
Useless use of reference constructor in void context at caveat.pl line 10.
Useless use of a constant in void context at caveat.pl line 6.
Name "main::list" used only once: possible typo at caveat.pl line 7.
Name "main::default_list" used only once: possible typo at caveat.pl line 10.
Name "main::TTY" used only once: possible typo at caveat.pl line 4.
Name "main::digits" used only once: possible typo at caveat.pl line 11.
Name "main::i" used only once: possible typo at caveat.pl line 7.
Use of uninitialized value in range (or flip) at caveat.pl line 2.
readline() on unopened filehandle TTY at caveat.pl line 4.
Argument "100" isn't numeric in repeat (x) at caveat.pl line 6.
Use of uninitialized value in array element at caveat.pl line 7.
Use of uninitialized value in print at caveat.pl line 7.
```

Note that it may still be appropriate to comment out the use warnings line when your application or module is deployed, especially if non-technical users will interact with it, or if it will run in a CGI or other embedded environment. Issuing warnings in these contexts can needlessly alarm users, or cause server errors.

Don't remove the use warnings completely, though; when something goes wrong, you'll want to uncomment it again so the reinstated warnings can help you locate and fix the problem.

Correctness

Never assume that a warning-free compilation implies correctness.

---

use strict and use warnings are powerful developments aids, whose insights into the foibles of the typical programmer sometimes border on the magical. It is a serious mistake not to use them at all times.

But, as the examples in the previous guidelines illustrate, they are neither infallible nor omniscient. It may seem counterintuitive, but Perl's extensive list of warnings and strictures can sometimes result in code that is *less* robust than it otherwise might have been. The comforting knowledge that "use strict will pick up any problems" often engenders a false sense of security, and promotes the illusion that a silent compilation implies a correct compilation.

But no Perl pragma will ever be able to pick out the serious bug in this subroutine:

```
sub is_monotonic_increasing {
    my ($data_ref) = @_;
    for my $i (1..$#{$data_ref}) {
        return 0 unless $data_ref->[$i-1] > $data_ref->[$i];
    }
    return 1;
}
```

It's foolish not to make use of the very real protections that use strict and use warnings provide. Just don't let those protections make you complacent*.

Overriding Strictures

Turn off strictures or warnings explicitly, selectively, and in the smallest possible scope.

Sometimes you really do need to implement something arcane; something that would cause use strict or use warnings to complain. In this case, because you'll always be using both those pragmas (see the previous three guidelines, "Strictures", "Warnings", and "Correctness"), you'll need to turn them off temporarily.

The key to doing that without compromising the robustness of your code is to turn off warnings and strictures in the smallest possible scope. And to turn off only the particular warnings you intend to cause or those specific strictures that you're intentionally violating.

For example, suppose you needed a Sub::Tracking module that, when passed the name of a subroutine, would modify that subroutine so that any subsequent call to it was logged. For example:

```
use Digest::SHA qw( sha512_base64 );

use Sub::Tracking qw( track_sub );
track_sub('sha512_base64');

# and later...

my $text_key
    = sha512_base64($original_text);  # Use of subroutine automatically logged
```

Such a module might be implemented as in Example 18-1.

Example 18-1. A module for tracking subroutine calls

```
package Sub::Tracking;

use version; our $VERSION = qv(0.0.1);

use strict;
use warnings;
use Carp;
use Perl6::Export::Attrs;
use Log::Stdlog {level => 'trace'};
```

---

* By the way, that serious bug was that the conditions under which a return 0 occurs is the wrong way round. The unless should be an if.

Example 18-1. A module for tracking subroutine calls (continued)

```perl
# Utility to create a tracked version of an existing subroutine...
sub _make_tracker_for {
    my ($sub_name, $orig_sub_ref) = @_;

    # Return a new subroutine...
    return sub {

        # ...which first determines and logs its call context
        my ($package, $file, $line) = caller;
        print {*STDLOG} trace =>
            "Called $sub_name(@_) from package $package at '$file' line $line";

        # ...and then transforms into a call to the original subroutine
        goto &{$orig_sub_ref};
    }
}


# Replace an existing subroutine with a tracked version...
sub track_sub : Export {
    my ($sub_name) = @_;

    # Locate the (currently untracked) subroutine in the caller's symbol table...
    my $caller = caller;
    my $full_sub_name = $caller.'::'.$sub_name;
    my $sub_ref = do { no strict 'refs'; *{$full_sub_name}{CODE} };

    # Or die trying...
    croak "Can't track nonexistent subroutine '$full_sub_name'"
        if !defined $sub_ref;

    # Then build a tracked version of it...
    my $tracker_ref = _make_tracker_for($sub_name, $sub_ref);

    # And install that version back in the caller's symbol table...
    {
        no strict 'refs';
        *{$full_sub_name} = $tracker_ref;
    }

    return;
}

1; # Magic true value required at end of module
```

The _make_tracker_for( ) utility subroutine creates a new anonymous subroutine that first logs the fact that it has been called:

```perl
print {*STDLOG} trace =>
    "Called $sub_name(@_) from package $package at '$file' line $line";
```

then turns itself into the original subroutine instead[*]:

```
goto &{$orig_sub_ref};
```

The Sub::Tracking::track_sub( ) subroutine expects to be passed the name of the subroutine to be tracked. It takes that name, prepends the caller's package name ($caller.'::'.$sub_name), and then looks up that fully qualified name to see if there is a corresponding subroutine entry in the caller's symbol table (*{$full_sub_name}{CODE}). The result of this look-up will be either a reference to the named subroutine or undef (if no such subroutine exists).

track_sub( ) then creates a new tracking version of the subroutine:

```
my $tracker_ref = _make_tracker_for($sub_name, $sub_ref);
```

and installs it back in the caller's symbol table:

```
*{$full_sub_name} = $tracker_ref;
```

The problem here is that both the symbol table look-up and the symbol table assignment use a string ($full_sub_name) as the name of the symbol table entry, rather than a hard reference to it. Using a string instead of a real reference would normally incur the wrath of use strict, but the no strict 'refs' declarations tell the compiler to turn a blind eye.

Of course, it's particularly tedious to have to set up those tiny block scopes to contain the no strict declarations, especially when you could get the same effect simply by omitting the use strict at the start of the module:

```
package Sub::Tracking;
# use strict   -- Disabled because symbolic references needed below
use warnings;
use Carp;
use Stdlog;
use version; our $VERSION = qv(0.0.1);

# etc.
```

But that's a bad practice, because it would remove the strictures not only from the two lines where they're not wanted, but from every other line as well. That could easily mask other strictness violations that you would still like to be informed of.

Nor would it have been acceptable to turn off strict references throughout the track_sub( ) subroutine:

```
sub track_sub : Export {
    my ($sub_name) = @_;
```

---

[*] This is known as a "magic goto". It replaces the current subroutine call with a call to whatever subroutine you tell it to go to. It's very useful when you're installing a wrapper around an existing subroutine. Your wrapper call can do whatever it needs to do, then silently transform itself into a call to the wrapped subroutine. After which, even caller won't be able to tell the difference. See the entry for goto in *perlfunc*.

```perl
    no strict 'refs';

    # Locate the (currently untracked) subroutine in the caller's symbol table...
    my $caller = caller;
    my $full_sub_name = $caller.'::'.$sub_name;
    my $sub_ref = *{$full_sub_name}{CODE};

    # Or die trying...
    croak "Can't track nonexistent subroutine '$full_sub_name'"
        if !defined $sub_ref;

    # Then build a tracked version of it...
    my $tracker_ref = _make_tracker_for($sub_name, $sub_ref);

    # And install that version back in the caller's symbol table...
    *{$full_sub_name} = $tracker_ref;

    return;
}
```

That would still exclude far more code from strictness-checking than was (ahem) strictly necessary.

Wrapping extra do blocks or raw blocks tightly around any statement that is deliberately violating strictness *is* tedious, but not as tedious as spending an hour debugging some unexpected symbolic reference, unauthorized package variable, or undeclared subroutine that use strict would otherwise have caught.

The Debugger

Learn at least a subset of the *perl* debugger.

Perl's integrated debugger makes it very easy to watch your program's internal state change as it executes. At the very least, you should be familiar with the basic features summarized in Table 18-1.

Table 18-1. Debugger basics

Debugging task	Debugger command
To run a program under the debugger	> `perl -d `*`program.pl`*
To set a **b**reakpoint at the current line	DB<1> **b**
To set a **b**reakpoint at line 42	DB<1> **b 42**
To **c**ontinue executing until the next break-point is reached	DB<1> **c**
To **c**ontinue executing until line 86	DB<1> **c 86**
To **c**ontinue executing until subroutine *foo* is called	DB<1> **c** *foo*
To execute the **n**ext statement	DB<1> **n**
To **s**tep into any subroutine call that's part of the next statement	DB<1> **s**

Table 18-1. Debugger basics (continued)

Debugging task	Debugger command
To **r**un until the current subroutine returns	DB<1> **r**
To e**x**amine the contents of a variable	DB<1> **x** *$variable*
To have the debugger **w**atch a variable or expression, and inform you whenever it changes	DB<1> **w** *$variable* DB<1> **w** *expr($ess)*$ion*
To **v**iew where you are in the source code	DB<1> **v**
To **v**iew line 99 of the source code	DB<1> **v 99**
To get **h**elpful **h**ints on the many other features of the debugger	DB<1> **|h h**

The standard *perldebug* and *perldebtut* documentation provide much more detail on using the debugger. You can also download and print out a handy free summary of the most commonly used commands from *http://www.perl.com/2004/11/24/debugger_ref.pdf*.

Manual Debugging

Use serialized warnings when debugging "manually".

Many developers prefer not to use the debugger. Maybe they don't like the command-line interface, or the way the debugger slows down the execution of their code, or the fact that it actually changes the code it's debugging[*]. Perhaps they just dislike the tedium of stepping through a program statement by statement.

The most popular alternative to using the debugger is to manually insert print statements at relevant points in the code. This has the distinct advantage of altering the code being debugged in limited and predictable ways.

But, if you're going to debug manually, don't use print for your print statements:

```
my $results  = $scenario->project_outcomes();

print "\$results: $results\n";  # debugging only
```

Use warn instead:

```
my $results  = $scenario->project_outcomes();

warn "\$results: $results";
```

---

[*] The subtle changes that the debugger surreptitiously makes to any code it's executing usually pass unnoticed. However, very occasionally those manipulations can actually make debugging even more difficult, by introducing arcane phenomena like *heisenbugs* (errors that vanish when you try to debug them), *schrödinbugs* (errors that manifest only when you're trying to debug something else), and *mandelbugs* (complex errors that seem to fluctuate more and more chaotically, the closer you look at them).

Because warn statements will not be used anywhere else in your code (see "Reporting Failure" in Chapter 13), using them for debugging makes it very easy to subsequently find your debugging statements. Using warn also conveniently ensures that debugging messages are printed to *STDERR, rather than *STDOUT.

In addition, it's a good practice always to serialize the data structure you're reporting, using Data::Dumper:

```
my $results  = $scenario->project_outcomes();

use Data::Dumper qw( Dumper );
warn '$results:', Dumper($results);
```

By printing the value you're reporting in a structured format, you maximize the information that's subsequently available to help you debug. For example, if the project_outcomes() method was expected to return an Achievements object, then debugging with:

```
warn "\$results: $results\n";
```

might print:

```
$results: Achievements=SCALAR(0x811130)
```

It looks like the method is working correctly, sending back an inside-out object of class Achievements. However, adding Data::Dumper serialization to the debugging statement:

```
warn '$results: ', Dumper($results);
```

reveals a subtle problem:

```
$results: $VAR1 = 'Achievements=SCALAR(0x811130)'
```

That is, instead of returning an actual Achievements object, the call to project_outcomes() is returning a string instead. The expected object reference is undergoing a spurious stringification before being returned. If the method had been behaving properly, the serialized output would have indicated that there was a real object in $results:

```
$results: $VAR1 = bless( do{\(my $o = undef)}, 'Achievements' )
```

So always serialize any data structure you're debugging*.

If you prefer this kind of manual debugging, you may find it useful to set up a macro in your editor to insert suitably serialized print statements automatically. For example, adding the following in *vim*:

```
:iab dbg use Data::Dumper qw( Dumper );^Mwarn Dumper [];^[hi
```

replaces any instance of 'dbg' you might insert in your program with:

---

* For the same reasons, it's also a mistake to use the p (print) command in the debugger. Always use the x (examine) command instead; it serializes its output.

```
use Data::Dumper qw( Dumper );
warn Dumper [_];
```

The macro then repositions the insertion point between the square brackets (represented by the underscore in the previous example) and allows you to continue to insert the data structure you want to debug. You can achieve a similar effect in *Emacs* with an entry in the global abbreviation table of your *~/.abbrev_defs* file:

```
(define-abbrev-table 'global-abbrev-table '(
    ("pdbg"  "use Data::Dumper qw( Dumper );\nwarn Dumper[];"  nil  1)
  ))
```

Semi-Automatic Debugging

**Consider using "smart comments" when debugging,
rather than warn statements.**

Serialized warnings work well for manual debugging, but they can be tedious to code correctly[*]. And, even with the editor macro suggested earlier, the output of a statement like:

```
warn 'results: ', Dumper($results);
```

still leaves something to be desired in terms of readability:

```
results: $VAR1 = bless( do{\(my $o = undef)}, 'Achievements' )
```

The Smart::Comments module (previously described under "Automatic Progress Indicators" in Chapter 10) supports a form of smart comment that can help your debugging. For example, instead of:

```
use Data::Dumper qw( Dumper );

my $results  = $scenario->project_outcomes();

warn '$results: ', Dumper($results);
```

you could just write:

```
use Smart::Comments;

my $results = $scenario->project_outcomes();

### $results
```

which would then output either:

```
### $results: <opaque Achievements object (blessed scalar)>
```

---

[*] Which is vital. If there's anything less enjoyable than beating your head against a bug for several hours, it's finally discovering that your debugging print statement was itself buggy, and the problem isn't anywhere near where you thought it was. This is presumably a *homerbug*.

or:

```
### $results: 'Achievements=SCALAR(0x811130)'
```

depending on whether $results is an actual object reference or merely its stringification.

Smart::Comments also supports comment-based assertions:

```
### check: @candidates >= @elected
```

which issue warnings when the specified condition is not met. For example, the previous comment might print:

```
### @candidates >= @elected was not true at ch18/Ch18.049_Best line 23.
###       @candidates was: [
###                           'Smith',
###                           'Nguyen',
###                           'Ibrahim'
###                         ]
###       @elected was: [
###                       'Smith',
###                       'Nguyen',
###                       'Ibrahim',
###                       'Nixon'
###                     ]
```

The module also supports stronger assertions:

```
### require: @candidates >= @elected
```

which prints the same warning as the ### check:, but then immediately terminates the program.

Apart from producing more readable debugging messages, the major advantage of this approach is that you can later switch off all these comment-based debugging statements simply by removing (or commenting out) the use Smart::Comments line. When Smart::Comments isn't loaded, those smart comments become regular comments, which means you can leave the actual debugging statements in your source code[*] without incurring any performance penalty.

---

[*] If you needed them once, you'll almost certainly need them again.

## CHAPTER 19

Miscellanea

Advice is what we ask for when we already know
the answer but wish we didn't.

—Erica Jong
How to Save Your Own Life

This chapter contains a handful of guidelines that do not fit cleanly into any of the previous categories. They cover reasons for revision control, the intricacies of interfacing with other languages, the care and feeding of configuration files, the trouble with tied variables, the complexities of caching, flaws in formats, optimal optimization, and the cunning cruelty of cleverness.

Revision Control

Use a revision control system.

Maintaining control over the creation and modification of your source code[*] is utterly essential for robust team-based development. Just as you wouldn't use an editor without an Undo button or a word processor that can't merge documents, so too you shouldn't use a filesystem you can't rewind, or a development environment that can't integrate the work of many contributors.

Programmers make mistakes, and occasionally those mistakes will be catastrophic. They will reformat the disk with the most recent version of the code. Or they'll mistype an editor macro and write zeros all through the source of a critical core module. Or two developers will unwittingly edit the same file at the same time and half their changes will be lost. Revision control systems can prevent those kinds of problems.

---

[*] And documentation, and data files, and document templates, and makefiles, and style sheets, and change logs, and any other resources your system requires. Revision control isn't only for source.

Moreover, occasionally the very best debugging technique is to just give up, stop trying to get yesterday's modifications to work correctly, roll the code back to a known stable state, and start over again. Less drastically, comparing the current condition of your code with the most recent stable version from your repository (even just a line-by-line *diff*) can often help you isolate your recent "improvements" and work out which of them is the problem.

Revision control systems such as *RCS*, *CVS*, *Subversion*, *Monotone*, *darcs*, *Perforce*, *GNU arch*, or *BitKeeper* can protect against calamities, and ensure that you always have a working fallback position if maintenance goes horribly wrong. The various systems have different strengths and limitations, many of which stem from fundamentally different views on what exactly revision control is. So it's a good idea to audition the various revision control systems and find the one that works best for you. *Pragmatic Version Control Using Subversion*, by Mike Mason (Pragmatic Bookshelf, 2005) and *Essential CVS*, by Jennifer Vesperman (O'Reilly, 2003) are useful starting points.

After all, rm * is never more than half a dozen keystrokes away.

Other Languages

Integrate non-Perl code into your applications
via the Inline:: modules.

Occasionally you may need to use code resources that are not written in Perl. Most often this will be C code, but it might also be C++, Java, Python, Ruby, Tcl, Scheme, AWK, or even Basic.

The CPAN provides interface tools for hooking all of these languages up to a Perl program, but most of those tools are very challenging to use correctly. By far the most frequently used is *xsubpp*, a compiler for Perl's own "XS" interface description language (see the *perlxstut* manpage[*]).

Hooking Perl to C using XS requires you to write a shell *.pm* module to bootstrap an object file that has been compiled from C code, which was in turn generated by *xsubpp* from a *.xs* source file containing pseudo-C annotated with an XS interface description. If that sounds horribly complicated, then you have achieved an accurate understanding of the use of *xsubpp*. Example 19-1 shows just how much work is involved in even a very simple example.

---

[*] If you *dare!*

Example 19-1. Creating a fast C-based rounding subroutine using XS

> **cat Round.pm**

```
package Round;
use strict;
use warnings;

use base qw( Exporter DynaLoader );
our $VERSION = '0.01';

@EXPORT = qw( round );

bootstrap Round $VERSION;

1;
__END__
```

> **cat rounded.pl**

```
use Round;
use IO::Prompt;

while (my $num = prompt -num => 'Enter a number: ') {
    print rounded($num), "\n";
}
```

> **cat Round.xs**

```
#include "EXTERN.h"
#include "perl.h"
#include "XSUB.h"

MODULE = Round      PACKAGE = Round

int
rounded(arg)
    double  arg
CODE:
    int res;
    /* Round towards zero... */
    if (arg > 0.0)      { res = floor(arg + 0.5); }
    else if (arg < 0.0) { res = ceil(arg - 0.5); }
    else                { res = 0; }
OUTPUT:
    res
```

> **cat Makefile.PL**

```
use ExtUtils::MakeMaker;
WriteMakefile(
    NAME         => 'Round',
    VERSION_FROM => 'Round.pm',
    LIBS         => ['-lm'],
);
```

Example 19-1. Creating a fast C-based rounding subroutine using XS (continued)

```
> perl Makefile.PL

Checking if your kit is complete...
Looks good
Writing Makefile for Mytest

> make install

umask 0 && cp Mytest.pm ./blib/Mytest.pm
perl xsubpp -typemap typemap Mytest.xs >Mytest.tc && mv Mytest.tc Mytest.c
Please specify prototyping behavior for Mytest.xs (see perlxs man)
cc -c Mytest.c
Running Mkbootstrap for Mytest ()
chmod 644 Mytest.bs
LD_RUN_PATH="" ld -o ./blib/auto/Mytest/Mytest.sl -b M ytest.o
chmod 755 ./blib/auto/Mytest/Mytest.sl
cp Mytest.bs ./blib/auto/Mytest/Mytest.bs
chmod 644 ./blib/PA-RISC1.1/auto/Mytest/Mytest.bs
Manifying ./blib/man3/Mytest.3
```

It's probably not surprising that most Perl programmers recoil from that approach. A much less demanding alternative is to use the Inline module, which allows you to include standard C code directly in your Perl application. Example 19-2 shows the *rounded.pl* application from Example 19-1, but now reimplemented using Inline.

Example 19-2. Creating a fast C-based rounding subroutine using Inline::C

```
> cat rounded.pl

use Inline C => q{
    int
    rounded(double arg) {
        /* Round towards zero... */
        if (arg > 0.0)      { return floor(arg + 0.5); }
        else if (arg < 0.0) { return ceil(arg - 0.5);  }
        else                { return 0;                }
    }
};

use IO::Prompt;
while (my $num = prompt -num => 'Enter a number: ') {
    print rounded($num), "\n";
}
```

Notice that, in this second version, there's no need for a separate *.xs* file, or a *.pm* wrapper module, or any explicit translation process, or compilation step. You just type your C code into your Perl source, as part of the use Inline C statement. Then, when *rounded.pl* is executed, Inline's import( ) subroutine parses the C code, builds a suitable XS representation, compiles it with the local C compiler, and loads the resulting object file back into the running process.

Of course, if that happened every time you ran the program, any performance benefit you might have gained by writing rounded( ) in C would clearly be more than overwhelmed by the costs of continually reparsing and recompiling. Fortunately, Inline caches any object files it builds and reparses and recompiles the original C source code only when that code actually changes. The very first time *rounded.pl* was run there would be a noticeable compilation delay, but thereafter the application would start almost instantly and reap the full performance benefits of its partial C implementation.

The second great advantage of using Inline is that there are other CPAN modules that allow it to also handle inlined C++, Java, Python, Ruby, Tcl, Scheme, AWK, bc, Basic, Parrot, and assembler[*]. You can even mix and match multiple languages within the same Perl program. For example, you might implement the number-crunching components in C, the GUI in Java, and the embedded artificial intelligence in Scheme.

Configuration Files

Keep your configuration language uncomplicated.

If you're going to provide a configuration mechanism for your application, make it declarative and minimal. Keep in mind that configuration files are one of the few components of your system that are directly read by end-users, so they need to be simple. They're also one of the few components of your system that are directly *written* by end-users. So they need to be even simpler.

It's almost always enough to just support some variation on the widely used *INI* file format: named sections, individual key/value pairs, multiline values, repeated values (or lists), and comments. Example 19-3 shows a typical configuration file with all of those features.

Example 19-3. A simple configuration language

```
> cat ~/.demorc

[Interface]
# Configurable bits that others will see...

Author: Jan-Yu Eyrie
E-mail: eju@calnet

Disclaimer: This code is provided AS IS, and comes with
          : ABSOLUTELY NO WARRANTY OF ANY KIND WHATSOEVER!
```

---

[*] For an up-to-date list, see *http://search.cpan.org/search?q=Inline*.

Example 19-3. A simple configuration language (continued)

```
          : It's buggy, slow, and will almost certainly
          : break your computer. Use at your own risk!

[Internals]
# Stuff no-one else sees...

# Look-up path for plug-ins...
lib: ~/lib/perl5
lib: ~/lib/perl
lib: /usr/share/lib/perl

[strict]    # Don't allow malformed inputs
[verbose]   # Report every step
[log]       # And log every transaction
```

Fancier features like nested or hierarchical data structures, separate syntaxes for lists and scalar values, special notations for boolean configuration variables, or character escapes, are almost always a bad idea. The extra syntax will confuse most users and—worse—make it far more likely that they'll inadvertently type something that's valid, but not what they intended.

Don't use XML as your configuration file format. It may be human-readable, but it's almost never human-comprehensible, and the ratio of mark-up to content is vastly too high. No-one wants to write or maintain a configuration file that looks like Example 19-4.

Example 19-4. An XML-based configuration language

> **cat ~/.demoxml**

```
<section name="Interface">
    <!-- Configurable bits that others will see... -->
    <var> <name>author</name> <value>Jan-Yu Eyrie</value> </var>
    <var> <name>e-mail</name> <value>eju@calnet</value> </var>
    <var>
        <name>disclaimer</name>
        <value>
            This code is provided AS IS, and comes with
            ABSOLUTELY NO WARRANTY OF ANY KIND WHATSOEVER!
            It's buggy, slow, and will almost certainly
            break your computer. Use at your own risk!
        </value>
    </var>
</section>
<section name="Internals">
    <!-- Stuff no-one else sees... -->
    <!-- Look-up path for plug-ins... -->
    <var>
        <name>lib</name>
        <value>
```

Example 19-4. An XML-based configuration language (continued)

```
        <list>
            <item>~/lib/perl5</item>
            <item>~/lib/perl</item>
            <item>~/lib/perl5</item>
            <item>/usr/share/lib/perl</item>
        </list>
        </value>
    </var>
</section>
<section name="strict">     <!-- Don't allow malformed inputs --> </section>
<section name="verbose">    <!-- Report</comment -->              </section>
<section name="log">        <!-- Report every step -->           </section>
```

Whatever format you choose, don't ever parse configuration files "manually" (i.e., with readlines and regexes and loops and all the other associated forms of torture). Don't write your own configuration file parsing module, either; there are already far too many configuration-file tools available on CPAN (see *http://search.cpan.org/ search?q=Config*).

Evaluating the available modules to determine the best fit for your particular application is an onerous task, but in most cases it's probably sufficient to look at just three of them:

Config::General

> This is a very powerful configuration file processor that covers almost all configuration needs very thoroughly. The configuration syntax it supports is fixed, but includes XML-ish blocks, Perl-like heredocs, and recursive file inclusion. The resulting configuration file format is therefore considerably more sophisticated than the style recommended earlier.

Config::Std

> This configuration language and parser was specifically designed using the criteria suggested in this guideline (and elsewhere in this book). It supports a fixed syntax that is identical to that shown in Example 19-3.

Config::Tiny

> This module is by far the smallest and fastest of the three. It parses the basic Windows INI format, which may be too minimal for some applications, as it doesn't support repeated or multiline values.

All three of these alternatives allow you to read configuration files into an internal data structure, update that data structure, and then write it back in the appropriate configuration file syntax. For example, the program:

```
use Config::Std;

# Read in the config file...
read_config '~/.demorc' => my %config;
```

```
# Update the library path and disclaimer...
$config{Internals}{lib} = ['~/.plugins', '/lib/share/plugins'];
$config{Interface}{Disclaimer} = 'Whatever, dude!';

# Delete the verbose option...
delete $config{verbose};

# Add a "Limits" section...
$config{Limits}{max_time}  = 1000;
$config{Limits}{max_space} = 1e6;

# Write back config file...
write_config %config;
```

would update the configuration file shown in Example 19-3, to produce the file shown in Example 19-5.

Example 19-5. The configuration file, reloaded

```
> cat ~/.demorc

[Interface]
# Configurable bits that others will see...

Author: Jan-Yu Eyrie
E-mail: eju@calnet

Disclaimer: Whatever, dude!

[Internals]
# Stuff no-one else sees...

# Look-up path for plug-ins...
lib: ~/.plugins
lib: /lib/share/plugins

[strict]    # Don't allow malformed inputs

[log]       # And log every transaction

[Limits]

max_time: 1000

max_space: 1000000
```

Note that Config::Std has an important advantage here compared to most other configuration-file parsers. When it writes back the configuration file, it always preserves the original comments, as well as the order in which sections and their associated configuration variables appear.

Formats

Don't use formats.

The `format` statement is one of the oldest and most fundamental features of Perl. It implements the original "R" of the "Practical Extraction and Reporting Language".

And even here in the 21st century—where data is more typically restructured, marked-up, CSS'd, JavaScripted, hyperlinked, and finally browsed—a simple text-based report is still often a cleaner and more usable alternative, especially in command-line environments:

```
> contacts -find 'Damian'

===================================
| NAME            | AGE | ID NUMBER |
|-----------------+-----+-----------|
| Damian M.       | 40  |    869942 |
| Conway          |     |           |
|===================================|
| COMMENTS                          |
|-----------------------------------|
| Do not feed after midnight. Do    |
| not mix with quantum physics. Do  |
| not allow subject to talk for     |
| "as long as he likes".            |
===================================
```

But building such a report with `format`, as in Example 19-6, has some serious drawbacks, especially in terms of best-practice programming. For a start, formats are statically defined (i.e., specified at compile time), so it's difficult to build a format as your program executes; you have to resort to a string eval (see Chapter 9). Formats rely on global variables for configuration, and on package variables for the data they are to format (see Chapter 5). They also have to write their formatted text to a named filehandle (see Chapter 10). That's three best-practice strikes against formats already.

Example 19-6. Building a report with format

```
# Predeclare report format with the necessary package variables...
our ($name, $ID, $age, $comments);

format CONTACT =
 ===================================
| NAME            | AGE | ID NUMBER |
|-----------------+-----+-----------|
| ^<<<<<<<<<<<<<<< | ^|| | ^>>>>>>>> |~~
  $name,            $age, $ID,
|===================================|
| COMMENTS                          |
|-----------------------------------|
```

Example 19-6. Building a report with format (continued)

```
|  ^<<<<<<<<<<<<<<<<<<<<<<<<<<<<<<<<<  |~~
   $comments,
   ===================================
.
```

```
# and later...

# Grab contact information...
($ID, $name, $age, my $comments_ref) = get_contact($search_string);

# Massage comments into a single string...
$comments = join "\n", @{$comments_ref};

# Open output stream to STDOUT and write formatted data...
open *CONTACT, q{>-} or croak "Can't open stdout: $OS_ERROR";
write *CONTACT;
```

Formats aren't re-entrant or recursive either, so you can't use a format to format the page header of another format. And you can't (easily) pre-format data that's going to be squeezed into a particular field.

Formats only provide a limited (and non-extensible) range of field types; they can't (easily) format bulleted lists, tables, comma'd numbers, monetary amounts, fully justified text, or verbatim data (i.e., with no line filling). And although it's easy to give each formatted page a header, page footers are difficult to produce.

Perl 6 will remedy all these problems and deficiencies by replacing the format declaration with a form( ) function, which can be called at run time to produce a formatted string that can be either printed at once or used in further formatting operations.

This new approach to text-based report generation is also available in Perl 5, via the Perl6::Form CPAN module. For example, a report like that generated by Example 19-6 could also be produced without package variables, named filehandles, or explicit list flattening by the code in Example 19-7.

Example 19-7. Building a report with Perl6::Form

```
use Perl6::Form;

my ($ID, $name, $age, $comments_ref) = get_contact($search_string);

print form   {bullet=>'*'},
    '  ===================================  ',
    '| NAME              | AGE | ID NUMBER |',
    '|-----------------+-----+-----------|',
    '| {[[[[[[[[[[[[[} | {|} | {>>>>>>>} |',
       $name,            $age, $ID,
    '|===================================|',
    '| COMMENTS                          |',
    '|-----------------------------------|',
    '| * {[[[[[[[[[[[[[[[[[[[[[[[[[[[[[} |',
```

Example 19-7. Building a report with Perl6::Form (continued)

```
        $comments_ref,
'  ================================= ',
;
```

Note the use of an asterisk as a bullet to improve the readability of the comments:

```
===================================
| NAME           | AGE | ID NUMBER |
|----------------+-----+-----------|
| Damian M.      | 40  |    869942 |
| Conway         |     |           |
|=================================|
| COMMENTS                        |
|---------------------------------|
| * Do not feed after midnight.   |
| * Do not mix with quantum       |
|   physics.                      |
| * Do not allow subject to talk  |
|   for "as long as he likes".    |
===================================
```

Ties

Don't tie variables or filehandles.

Ties provide a way of replacing the behaviour any type of variable, or of a filehandle. The full mechanism is described in the standard *perltie* documentation[*].

Tied variables look exactly like ordinary scalars, arrays, or hashes, but they don't act exactly like them. Their whole purpose is to hide special non-standard behaviour inside a familiar interface. As such, they can be wonderfully Perlish and Lazy, making it easy (for example) to create a variable that automatically self-increments every time its value is accessed:

```
# Create a variable whose value cycles from zero to five...
use Tie::Cycle;
tie my $next_index, 'Tie::Cycle', [0..5];

# Read in monthly results...
my @cyclic_buffer;
while (my $next_val = prompt 'Next: ') {
    # Saving them in a six-month cyclic buffer...
    $cyclic_buffer[$next_index] = $next_val;
```

---

[*] And more extensively explained in Chapter 9 of *Object Oriented Perl* (Manning, 1999) or Chapter 14 of *Programming Perl* (O'Reilly, 2000).

```
    # And printing the moving average each month...
    print 'Half-yearly moving average: ',
        sum(@cyclic_buffer)/@cyclic_buffer, "\n";
}
```

Every time $next_index is used as an index into @cyclic_buffer, it moves on to the next value in [0..5]. When there are no more values, it loops back to zero and starts again. So $cyclic_buffer[$next_index] is always the next element in the cyclic buffer, even though $next_index is never explicitly incremented or reset.

And that's the problem. If $next_index had been tied further away from the loop*, it might easily seem to some maintainer that every new value is being assigned into the same element of the buffer. Tied variables make any code that uses them less maintainable, because they make normal variable operations behave in unexpected, non-standard ways.

They're also less efficient. A tied variable is actually a wrapper around some blessed object, and so every access on any tied variable requires a method call (instead of being implemented in highly optimized C code).

Finally, tied variables can sometimes make your code less robust, as it's very easy to subtly misimplement some aspect of the expected variable behaviour.

Tied variables can always be replaced with method calls on objects:

```
    # Create an iterator object whose value cycles from zero to five...
    use List::Cycle;
    my $index = List::Cycle->new({ vals => [0..5] });

    # Read in monthly results...
    my @cyclic_buffer;
    while (my $next_val = prompt 'Next: ') {
        # Saving them in a six-month cyclic buffer...
        $cyclic_buffer[$index->next()] = $next_val;

        # And printing the moving average each month...
        print 'Half-yearly moving average: ',
            sum(@cyclic_buffer)/@cyclic_buffer, "\n";
    }
```

Often they can also be replaced with a simple subroutine:

```
    # Create a subroutine whose value cycles from zero to five...
    {
        my $next   = -1;
        my @values = (0..5);

        sub next_index { return $next = ($next+1) % @values }
    }
```

---

* And as the code is maintained and extended, that critical tying of the variable *will* drift away from the code where the magic variable is used.

```
# Read in monthly results...
my @cyclic_buffer;
while (my $next_val = prompt 'Next: ') {
    # Saving them in a six-month cyclic buffer...
    $cyclic_buffer[next_index()] = $next_val;

    # And printing the moving average each month...
    print 'Half-yearly moving average: ',
        sum(@cyclic_buffer)/@cyclic_buffer, "\n";
}
```

Either way, the distinctive syntax of the method or subroutine calls provides an essential clue to the distinctive behaviour of the buffer index. So either of the previous solutions will be much more comprehensible, maintainable, and reliable than a tied variable.

Cleverness

Don't be clever.

Tied variables are a clever idea, but "cleverness" is the natural enemy of maintainable code. Unfortunately, Perl provides endless opportunities for cleverness.

For example, imagine coming across this result selector in production code:

```
$optimal_result = [$result1=>$result2]->[$result2<=$result1];
```

The syntactic symmetry is very elegant, of course, and devising it obviously provided the original developer with a welcome diversion from the tedium of everyday coding. But a clever line of code like that is a (recurring) nightmare to understand and to maintain, and imposes an unnecessary burden on everyone in the development and maintenance teams.

Cleverness doesn't have to be nearly that flagrant either. Having finally deduced that the example expression returns the smaller of the two results*, you would almost certainly be tempted to immediately replace it with something like the following:

```
$optimal_result = $result1 <= $result2 ? $result1 : $result2;
```

---

* The first square brackets ([$result1=>$result2]) create an anonymous array containing the two results in order. Then the second brackets index into that array. The index they use is the integer result of the less-than-or-equal-to comparison: $result2<=$result1. That comparison is true (1) if $result2 is no bigger than $result1, in which the resulting index (1) selects the second element ($result2) from the anonymous array. If $result1 is smaller than $result2, then the result of the comparison is false, which becomes zero when used as an index, which selects the first element ($result1) from the anonymous array. So the entire expression always selects whichever of the two results is smaller. Of course, it takes seven lines of careful analysis to work that out, but that's a small price to pay to enjoy High Art.

While that's certainly an improvement in both readability and efficiency, it still requires some careful thought to verify that it's doing the right (i.e., minimizing) thing. And everyone who maintains this code will still have to decode that expression—possibly every time they come across it.

However, it's also possible to write that same expression in a way that's so obvious, straightforward, and plain-spoken that it requires no effort at all to verify that it implements the desired behaviour:

```
use List::Util qw( min );

$optimal_result = min($result1, $result2);
```

It's not "clever" and it's even marginally slower, but it *is* clean, clear, efficient, scalable, and easy to maintain. And that's always a much better choice.

Encapsulated Cleverness

If you *must* rely on cleverness, encapsulate it.

Very occasionally a genuine need for efficiency may (appear to) make it essential to use non-obvious Perl idioms such as:

```
# Make sure the requests are unique...
@requests  = keys %{ {map {$_=>1} @raw_requests} };
```

This statement takes each request in @raw_requests, converts it to a pair ($_=>1) in which the request is now the key, and uses that list of pairs to initialize an anonymous hash ({map {$_=>1} @raw_requests }), which folds every repeated request into the same hash key. The hash is then dereferenced (%{ {map {$_=>1} @raw_requests}), and its unique keys are retrieved (keys %{ {map {$_=>1} @raw_requests} }) and finally assigned into @requests.

But an expression that complex should never be left raw in code. If it's kept at all, it should be kept as a dirty little secret, shamefully hidden away in a subroutine in some dark corner of your code:

```
sub unique {
    return keys %{ { map {$_=>1} @_ } };   # Mea culpa!
}

# and later...

@requests = unique(@raw_requests);
```

Apart from the obvious advantage that the request-handling code becomes vastly more readable, encapsulating the cleverness has another important benefit: when the cleverness proves not to be as clever as you first thought, it's very easy to replace it with something that's both slightly more readable and very much more efficient:

```
sub unique {
    my %uniq;            # Use keys of this hash to track unique values
    @uniq{@_} = ();      # Use the args as those keys (the values don't matter)
    return keys %uniq;   # Return those unique values
}
```

In this version, the list of values that's passed in (@_) is used as the list of keys in a hash slice (@uniq{@_}) of the %uniq hash. Slicing that hash creates all the requested keys within the hash, with the values for repeated keys overwriting earlier ones. The slice produces a list of entries, which is assigned an empty list (@uniq{@_} = ( )), as only the keys themselves matter. The assignment is required, though, because the hash keys are created only when the slice is an lvalue. The keys of the post-sliced hash are therefore the unique values from the original argument list, which the subroutine then simply returns (return keys %uniq).

This version is faster than the previous one because it doesn't have to build an interim key/value/key/value... list and then use that to initialize the hash. Instead, the slicing operation creates all the required keys at once, and the empty list assignment means that no values need to be assigned (or have space allocated for them).

Outside the subroutine there are important benefits too. Because the "clever" code remains hidden away, every line of client code that uses unique( ) will immediately benefit from the improved performance, but without needing to be rewritten in any way.

Of course, later you'll probably realize that both versions of unique( ) share two flaws: they don't preserve the order of any list they're given (which is a problem if that list is a search path), and they convert all the list data to strings (which is a problem if that data was originally a list of objects or references).

However, once you realize that, you *still* won't have to change the client code, because you can just rewrite the encapsulated nastiness once again:

```
sub unique {
    my %seen;                        # Keys track values already seen
    return grep {!$seen{$_}++} @_;   # Keep only those not yet seen
}
```

This version uses a hash (%seen) merely as a look-up table indicating which values have already been encountered. Then it filters the original argument list, keeping only those values that have not yet been seen and incrementing the count of "sightings" for each element as it's examined ($seen{$_}++). The use of a post-increment is critical here as it's essential that the count be incremented every time, but that the count be zero the first time the grep encounters a particular element, so the filter will let that first instance through.

Because grep is merely a filter which passes acceptable values through unchanged, this version of unique( ) preserves both the type and the order of the arguments it's given. And, though it's not quite as fast as the sliced solution shown earlier, it still runs faster than the "clever" anonymous hash version.

Benchmarking

Don't optimize code—benchmark it.

It's natural to think that a single expression like:

```
keys %{ { map {$_=>1} @_ } }
```

will be more efficient than two statements:

```
my %seen;
return grep {!$seen{$_}++} @_;
```

But, unless you are deeply familiar with the internals of the Perl interpreter[*], intuitions about the relative performance of two constructs are exactly that: unconscious guesses.

The only way to know for sure which of two—or more—alternatives will perform better is to actually time each of them. The standard Benchmark module makes that easy, as Example 19-8 illustrates.

Example 19-8. Benchmarking the uniqueness functions

```
# A short list of not-quite-unique values...
our @data = qw( do re me fa so la ti do );

# Various candidates...
sub unique_via_anon {
    return keys %{ { map {$_=>1} @_ } };
}

sub unique_via_grep {
    my %seen;
    return grep { !$seen{$_}++ } @_;
}

sub unique_via_slice {
    my %uniq;
    @uniq{@_} = ();
    return keys %uniq;
}
```

---

[*] In which case you already have far more serious personal issues to deal with.

Example 19-8. Benchmarking the uniqueness functions (continued)

```perl
# Compare the current set of data in @data
sub compare {
    my ($title) = @_;

    print "\n[$title]\n";

    # Create a comparison table of the various timings, making sure that
    # each test runs at least 10 CPU seconds...
    use Benchmark qw( cmpthese );
    cmpthese -10, {
        anon   => 'my @uniq = unique_via_anon(@data)',
        grep   => 'my @uniq = unique_via_grep(@data)',
        slice  => 'my @uniq = unique_via_slice(@data)',
    };

    return;
}

compare('8 items, 10% repetition');

# Two copies of the original data...
@data = (@data) x 2;
compare('16 items, 56% repetition');

# One hundred copies of the original data...
@data = (@data) x 50;
compare('800 items, 99% repetition');
```

The cmpthese( ) subroutine is passed a number, followed by a reference to a hash of tests. The number specifies either the exact number of times to run each test (if the number is positive) or the absolute number of CPU seconds to run the test for (if the number is negative). Typical values are around 10,000 repetitions or 10 CPU seconds, but the module will warn you if the test is too short to produce an accurate benchmark.

The keys of the test hash are the names of your tests, and the corresponding values specify the code to be tested. Those values can be either strings (which are eval'd to produce executable code) or subroutine references (which are called directly).

Specifying your tests as strings usually produces results that are more accurate. Subroutine references have to be re-invoked each time each test is repeated, which adds a subroutine call overhead to every test and tends to obscure small relative differences in performance. So benchmarking via eval'd strings is the better practice here (despite the general exhortations against them in Chapter 8).

Unfortunately, eval'd code can see only those lexical variables in the scope where the eval is executed, not those in the scope where the string is created. That means the string eval inside cmpthese( ) cannot see lexicals in the scope where cmpthese( ) was called. So for accurate benchmarking, it's necessary to also ignore the strong admonitions in Chapter 5, and pass data to Benchmark tests using package variables (e.g. our @data) rather than lexicals.

Of course, if you use anonymous subroutines for your tests, they *can* see any lexicals in their declaration scope, in which case you can avoid both globals and eval, the only problem being that your results may be badly skewed by the extra subroutine call costs.

The benchmarking code in Example 19-8 would print out something like the following:

```
[8 items, 10% repetitions]
          Rate  anon  grep slice
anon  28234/s    --  -24%  -47%
grep  37294/s   32%    --  -30%
slice 53013/s   88%   42%    --

[16 items, 50% repetitions]
          Rate  anon  grep slice
anon  21283/s    --  -28%  -51%
grep  29500/s   39%    --  -32%
slice 43535/s  105%   48%    --

[800 items, 99% repetitions]
        Rate  anon  grep slice
anon    536/s    --  -65%  -89%
grep   1516/s  183%    --  -69%
slice  4855/s  806%  220%    --
```

Each of the tables printed has a separate row for each named test. The first column lists the absolute speed of each candidate in repetitions per second, while the remaining columns allow you to compare the relative performance of any two tests. For example, in the final test, tracing across the grep row to the anon column reveals that the grepped solution was 1.83 times (183%) faster than using an anonymous hash. Tracing further across the same row also indicates that grepping was 69% slower (-69% faster) than slicing.

Overall, the indication from the three tests is that the slicing-based solution is consistently the fastest for this particular set of data on this particular machine. It also appears that as the data set increases in size, slicing also scales much better than either of the other two approaches.

However, those two conclusions are effectively drawn from only three data points (namely, the three benchmarking runs). To get a more definitive comparison of the three methods, you'd also need to test other possibilities, such as a long list of non-repeating items or a short list with nothing but repetitions.

Better still, test on the real data that you'll actually be "unique-ing".

For example, if that data is a sorted list of a quarter million words, with only minimal repetitions, and which has to remain sorted, then test exactly that:

```
our @data = slurp '/usr/share/biglongwordlist.txt';

use Benchmark qw( cmpthese );
    cmpthese 10, {
```

```
    # Note:the non-grepped solutions need a post-uniqification re-sort
    anon  => 'my @uniq = sort(unique_via_anon(@data))',
    grep  => 'my @uniq =      unique_via_grep(@data)',
    slice => 'my @uniq = sort(unique_via_slice(@data))',
};
```

Not surprisingly, this benchmark indicates that the grepped solution is markedly superior on a large sorted data set:

```
       s/iter anon slice  grep
anon    4.28   --   -3%  -46%
slice   4.15   3%    --  -44%
grep    2.30  86%   80%    --
```

Perhaps more interestingly, the grepped solution still benchmarks as being marginally faster when the two hash-based approaches *aren't* re-sorted. This suggests that the better scalability of the sliced solution that was seen in the earlier benchmark is a localized phenomenon, and is eventually undermined by the growing costs of allocation, hashing, and bucket-overflows as the sliced hash grows very large.

Above all, that last example demonstrates that benchmarks only benchmark the cases you actually benchmark. And that useful conclusions about performance can only be drawn from benchmarking real data.

Memory

Don't optimize data structures—measure them.

Intuitions about the relative space efficiency of different data structures aren't very reliable, either. If you are concerned about the memory footprint of a data structure that you are using, the Devel::Size module makes it easy to see how heavy the burden actually is:

```perl
# This look-up table is handy, but seems to be too bloated...
my %lookup = load_lookup_table($file);

# So let's look at how much memory it's using...
use Devel::Size qw( size total_size );
use Perl6::Form;

my $hash_mem  = size(\%lookup);        # Storage overheads only
my $total_mem = total_size(\%lookup);  # Overheads plus actual data
my $data_mem  = $total_mem - $hash_mem; # Data only

print form(
    'hash alone: {>>>,>>>,>>} bytes', $hash_mem,
    'data alone: {>>>,>>>,>>} bytes', $data_mem,
    '=============================',
    'total:      {>>>,>>>,>>} bytes', $total_mem,
);
```

That might print something like:

```
hash alone:    8,704,075 bytes
data alone:    8,360,250 bytes
==============================
total:        17,064,325 bytes
```

which indicates that storing your 8.36MB of data in a hash has incurred an overhead of an additional 8.70MB for buckets, hash tables, keys, and other internals.

The total_size( ) subroutine takes a reference to a variable and returns the total number of bytes of memory used by that variable. This includes both:

- The memory that the variable uses for its own implementation. For example, the buckets that are needed to implement a hash, or the flag bits that are used inside every scalar.

- The memory used by the data that the variable stores. For example, the space required for the keys and values in a hash, or for the value in a scalar.

The size( ) subroutine also takes a variable reference, but returns only the number of bytes that the variable uses for itself, excluding the memory required to store its data.

Caching

Look for opportunities to use caches.

It makes sense not to do the same calculation twice, if the result is small enough that it can reasonably be stored for reuse. The simplest form of that is putting a result into an interim variable whenever it will be used more than once. That is, instead of calling the same functions twice on the same data:

```
print form(
    'hash alone: {>>>,>>>,>>} bytes', size(\%lookup),
    'data alone: {>>>,>>>,>>} bytes', total_size(\%lookup)-size(\%lookup),
    '==============================',
    'total:      {>>>,>>>,>>} bytes', total_size(\%lookup),
);
```

call them once, store the results temporarily, and retrieve them each time they're needed:

```
my $hash_mem  = size(\%lookup);
my $total_mem = total_size(\%lookup);
my $data_mem  = $total_mem - $hash_mem;

print form(
    'hash alone: {>>>,>>>,>>} bytes',  $hash_mem,
    'data alone: {>>>,>>>,>>} bytes',  $data_mem,
    '==============================',
```

```
        'total:     {>>>,>>>,>>} bytes', $total_mem,
    );
```

This often has the additional benefit of allowing you to name the interim values in ways that make the code more comprehensible.

Subroutines like size( ) and total_size( ) and functions like rand( ) or readline( ) don't always return the same result when called with the same arguments. Such subroutines are good candidates for temporary and localized reuse of results, but not for longer-term caching.

On the other hand, *pure functions* like sqrt( ) and int( ) and crypt( ) *do* always return the same result for the same list of arguments, so their return values can be stored long-term and reused whenever they're needed again. For example, if you have a subroutine that returns a case-insensitive SHA-512 digest:

```
sub lc_digest {
    my ($text) = @_;

    use Digest::SHA qw( sha512 );
    return sha512(lc $text);
}
```

then you could (potentially) speed it up over many calls by giving it a private look-up table in which results can be cached as they're computed, as shown in Example 19-9.

Example 19-9. Adding a cache to a digest subroutine

```
{
    my %cache;

    sub lc_digest {
        my $text = lc shift;

        # Compute the answer only if it's not already known...
        if (!exists $cache{$text}) {
            use Digest::SHA qw( sha512 );
            $cache{$text} = sha512($text);
        }

        return $cache{$text};
    }
}
```

On the other hand, if the range of possible data for a computation is small and the number of computations is large, then it's often simpler and more efficient to pre-compute the entire look-up table and then access it directly, thereby eliminating the cost of a subroutine call. For example, suppose you were doing some kind of image processing and needed square roots for pixel intensity values in the range 0 to 255. You could write:

```
for my $row (@image_rows) {
    for my $pixel_value (@{$row}) {
        $pixel_value = sqrt($pixel_value);
```

```
        }
    }
```

or you could dramatically reduce the number of sqrt operations by precomputing all possible values and creating a look-up table:

```
my @sqrt_of = map { sqrt $_ } 0..255;

for my $row (@image_rows) {
    for my $pixel_value (@{$row}) {
        $pixel_value = $sqrt_of[$pixel_value];
    }
}
```

For a thorough discussion of the many applications and advantages of caching, see Chapter 3 of *Higher-Order Perl*, by Mark Jason Dominus (Morgan Kaufmann, 2005)

Memoization

Automate your subroutine caching.

The logic required to implement a caching strategy is always the same: *check whether the result is already cached; otherwise, compute and cache it; either way, return the cached result*. So, as usual, there's a CPAN module that automates the task: Memoize.

To add caching to a subroutine (a process called *memoization*), you simply define the subroutine without any caching, and load Memoize. The module will automatically export a memoize( ) subroutine, which you then call, passing it a string containing the name of the subroutine you want cached. Like so:

```
sub lc_digest {
    my ($text) = @_;

    use Digest::SHA qw( sha512 );
    return sha512(lc $text);
}

use Memoize;
memoize( 'lc_digest' );
```

Notice how much cleaner this is than the "manually cached" version in Example 19-9.

It's also more reliable, as you can focus on getting the computation correct, and leave the details of the caching strategy to Memoize. For example, the caches that the module installs correctly differentiate between subroutine calls in list and scalar context. This is important, because the same subroutine called with the same arguments might still return different values, depending on whether it was expected to return a list or a single value. Forgetting this distinction is a very common error when implementing caching manually[*].

The `memoize( )` subroutine has many other options for fine-tuning the kinds of caching it confers. The module documentation provides detailed descriptions of the many possibilities, including caching results in a database so that the cache persists between executions of your program.

Caching for Optimization

Benchmark any caching strategy you use.

Caching is a strategy that would seem to have no downside. After all, computing a value only once is obviously always going to be quicker than recomputing it many times[†]. That's true, of course, but it isn't the whole story. Occasionally, caching can backfire and actually make a computation slower.

It's certainly the case that computing once is always quicker than recomputing every time. However, caching isn't quite a case of *computing-once*; it's actually a case of *computing-once-and-forever-after-rechecking-whether-you've-already-computed-and-if-so-then-accessing-the-previously-computed-value*. That more complicated process may not always be quicker than recomputing every time. Searching and then accessing a look-up table has an intrinsic cost, which can occasionally be greater than redoing the entire calculation. Especially if the look-up table is a hash.

So, whenever you decide to add caching to a computation, it's essential to benchmark the resulting code, to make sure that the cache look-up costs aren't more expensive that the computation itself. For example, for the pixel square roots from the previous guideline, a simple speed comparison:

```
use Benchmark qw( cmpthese );

my @sqrt_of = map {sqrt $_} 0..255;

cmpthese -30, {
    recompute      => q{ for my $n (0..255) { my $res = sqrt $n      } },
    look_up_array  => q{ for my $n (0..255) { my $res = $sqrt_of[$n] } },
};
```

---

[*] It's not, however, a defect in the manually cached version of `lc_digest( )` in Example 19-9, because `sha512( )` always returns a single value, regardless of its call context.

[†] At least, until your calculations turn quantum.

reveals that, in this instance, using a look-up table is only about 9% faster than just calling sqrt directly every time:

```
                 Rate      recompute   look_up_array
recompute       3951/s        --          -8%
look_up_array   4291/s        9%           --
```

You then need to decide whether that marginal performance improvement is enough to warrant the additional complexity in the code.

By the way, if you're using Memoize to install your caching, you can tell it to install the memoized version of your subroutine under a different name by using the INSTALL option. This makes it easy to benchmark the relative performance of two versions:

```perl
# Install a memoized version of lc_digest() as fast_lc_digest()...
memoize( 'lc_digest', INSTALL=>'fast_lc_digest' );

# See if it is actually any faster on real data sets...
cmpthese -30, {
    nomemo => q{ for my $text (@real_data) { my $res = lc_digest($text); }      },
    memo   => q{ for my $text (@real_data) { my $res = fast_lc_digest($text); } },
};
```

Profiling

Don't optimize applications—profile them.

In the previous guideline, the benchmarked comparison between repeatedly computing sqrt $pixel_value and repeatedly looking up $sqrt_of[$pixel_value] indicated that caching provided a 9% improvement:

```
                 Rate      recompute   look_up_array
recompute       3951/s        --          -8%
look_up_array   4291/s        9%           --
```

That sounds impressive, but it's important to keep those numbers in perspective. Each iteration of the test did 256 square root retrievals. So, overall, the test was achieving 1,011,456 (i.e., 3951 × 256) sqrt calls per second, compared to 1,098,496 @sqrt_of look-ups per second.

Suppose you were processing the 786,432 pixels of a typical 1024 × 768 image. Using the example performance figures, the repeated sqrt calls would require around 0.78 seconds to process that many pixels, whereas the look-up table would take only about 0.72 seconds. Adding a cache to this section of your code would save you a grand total of 0.06 seconds per image.

That's an all-too-common outcome when code is optimized: developers focus their efforts on those components that are easy to optimize, rather than on those components in which improvements will produce the greatest benefit.

How do you find those places where optimization will do the most good? By understanding where your application spends most of its time. And the easiest way to do that is to *profile* your program using the standard `Devel::DProf` module, which can determine how long your application spends within each subroutine in your source code. That is, instead of running your program in the usual way:

```
> perl application.pl datafile
```

run it under the auspices of the profiler module:

```
> perl -d:DProf application.pl datafile
```

The `-d:` debugging flag is a shorthand for `-MDevel::`, so specifying `-d:DProf` is the same as specifying `-MDevel::DProf`. That tells *perl* to include that profiling module before the start of the *application.pl* source.

The module itself simply watches every subroutine call within your code, noting how much time elapses between the invocation and return, and adding that duration to a record of the total time spent in each subroutine. At the end of the program, the module creates a file called *tmon.out* in the current directory.

It's possible to directly interpret the raw data in the file (see the module docs for details), but much easier to understand it by passing it through the standard *dprofpp* application.

For example, you could use `Devel::DProf` to profile a call to your new *autoformat* application, and then summarize the results with *dproffpp* like so:

```
> perl -d:DProf ~/bin/autoformat < Ch_19.txt > Ch_19_formatted.txt

> dprofpp tmon.out
```

```
Total Elapsed Time = 3.212516 Seconds
  User+System Time = 0.722516 Seconds
Exclusive Times
%Time ExclSec CumulS #Calls sec/call Csec/c  Name
 16.6   0.120  0.416      3   0.0399 0.1387  main::BEGIN
 11.0   0.080  0.138      9   0.0089 0.0153  Text::Autoformat::BEGIN
 8.30   0.060  0.066      1   0.0600 0.0665  Getopt::Declare::parse
 7.89   0.057  0.057    221   0.0003 0.0003  Text::Balanced::_failmsg
 6.09   0.044  0.075      1   0.0437 0.0749  Text::Autoformat::autoformat
 5.54   0.040  0.089      3   0.0133 0.0298  Getopt::Declare::Arg::BEGIN
 5.26   0.038  0.252      1   0.0381 0.2516  Getopt::Declare::new
 4.01   0.029  0.059     26   0.0011 0.0023  Getopt::Declare::BEGIN
 3.88   0.028  0.111     70   0.0004 0.0016  Text::Balanced::extract_codeblock
 3.60   0.026  0.074    133   0.0002 0.0006  Text::Balanced::_match_codeblock
 2.77   0.020  0.020      1   0.0200 0.0199  Text::Balanced::ErrorMsg::BEGIN
 2.77   0.020  0.030      3   0.0066 0.0099  vars::BEGIN
 2.77   0.020  0.020      5   0.0040 0.0040  Exporter::as_heavy
 2.77   0.020  0.020     17   0.0012 0.0012  Exporter::import
 1.38   0.010  0.010      1   0.0100 0.0100  AutoLoader::AUTOLOAD
```

For each subroutine, the table produced by *dprofpp* shows (amongst other details):

- The total time spent in the subroutine (%Time), as a percentage of the total time spent running the application
- The actual amount of time spent within the subroutine (ExclSec)
- The actual amount of time spent within the subroutine and any subroutines it called (CumulS)
- The number of calls made to the subroutine (#Calls)

Looking at the output of the previous example, you can see that the program spends about 8% of its time in Text::Balanced::_failmsg( ), making a total of 221 calls to that subroutine. In contrast, it spends only about half that amount of time in 70 calls to Text::Balanced::extract_codeblock( ). So it probably makes sense to focus any optimization efforts on _failmsg( ) first.

If you need finer-grained profiling, the Devel::SmallProf CPAN module allows you to count how many times each line of your program is executed, which makes it easier to determine precisely what statement is causing a particular subroutine to be expensive:

```
> perl -d:SmallProf application.pl datafile
```

The result is a file named smallprof.out, which is actually a copy of your source code with each line prefixed by the number of times it was executed, the total amount of time spent executing the line, and the line number. Although the module lacks a utility like *dprofpp* to summarize its output, it is an excellent investigative tool once you have identified the main suspects using Devel::DProf.

Enbugging

Be careful to preserve semantics when refactoring syntax.

The guidelines in this book are designed to improve the robustness, efficiency, and maintainability of your code. However, you need to take extra care when applying them retrospectively to the source of existing applications.

If you're rewriting existing code to bring it into line with the practices suggested here, be sure that you preserve the existing *behaviour* of the code through the changes you make. For example, if you have a loop such as:

```
for (@candidates) { next unless m/^Name: (.+?); $/; $target_name = $1 and last }
```

you might refactor it to:

```
# Find the first candidate with a valid Name: field...
CANDIDATE:
for my $candidate (@candidates) {
    # Extract the contents of the Name: field...
    my ($name)
        = $candidate =~ m/^Name: (.+?); $/xms;

    # ...or try elsewhere...
    next CANDIDATE if !defined $name;

    # If name found, save it and we're done...
    $target_name = $name;
    last CANDIDATE;
}
```

However, adding the /xms (as recommended in Chapter 12) will alter the semantics of the pattern inside the regular expression. Specifically, it will change the meaning of ^, $, .+?, and the space character. Even though the pattern's syntax didn't change, its behaviour did. That's a particularly subtle way to break a piece of code.

In this case, you have to make sure that you apply *all* of the guidelines in Chapter 12, changing the pattern as well as the flags, so as to preserve the original behaviour:

```
# Find the first candidate with a valid Name: field...
CANDIDATE:
for my $candidate (@candidates) {
    # Extract the Name: field...
    my ($name)
        = $candidate =~ m{\A Name: \s+ ([^\N]+) ; \s+ \n? \z}xms;

    # ...or try elsewhere...
    next CANDIDATE if !defined $name;

    # If name found, save it and we're done...
    $target_name = $name;
    last CANDIDATE;
}
```

Good intentions don't prevent bad outcomes, especially when you're renovating existing code. Making obvious improvements can also introduce unobvious bugs. However, the recommendations in Chapter 18 can help you detect when virtue has become its own punishment. For example, having rewritten that statement, you could immediately rerun prove -r, which—assuming your test suite was sufficiently comprehensive—would highlight the unintended change in behaviour.

Essential Perl Best Practices

Ten Essential Development Practices

1. Design the module's interface first.
   [Chapter 17: *Interfaces*]
2. Write the test cases before the code.
   [Chapter 18: *Test Cases*]
3. Create standard POD templates for modules and applications.
   [Chapter 7: *Boilerplates*]
4. Use a revision control system.
   [Chapter 19: *Revision Control*]
5. Create consistent command-line and configuration interfaces.
   [Chapter 14: *Command-Line Structure*, Chapter 19: *Configuration Files*]
6. Agree upon a coherent layout style and automate it with *perltidy*.
   [Chapter 2: *Automated Layout*]
7. Code in commented paragraphs.
   [Chapter 2: *Chunking*]
8. Throw exceptions instead of returning special values or setting flags.
   [Chapter 13: *Exceptions*]
9. Add new test cases before you start debugging.
   [Chapter 18: *Debugging and Testing*]
10. Don't optimize code—benchmark it.
    [Chapter 19: *Benchmarking*]

Ten Essential Coding Practices

1. Always use `strict` and use `warnings`.
   [Chapter 18: *Strictures*, *Warnings*]

2. Use grammatical templates when forming identifiers.
   [Chapter 3: *Identifiers, Booleans, Reference Variables, Arrays and Hashes*]

3. Use lexical variables, not package variables.
   [Chapter 5: *Lexical Variables*]

4. Label every loop that is exited explicitly, and every `next`, `last`, or `redo`.
   [Chapter 6: *Loop Labels*]

5. Don't use bareword filehandles; use indirect filehandles.
   [Chapter 10: *Filehandles, Indirect Filehandles*]

6. In a subroutine, always unpack `@_` first, using a hash of named arguments if there are more than three parameters.
   [Chapter 9: *Argument Lists, Named Arguments*]

7. Always return via an explicit `return`.
   [Chapter 9: *Implicit Returns*]

8. Always use the `/x`, `/m`, and `/s` flags, and the `\A` and `\z` anchors.
   [Chapter 12: *Extended Formatting, Line Boundaries, Matching Anything, String Boundaries*]

9. Use capturing parentheses in regexes only when deliberately capturing, then give the captured substrings proper names.
   [Chapter 12: *Capturing Parentheses, Capture Variables*]

10. Never make variables part of a module's interface.
    [Chapter 17: *Interface Variables*]

Ten Essential Module Practices

1. Write tests using the `Test::Simple` or `Test::More` modules.
   [Chapter 18: *Modular Testing*]
2. use `English` for the less familiar punctuation variables.
   [Chapter 5: *Punctuation Variables*]
3. Use named constants created with the `Readonly` module.
   [Chapter 4: *Constants*]
4. Use the "non-builtin builtins" from `Scalar::Util`, `List::Util`, and `List::MoreUtils`.
   [Chapter 8: *Utilities*]
5. Use `IO::Prompt` when prompting for interactive input.
   [Chapter 10: *Simple Prompting, Power Prompting*]
6. Use the `Carp` and `Exception::Class` modules to create OO exceptions that report from the caller's location.
   [Chapter 13: *Reporting Failure, Exception Classes*]
7. Use the `Fatal` module to make builtins throw exceptions on failure.
   [Chapter 13: *Builtin Failures, Contextual Failure*]
8. Create aliases using the `Data::Alias` or `Lexical::Alias` module.
   [Chapter 6: *Necessary Subscripting*]
9. Use `Regexp::Common` instead of writing your own regexes.
   [Chapter 12: *Canned Regexes*]
10. Use the `Class::Std` module to create properly encapsulated classes.
    [Chapter 16: *Automating Class Hierarchies, Attribute Demolition, Attribute Building*]

Perl Best Practices

This appendix lists the complete set of 256 guidelines presented in this book. The section heading under which each guideline appears is also provided in square brackets.

Chapter 2, *Code Layout*

- Brace and parenthesize in K&R style. [*Bracketing*]
- Separate your control keywords from the following opening bracket. [*Keywords*]
- Don't separate subroutine or variable names from the following opening bracket. [*Subroutines and Variables*]
- Don't use unnecessary parentheses for builtins and "honorary" builtins. [*Builtins*]
- Separate complex keys or indices from their surrounding brackets. [*Keys and Indices*]
- Use whitespace to help binary operators stand out from their operands. [*Operators*]
- Place a semicolon after every statement. [*Semicolons*]
- Place a comma after every value in a multiline list. [*Commas*]
- Use 78-column lines. [*Line Lengths*]
- Use four-column indentation levels. [*Indentation*]
- Indent with spaces, not tabs. [*Tabs*]
- Never place two statements on the same line. [*Blocks*]
- Code in paragraphs. [*Chunking*]
- Don't cuddle an else. [*Elses*]
- Align corresponding items vertically. [*Vertical Alignment*]
- Break long expressions before an operator. [*Breaking Long Lines*]
- Factor out long expressions in the middle of statements. [*Non-Terminal Expressions*]
- Always break a long expression at the operator of the lowest possible precedence. [*Breaking by Precedence*]

- Break long assignments before the assignment operator. [*Assignments*]
- Format cascaded ternary operators in columns. [*Ternaries*]
- Parenthesize long lists. [*Lists*]
- Enforce your chosen layout style mechanically. [*Automated Layout*]

Chapter 3, *Naming Conventions*

- Use grammatical templates when forming identifiers. [*Identifiers*]
- Name booleans after their associated test. [*Booleans*]
- Mark variables that store references with a _ref suffix. [*Reference Variables*]
- Name arrays in the plural and hashes in the singular. [*Arrays and Hashes*]
- Use underscores to separate words in multiword identifiers. [*Underscores*]
- Distinguish different program components by case. [*Capitalization*]
- Abbr idents by prefx. [*Abbreviations*]
- Abbreviate only when the meaning remains unambiguous. [*Ambiguous Abbreviations*]
- Avoid using inherently ambiguous words in names. [*Ambiguous Names*]
- Prefix "for internal use only" subroutines with an underscore. [*Utility Subroutines*]

Chapter 4, *Values and Expressions*

- Use interpolating string delimiters only for strings that actually interpolate. [*String Delimiters*]
- Don't use "" or '' for an empty string. [*Empty Strings*]
- Don't write one-character strings in visually ambiguous ways. [*Single-Character Strings*]
- Use named character escapes instead of numeric escapes. [*Escaped Characters*]
- Use named constants, but don't use constant. [*Constants*]
- Don't pad decimal numbers with leading zeros. [*Leading Zeros*]
- Use underscores to improve the readability of long numbers. [*Long Numbers*]
- Lay out multiline strings over multiple lines. [*Multiline Strings*]
- Use a heredoc when a multiline string exceeds two lines. [*Here Documents*]
- Use a "theredoc" when a heredoc would compromise your indentation. [*Heredoc Indentation*]
- Make every heredoc terminator a single uppercase identifier with a standard prefix. [*Heredoc Terminators*]
- When introducing a heredoc, quote the terminator. [*Heredoc Quoters*]
- Don't use barewords. [*Barewords*]

- Reserve => for pairs. [*Fat Commas*]
- Don't use commas to sequence statements. [*Thin Commas*]
- Don't mix high- and low-precedence booleans. [*Low-Precedence Operators*]
- Parenthesize every raw list. [*Lists*]
- Use table-lookup to test for membership in lists of strings; use any( ) for membership of lists of anything else. [*List Membership*]

Chapter 5, *Variables*

- Avoid using non-lexical variables. [*Lexical Variables*]
- Don't use package variables in your own development. [*Package Variables*]
- If you're forced to modify a package variable, localize it. [*Localization*]
- Initialize any variable you localize. [*Initialization*]
- use English for the less familiar punctuation variables. [*Punctuation Variables*]
- If you're forced to modify a punctuation variable, localize it. [*Localizing Punctuation Variables*]
- Don't use the regex match variables. [*Match Variables*]
- Beware of any modification via $_. [*Dollar-Underscore*]
- Use negative indices when counting from the end of an array. [*Array Indices*]
- Take advantage of hash and array slicing. [*Slicing*]
- Use a tabular layout for slices. [*Slice Layout*]
- Factor large key or index lists out of their slices. [*Slice Factoring*]

Chapter 6, *Control Structures*

- Use block if, not postfix if. [*If Blocks*]
- Reserve postfix if for flow-of-control statements. [*Postfix Selectors*]
- Don't use postfix unless, for, while, or until. [*Other Postfix Modifiers*]
- Don't use unless or until at all. [*Negative Control Statements*]
- Avoid C-style for statements. [*C-Style Loops*]
- Avoid subscripting arrays or hashes within loops. [*Unnecessary Subscripting*]
- Never subscript more than once in a loop. [*Necessary Subscripting*]
- Use named lexicals as explicit for loop iterators. [*Iterator Variables*]
- Always declare a for loop iterator variable with my. [*Non-Lexical Loop Iterators*]
- Use map instead of for when generating new lists from old. [*List Generation*]
- Use grep and first instead of for when searching for values in a list. [*List Selections*]
- Use for instead of map when transforming a list in place. [*List Transformation*]

- Use a subroutine call to factor out complex list transformations. [*Complex Mappings*]
- Never modify $_ in a list function. [*List Processing Side Effects*]
- Avoid cascading an if. [*Multipart Selections*]
- Use table look-up in preference to cascaded equality tests. [*Value Switches*]
- When producing a value, use tabular ternaries. [*Tabular Ternaries*]
- Don't use do...while loops. [*do-while Loops*]
- Reject as many iterations as possible, as early as possible. [*Linear Coding*]
- Don't contort loop structures just to consolidate control. [*Distributed Control*]
- Use for and redo instead of an irregularly counted while. [*Redoing*]
- Label every loop that is exited explicitly, and use the label with every next, last, or redo. [*Loop Labels*]

Chapter 7, *Documentation*

- Distinguish user documentation from technical documentation. [*Types of Documentation*]
- Create standard POD templates for modules and applications. [*Boilerplates*]
- Extend and customize your standard POD templates. [*Extended Boilerplates*]
- Put user documentation in source files. [*Location*]
- Keep all user documentation in a single place within your source file. [*Contiguity*]
- Place POD as close as possible to the end of the file. [*Position*]
- Subdivide your technical documentation appropriately. [*Technical Documentation*]
- Use block templates for major comments. [*Comments*]
- Use full-line comments to explain the algorithm. [*Algorithmic Documentation*]
- Use end-of-line comments to point out subtleties and oddities. [*Elucidating Documentation*]
- Comment anything that has puzzled or tricked you. [*Defensive Documentation*]
- Consider whether it's better to rewrite than to comment. [*Indicative Documentation*]
- Use "invisible" POD sections for longer technical discussions. [*Discursive Documentation*]
- Check the spelling, syntax, and sanity of your documentation. [*Proofreading*]

Chapter 8, *Built-in Functions*

- Don't recompute sort keys inside a sort. [*Sorting*]
- Use reverse to reverse a list. [*Reversing Lists*]

- Use scalar reverse to reverse a scalar. [*Reversing Scalars*]
- Use unpack to extract fixed-width fields. [*Fixed-Width Data*]
- Use split to extract simple variable-width fields. [*Separated Data*]
- Use Text::CSV_XS to extract complex variable-width fields. [*Variable-Width Data*]
- Avoid string eval. [*String Evaluations*]
- Consider building your sorting routines with Sort::Maker. [*Automating Sorts*]
- Use 4-arg substr instead of lvalue substr. [*Substrings*]
- Make appropriate use of lvalue values. [*Hash Values*]
- Use glob, not <...>. [*Globbing*]
- Avoid a raw select for non-integer sleeps. [*Sleeping*]
- Always use a block with a map and grep. [*Mapping and Grepping*]
- Use the "non-builtin builtins". [*Utilities*]

Chapter 9, *Subroutines*

- Call subroutines with parentheses but without a leading &. [*Call Syntax*]
- Don't give subroutines the same names as built-in functions. [*Homonyms*]
- Always unpack @_ first. [*Argument Lists*]
- Use a hash of named arguments for any subroutine that has more than three parameters. [*Named Arguments*]
- Use definedness or existence to test for missing arguments. [*Missing Arguments*]
- Resolve any default argument values as soon as @_ is unpacked. [*Default Argument Values*]
- Always return scalar in scalar returns. [*Scalar Return Values*]
- Make list-returning subroutines return the "obvious" value in scalar context. [*Contextual Return Values*]
- When there is no "obvious" scalar context return value, consider Contextual::Return instead. [*Multi-Contextual Return Values*]
- Don't use subroutine prototypes. [*Prototypes*]
- Always return via an explicit return. [*Implicit Returns*]
- Use a bare return to return failure. [*Returning Failure*]

Chapter 10, *I/O*

- Don't use bareword filehandles. [*Filehandles*]
- Use indirect filehandles. [*Indirect Filehandles*]
- If you have to use a package filehandle, localize it first. [*Localizing Filehandles*]

- Use either the IO::File module or the three-argument form of open. [*Opening Cleanly*]
- Never open, close, or print to a file without checking the outcome. [*Error Checking*]
- Close filehandles explicitly, and as soon as possible. [*Cleanup*]
- Use while (<>), not for (<>). [*Input Loops*]
- Prefer line-based I/O to slurping. [*Line-Based Input*]
- Slurp a filehandle with a do block for purity. [*Simple Slurping*]
- Slurp a stream with Perl6::Slurp for power and simplicity. [*Power Slurping*]
- Avoid using *STDIN, unless you really mean it. [*Standard Input*]
- Always put filehandles in braces within any print statement. [*Printing to Filehandles*]
- Always prompt for interactive input. [*Simple Prompting*]
- Don't reinvent the standard test for interactivity. [*Interactivity*]
- Use the IO::Prompt module for prompting. [*Power Prompting*]
- Always convey the progress of long non-interactive operations within interactive applications. [*Progress Indicators*]
- Consider using the Smart::Comments module to automate your progress indicators. [*Automatic Progress Indicators*]
- Avoid a raw select when setting autoflushes. [*Autoflushing*]

Chapter 11, *References*

- Wherever possible, dereference with arrows. [*Dereferencing*]
- Where prefix dereferencing is unavoidable, put braces around the reference. [*Braced References*]
- Never use symbolic references. [*Symbolic References*]
- Use weaken to prevent circular data structures from leaking memory. [*Cyclic References*]

Chapter 12, *Regular Expressions*

- Always use the /x flag. [*Extended Formatting*]
- Always use the /m flag. [*Line Boundaries*]
- Use \A and \z as string boundary anchors. [*String Boundaries*]
- Use \z, not \Z, to indicate "end of string". [*End of String*]
- Always use the /s flag. [*Matching Anything*]
- Consider mandating the Regexp::Autoflags module. [*Lazy Flags*]

- Use m{...} in preference to /.../ in multiline regexes. [*Brace Delimiters*]
- Don't use any delimiters other than /.../ or m{...}. [*Other Delimiters*]
- Prefer singular character classes to escaped metacharacters. [*Metacharacters*]
- Prefer named characters to escaped metacharacters. [*Named Characters*]
- Prefer properties to enumerated character classes. [*Properties*]
- Consider matching arbitrary whitespace, rather than specific whitespace characters. [*Whitespace*]
- Be specific when matching "as much as possible". [*Unconstrained Repetitions*]
- Use capturing parentheses only when you intend to capture. [*Capturing Parentheses*]
- Use the numeric capture variables only when you're sure that the preceding match succeeded. [*Captured Values*]
- Always give captured substrings proper names. [*Capture Variables*]
- Tokenize input using the /gc flag. [*Piecewise Matching*]
- Build regular expressions from tables. [*Tabular Regexes*]
- Build complex regular expressions from simpler pieces. [*Constructing Regexes*]
- Consider using Regexp::Common instead of writing your own regexes. [*Canned Regexes*]
- Always use character classes instead of single-character alternations. [*Alternations*]
- Factor out common affixes from alternations. [*Factoring Alternations*]
- Prevent useless backtracking. [*Backtracking*]
- Prefer fixed-string eq comparisons to fixed-pattern regex matches. [*String Comparisons*]

Chapter 13, *Error Handling*

- Throw exceptions instead of returning special values or setting flags. [*Exceptions*]
- Make failed builtins throw exceptions too. [*Builtin Failures*]
- Make failures fatal in all contexts. [*Contextual Failure*]
- Be careful when testing for failure of the system builtin. [*Systemic Failure*]
- Throw exceptions on all failures, including recoverable ones. [*Recoverable Failure*]
- Have exceptions report from the caller's location, not from the place where they were thrown. [*Reporting Failure*]
- Compose error messages in the recipient's dialect. [*Error Messages*]
- Document every error message in the recipient's dialect. [*Documenting Errors*]
- Use exception objects whenever failure data needs to be conveyed to a handler. [*OO Exceptions*]

- Use exception objects when error messages may change. [*Volatile Error Messages*]
- Use exception objects when two or more exceptions are related. [*Exception Hierarchies*]
- Catch exception objects in most-derived-first order. [*Processing Exceptions*]
- Build exception classes automatically. [*Exception Classes*]
- Unpack the exception variable in extended exception handlers. [*Unpacking Exceptions*]

Chapter 14, *Command-Line Processing*

- Enforce a single consistent command-line structure. [*Command-Line Structure*]
- Adhere to a standard set of conventions in your command-line syntax. [*Command-Line Conventions*]
- Standardize your meta-options. [*Meta-options*]
- Allow the same filename to be specified for both input and output. [*In-situ Arguments*]
- Standardize on a single approach to command-line processing. [*Command-Line Processing*]
- Ensure that your interface, run-time messages, and documentation remain consistent. [*Interface Consistency*]
- Factor out common command-line interface components into a shared module. [*Interapplication Consistency*]

Chapter 15, *Objects*

- Make object orientation a choice, not a default. [*Using OO*]
- Choose object orientation using appropriate criteria. [*Criteria*]
- Don't use pseudohashes. [*Pseudohashes*]
- Don't use restricted hashes. [*Restricted Hashes*]
- Always use fully encapsulated objects. [*Encapsulation*]
- Give every constructor the same standard name. [*Constructors*]
- Don't let a constructor clone objects. [*Cloning*]
- Always provide a destructor for every inside-out class. [*Destructors*]
- When creating methods, follow the general guidelines for subroutines. [*Methods*]
- Provide separate read and write accessors. [*Accessors*]
- Don't use lvalue accessors. [*Lvalue Accessors*]
- Don't use the indirect object syntax. [*Indirect Objects*]
- Provide an optimal interface, rather than a minimal one. [*Class Interfaces*]

- Overload only the isomorphic operators of algebraic classes. [*Operator Overloading*]
- Always consider overloading the boolean, numeric, and string coercions of objects. [*Coercions*]

Chapter 16, *Class Hierarchies*

- Don't manipulate the list of base classes directly. [*Inheritance*]
- Use distributed encapsulated objects. [*Objects*]
- Never use the one-argument form of bless. [*Blessing Objects*]
- Pass constructor arguments as labeled values, using a hash reference. [*Constructor Arguments*]
- Distinguish arguments for base classes by class name as well. [*Base Class Initialization*]
- Separate your construction, initialization, and destruction processes. [*Construction and Destruction*]
- Build the standard class infrastructure automatically. [*Automating Class Hierarchies*]
- Use Class::Std to automate the deallocation of attribute data. [*Attribute Demolition*]
- Have attributes initialized and verified automatically. [*Attribute Building*]
- Specify coercions as :STRINGIFY, :NUMERIFY, and :BOOLIFY methods. [*Coercions*]
- Use :CUMULATIVE methods instead of SUPER:: calls. [*Cumulative Methods*]
- Don't use AUTOLOAD( ). [*Autoloading*]

Chapter 17, *Modules*

- Design the module's interface first. [*Interfaces*]
- Place original code inline. Place duplicated code in a subroutine. Place duplicated subroutines in a module. [*Refactoring*]
- Use three-part version numbers. [*Version Numbers*]
- Enforce your version requirements programmatically. [*Version Requirements*]
- Export judiciously and, where possible, only by request. [*Exporting*]
- Consider exporting declaratively. [*Declarative Exporting*]
- Never make variables part of a module's interface. [*Interface Variables*]
- Build new module frameworks automatically. [*Creating Modules*]
- Use core modules wherever possible. [*The Standard Library*]
- Use CPAN modules where feasible. [*CPAN*]

Chapter 18, *Testing and Debugging*

- Write the test cases first. [*Test Cases*]
- Standardize your tests with `Test::Simple` or `Test::More`. [*Modular Testing*]
- Standardize your test suites with `Test::Harness`. [*Test Suites*]
- Write test cases that fail. [*Failure*]
- Test both the likely and the unlikely. [*What to Test*]
- Add new test cases before you start debugging. [*Debugging and Testing*]
- Always use `strict`. [*Strictures*]
- Always turn on warnings explicitly. [*Warnings*]
- Never assume that a warning-free compilation implies correctness. [*Correctness*]
- Turn off strictures or warnings explicitly, selectively, and in the smallest possible scope. [*Overriding Strictures*]
- Learn at least a subset of the *perl* debugger. [*The Debugger*]
- Use serialized warnings when debugging "manually". [*Manual Debugging*]
- Consider using "smart comments" when debugging, rather than `warn` statements. [*Semi-Automatic Debugging*]

Chapter 19, *Miscellanea*

- Use a revision control system. [*Revision Control*]
- Integrate non-Perl code into your applications via the `Inline::` modules. [*Other Languages*]
- Keep your configuration language uncomplicated. [*Configuration Files*]
- Don't use formats. [*Formats*]
- Don't tie variables or filehandles. [*Ties*]
- Don't be clever. [*Cleverness*]
- If you must rely on cleverness, encapsulate it. [*Encapsulated Cleverness*]
- Don't optimize code—benchmark it. [*Benchmarking*]
- Don't optimize data structures—measure them. [*Memory*]
- Look for opportunities to use caches. [*Caching*]
- Automate your subroutine caching. [*Memoization*]
- Benchmark any caching strategy you use. [*Caching for Optimization*]
- Don't optimize applications—profile them. [*Profiling*]
- Be careful to preserve semantics when refactoring syntax. [*Enbugging*]

APPENDIX C
Editor Configurations

A suitably configured editor can make coding much easier, and code much more robust. Automating common tasks ensures that those tasks are done correctly every time, and automating common formatting requirements means that those requirements can be followed consistently without effort.

The following sections provide additions for the configuration files of five popular text editors. These additions support many of the layout and debugging guidelines recommended in this book.

vim

vim is one of several successors to the classic Unix text editor *vi*. You can learn about *vim* and download the latest open source version for all major operating systems from *http://www.vim.org*.

The following commands might make useful additions to your *.vimrc* file:

```
set autoindent                  "Preserve current indent on new lines
set textwidth=78                "Wrap at this column
set backspace=indent,eol,start  "Make backspaces delete sensibly

set tabstop=4                   "Indentation levels every four columns
set expandtab                   "Convert all tabs typed to spaces
set shiftwidth=4                "Indent/outdent by four columns
set shiftround                  "Indent/outdent to nearest tabstop

set matchpairs+=<:>             "Allow % to bounce between angles too

"Inserting these abbreviations inserts the corresponding Perl statement...
iab phbp  #! /usr/bin/perl -w
iab pdbg  use Data::Dumper 'Dumper';^Mwarn Dumper [];^[hi
iab pbmk  use Benchmark qw( cmpthese );^Mcmpthese -10, {};^[O
iab pusc  use Smart::Comments;^M^M###
iab putm  use Test::More qw( no_plan );

iab papp  ^[:r ~/.code_templates/perl_application.pl^M
iab pmod  ^[:r ~/.code_templates/perl_module.pm^M
```

For many more ways to customize and enhance *vim*, see *http://www.vim.org/tips/*.

vile

vile is another major successor to *vi*. For more information about *vile*, including source code and various precompiled distributions, see *http://dickey.his.com/vile/vile.html*. The following commands might make useful additions to your *.vilerc* file:

```
;Preserve current indent on new lines
set autoindent

;Wrap at the 78th column
set fillcol=78
set wrapwords

; Use 4-space indents, not tabs
set tabspace=4
set shiftwidth=4
set noti

;Allow % to bounce between angles too
set fence-pairs="()[]{}<>"

;Inserting these abbreviations inserts the corresponding Perl statement...
abb phbp  #! /usr/bin/perl -w
abb pdbg  use Data::Dumper 'Dumper';^Mwarn Dumper [];^[hi
abb pbmk  use Benchmark qw( cmpthese );^Mcmpthese -10, {};^[0
abb pusc  use Smart::Comments;^M^M###
abb putm  use Test::More qw( no_plan );

abb papp  ^[:r ~/.code_templates/perl_application.pl^M
abb pmod  ^[:r ~/.code_templates/perl_module.pm^M
```

Emacs

Emacs is an "extensible, customizable, self-documenting real-time display editor". To learn about Emacs and download its free source code for just about any operating system, see *http://www.gnu.org/software/emacs/emacs.html*.

The following configuration commands might be useful in your *.emacs* file:

```
;; Use cperl mode instead of the default perl mode
(defalias 'perl-mode 'cperl-mode)

;; turn autoindenting on
(global-set-key "\r" 'newline-and-indent)

;; Use 4 space indents via cperl mode
(custom-set-variables
  '(cperl-close-paren-offset -4)
  '(cperl-continued-statement-offset 4)
  '(cperl-indent-level 4)
```

```lisp
 '(cperl-indent-parens-as-block t)
 '(cperl-tab-always-indent t))

;; Insert spaces instead of tabs
(setq-default indent-tabs-mode nil)


;; Set line width to 78 columns...
(setq fill-column 78)
(setq auto-fill-mode t)


;; Use % to match various kinds of brackets...
;; See: http://www.lifl.fr/~hodique/uploads/Perso/patches.el
(global-set-key "%" 'match-paren)
(defun match-paren (arg)
  "Go to the matching paren if on a paren; otherwise insert %."
  (interactive "p")
  (let ((prev-char (char-to-string (preceding-char)))
        (next-char (char-to-string (following-char))))
    (cond ((string-match "[[{(<]" next-char) (forward-sexp 1))
          ((string-match "[\]})>]" prev-char) (backward-sexp 1))
          (t (self-insert-command (or arg 1))))))


;; Load an application template in a new unattached buffer...
(defun application-template-pl ()
  "Inserts the standard Perl application template"  ; For help and info.
  (interactive "*")                                 ; Make this user accessible.
  (switch-to-buffer "application-template-pl")
  (insert-file "~/.code_templates/perl_application.pl"))
;; Set to a specific key combination...
(global-set-key "\C-ca" 'application-template-pl)


;; Load a module template in a new unattached buffer...
(defun module-template-pm ()
  "Inserts the standard Perl module template"       ; For help and info.
  (interactive "*")                                 ; Make this user accessible.
  (switch-to-buffer "module-template-pm")
  (insert-file "~/.code_templates/perl_module.pm"))
;; Set to a specific key combination...
(global-set-key "\C-cm" 'module-template-pm)


;; Expand the following abbreviations while typing in text files...
(abbrev-mode 1)

(define-abbrev-table 'global-abbrev-table '(
    ("pdbg"   "use Data::Dumper qw( Dumper );\nwarn Dumper[];"   nil 1)
    ("phbp"   "#! /usr/bin/perl -w"                              nil 1)
    ("pbmk"   "use Benchmark qw( cmpthese );\ncmpthese -10, {};" nil 1)
    ("pusc"   "use Smart::Comments;\n\n### "                     nil 1)
    ("putm"   "use Test::More 'no_plan';"                        nil 1)
    ))


(add-hook 'text-mode-hook (lambda () (abbrev-mode 1)))
```

For other handy Emacs configuration tips, see *http://www.emacswiki.org/cgi-bin/wiki*.

BBEdit

BBEdit is a popular commercial text editor for Apple computers, considered by many Mac developers to be the best available. You can read about its extensive features, download a demonstration copy of the application, or purchase a full license for the software from *http://www.barebones.com/products/bbedit/*.

To configure BBEdit with the extra editor features suggested in this book, you might first need to create some local folders (in order to pre-empt the application's default support folder). See the application's user manual for more information.

Then, adjust your preferences settings. In the Preferences → Editor Defaults screen:

- Turn on Auto-Indent.
- Turn on Balance While Typing.
- Turn on Auto-Expand Tabs.
- Turn on Show Invisibles.

Adjust your tab stops to four spaces. For BBEdit 7, use the configuration panel under Text → Fonts&Tabs. For BBEdit 8, the option is under Text → Show Fonts.

You can create stationery for any boilerplate file templates you wish to be able to load by using BBEdit to create a file containing the desired code. When the code template is ready, select File → Save As... and turn on the "Save as Stationery" option. Save the file to the folder *~/Library/Application Support/BBEdit Support/Stationery/* and it will then be available from the Stationery palette, or via the standard menu item File → "New with Stationery". You might, for example, create the stationery files *~/Library/ Application Support/BBEdit Support/Stationery/perl application.pl* and *~/Library/ Application Support/BBEdit Support/Stationery/perl module.pm*.

To use an abbreviation in BBEdit, you need to install a Glossary item. First, create the folder *~/Library/Application Support/BBEdit Support/Glossary/Perl.pl/*. Then, add a file named *debug*, with the following contents:

```
use Data::Dumper qw( Dumper );
warn Dumper [ #SELECT##INSERTION# ];
```

The Glossary will now contain a debug item whenever a Perl file is opened. Selecting that item will wrap the specified text around the current selection, which will be inserted in place of the #SELECT# marker. The insertion point will then be placed wherever the #INSERTION# marker was, and the marker will be removed.

You can create as many glossary entries as you wish. For example, a *~/Library/ Application Support/BBEdit Support/Glossary/Perl.pl/benchmark* file might contain:

```
use Benchmark qw( cmpthese );
cmpthese -10, {
    #INSERTION#
};
```

TextWrangler

TextWrangler is a free text editor from the makers of BBEdit. Although it has a comparatively restricted set of features, it is still extremely capable and easy to use. You can download a free copy of it from *http://www.barebones.com/products/textwrangler/*.

First, adjust your preferences settings. In the Editor Defaults screen under Preferences:

- Turn on Auto-Indent.
- Turn on Balance While Typing.
- Turn on Auto-Expand Tabs.
- Turn on Show Invisibles.

Adjust your tab stops to four spaces using the option under Text → Show Fonts.

You can create stationery for any boilerplate file templates you wish to load by using TextWrangler to create a file containing the desired code. When the code template is ready, select File → Save As... and turn on the "Save as Stationery" option. Save the file to the folder *~/Library/Application Support/TextWrangler Support/Stationery/*. It will then be available from the Stationery palette, or via the standard menu item File → "New with Stationery". For example, you might create the stationery files *~/Library/Application Support/TextWrangler Support/Stationery/perl application.pl* and *~/Library/Application Support/TextWrangler Support/Stationery/perl module.pm*.

To use abbreviations in TextWrangler, you need to write a small Perl script that will generate the text you want by filtering the current selection. First, create the folder *~/Library/Application Support/TextWrangler Support/Unix Support/Unix Filters/*. Then, add a file named *debug.pl*, with the following contents:

```
#! /usr/bin/perl --
print 'use Data::Dumper qw( Dumper );\nwarn Dumper [ ', <>, ' ]';
```

You can then assign this filter to a particular keystroke using the palette available from the Windows → Palettes → Unix Filters menu. Thereafter, typing that keystroke will take the current selection, pass it to the standard input of *debug.pl*, and replace the selection with the output of that script.

Create as many text filters as you wish. For example, a *~/Library/Application Support/TextWrangler Support/Unix Support/Unix Filters/benchmark.pl* file might contain:

```
#! /usr/bin/perl --
use Perl6::Slurp;

my $selection = slurp;

print <<"END_REPLACEMENT"
use Benchmark qw( cmpthese );
cmpthese -10, {
    $selection
};
END_REPLACEMENT
```

Recommended Modules and Utilities

Recommended Core Modules

Module name	Description	In core since
base	Specifies the base classes of the current package at compile time (see Chapter 16)	5.005
Benchmark	Provides utilities to time fragments of Perl code (see Chapter 19)	5.003
Carp	Provides subroutines that warn or throw exceptions, reporting the problem from the caller's location (see Chapter 13)	5.6
charnames	Enables the use of character names via \N{CHARNAME} string literal escapes (see Chapter 4)	5.6
CPAN	Simplifies the downloading and installation of CPAN modules	5.004
Data::Dumper	Converts data structures into string representations of Perl code (see Chapters 15, 17, and 18)	5.005
Devel::DProf	Profiles Perl code (see Chapter 19)	5.6
English	Defines readable English names for special variables (see Chapter 5)	5.003
Fatal	Replaces functions and subroutines with equivalents that either succeed or throw an exception (see Chapter 13)	5.005
File::Glob	Implements command-line filename globbing (see Chapter 8)	5.6
File::Temp	Provides a safe and efficient way to create temporary files (see Chapter 17)	5.6
Getopt::Long	Parses command-line options (see Chapter 14)	5.003
IO::File	Creates I/O objects connected to files (see Chapter 10)	5.004
IO::Handle	Acts as the base class for filehandles and objects (see Chapter 5)	5.004
List::Util	Provides additional list-processing utilities missing from the core language (see Chapters 2 and 8)	5.8
Memoize	Optimizes subroutines by caching their return values and reusing them (see Chapters 8 and 19)	5.003
overload	Allows existing Perl operators to be redefined for objects of the current class (see Chapter 15)	5.003
Scalar::Util	Provides additional scalar-processing utilities missing from the core language (see Chapters 8, 10, and 15)	5.8

Module name	Description	In core since
strict	Prohibits unsafe uses of package variables, symbolic references, and barewords (see Chapters 4 and 18)	5.8
Test::Harness	Executes and summarizes Perl test suites (see Chapter 18)	5.8
Test::More	Provides more sophisticated utilities for writing tests (see Chapter 18)	5.8
Test::Simple	Provides basic utilities for writing tests (see Chapter 18)	5.8
Time::HiRes	Installs high-resolution versions of Perl's built-in time-keeping functions (see Chapter 8)	5.8
version	Allows multipart versions to be specified as objects (see Chapter 17)	5.10

Recommended CPAN Modules

Module name	Description	Recommended version
Attribute::Types	Provides markers that confer type constraints on variables (see Chapter 3)	0.10 or later
Class::Std	Implements encapsulated class hierarchies (see Chapter 16)	Any
Class::Std::Utils	Provides utility functions for producing unique identifiers for any object, for creating anonymous scalars, and for extracting initialization values from a hierarchical initializer list (see Chapter 15)	Any
Config::General	Reads and writes almost any type of configuration file (see Chapter 19)	2.27 or later
Config::Std	Reads and writes simple configuration files, preserving their structure and comments (see Chapter 19)	Any
Config::Tiny	Reads and writes simple "INI" format configuration files with as little code as possible (see Chapter 19)	2.01 or later
Contextual::Return	Simplifies returning different values in different contexts (see Chapter 9)	Any
Data::Alias	Provides a comprehensive set of operations for aliasing variables (see Chapter 6)	0.04 or later
DateTime	Creates powerful date and time objects	0.28 or later
DBI	Provides a generic interface to a large number of databases (see also the many DBD:: modules)	1.48 or later
Devel::Size	Reports the amount of memory a variable uses (see Chapter 19)	0.59 or later
Exception::Class	Simplifies the creation of exception class hierarchies (see Chapter 13)	1.20 or later
File::Slurp	Permits efficient reading and writing of entire files (see Chapter 10)	Any
Filter::Macro	Converts a module into a macro that is expanded inline when the module is loaded	0.02 or later
Getopt::Clade	Builds command-line parsers from an WYSIWYG declaration (see Chapter 14)	Any

Module name	Description	Recommended version
Getopt::Euclid	Builds command-line parsers from command-line documentation (see Chapter 14)	Any
HTML::Mason	Builds web sites from modular Perl/HTML specifications (see Chapter 14)	1.28 or later
Inline	Enables Perl subroutines to be written in other programming languages (see Chapter 19)	0.44 or later
IO::InSitu	Allows a file to be modified in place with backup protection (see Chapter 14)	Any
IO::Interactive	Supplies handy subroutines for testing interactivity (see Chapter 10)	Any
IO::Prompt	Simplifies interactive prompting for user input (see Chapters 10 and 17)	0.02 or later
Lexical::Alias	Provides a smaller set of operations for aliasing variables (see Chapter 6)	0.04 or later
List::Cycle	Creates objects that can cycle through lists of values (see Chapter 19)	Any
List::MoreUtils	Provides additional list-processing utilities missing from the core language and the List::Util module (see Chapters 4 and 8)	0.09 or later
Log::Stdlog	Allows simple event logging via a special filehandle (see Chapter 6)	Any
Module::Build	Builds, tests, and installs Perl modules	0.2609 or later
Module::Starter	Creates the directory structures and starter files needed to develop a Perl module (see Chapters 17 and 18)	1.38 or later
Module::Starter:: PBP	Creates the directory structures and starter files needed to develop a Perl module conforming to the guidelines presented in this book (see Chapters 17 and 18)	Any
only	Loads only specific versions of a module (see Chapter 17)	0.27 or later
Parse::RecDescent	Creates recursive-descent parsers (see Chapter 3)	1.94 or later
Perl6::Builtins	Provides updated versions of several Perl builtins, notably the system command, with extra features that will be standard in Perl 6 (see Chapter 13)	Any
Perl6::Export:: Attrs	Provides a simple and robust way to export subroutines from modules (see Chapter 17)	Any
Perl6::Form	Implements a replacement for Perl format statements (see Chapter 19)	0.04 or later
Perl6::Slurp	Opens a file and reads its contents in one statement (see Chapters 10 and 17)	0.03 or later
POE	Implements a portable multitasking and networking framework for Perl	0.3009 or later
Readonly	Creates read-only scalars, arrays, and hashes (see Chapter 14)	1.03 or later
Regexp::Autoflags	Automatically appends /xms to all regexes (see Chapter 12)	Any
Regexp::Assemble	Combines simple patterns into a single complex pattern (see Chapter 12)	0.10 or later

Module name	Description	Recommended version
Regexp::Common	Generates many commonly needed regular expressions (see Chapter 12)	2.120 or later
Regexp::MatchContext	Defines "match variables" that aren't prohibitively expensive (see Chapter 5)	Any
Smart::Comments	Enables special comments for debugging and reporting the progress of non-interactive loops (see Chapters 10 and 18)	Any
Sort::Maker	Creates efficient sorting subroutines from simple descriptions (see Chapter 8)	Any
Sub::Installer	Installs subroutines in packages (see Chapters 6 and 8)	Any
Text::Autoformat	Automatically wraps and reformats plain text based on its content (see Chapter 18)	1.12 or later
Text::CSV	Provides tools to manipulate comma-separated value strings (see Chapter 8)	Any
Text::CSV::Simple	Simplifies parsing of CSV files (see Chapter 8)	0.20 or later
Text::CSV_XS	Provides faster 8-bit-clean tools to manipulate comma-separated value strings (see Chapter 8)	0.23 or later
XML::Parser	Parses XML documents using the Expat library	2.34 or later
YAML	Serializes Perl data structures to a compact and readable string representation (see Chapter 5)	0.38

Utility Subroutines

Subroutine	Description	Available From
all()	Returns true if all its arguments are true (see Chapter 8)	List::MoreUtils
anon_scalar()	Returns a reference to an anonymous scalar (see Chapters 15 and 16)	Class::Std::Utils
any()	Returns true if any of its arguments are true (see Chapters 4 and 8)	List::MoreUtils
apply()	Applies a transformation to its list of arguments (see Chapter 8)	List::MoreUtils
blessed()	Returns true if its argument is a reference to a blessed object (see Chapter 8)	Scalar::Util
carp()	Prints a warning like warn does, but reports it from the caller's location (see Chapters 2, 6, 9, and 13)	Carp
cmp_these()	Times a set of alternative code fragments and compares the results in a table (see Chapter 19)	Benchmark
croak()	Throws an exception like die does, but reports it from the caller's location (see Chapters 2, 6, 9, and 13)	Carp
first()	Returns the first of its arguments that satisfies some test (see Chapters 2 and 8)	List::Util
first_index()	Returns the index of the first of its arguments that satisfies some test (see Chapter 8)	List::MoreUtils
form()	Formats data into fixed-field reports (see Chapters 5 and 19)	Perl6::Form
ident()	Returns a unique identifier for an object (see Chapters 15 and 16)	Class::Std::Utils

Subroutine	Description	Available From
interactive()	Returns an output filehandle that ignores output unless the current process is interactive (see Chapter 10)	IO::Interactive
is()	Tests whether its arguments are equal and reports accordingly (see Chapters 17 and 18)	Test::More
is_interactive()	Returns true if the current process is interactive (see Chapter 10)	IO::Interactive
is_weak()	Returns true if its argument is a reference that is invisible to the garbage collector (see Chapter 8)	Scalar::Util
looks_like_number()	Returns true if the argument is something Perl could convert to a number (see Chapter 8)	Scalar::Util
make_sorter()	Generates efficient sorting routines (see Chapter 8)	Sort::Maker
max()	Returns the maximum of a list of numbers (see Chapters 2 and 8)	List::Util
maxstr()	Returns the lexicographically last value from a list of strings (see Chapter 8)	List::Util
memoize()	Causes a subroutine to cache its return values (see Chapter 19)	Memoize
min()	Returns the minimum of a list of numbers (see Chapter 8)	List::Util
minstr()	Returns the lexicographically first value from a list of strings (see Chapter 8)	List::Util
none()	Returns true if none of its arguments is true (see Chapter 8)	List::MoreUtils
notall()	Returns true if any of its arguments is false (see Chapter 8)	List::MoreUtils
ok()	Tests whether a condition is true and reports accordingly (see Chapters 17 and 18)	Test::Simple
openhandle()	Returns true if its argument is an open filehandle (see Chapter 8)	Scalar::Util
pairwise()	Applies a specified binary operation between corresponding elements of two arrays (see Chapter 8)	List::MoreUtils
prompt()	Prints a prompt, reads some input, verifies it, and returns it (see Chapters 10 and 17)	IO::Prompt
qv()	Creates a version number object (see Chapter 17)	version
readonly()	Returns true if its argument is not assignable (see Chapter 8)	Scalar::Util
read_file()	Reads and returns the entire contents of a file (see Chapters 8 and 10)	File::Slurp
reduce()	Applies a specified binary operation between every adjacent element in a list (see Chapter 8)	List::Util
refaddr()	Returns the address of a reference, as an integer (see Chapters 8 and 15)	Scalar::Util
reftype()	Returns a string representing the underlying type of a reference (see Chapter 8)	Scalar::Util
shuffle()	Returns its arguments in a (pseudo)random order (see Chapter 8)	List::Util
size()	Returns the amount of memory used to store the data in its argument (see Chapter 19)	Devel::Size
slurp()	Reads the entire contents of a file (see Chapters 10 and 17)	Perl6::Slurp
sum()	Returns the numeric sum of its arguments (see Chapter 8)	List::Util

Subroutine	Description	Available From
tainted( )	Returns true if its argument is tainted (see Chapter 8)	Scalar::Util
total_size( )	Returns the amount of memory used to store the data and implementation of its argument (see Chapter 19)	Devel::Size
uniq( )	Returns its list of arguments with any duplicates removed (see Chapter 8)	List::MoreUtils
usleep( )	Sleeps a specified number of microseconds (see Chapter 8)	Time::HiRes
weaken( )	Hides a reference from the garbage collector (see Chapters 8 and 11)	Scalar::Util
zip( )	Interleaves values from two or more arrays (see Chapter 8)	List::MoreUtils

Bibliography

Perl Coding and Development Practices

Testing and Debugging

Perl Debugged. Peter J. Scott and Ed Wright. Addison-Wesley, 2001, ISBN: 0-201-70054-9.

Perl Medic: Transforming Legacy Code. Peter J. Scott. Addison-Wesley, 2004, ISBN: 0-201-79526-4.

Perl Testing: A Developer's Notebook. Ian Langworth and chromatic. O'Reilly, 2005, ISBN: 0-59610-092-2.

Algorithms and Efficiency

Data Munging with Perl. David Cross. Manning Publications, 2001, ISBN: 1-930110-00-6.

Effective Perl Programming: Writing Better Programs with Perl. Joseph N. Hall with Randal Schwartz. Addison-Wesley, 1997, ISBN: 0-201-41975-0.

Higher-Order Perl: Transforming Programs with Programs. Mark Jason Dominus. Morgan Kaufmann, 2005, ISBN: 1-55860-701-3.

Mastering Algorithms with Perl. Jon Orwant, Jarkko Hietaniemi, and John Macdonald. O'Reilly, 1999, ISBN: 1-56592-398-7.

Mastering Regular Expressions, Second Edition. Jeffrey E. F. Friedl. O'Reilly, 2002, ISBN: 0-596-00289-0.

Object Oriented Perl. Damian Conway. Manning, 1999, ISBN: 1-884777-79-1.

Perl Cookbook, Second Edition. Tom Christiansen and Nathan Torkington. O'Reilly, 2003, ISBN: 0-59600-313-7.

Coding Style and Common Mistakes

The *perlstyle* manpage

The *perltrap* manpage

General Coding and Development Practices

Coding Standards

C Style: Standards and Guidelines. David Straker. Prentice Hall, 1992, ISBN: 0-13-116898-3.

The Elements of Programming Style, 2nd edition. Brian W. Kernighan and P. J. Plauger. McGraw-Hill, 1978, ISBN: 0-07-034207-5.

Development Practices

The Mythical Man-Month: Essays on Software Engineering, 20th Anniversary Edition. Frederick P. Brooks. Addison-Wesley, 1995, ISBN: 0-201-83595-9.

The Practice of Programming. Brian W. Kernighan and Rob Pike. Addison-Wesley, 1999, ISBN: 0-201-61586-X.

The Pragmatic Programmer: From Journeyman to Master. Andrew Hunt and David Thomas. Addison-Wesley, 1999, ISBN: 0-201-61622-X.

Text Editors

Learning the vi Editor, Sixth Edition. Linda Lamb and Arnold Robbins. O'Reilly, 1998, ISBN: 1-56592-426-6.

Learning GNU Emacs, Third Edition. Debra Cameron, James Elliott, and Marc Loy. O'Reilly Media, 2004, ISBN: 0-596-00648-9.

Index

Numbers and Symbols

{ } (see braces)
( ) (see parentheses)
[ ] (see square brackets)
& (ampersand), 175–177
@_ array, 178–181, 185, 470
* (asterisk), 206
\ (backslash), 52, 54, 243
character, 236
: (colon), 31
, (comma) (see commas)
- (dash), 302, 303
$ (dollar sign), 89, 195
. (dot) operator, 355
" (double quotation) (see double quotation)
= (equals sign), 302
/ (forward slash), 243
- (hyphen), 44, 302
$ metacharacter, 237, 238, 239, 241
. metacharacter, 240
^ metacharacter, 237, 238, 239, 241
- (minus sign), 88
-> notation, 227
<> operation (see slurping)
! operator, 70, 356
** operator, 15
|| operator, 70, 185
||= operator, 185
+ (plus) operator, 356
+ (plus sign), 15
? (question mark), 31, 32, 262
<> (see angle brackets)
@ (see at sign)

$_ (see dollar-underscore)
; (see semicolons)
_ (see underscore)
' (single quotation) (see single quotation)
$/ variable, 213, 215

A

\A anchor, 239, 257, 470
$a variable, 74, 430
abbreviations, 46–47, 473
abs function, 106
"abstract" as ambiguous name, 48
accessors
    best practice, 479
    lvalue, 346–349
    overview, 340–346
ACKNOWLEDGEMENTS template, 139
adjectives, naming conventions, 38
algorithms, documenting, 142, 143
alias function, 104
alias variables, 104
aliases
    @_ array and, 180
    best practices, 471
    defined, 103
    dollar-underscore, 114
    each function and, 105
    in-situ files and, 305
    values function, 102
    (see also Data::Alias module;
        Lexical::Alias module)
aliasing, 103, 104
@alist argument, 173

We'd like to hear your suggestions for improving our indexes. Send email to *index@oreilly.com*.

G

\G metacharacter, 257
garbage collection
    hashes, 234, 332, 337
    inside-out objects and, 337
/gc flag, 257–259, 307
gensym( ) subroutine, 204
Getopt::Clade module (CPAN)
    command-line processing, 310
    description, 488
    interapplication consistency, 314
    interface consistency, 311, 314
Getopt::Euclid module (CPAN), 311, 314,
       315, 489
Getopt::Long module (CPAN), 308, 309,
       314, 487
Getopt::Std module (CPAN), 308
getpwent function, 191
glob function, 167, 168, 476
global variables, 82, 297, 449
gmtime function, 191
GNU bracketing, 10, 11
goto statement, 94
grammar rules, identifiers and, 37, 38, 39
grep function
    aliases and, 115
    arrays and, 43
    benchmarking and, 455, 458, 459
    best practice, 476
    complex mappings, 113
    contextual return values, 189
    dollar-underscore and, 87, 114, 115, 116
    first function and, 110
    homogeneous list-returning
        subroutine, 190
    keys in, 103
    looping and, 112
    overview, 169, 170
    scalar return values, 187
    semicolons and, 17
    spacing statements, 22
Guttman-Rosler Transform, 164

H

hash algorithms, one-way, 150
hash functions, cryptographic, 150
hashes
    anonymous, 324, 330, 331, 454
    base class initialization and, 371–376
    best practices, 470, 473, 476, 479

    built-in functions and, 166
    constructor arguments and, 367–370
    empty, 374
    fat commas and, 66
    grammar rules, 39
    inside-out objects and, 324, 330
    iterating, 104
    keys and indices, 14
    as look-up tables, 118
    multi-contextual return values and, 192
    named arguments and, 182, 183
    naming conventions, 43
    pseudohashes, 322, 479
    reclaiming, 337
    references to, 233, 234
    restricted, 322, 323
    slicing, 89, 90, 102, 193, 455
    sort function and, 151
    unnecessary subscripting, 101–103
    vertical alignment and, 27
hash-ref values, 192
Hash::Util module, 322, 323
--help option, 303, 306, 310, 311
here documents (heredoc)
    best practice, 473
    indentation in, 61–62
    quotes in, 64, 65
    terminators in, 62–64
    values and expressions, 61
heterogeneous list-returning subroutine, 191
hierarchies, 320, 322
    (see also class hierarchies)
homogeneous list-returning subroutine, 190
homonyms
    ambiguous names and, 48
    best practice, 476
    methods and, 338
    in subroutines, 177, 178
HTML::Mason module (CPAN), 418, 489
hyphen (-), 44, 302, 303

I

ident( ) subroutine, 330, 490
identifiers
    abbreviating, 46
    best practices, 470, 473
    capitalization of, 45, 46
    keys and, 66
    naming conventions, 37–40
    spaces and hyphens in, 44
    unrecognized, 65

max( ) subroutine, 13, 172, 491
maxstr( ) subroutine, 172, 174, 491
memoization, 152, 462, 463, 481
memoize( ) subroutine, 462, 463, 491
Memoize module (CPAN), 152, 462, 463, 487
memory
    best practice, 481
    inside-out objects and, 332, 337
    map function and, 113
    recommendations, 459, 460
    slurping and, 212
metacharacters, 247, 478
meta-options, 303, 304
method calls, 292, 321, 349, 452
methods
    accessing attributes, 340–346
    best practice, 479
    capitalization of, 45
    cloning and, 334
    convenience, 354
    cumulative, 389–393, 480
    grammar rules, 40
    lvalue, 347
    overview, 338–340
    sub keyword, 142
min( ) subroutine, 172, 491
minstr( ) subroutine, 172, 491
minus sign (-), 88
missing arguments, 184–185
Module::Build module (CPAN), 404, 489
modules
    best practices, 469, 480
    core, 487, 488
    CPAN and, 397, 418, 419
    creating, 415–417
    declarative exporting, 409–410
    exporting, 407–408
    interface variables, 411–414
    interfaces and, 397–401, 407
    refactoring, 397, 401–404
    standard library, 417, 418
    testing considerations, 427
    version numbers, 404, 405
    version requirements, 405–407
Module::Starter module (CPAN), 416, 489
Module::Starter::PBP module (CPAN), 416, 417, 489
mutators, 341, 351
my keyword, 108–110

N

NAME template, 134, 136
named arguments, 182–183, 470, 476
named characters, 247, 248
named escapes, 54
nameless scalars, 331
names
    ambiguous, 48
    arguments and, 182–183
    best practice, 473
    capture variables and, 254
    constants and, 56
    for methods, 339
    lexical variables, 331
name/value pairs, 66, 182
naming conventions
    abbreviations, 46–47
    advantages of, 36
    ambiguous names, 48
    arrays and hashes, 43
    best practice, 473
    boolean values, 40–41
    capitalization, 45, 46
    filenames, 304–305
    identifiers, 37–40
    methods and, 338
    reference variables, 41, 42
    underscores, 44
    utility subroutines, 49
negative indices, 88–89
nesting
    abbreviations in loops, 47
    conditional tests, 96
    loops and, 131
new( ) method
    attribute building and, 388
    construction/destruction and, 379
    constructors and, 333–336
    indirect objects and, 350
    inheritance and, 376
    UNIVERSAL class and, 381
newline character, 60, 236
NEXT module, 389
next statement, 94, 129, 470
"no" as ambiguous name, 48
none( ) subroutine, 173, 491
not operator, 70
notall( ) subroutine, 173, 491
nouns, naming conventions, 38
numbers
    best practice, 473

conversion subroutines for, 388
long, 59, 60
:NUMERIFY method, 388

O

Object:: namespace, 318
object orientation
appropriate criteria, 320–321
best practice, 479
as choice, 319
error handling, 287–290
objects
accessors, 340–346
best practice, 479, 480
blessing, 365–367
building, 318
class hierarchies and, 361–365
class interfaces, 351–354
cloning, 334–336
coercions, 356–358
constructors, 333
destructors, 336–338
encapsulation and, 321, 323–333
indirect, 349–351, 479
lvalue accessors, 346–349
methods, 338–340
object orientation as choice, 319
operator overloading, 354–356
pseudohashes and, 322
restricted hashes, 322
(see also inside-out objects)
Occam's Razor, 351
oct function, 59
octal numbers, 59
ok( ) subroutine
declarative exporting and, 410
description, 491
modular testing and, 422
testing and, 407
one-way hash algorithms, 150
only module (CPAN), 406, 407, 489
open statement
debugging, 204
error checking and, 208, 209
error handling, 274
opening cleanly, 207, 208
recoverable failure and, 281
scalar variables and, 204
openhandle( ) subroutine, 171, 491
operators
best practice, 472, 474, 480
breaking by precedence, 29, 30

breaking expressions before, 27–29
code layout and, 14
comma and, 69, 71
isomorphic, 354–356
low-precedence, 70–71
object orientation and, 321
overloading, 354–356
sub keyword and, 142
ternary, 31, 32, 121–123
types of, 51
vertical alignment of, 26, 27
OPTIONS section (documentation), 311
OPTIONS template, 137
or operator, 70, 185
Orcish Manœuvre, 150, 164
overload module, 487

P

(?p) marker, 84
package filehandles
autoflushing, 226
braces and, 217
clean-up, 209
localizing, 205, 206
naming considerations, 203, 204
package variables
benchmarking and, 457
best practices, 470, 474
converting to, 306
declarative exporting and, 409
formats and, 449
interfaces and, 414
localization, 77, 78
overview, 75–77
self-declaring, 73
strictures and, 430
packages
capitalization of, 45
grammar rules, 39
naming conventions, 37
pairwise( ) subroutine, 173, 491
paragraphs
chunking and, 23, 24
defined, 23
documenting, 142
parameters
best practices, 470
methods and, 338
named arguments and, 182–183
numbered, 179
testing, 426

prompt( ) subroutine
  as builtin, 13
  description, 491
  interfaces and, 399, 400
  power prompting and, 220, 221
prompting
  best practice, 477
  power, 220–221
  simple, 217
proofreading, 148, 475
properties
  best practice, 478
  naming conventions, 40
  regular expressions and, 248, 249
prototypes, 194–196, 476
prove utility, 424, 425
pseudohashes, 322, 479
punctuation variables
  autoflushing, 225
  best practices, 471, 474
  listed, 73
  localization, 81, 82
  overview, 79–81
  regex and, 82
push( ) method, 110, 111, 339

Q

q{} string, 262
qq{} string, 262
qr{} string, 262
question mark (?), 31, 32, 262
quicksort algorithm, 149
quotes in heredocs, 64, 65, 473
qv( ) subroutine, 404, 405, 406, 491

R

rand function, 461
%RE hash, 263
readability
  abbreviations and, 47
  assignments and, 31
  built-in functions and, 13
  cleverness and, 454
  comments and, 451
  complex mappings, 114
  cuddling and, 24
  debugging and, 439
  of expressions, 14
  fat commas and, 66
  of lists, 26
  look-up tables and, 120

multiline strings and, 60
named constants and, 56
negative control statements, 97–99
optimizing for, 4
semicolons and, 16
slice layout, 90
statements on lines, 22
string delimiters and, 52
tabular ternaries and, 122
underscores and, 59, 60
use English pragma, 79, 80
variables and, 105
readdir function, 191
read_file( ) subroutine, 491
readline function
  caching and, 461
  configuration files and, 447
  contextual return values, 189
  globbing and, 167
  iterative subroutines and, 191
  module interfaces and, 399
  scalar variables, 167
  simple slurping, 213
  slurp( ) subroutine and, 215
README file, 416
readonly( ) subroutine, 171, 491
Readonly module (CPAN), 55, 58, 471, 489
readpipe function, 189
"record" as ambiguous name, 48
$RECORD_SEPARATOR argument, 158
redo statement
  best practices, 470
  flow of control and, 94
  loop labels and, 128, 129
  while statement and, 128, 129
reduce( ) subroutine, 172, 491
_ref suffix, 41, 42
refactoring
  best practice, 480
  considerations, 466, 467
  modules and, 397, 401–404
refaddr( ) subroutine, 171, 330, 491
reference variables, 41, 42, 473
references
  best practice, 477
  braced, 228–229
  cyclic, 232–234
  dereferencing, 227, 228
  symbolic, 230–231
reftype( ) subroutine, 171, 491
regex (see regular expressions)
Regexp::Assemble module (CPAN), 262, 489

sub keyword, 142
Sub::Installer module (CPAN), 163, 490
subroutine calls
    barewords and, 205
    complex mappings, 113–114
    error handling and, 276, 280
    extracting values, 105
    misreading, 11, 12
    parentheses and, 13
SUBROUTINE/METHODS template, 134
subroutines
    anonymous, 163
    argument lists, 178–181
    best practices, 470, 472, 476
    boolean values and, 40
    as builtins, 13
    caching and, 461, 462, 463
    call syntax, 175–177
    capitalization of, 45
    code layout and, 12
    contextual return values, 188–191
    conversion, 388
    declarative exporting and, 409
    decomposition and, 175
    default argument values, 185–186
    documenting, 141, 142
    exporting and, 407–410
    grammar rules, 40
    heredocs and, 62
    homonyms, 177, 178
    implicit returns, 197–199
    interface variables and, 411–414
    lvalues and, 346
    magic goto, 435
    memoizing, 152
    methods and, 338
    missing arguments, 184–185
    multi-contextual return values, 191–194
    name templates for, 37
    named arguments, 66, 182–183
    parentheses and, 176
    prototypes in, 194–196
    refactoring, 401–404
    regular expressions as, 236
    returning failure, 199, 201
    scalar return values, 186–188
    sub keyword, 142
    tied variables and, 452
    utility, 490–492
    wrapper, 181
    (see also utility subroutines)

subscripting
    best practice, 474
    necessary, 103–105
    unnecessary, 101–103
substr function
    arguments, 170
    fixed-width data and, 154
    four-argument substr, 166
    lvalue substr, 165, 166
    overview, 165, 166
substrings
    best practice, 476
    built-in functions and, 165, 166
    unpack function and, 155
suffixes, naming conventions, 41, 42, 46
sum( ) subroutine, 172, 491
SUPER pseudoclass, 389–393
Symbol module, 204
symbolic references, 230–231, 409, 430, 477
SYNOPSIS section (documentation), 311
SYNOPSIS template, 134
syntactic consistency, 36
system function, 274, 280, 281

T

.t file extension, 423, 424, 425
-T function, 106
\t instead of tab, 22, 53
t/ subdirectory, 416, 423, 424
tables
    array naming conventions, 43
    best practice, 475
    command-line processing and, 308
    look-up, 118–121, 455, 464
    regular expressions and, 259–261
    slice factoring and, 90
    ternary operator and, 32, 121–123
    vertical alignment, 26–27
tabs
    best practice, 472
    code layout and, 20, 22
    empty strings and, 53
tainted( ) subroutine, 171, 492
technical documentation, 133, 141, 475
templates
    BBEdit editor and, 485
    best practices, 469, 470, 475
    for comments, 141, 142
    creating modules, 416
    for documentation, 133–139
    grammar rules and, 37

variable-width data, 157, 158–161
verbose option (Carp), 284
version module (CPAN), 404, 405, 488
version numbers
    best practice, 480
    modules and, 404, 405
    requirements, 405–407
--version option, 303, 310
VERSION template, 134, 136
$VERSION variable, 404, 405, 406
vertical alignment
    best practice, 472
    code layout and, 26–27
    importance of, 24
    leading zeros and, 58
vi editor, 10, 18
vile editor, 483
vim editor, 21, 438, 482, 483
:void marker, 279, 280
vstrings, 404

W

wantarray function, 193
warehoused attributes, 324
warn function, 284
warn statement, 438
warnings
    best practices, 470, 481
    testing/debugging, 431, 432, 433
$WARNINGS variable, 431
weaken( ) subroutine, 171, 234, 492
WeakRef module (CPAN), 234
while statement
    checking CSV syntax, 160
    for loops and, 101
    implicit returns and, 198
    input loops and, 211–212
    module interfaces and, 399

postfix looping and, 96–97
readability, 97–98
redo statement and, 128, 129
Smart::Comments module and, 224
whitespace (see spaces)
WIFEXITED( ) subroutine, 281

X

x command, 438
/x flag
    best practice, 470
    brace delimiters, 243
    extended formatting, 236, 237
    tabular regexes, 260
X::EOF exception handler
    exception classes and, 293, 296
    OO exceptions and, 289
    unpacking exceptions, 296–298
XML, 446, 447
XML::Parser module (CPAN), 418, 490
/xms flag, 242, 467
.xs file extension, 442
xsubpp tool, 442

Y

YAML module (CPAN), 490

Z

\z anchor, 239, 240, 252, 470
zeros
    best practice, 473
    leading, 58, 59
    module interfaces and, 399
    testing considerations, 426
zip( ) subroutine, 173, 492

About the Author

Damian Conway holds a PhD in computer science and is an honorary Associate Professor with the School of Computer Science and Software Engineering at Monash University, Melbourne, Australia.

Currently he runs an international IT training company—Thoughtstream—which provides programmer development from beginner to masterclass level throughout Europe, North America, and Australasia.

Damian was the winner of the 1998, 1999, and 2000 Larry Wall Awards for Practical Utility. The best technical paper at the annual Perl Conference was subsequently named in his honour. He has been a member of the technical committee for The Perl Conference, a keynote speaker at many Open Source conferences, is a former columnist for *The Perl Journal*, and is author of the book *Object Oriented Perl*. In 2001 Damian received the first "Perl Foundation Development Grant" and spent 20 months working on projects for the betterment of Perl.

A popular speaker and trainer, he is also the author of numerous well-known Perl modules, including Parse::RecDescent (a sophisticated parsing tool), Class::Contract (design-by-contract programming in Perl), Lingua::EN::Inflect (rule-based English transformations for text generation), Class::Multimethods (multiple dispatch polymorphism), Text::Autoformat (intelligent automatic reformatting of plaintext), Switch (Perl's missing case statement), NEXT (resumptive method dispatch), Filter::Simple (Perl-based source code manipulation), Quantum::Superpositions (auto-parallelization of serial code using a quantum mechanical metaphor), and Lingua::Romana::Perligata (programming in Latin).

Most of Damian's time is now spent working with Larry Wall on the design of the new Perl 6 programming language.

Colophon

Our look is the result of reader comments, our own experimentation, and feedback from distribution channels. Distinctive covers complement our distinctive approach to technical topics, breathing personality and life into potentially dry subjects.

The animal on the cover of *Perl Best Practices* is an American staghound, a hybrid of the greyhound and the Scottish deerhound that is bred specifically for coursing, or hunting by sight. Coursing is one of the world's oldest field sports, and "gazehounds," or "sighthounds," have been tested in competition since as early as AD 116.

The staghound is not recognized as a breed, but is considered a type of sighthound. Although some lines of staghounds have been bred together since the 1700s—longer than some modern breeds—most huntsmen don't push for breed recognition. They believe the staghound should be left unrecognized in order to preserve it as a coursing animal bred for function and not form. As a result, there are no breed standards. Staghounds come in any color or pattern found in either the greyhound or Scottish deerhound and have three coat types: "shag," "slick," and "broken" (which is between shag and slick).

The staghound exhibits many of the same physical characteristics as the greyhound, with long legs, strong muscles, a deep chest, and keen eyesight, and has the endurance and scenting ability of the Scottish deerhound. The staghound's coursing instinct is so strong that anything that runs—rabbits, deer, coyotes, etc.—may be considered quarry. Because these dogs are fast and alert but not hyper or aggressive, they are also said to make excellent pets if exercised regularly.

Genevieve d'Entremont was the production editor and proofreader for *Perl Best Practices*. Nancy Kotary copyedited the book. Darren Kelly and Claire Cloutier provided quality control. Lucie Haskins wrote the index.

Ellie Volckhausen designed the cover of this book, based on a series design by Edie Freedman. The cover image is a 19th-century engraving from Richard Lydekker's *The Royal Natural History*. Karen Montgomery produced the cover layout with Adobe InDesign CS using Adobe's ITC Garamond font.

David Futato designed the interior layout. This book was converted by Keith Fahlgren to FrameMaker 5.5.6 with a format conversion tool created by Erik Ray, Jason McIntosh, Neil Walls, and Mike Sierra that uses Perl and XML technologies. The text font is Linotype Birka; the heading font is Adobe Myriad Condensed; and the code font is LucasFont's TheSans Mono Condensed. The technical illustration that appears in this book was produced by Robert Romano using Macromedia FreeHand MX and Adobe Photoshop CS. This colophon was written by Lydia Onofrei.

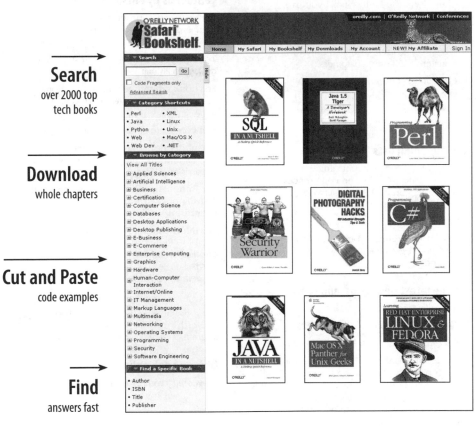

Keep in touch with O'Reilly

Download examples from our books

To find example files from a book, go to: *www.oreilly.com/catalog* select the book, and follow the "Examples" link.

Register your O'Reilly books

Register your book at *register.oreilly.com* Why register your books? Once you've registered your O'Reilly books you can:

- Win O'Reilly books, T-shirts or discount coupons in our monthly drawing.

- Get special offers available only to registered O'Reilly customers.

- Get catalogs announcing new books (US and UK only).

- Get email notification of new editions of the O'Reilly books you own.

Join our email lists

Sign up to get topic-specific email announcements of new books and conferences, special offers, and O'Reilly Network technology newsletters at:

elists.oreilly.com

It's easy to customize your free elists subscription so you'll get exactly the O'Reilly news you want.

Get the latest news, tips, and tools

www.oreilly.com

- "Top 100 Sites on the Web"—PC Magazine
- CIO Magazine's Web Business 50 Awards

Our web site contains a library of comprehensive product information (including book excerpts and tables of contents), downloadable software, background articles, interviews with technology leaders, links to relevant sites, book cover art, and more.

Work for O'Reilly

Check out our web site for current employment opportunities:

jobs.oreilly.com

Contact us

O'Reilly Media, Inc.
1005 Gravenstein Hwy North
Sebastopol, CA 95472 USA
Tel: 707-827-7000 or 800-998-9938
   (6am to 5pm PST)
Fax: 707-829-0104

Contact us by email

For answers to problems regarding your order or our products:
order@oreilly.com

To request a copy of our latest catalog:
catalog@oreilly.com

For book content technical questions or corrections: **booktech@oreilly.com**

For educational, library, government, and corporate sales: **corporate@oreilly.com**

To submit new book proposals to our editors and product managers:
proposals@oreilly.com

For information about our international distributors or translation queries:
international@oreilly.com

For information about academic use of O'Reilly books:
adoption@oreilly.com
or visit:
academic.oreilly.com

For a list of our distributors outside of North America check out:
international.oreilly.com/distributors.html

Order a book online

www.oreilly.com/order_new

Our books are available at most retail and online bookstores.
To order direct: 1-800-998-9938 • *order@oreilly.com* • *www.oreilly.com*
Online editions of most O'Reilly titles are available by subscription at *safari.oreilly.com*